HISTORIC PRESERVATION FOR DESIGNERS

PETER B. DEDEK

FAIRCHILD BOOKS

New York

SEC

HISTORIC PRESERVATION FOR DESIGNERS

PETER B. DEDEK

FAIRCHILD BOOKS

New York

Fairchild Books
An imprint of Bloomsbury Publishing Inc

1385 Broadway   50 Bedford Square
New York   London
NY 10018   WC1B 3DP
USA   UK

www.fairchildbooks.com

First published 2014

Library of Congress Cataloging-in-Publication Data
A catalog record for this book is available from the Library of Congress
2013938690

ISBN: PB: 978-1-60901-509-1

Text Design by Kendrek Lyons
Typeset by Precision Graphics
Cover Design Sarah Silberg
Printed and bound in the United States of America

TABLE OF CONTENTS

PREFACE

People are attracted to historic architecture for a variety of reasons. Some see it as beautiful, others are interested in the heritage it represents, and some individuals see it in environmental terms as offering opportunities to recycle whole structures, landscapes, entire neighborhoods, and cities. Historic buildings come in all shapes and sizes and represent a plethora of styles, periods of history, irreplaceable building materials, and unique craftsmanship. In a world so often dominated by uniformity and reproduction, historic sites offer variety and authenticity. Unlike contrived modern environments, such as shopping centers, resorts, and Disney World, historic places show us the quirky, the unexpected, the grand statements and intricate details left by previous generations. This creates a sense of identification with the past and the feeling that a particular place is special in a way no other could be.

Because of their variety and complexity, working with historic buildings can be challenging and complicated. With factors such as building codes, space planning, accessibility requirements, and aesthetics, designing new built environments is difficult enough, but rehabilitating historic buildings also involves protecting fragile decorative elements, remediating decay, shoring up obsolete and often complicated structural systems, and modifying historic floor plans designed for uses and lifestyles that sometimes no longer exist. Historic design is as much a process of conservation and stewardship as expression and construction. Historic design combines many skills and talents: creativity, curation, research, planning, negotiation. The field of historic preservation is dynamic and multidisciplinary. Preservation intersects with many other disciplines, including architecture, landscape architecture, interior design, urban planning, history, and law. Working in concert with these diverse fields, preservationists seek to save unique, often beautiful places, large and small, which help define the American character.

Preservationists engage in a vast array of endeavors, performing activities such as renovating and rehabilitating historic buildings and interiors, creating historic districts, promoting urban revitalization, studying the history and significance of old buildings and sites, reviewing and creating land-use regulations, and pursuing preservation law cases. What all preservationists have in common is an ethic, the belief that saving and caring for historic places serves society as a whole and enriches the lives of all Americans by providing a direct connection to history and creating a unique sense of place. Historic landmarks cultivate personal and civic identities. Preservationists believe that the interests of corporations, governmental agencies, and individuals should sometimes be tempered by the need to retain historic places.

Historic preservation not only concerns history; if practiced well, it also conserves the environment and natural resources. The preservation of historic sites, neighborhoods, and landscapes can save vast amounts of energy and prevents perfectly serviceable building materials, such as historic brick and stone and old-growth timber, from going to the landfill. Because it works on such a grand scale, preservation can form the basis of the ultimate re-use and recycling program.

This book focuses on how historic preservation impacts the education and work of architects and interior designers. Because the preservation field is so broad, involving problems as diverse as conserving old wallpaper, planning traffic patterns, and educating visitors at historic sites, attempting to provide a sufficient survey of the entire field in a manageable book would be difficult if not impossible. By concentrating on preservation issues architects and interior designers are likely to encounter in the course their education and their professional lives, this book seeks to provide an introduction to preservation theory and practice as it relates to design. Although there is a great variety of historic sites and resources, such as districts, archeological sites, and historic cultural landscapes, this book emphasizes the identification, documentation, preferred treatments, and best practices in the rehabilitation and restoration of historic buildings and interiors.

Designed to be read from beginning to end in a linear fashion, the facts, terms, and concepts introduced in earlier chapters are often referenced and discussed in greater detail in later ones. However, this book can also be used as a reference for those working with historic design projects throughout the design process, from the initial identification and documentation of historic resources to design conception through schematic design, design development, construction documents, and construction.

As increasing numbers of aging buildings across America are being preserved and will require rehabilitation and modification for new uses sooner or later, it is important that architects and designers understand the rationale and methodology of historic preservation. In the past, the fields of architecture and interior design emphasized new construction and were sometimes hostile to preservation. One reason for this is that saving buildings was seen as bad for business, because preservation might reduce the need for new construction. Another reason for this is that many architects and designers embrace the design fields because they want to express their personal aesthetic and produce work that is contemporary or even revolutionary. As it turns out, historic buildings present many challenges for designers working with them, making rehabilitation projects as involved, or even more so than new construction. This creates plenty of work, and there are also a lot of situations where impressive design originality and innovation can be appropriately expressed within historic buildings or in their proximity. The following chapters describe many of the pitfalls and opportunities designers encounter when working with historic architecture.

This book starts with a history of historic preservation in the United States. Then it discusses governmental involvement in preservation at the national, state, and local levels, and also outlines private sector preservation activities. The text also has a discussion of the factors that make a property historic and outlines methods of researching historic sites. The book's main focus, however, is on the design-related aspects of the field, such as building restoration and rehabilitation, adaptive-use, conserving historic building materials, researching and inspecting historic buildings, managing the historical design process, promoting accessibility in historic buildings, and green design in historic architecture.

The text is divided into three sections that build on each other in a logical order. The first introduces the field of historic preservation with a brief history of its practice in the United States in Chapter 1, and Chapters 2 and 3 cover the roles of government and the private sector. Because it does not contain a review of architectural styles, this book is intended to be used in conjunction with a book or website that identifies and describes the styles of historic American architecture.

Section Two focuses on the practice of historic preservation, beginning in Chapter 4, with defining what makes a property historic and outlines methods of researching and documenting historic properties. Chapter 5 reviews the practice and theory of historic preservation law.

Chapter 6 examines approaches to the management and rehabilitation of historic buildings. The second half of Section Two covers technological aspects of historic preservation with a survey of the properties and methods of caring for a range of historic building materials in Chapter 7, a survey of common natural and man-made threats to historic buildings in Chapter 8, and methods of investigating a building to determine its date of construction in Chapter 9.

Section Three addresses issues and methods of preservation design. Chapter 10 discusses the *Secretary of the Interior's Standards* and their appropriate application in design projects. Chapter 11 covers programming and managing historic design projects. Chapters 12 and 13 consider two aspects of socially responsible preservation design: universal design and green building.

The book concludes with a brief look at emerging trends in historic preservation. Each chapter begins with a list of objectives that preview the topics of discussion and ends study questions and, where appropriate, with visual quizzes to help students internalize and retain the chapter content. A list of references provides sources for further research. Within each chapter, new terms are highlighted in boldface and defined where they are introduced.

SOURCE

National Park Service (NPS). "National Register Bulletin, Guidelines for Local Surveys, A Basis for Preservation Planning." accessed November 13, 2012. http://www.nps.gov/nr/publications/bulletins/nrb24/intro.htm

A SHORT HISTORY OF HISTORIC PRESERVATION IN THE UNITED STATES

OBJECTIVES

- Introduce the field of historic preservation.

- Outline a number of fundamental terms used in preservation.

- Describe the development of historic preservation in the United States from the preservation of Independence Hall in 1816 to the plethora of private and public efforts that make up the preservation movement today.

- Outline how this unique history has affected and continues to influence the design fields, particularly architecture and interior design.

- Introduce a number of key governmental and private preservation initiatives.

The field of historic preservation in the United States began with the efforts of a small number of private individuals in the 1800s working to save historic sites associated with elite individuals. Despite its limited beginnings, the field grew in the 20th century to involve governments, nonprofits, and a wide range of activists working to preserve thousands of historic sites, districts, and entire landscapes. In recent decades, the scope of the field broadened further to include a more diverse range of historic resources, including many associated with common people.

KEY PRESERVATION TERMS

A number of important terms that define distinct types of historic resources are critical to understanding the preservation field. One of these terms is "historic property." The National Park Service (NPS), the federal governmental agency that oversees many of the historic preservation activities in the United States, defines a **historic property** as "any building, structure, site, object, or district that has historical, architectural, archeological, or cultural significance." The specific factors used to determine which properties have historical significance are discussed in Chapter 4. The NPS has the following definitions for types of historic properties:

- **Building:** A *building* is a relatively permanent construction built to shelter any type of human activity, such as living, selling goods, or producing goods. Buildings include houses, barns, churches, factories, and office blocks and other types of shelters that are designed to be fixed to one location (although buildings are sometimes moved) and are usually made of heavy materials such as wood, brick, metal, stone, or concrete.

- **Structure:** In historic preservation, the term *structure* refers to any durable man-made construction designed to occupy a particular location that does not shelter human activity or at least was not designed to do so. Examples include bridges, most monuments, radio transmission towers, tombs, tunnels, and retaining or garden walls: any large-scale piece of human-built engineering that was not designed to move or be moved, so long as its purpose was not to shelter or house humans.

- **Object:** *Objects* are different from buildings and structures. Objects are often artistic in nature and usually relatively small in scale compared to buildings and are constructed in a simple manner. Although an object may be movable, it is normally associated with a specific setting or environment, such as statuary placed in a designed landscape; although a historic ship, which was obviously designed to move, would be considered an object in NPS preservation terminology.

- **Historic site:** *Historic site* refers to the physical location where a historically significant event took place; where a prehistoric or historic occupation or activity happened; or where buildings, structures or objects, whether intact, in ruins, or no longer evident, stand or stood. The land or site itself possesses historical, cultural, or archeological value regardless of the historical value of any construction that may exist there.

- **Historic district:** A *historic district* is a defined geographical area made up of a significant concentration, linkage, or continuity of sites, buildings, structures, or objects that are united historically or stylistically by events, design, function, or physical development (National Park Service 2012). Preservationists create historic districts by surveying an area of a settlement, town, or city, determining which buildings within the area are historic or "contributing" and which are not, and then defining and outlining the district based on these data. The historic resources located in a district normally constitute the majority of all of the buildings and structures to be found within the designated boundaries of the district.

Even though many different types and ages of buildings and structures may exist in a single historic district, they usually have some unifying factor related to common themes in their development over time. For example, the historic buildings and structures in a historic district may be linked by a common thread of history, such as the development of a local railroad hub or a single planned subdivision, or they might be linked by having a majority of buildings in a particular style, such as a district of 1920s bungalows or one of 1950s ranch houses.

In the United States, historic districts come in two basic varieties: those listed on the National Register and those created by local authorities, although some districts share both designations.

Similarly designated historic neighborhoods are known as *conservation areas* in England and in many other English-speaking countries.

EARLY PRESERVATION EFFORTS IN THE UNITED STATES

Private citizens began the field of historic preservation in the United States in the early 19th century. Most of the places these early preservationists worked to protect were associated with so-called "great white men": presidents, senators, planters, top generals, and the like. The majority had historical significance at the national level. The first of these sites was Independence Hall.

INDEPENDENCE HALL

The story of Independence Hall—then known as the Old State House—in Philadelphia, Pennsylvania, illustrates the almost complete lack of a preservation ethic in the early 19th century (Figure 1.1). The building was nearly destroyed in 1813, only two generations after the American Revolution, because the government of Pennsylvania, which had moved its capital from Philadelphia to Harrisburg by this time, viewed the building and its grounds as little more than surplus property. At the time, the Pennsylvania state legislature proposed demolishing the building and selling the property off as building lots (Hosmer 1965).

In what may be the first public appeal for historic preservation in American history, the Philadelphia city council opposed the proposed demolition stating, "The spot which the bill proposes to cover with private buildings is hallowed . . . by many strong and impressive public

Figure 1.1 Historic image of Independence Hall in the 1700s with its original tower and wings. Source: U.S. History Images, http://ushistoryimages.com.

acts . . . which embraced the whole United States and has given birth to the only free republic the world has seen. . . ." Despite the building's tremendous historical significance, the city council felt it necessary to go even further and advance the notion that preserving the open space around the building would help keep air moving near the city center, which they claimed might protect the city from outbreaks of yellow fever. Fortunately for the building, the state senate voted to postpone selling the land in 1813. In 1816, in the midst of another attempt to demolish the building, a number of early historical associations appealed to the city of Philadelphia, which responded by purchasing the property from the state with the intention of preserving it (Mires 2002). Although Independence Hall was saved, both of its original wings were demolished to make room for new "fireproof" buildings to be designed by architect John Mills, and the irreplaceable woodwork in the room in which the Declaration of Independence was signed had been torn out (Figure 1.2) (Hosmer 1965).

The fact that a building as historically significant as Independence Hall was threatened with demolition in the first place shows how the cultural, educational, and aesthetic value of historic sites had not yet been established except in the minds of a small number of visionaries. Despite this, after 1824 additional people became interested in the building and began to replace some of its lost features, including the tower, which had been removed shortly after the American Revolution. Architect William Strickland designed a reasonably accurate reconstruction of the tower in 1828, creating one of the earliest historic reconstructions in America.

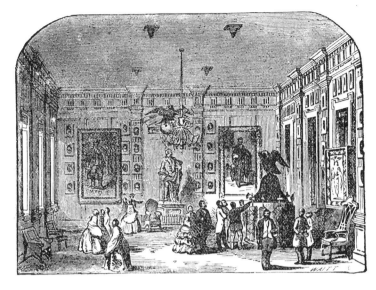

Figure 1.2 Interior of Independence Hall in the 1870s. Source: U.S. History Images, http://ushistoryimages.com.

HASBROUCK HOUSE

Aside from a few isolated private efforts, such as the preservation of the Touro Synagogue in Newport, Rhode Island, by Abraham Touro in 1822, it would be 34 years until another significant American historic site was deliberately preserved (Hosmer 1965). The Hasbrouck House, built in 1750 (Figure 1.3), was the first historic site to be preserved with the support of a state government. This relatively humble stone house functioned as George Washington's military headquarters in Newburgh, New York, from April 1, 1782, until August 19, 1783. The state of New York purchased the building and a few acres of surrounding land in 1850 for the purposes

Figure 1.3. The Hasbrouck House built in 1750 in Newburgh, New York, was the first historic site to be preserved with government support. Source: Photograph by Peter B. Dedek, 2010.

of preserving the site, and today, the property continues to function as a state-owned historic site. This modest example of preservation by the state of New York set an early precedent for the creation of many state-owned historic sites across the nation. Like most other early historic sites, the house was associated with a member of the elite and had national significance.

MOUNT VERNON

The effort to save Mount Vernon, the ancestral home of George Washington, was probably the most significant exception to the usual disregard of American historic sites during the 19th century.

MOUNT VERNON

In the early 1850s, Ann Pamela Cunningham from South Carolina became interested in George Washington's home at Mount Vernon after her mother wrote in a letter that the house was in danger due to neglect and someone ought to save it (Figure 1A). Because of spinal injuries received in a horse accident at age seventeen, Cunningham had spent twenty years "confined to her couch," relegated to the sidelines of plantation society, and welcomed the opportunity to pursue a cause. She founded the Mount Vernon Ladies Association of the Union in 1854 to preserve the Georgian-style plantation house in Virginia, built in 1741.

Figure 1A Mount Vernon in disrepair c. 1855. Source: Clements Library, University of Michigan.

As with many women whose abilities and talents were unrecognized and underutilized during the 1800s, once given the opportunity, Ann Pamela Cunningham proved to be very competent. She organized members and garnered resources from all parts of the United States to save Mount Vernon. Part of her motivation for saving the mansion was to help rally the nation around Washington's memory in an attempt to repair the growing sectarian rift between North and South in the run up to the Civil War (Mount Vernon Backgrounders 2006). She also wanted to memorialize George Washington and his contributions during the founding of the United States as commander of the rebel forces and as the first American president.

Initially, the Mount Vernon Ladies Association tried to interest the federal government and the state of Virginia in buying the property, but neither showed interest. Not deterred, Cunningham decided to raise the money herself and buy the house with private funds. With the help of influential friends and associates, such as Edward Everett of Boston, a nationally famous orator, she raised the money needed make an offer to buy the estate from John Augustine Washington III, a relative of George Washington, who refused to sell. However, after Cunningham met with Washington's wife, he agreed to sell the house for $200,000 (about $5,500,000 in 2012 dollars) (Inflation Calculator 2013) partly on credit, which the Mount Vernon Ladies Association paid in full within the next few years (Mount Vernon Backgrounders 2006), after restoring the property and opening it to the public (Figure 1B).

Figure 1B Mount Vernon House, restored. Source: Photograph by Peter B. Dedek, 2012.

Cunningham's solution, the use of private money for her preservation project rather than relying on the government, set a precedent that would continue in American preservation efforts throughout the 19th and early 20th centuries. Historic preservation remained mostly a pursuit of the well-heeled far into the 20th century. In addition, the Mount Vernon Ladies Association laid the foundations for how restoration was to be performed in America. The association meticulously preserved, restored, and interpreted the house and its surroundings to a specific period in history: the end of the 18th century, the last few years George Washington lived there before his death. They recreated that period throughout much of the property, including interiors and outbuildings. The effort succeeded, and the site was conserved and restored and became a precedent for other early preservation projects. The practice of restoring historic properties to interpret a specific time period using as much historical documentation as possible continued for many decades and is still practiced today in some places.

EARLY FEDERAL EFFORTS

The federal government did little to support the historic built environment in the 19th century. However, it became the first government in the world to act significantly to preserve natural areas when it established the world's first national park, Yellowstone, in 1872. The creation of Yellowstone and subsequent national parks established the precedent for later efforts on the part of the federal government to protect not just natural areas, but sites significant to history and prehistory as well.

As easterners visited and settled the American Southwest in greater numbers, the ruins of graves and pueblos built by the Anasazi, ancient Native Americans who occupied areas of the Southwest well before European settlement, came under increasing threat from looters. Enthusiast organizations, such as the Archeological Institute of America and the Colorado Cliff Dwellers Association, began protesting against the destruction of sites like Casa Grande, ruins

Figure 1.4 Casa Grande Ruins. Source: The National Park Service.

of an ancient Native American settlement, to the government (Figure 1.4) (Special Committee on Historic Preservation 1966). In one of the first federal historic preservation efforts, in 1889 the United States Congress allocated $2,000 (about $50,000 in 2012 dollars) to protect the Casa Grande ruin in Arizona from destruction due to rampant commercial pot hunting (Inflation Calculator 2013).

In that same year, following Ann Pamela Cunningham's example, the Ladies Hermitage Association convinced the state of Tennessee to deed the Hermitage, the home of President Andrew Jackson, built around 1820 near Nashville, to their organization for purposes of preservation (Hermitage 2012). Eighteen years later in 1907, President Theodore Roosevelt visited the site and convinced Congress to provide funds to have a water system installed and to make repairs to the house in one of only a few early federal appropriations to preserve a historic site (Bucy 2009).

Another federal preservation effort began in 1890, when the government designated Chickamauga Battlefield in Georgia as the first national military park in an effort to memorialize the Civil War. Soon thereafter, the Gettysburg and Shiloh Battlefields were so designated, creating a new type of federally owned and designated historic site. The battlefields were eventually transferred to the National Park Service after it was established in 1916.

PRESERVATION IN THE EARLY 20TH CENTURY

The field of historic preservation developed and reached maturity in the 20th century. Preservation standards were developing in Europe as well; for example, the United Kingdom passed its first preservation law, the Ancient Monuments Protection Act, in 1882. The act initially protected just 50 monuments in all of Great Britain, but the British Parliament passed more comprehensive preservation laws in 1900 and again in 1910. In the century's early decades, the foundations of both the private and the public institutions of preservation in many parts of Europe and North America were established.

THE ANTIQUITIES ACT OF 1906

In 1906, the federal government took its first significant step toward playing a meaningful role in historic preservation. In response to public pressure over the looting of historic Native American graves and other sites in the West, Congress passed the Antiquities Act of 1906. The Antiquities Act allowed the president to set aside Native American ruins and other places "of historical or scientific interest" located on federal lands to protect them from looting and other kinds of destruction (Rothman 1989). These new reserves were called *national monuments*. Many early national monuments have since evolved into national parks. The national monument program formed the backbone of direct federal protection of historic and natural sites. The act also made it illegal for unauthorized people to excavate or rob archeological sites located on federal land and levied a fine on violators.

As it turned out, the 1906 act did little to deter looting, but it *did* initiate a long-standing federal trend in preservation of mostly focusing on the government's own activities and concentrating on historic resources located on federal land, rather than attempting to regulate the treatment of historic properties in private hands. To this day, with the notable exception of the Historic Preservation Tax Incentives program discussed later in this chapter, federal preservation laws usually govern only the activities of federal agencies, and concern projects directly controlled or funded by the federal government.

The Antiquities Act was a product of the Progressive era, which emphasized the regulation and "wise use" of resources overseen by academically trained experts and bureaucrats with the idea that when properly managed, natural and cultural resources would not be wastefully destroyed or uselessly squandered by unbridled economic exploitation and could therefore be studied by scientists and enjoyed by the public.

SOCIETY FOR THE PRESERVATION
OF NEW ENGLAND ANTIQUITIES

With the exception of the creation of the National Park Service in 1916, between 1906 and the Great Depression, historic preservation changed little at the federal level. However, during the 1910s and 1920s, private preservation efforts increased in frequency and scale. In 1910, William Sumner Appleton founded the Society for the Preservation of New England Antiquities with the mission of preserving the "most interesting" historic buildings in New England (Cooke 1987). In 1941, Appleton described his reasons for founding the Society:

When the writer was a boy it was possible for the visitor to Boston to wander around the older streets of the city and to have pointed out some fifty interesting old structures, all of them worthy of interest because of their architectural excellence, extreme old age, or connection to some event of historical significance. This list of fifty, within the author's memory has dwindled down to about ten . . . (Appleton 1941).

In this quote, Appleton cites three reasons to preserve a historic property: architectural excellence, old age, and connection to significant historical events. These justifications resemble the criteria for evaluation of historic properties developed by the National Park Service for the National Register of Historic Places in the early 1970s (see Chapter 4). Today, these same criteria are used across the nation to determine which buildings and sites should be considered historic. Since 1910, the Society for the Preservation of New England Antiquities—now called Historic New England—has purchased and operated a number of house museums, collected more than 100,000 historic objects, created and managed a large historical archive, and provided preservation services to assist New Englanders in preservation projects (Historic New England 2010).

COLONIAL WILLIAMSBURG

William Sumner Appleton was part of a growing trend in private preservation efforts. In 1923 the Reverend Doctor W.A.R. Goodwin began a campaign to restore the entire city center of Williamsburg, Virginia, the former colonial capital of Virginia. In that year, he became acquainted with John D. Rockefeller at a meeting of the Phi Beta Kappa Society in New York City and proposed that Rockefeller finance a Phi Beta Kappa Memorial Hall for Williamsburg's College of William and Mary. Soon after, Rockefeller toured Williamsburg with Goodwin and agreed to underwrite much of the restoration of the entire historic city. The idea was to create an open air historical museum based on European precedents such as Skansen, a living outdoor museum created in 1891 in Stockholm, Sweden, dedicated to showing visitors how Swedes lived and worked before industrialization.

Work at Williamsburg began in 1926 to take the city "back" to its colonial appearance, with many of the buildings carefully documented and some, such as the Wren Building (1695; Figure 1.5), restored by architect William Graves Perry. In the course of the heavy-handed citywide

Figure 1.5 Wren Building. Source: Special Collections, John D. Rockefeller, Jr. Library, The Colonial Williamsburg Foundation.

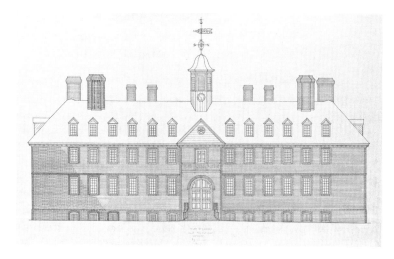

restoration, many buildings that Goodwin, Perry, and Rockefeller deemed "nonhistoric"—any building constructed after 1800—were demolished, while others were restored. A number of previously lost buildings, such as the colonial Virginia state capitol, were reconstructed based on a combination of historical records and pure speculation.

Goodwin, Perry, and Rockefeller were attempting to recreate and sometimes reinvent the historic town of Williamsburg to exhibit a colonial American city. Despite the demolition of century-old buildings and a few questionable reconstructions at Williamsburg, the project helped garner public interest in America's heritage and sparked widespread enthusiasm about historic architecture and places, allowing American preservation to evolve. The site operates today and has since adopted more sound preservation and historical interpretation practices than those used by its founders.

GREENFIELD VILLAGE

Henry Ford, another 20th-century millionaire industrialist, developed Greenfield Village in Michigan starting in 1929. Touting the idea that "history (as taught in schools) is bunk," Ford set out on a project to present his own version of American history directly to the public. An avid collector, Ford had accumulated a vast assortment of antique artifacts, such as tractors, old automobiles, and electronic equipment, and even entire historic buildings, which he had moved to the Greenfield site from locations far and wide.

To house his massive collection and educate the public about the development of American agricultural, industrial, and architectural technology, Ford established the Henry Ford Museum and Greenfield Village—initially called the Edison Institute, to honor his friend, Thomas Edison—to celebrate America's progress. Greenfield Village, which continues to function today, was intended to act as a kind of time capsule where Americans would be able to experience their history firsthand. Moving buildings from their original locations and displaying them as if they were museum pieces along with artifacts gathered from various times and places would not be considered good preservation practice today, but the development of Greenfield Village exposed a great number of Americans to the importance of historic buildings and artifacts and further advanced the concept of the outdoor history museum.

SIGNIFICANT FEDERAL EFFORTS

During the 1930s, the federal government began to take a more significant role in managing America's historic resources. This included a number of new programs, many of which were part of President Franklin D. Roosevelt's New Deal.

The Historic American Building Survey

Congress created the Historic American Building Survey (HABS) in 1933 to employ out-of-work architects, photographers, and historians as part of Roosevelt's New Deal. The idea was to document America's historic sites by having the participants make measured drawings and take

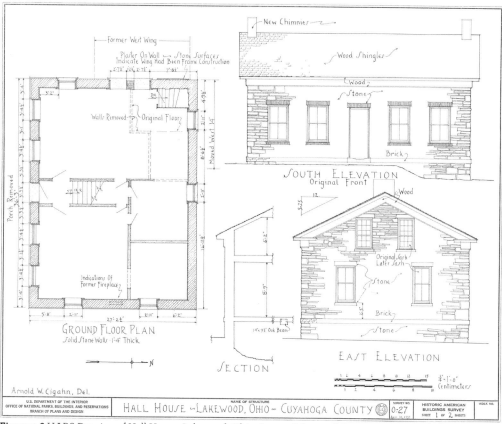

Figure 1.6 HABS Drawing of Hall House, Lakewood, Ohio. Source: Library of Congress, Prints and Photographs Division, Washington, DC, 20540 USA. http://hdl.loc.gov/loc.pnp/hhh.oh0213. Historic American Buildings Survey. Survey number HABS OH-27.

photographs of historic buildings across the nation (Figure 1.6). HABS historians wrote short histories of many of the buildings HABS architects and photographers documented. This represented the first large-scale attempt to record America's historic sites. HABS documented buildings of all types, from the grand and well-known to the small and obscure. Investment in HABS was reduced when America entered World War II, but the program was revived in the 1950s and has since become part of the Cultural Resources Stewardships and Partnerships Program of the National Park Service. HABS is the last New Deal program still active today.

The Historic Sites Act

In a more significant move, Congress passed the Historic Sites Act in 1935, which set in motion federal efforts to identify historic properties of national significance and to preserve a number of sites located on federal land. This effort later evolved into America's National Historic Landmarks program. The overall purpose of the Historic Sites Act was to make it "national policy to preserve for public use historic sites, buildings, and objects of national significance for the inspiration and benefit of the American people." The act placed many federally owned historic places in the care of the NPS, greatly increasing that agency's role in preservation. The Historic Sites Act also directed the Secretary of the Interior "through the National Park Service" to survey historic properties nationwide for the purpose of determining which "possess exceptional value as commemorating or illustrating the history of the United States," acquire, restore, and operate historic properties of national significance, enter into contracts with "states, municipal subdivisions, associations, or individuals" to preserve historic sites, erect historical markers, and develop historical education programs (Historic Sites Act 1935). The Historic Sites Act was the first federal law to establish preservation as a national priority and laid the foundations for the larger role the federal government would take later in the century.

EARLY EFFORTS BY LOCAL GOVERNMENTS

In the 1930s, a handful of local and state governments began to create **local historic districts**, which consist of multiple historic properties located within a specific and contiguous geographical area that are designated and regulated by local municipal law. The first two such districts were in Charleston, South Carolina, and the French Quarter of New Orleans, Louisiana.

Charleston, South Carolina: The Battery

In 1929, a group of residents of Charleston, South Carolina, lobbied their city government to limit demolitions in one of Charleston's most historic neighborhoods called The Battery, because developers were buying historic houses and demolishing them to build new commercial establishments, such as gas stations, and to loot them for architectural antiques (Figure 1.7).

Figure 1.7 Shackleford-Williams House, the Battery, Charleston, South Carolina. Source: Library of Congress, Prints and Photographs Division, Washington, DC, 20540 USA. http://hdl.loc.gov/loc.pnp/hhh.sc0888. Historic American Buildings Survey. Survey number HABS SC-683.

In 1931, in order to protect the historic qualities of this unique area of mostly 18th- and 19th-century mansions, the city of Charleston created the nation's first historic district with a board of architectural review to prevent further destruction.

The concept of historic districts was based on the practice of **zoning**, an urban planning tool that had been recently introduced by municipalities to separate residential, commercial, and industrial areas in order to increase the quality of life and the property values within protected areas (Morton 1987, 159). A historic district was essentially a new kind of urban zone, a clearly defined area where historic structures were to be protected.

The Charleston district established the first governmental architectural controls in the United States regulating both public and private demolitions, rehabilitations, and building projects involving the exteriors of historic buildings. The basic concept of a local historic district, such as the one created in Charleston, survives to this day. In the United States, local historic districts like this are the only type of historic district overseen by a board of architectural reviewers with the authority to regulate the actions of governments, private individuals, architectural designers, institutions, and corporations.

The French Quarter

In 1936, the Louisiana State Legislature authorized a similar district, located in the French Quarter of New Orleans, Louisiana, based on regulatory powers granted by a recent amendment to the Louisiana state constitution. The French Quarter, which consists of about 78 city blocks and constitutes the original city of New Orleans, was originally founded in 1718. The district contains a number of highly historic buildings, such as the Ursuline Convent (1745; Figure 1.8) and the Cabildo (1795), that date back to the 18th century and survive intact, along with hundreds of historically significant 19th-century buildings, in a cohesive context.

Figure 1.8 Ursuline Convent, New Orleans, 1745. The oldest building in the Mississippi Valley, the convent is the only remaining building dating from French Louisiana. Source: Photograph by Peter B. Dedek, 2010.

As with all local historic districts, state legislation was required to give local governments the police power necessary to establish and enforce standards for the treatment of buildings in the French Quarter, or *Vieux Carré* as it is also known. This enabling legislation, first passed by South Carolina and Louisiana, became a prototype for historic districts in other states. The legal validity of this new concept, a local historic district where a city government (backed by state law) could dictate to private landowners what they could do and what they could not do to their historic properties had never been tested in the courts, and it took several decades of legal precedents in state and federal courts to establish and define this authority. In the decades following the 1930s, other cities and towns, such as Alexandria, Virginia, in 1946, Georgetown in Washington, D.C., in 1950, and Philadelphia in 1955, created local historic districts. Also in 1955, the Massachusetts legislature passed bills creating historic districts on Beacon Hill in Boston and on the island of Nantucket.

The *Vieux Carré* historic district, which largely escaped damage in Hurricane Katrina in 2005, continues to function in much the same way as it did when established in 1936, protecting one of the largest intact 19th-century neighborhoods in North America.

PRESERVATION COMES OF AGE: THE POSTWAR ERA

After the Second World War, the preservation movement gradually coalesced. The key elements that define historic preservation in America today, such as the National Trust for Historic Preservation and the National Historic Preservation Act, emerged in the decades following the war, laying the foundations for the preservation movement's maturation in the 1970s.

NATIONAL TRUST FOR HISTORIC PRESERVATION

A coalition of private citizens and public officials largely associated with the National Park Service created the National Trust for Historic Preservation in 1949. The first significant cooperative effort between the public and private sectors in preservation in the United States, the National Trust, was, to some degree, modeled on the National Trust in the United Kingdom, which had been founded in 1895 with the purpose of acting "as a guardian for the nation in the acquisition and protection of threatened coastline, countryside and buildings" (British National Trust 2010). In protecting coastline and countryside, the British National Trust has a wider mission than its American cousin, which focuses only on historic preservation (Finley 1965, 1).

The United States' National Trust acquires and manages individual historic sites and acts as a major advocate for historic preservation in America. According to the organization's mission statement, "The National Trust for Historic Preservation is a private, nonprofit membership organization dedicated to protecting the irreplaceable. It provides leadership, education, and advocacy to save America's diverse historic places and revitalize communities" (National Trust for Historic Preservation 2010).

Although begun as a public-private partnership, today the National Trust is a completely private organization. While it received federal funding for over thirty years, after Congress cut the trust's federal appropriation in half in 1995, the organization decided to forgo Congressional funding entirely, which ceased in 1998 (discussed further in Chapter 3) (National Trust for Historic Preservation 2010).

THE NEED FOR PRESERVATION IN THE POSTWAR DECADES

Despite the gains in the preservation field described here, the 1930s through the 1960s were disastrous decades for America's historic architecture, neighborhoods, and landscapes. Thousands of historic sites were destroyed to make way for all manner of new development. Even buildings as famous and revered as the huge and magnificent Beaux-Arts style Pennsylvania Station in Midtown Manhattan, designed by the prestigious firm of McKim, Mead, and White in 1910, were lost in the 1960s (Figures 1.9a and 1.9b). Despite public outcry by such New York institutions as the *New York Times* and opposition from many of New York's elite, including many of its architects, the building fell to the wrecking ball in 1963 (Plosky 2000). The building was replaced by the architecturally banal Madison Square Garden and some boxy office buildings (Figure 1.9c). However, the loss of the Pennsylvania Station motivated the city of New York

Figure 1.9b Pennsylvania Station, circa 1911. Source: © Corbis.

Figure 1.9a Inside the current Pennsylvania Station in New York City, located in the basement of the architecturally banal 1960s Madison Square Garden, is a photograph of the magnificent 1915 Beaux-Arts Pennsylvania Station (Figure 1.9b) that was destroyed to make way for it. Such memorials are merely a sad reminder of the wastefulness of demolishing our architectural heritage. Source: Photograph by Peter B. Dedek, 2009.

Figure 1.9c Madison Square Garden, the building that replaced Pennsylvania Station. Source: Photograph by Peter B. Dedek, 2010.

to pass city landmarks legislation and later led to the successful preservation of other New York icons, including Grand Central Terminal (Figure 1.10), which had been slated for a similar fate.

Although some cities had established local historic districts and designated historic landmarks by the 1960s, the destruction of historic places as a whole only intensified. The federal government, which had acted in the 1930s to document and save historic sites with HABS and the Historic Sites Act, created programs and projects, such as urban renewal and the interstate highway system, which encouraged and even mandated the mass destruction of historic areas.

In the mid-20th century, the largest threat to historic buildings in the United States came from federally funded activities. The destruction was catastrophic. By 1966, over half of the 12,000 historic buildings documented by the Historic American Building's Survey (HABS) since 1933 had been demolished (U.S. Council of Mayors 1966). Federally financed urban renewal projects were tearing the hearts out of many American cities and towns as interstate highways blew through many of the historic areas still remaining. In Boston, massive federally-funded urban renewal projects wiped out entire neighborhoods in the late 1950s and early 1960s, including the city's entire historic west end, which fell to urban renewal in 1961 (Figure 1.11).

In some cases, the widespread use of urban renewal funds pitted architects and interior designers against preservationists, because design professionals saw all of the new construction that resulted as good for business. Many also supported urban renewal because in these times, many architects and designers admired the style and utopian schemes of modernists, such as Mies van der Rohe, Le Corbusier, and Walter Gropius, and held a modern ethic of "newer is

Figure 1.10 Interior, Grand Central Terminal. The Beaux-Arts building and its spectacular interior were preserved and eventually restored. Source: © Atlantide Phototravel/Corbis.

Figure 1.11 Historic Boston being demolished in the 1960s. Source: Bettmann Archive—UPI.

better." They believed the functional International Style was preferable to the older decorative historical styles. During the period of urban renewal, many Americans saw many older areas of cities as "blighted areas" that needed to be cleared for modern development, which they believed would be healthier and more efficient for the people who lived and worked in them.

THE HISTORIC PRESERVATION ACT OF 1966

Ironically, the federal government, singularly responsible for so much destruction, moved to take charge of historic preservation in 1966, a time when it was still financing the mass demolition of America's historic city centers. As different arms of federal government pursued contradictory policies relating to historic preservation, it took decades of laws, executive orders, court cases, and bureaucratic reforms for the federal government to gradually become more beneficial to historic resources than it had been earlier. For good reason, most federal historic preservation laws passed during this period were federal attempts to limit the harmful impacts of the government's own programs.

After the publication of Jane Jacobs's *The Death and Life of American Cities* in 1961, which pointed out the waste and failures of urban renewal, an ad hoc group called the Special Committee on Historic Preservation, which was under the auspices of the United States Conference of Mayors (with influential members, such as the Governor of Vermont and the chairman of the National Trust for Historic Preservation), published a report called "With Heritage So Rich" in 1964. In 1966 they developed it into a book with a forward by then-First Lady, Lady Bird Johnson. The publication of *With Heritage So Rich* represented one of the first national, high-profile protests against the sad state of preservation at the time (US Council of Mayors 1966). Later the same year, Congress passed the National Historic Preservation Act of 1966, which created the blueprint for the preservation field as it exists today in the United States. The 1966 Act built on the Historic Sites Act of 1935 but went much further.

The law established the National Advisory Council on Historic Preservation, an independent federal agency made up of 23 members, 21 of which are appointed by the president. The council's purpose is to promote the "preservation, enhancement, and productive use of our nation's historic resources" and to serve as the primary federal policy advisor to the president and Congress on historic preservation issues (Advisory Council 2010).

The National Historic Preservation Act also created the **National Register of Historic Places**, the nation's official list of historic properties deemed worthy of preservation (see Chapter 4). More than just a list, the National Register, which is maintained by the National Park Service, is a major component of a nationwide program to "identify, evaluate, and protect historic and archaeological resources." Properties listed on the National Register include "districts, sites, buildings, structures, and objects that are significant in American history, architecture, archaeology, engineering, and culture." Currently, well over one million individual properties (many within districts) located in all parts of the nation are listed on the National Register (FPI 2012).

The National Historic Preservation Act also contains **Section 106**, a law requiring all federal agencies or other entities that engage in projects or "undertakings" using federal funds or needing a federal license to allow the advisory council to have "the opportunity to comment" on the project before it is built. This requirement has evolved into a special review process to assess the potential effects on any possible historic properties before a project can begin. The act also established the basis for the creation of new state agencies called state historic preservation offices (SHPOs, discussed in Chapter 2).

SECTION 4(F)

The same year Congress passed the National Historic Preservation Act, it passed the Transportation Act, which included **Section 4(f)**, a legal clause that helps protect historic properties from the activities of the federal Department of Transportation (DOT) and any state DOTs using federal money. Section 4(f), which requires the engineers of transportation projects to take into account the protection of historic resources when planning them, has become an important tool in limiting the destruction of historic sites due to highway and other transportation-related projects (discussed further in Chapter 2).

PRESERVATION REACHES MATURITY, 1970s–2000s

With the implementation of the National Historic Preservation Act and the passage of additional federal and state laws, the preservation field began to take its present form in the late 20th century. As the provisions of the National Historic Preservation Act were implemented in the late 1960s and early 1970s, an entire new bureaucracy emerged around the state historic preservation offices, the National Park Service, and the Advisory Council on Historic Preservation. This bureaucracy, which operates at the state and federal levels, is both advisory and regulatory as it implements and manages major preservation tools, such as the National Register of Historic Places, the Historic American Building Survey, and Section 106. However, as the field evolved, additional governmental and nongovernmental programs and guidelines were created to complement those already in operation.

EXECUTIVE ORDER 11593

Despite the passage of the National Historic Preservation Act, by the early 1970s, many historic properties owned by the federal government were still not being maintained, causing President Richard M. Nixon to issue Executive Order 11593 in 1971, which requires federal agencies to take an active role in the preservation and care of cultural properties under their control. The executive order covers all federally owned historic properties, including buildings and archeological sites, to ensure they are actively preserved, maintained, and restored if necessary. Executive Order 11593 was essentially intended to provide executive enforcement of provisions of the National Historic Preservation Act of 1966.

FEDERAL HISTORIC PRESERVATION TAX INCENTIVES

In the mid-1970s, the federal government also acted to encourage preservation by private developers. In 1976 Congress enacted a 25 percent federal tax incentive designed to encourage private developers of commercial properties to rehabilitate historic buildings rather than tearing them down and replacing them. This law, called the Federal Historic Preservation Tax Incentives program, was passed mainly to compensate for existing tax codes that favored new construction over reusing existing buildings. In 1986, the law was weakened, but the program still provides a 20 percent tax credit (discussed in Chapter 2). The Federal Historic Preservation Tax Incentives program impacted the design fields significantly because it brought billions of dollars into preservation projects requiring architectural design services. Historic factories and warehouses, train stations, hotels, and other income-producing buildings were rehabilitated according to federal historic guidelines and converted into new uses, such as lofts and shopping centers.

CHANGES IN ATTITUDES ABOUT PRESERVATION: POSTMODERNISM

Besides more federal programs and local historic districts, another force influenced designers. By the late 1970s, the Modernist style of architecture, which had emphasized new construction, lack of decoration and, in theory at least, design focused solely on function, structure, materials, and proportion, was giving way to the postmodern style, which introduced new versions of historic architectural styles, forms, and decoration, often presented in ironic ways. The general resurgence of historic references in architecture that flowered in the 1980s helped to increase a general appreciation of historic architecture on the part of designers. An increase in the number and size of historic districts also made designers more aware of historic architecture.

New buildings constructed within historic neighborhoods are referred to as **infill** buildings. With the large number of local historic districts in the 1980s and 1990s, architects were increasingly compelled to design infill buildings that conformed to the historical design guidelines within those districts. This meant design elements of the infill buildings, such as their overall form or massing, scale, materials, and proportions were required to fit in and be contextual with the historic buildings around them. Also, with fewer old buildings being demolished and replaced, in part because of the popularity of the federal Preservation Tax Incentive program, architects and interior designers found themselves working directly with historic buildings more often than previously. Because more designers were doing renovations and rehabilitations, the title *historical architect* was created to describe architects who specialized in restorations and sensitive rehabilitations of historic buildings. Interior designers also began to specialize in historic design. Over time, the practice of historic preservation and building design became increasingly interconnected.

Penn Central Transportation Co. v. City of New York

Near the end of the 1970s, after decades of legal ambivalence as to whether governments possessed the legitimate police power to limit private activities for the purposes of historic preservation, the U.S. Supreme Court created a significant legal precedent in the arena of regulation. In 1978, the Supreme Court upheld the right of municipalities to enforce historic preservation ordinances in the landmark *Penn Central Transportation Co. v. City of New York* case that resulted from an attempt by the Penn Central Transportation Company to erect a giant glass office tower designed by modernist architect Marcel Breuer directly atop the historic Grand Central Terminal (discussed in Chapter 5) (Figures 1.12a and 1.12b).

Figure 1.12a Grand Central Terminal in 1913, shortly after its construction. Source: © CORBIS.

HERITAGE AREAS AND CORRIDORS

In 1984, Congress took a broader role in preservation when it began establishing National Heritage Areas and National Heritage Corridors. This expanded the scope of preservation from focusing on individual sites and districts. The first area so recognized was the Illinois & Michigan Canal National Heritage Area. These multi-county regions contain related historic properties and are designated and administered by the federal government, which has created more than 40 such areas to date, with the cooperation of state and local governments, private landowners, business people, and local activists (NPS Heritage Areas 2010). An example of one such national heritage area is the Path of Progress.

Figure 1.12b Marcel Breuer's 1969 proposal for an office tower to be built atop Grand Central Terminal. Source: Grand Central Air Rights Building, proposal drawing, ca. 1969 / unidentified artist. Marcel Breuer papers, Archives of American Art, Smithsonian Institution.

Authorized in 1988, the Path of Progress consists of a five-hundred-mile designated route through a nine-county region of southwestern Pennsylvania marked with distinctive road signs that guide visitors to significant sites associated with the area's historic industries of mining, railroading, and steel production.

An example of a National Heritage Corridor created by federal law is the Route 66 Corridor Preservation Program, which seeks to coordinate and provide funding for the preservation of historic sites and road-related architecture along the entire length of historic Route 66

Figure 1.13 Fancy motels such as this once lined the Route 66 Corridor. The few that exist today should be preserved as increasingly rare examples of 20th-century road-related architecture. Source: From Peter B. Dedek collection.

from Chicago to Los Angeles (Figure 1.13). Established in 1999, the initiative was designed to be a "program of technical assistance and grants [to] set priorities for the preservation of the Route 66 corridor" (Route 66 Corridor Act 1999). The vast scale of the area included (more than 2,400 miles) and the broad scope of resources considered historic—including aging bridges, old motels, ancient pueblos, and 1950s movie sets—makes the Route 66 Corridor program significant in the history of historic preservation. The use of heritage areas and historic corridors allows historic places to be preserved with their broad contexts and emphasizes the linkages among related historic sites over sometimes vast geographic areas.

INTERSTATE SURFACE TRANSPORTATION EFFICIENCY ACT

In an effort to provide direct funding for the preservation of transportation-related historic properties, Congress added enhancement grants to the Interstate Surface Transportation Efficiency Act (ISTEA), which it passed in 1991. This program provided federal funding for preservation projects involving buildings and structures located near highways, railroad tracks, or other transportation corridors. Enhancement grants were used in many restoration and rehabilitation projects, some with only a tangential connection with transportation. In 1998 Congress replaced ISTEA with the Transportation Equity Act for the 21st Century (TEA-21), which also included enhancement grants, but the rules relating to historic buildings and structures were tightened to include only resources directly related to transportation, such as historic bridges and railroad stations (discussed in Chapter 2).

NATIVE AMERICAN PRESERVATION PROGRAMS

By the 1990s, the scope of historic preservation had expanded far beyond the limited vision of preserving colonial cities and 19th-century neighborhoods.

In 1990, Congress enacted the Native American Graves Protection and Repatriation Act (NAGPRA) to "address the rights of lineal descendants, Indian tribes, and Native Hawaiian organizations to Native American cultural items, including human remains, funerary objects, sacred objects, and objects of cultural patrimony" (NPS National NAGPRA 2012). Managed by the Secretary of the Interior, the National NAGPRA Program was designed to protect Native American sacred artifacts and human remains from being looted and held in museums against the wishes of members of the tribes to which they are connected. The law broadened the scope of what kinds of artifacts and sites were worthy of preservation and was a significant step in giving Native Americans some control over their own heritage.

In 1992, the U.S. Congress passed amendments to the National Historic Preservation Act of 1966 (P.L. 102-575) that allowed interested federally recognized Native American tribes to adopt formal responsibility for the preservation of historic properties located on tribal lands. The amendments allow tribes to assume the functions of a State Historic Preservation Officer (SHPO), thus creating the Tribal Historic Preservation Offices (THPOs) (Advisory Council 2002).

In the mid-1990s, federal attention to Native American sites increased. Because of increasing concern for the preservation of Native American sites and the cultures that revere them, in 1996 President Bill Clinton issued Executive Order 13007, which instructed federal agencies dealing with Native American sacred sites to reevaluate their policies regarding them. Agencies were ordered to "accommodate access to and ceremonial use of Indian sacred sites by Indian religious practitioners and avoid adversely affecting the physical integrity of such sacred sites" (Advisory Council 2012).

SAVE AMERICA'S TREASURES

In the late 1990s, the federal government continued to expand and redefine its role in preservation. Established by a Presidential Executive Order by Bill Clinton in 1998, Save America's Treasures was a public-private partnership involving the National Trust for Historic Preservation, the National Park Service, and the President's Committee on the Arts and Humanities to fund the physical bricks-and-mortar preservation of sites with national historical significance. By 2008, the program had funded 1,600 projects and awarded over $300 million in public and private grants to preservation efforts located in every state (National Trust for Historic Preservation 2010). Despite its successes, Congress did not provide funding for fiscal years 2011 and 2012, and the program ceased operation (NPS Survey 2012).

PRESERVE AMERICA

In recent decades, historic preservation has been fortunate enough to be supported by politicians from both of the major political parties. In 2003, President George W. Bush signed Executive Order 13287, which created Preserve America, a program that "reaffirms the federal government's responsibility to show leadership in preserving America's heritage by actively advancing the protection, enhancement, and contemporary use of the historic properties owned by the federal government, and by promoting intergovernmental cooperation and partnerships for the preservation and use of historic properties" (Advisory Council 2012). Under the Preserve America program, the designation "Preserve America Community" was given to more than 500 "communities, including individual neighborhoods in large cities, that protect and celebrate their heritage, use their historic assets for economic development and community revitalization, and encourage people to experience and appreciate local historic resources through education and heritage tourism programs" (Advisory Council 2008). Preserve America focused on providing grants to support planning and studies rather than bricks-and-mortar projects. As of 2010, the program had provided "[m]ore than $20 million in matching grants awarded to 259 projects throughout the country" (Preserve America 2012). However, as with Save America's Treasures, funding for Preserve America was eliminated in the 2012 federal budget and was not being implemented at this writing.

THE FIELD OF HISTORIC PRESERVATION TODAY

Over the past two hundred years, historic preservation has evolved from a few isolated private efforts by a handful of concerned citizens trying to save individual sites into a highly sophisticated movement backed by law, governmental bureaucracy, and organized activism. Preservation has become an academic discipline with departments and undergraduate and advanced degrees related to preservation located in universities across the nation. Preservation has also become a profession that employs thousands of individuals who are educated in its theory and practice, including historical architects, architectural historians, preservation lawyers, and preservation specialists, who work in federal and state agencies, private advocacy groups, and design and consulting firms.

The field has moved from being concerned mainly with sites associated with the elite to one concerned with the history and material culture of diverse peoples from all economic levels and all ethnic groups throughout America. Not only has the scope of preservation widened to include the heritage of more and more people, it has also expanded to include sites from the recent past not traditionally considered historic (Figure 1.14). These include places such as gas stations, motels, and restaurants from the 1920s through the 1960s and novel building types, such as Lustron houses, a type of small metal suburban tract house produced by the Lustron Corporation for only two years from 1949 to 1950 (Figure 1.15).

Another way in which the focus of historic preservation has broadened is its gradual shift from concentrating on specific sites, such as Independence Hall and Mount Vernon, to entire districts, such as the Battery in Charleston and the French Quarter in New Orleans, to landscapes and eventually to the preservation of entire regions, such as the Path of Progress

Figure 1.14 Although still endangered, architecture such as this café in San Bruno, California, near San Francisco are increasingly receiving historic status and being preserved. Source: Photograph by Peter B. Dedek 2009.

Figure 1.15 Lustron House, Arlington, Virginia. Source: Library of Congress, Prints and Photographs Division, Washington, D.C. 20540 USA. http://hdl.loc.gov/ loc.pnp/hhh.va2032. Historic American Buildings Survey. Survey number HABS VA-1414.

in southwestern Pennsylvania and the historic Route 66 Corridor, which stretches across the American West from Chicago to Los Angeles.

In the 21st century, historic preservation has become an integral part of the fields of architecture and interior design. Although some designers may continue to be hostile to preservation, in reality, this expanding area of design is only going to continue to grow in importance given the increasing emphasis placed on preservation by clients and the public and the ever growing number of buildings becoming historic due to that fact that in the United States any building fifty years or older is considered potentially historic. In addition, many people are moving back into historic city centers, bringing capital and initiating historic design projects.

As preservation grows more sophisticated, it has become evident that the discipline is increasingly relevant to and connected with the environmental or "green" movement. Green architecture has been transforming the design fields in recent years. Because of its focus on recycling buildings and reusing existing neighborhoods and entire regions rather than building on pristine land, historic preservation has a clear role to play in efforts to solve the environmental and social issues facing our nation. As their discipline expands in scope and complexity, preservationists will continue to increase their cooperation and integration with a number of allied disciplines, including architecture, interior design, urban planning, public history, and environmental conservation.

Despite its successes, the challenges facing preservation today are significant. While the American preservation movement has saved countless buildings, districts, and sites from destruction, it has had mixed results in certain areas, such as the retention and care of historic interiors, many of which have been destroyed even when the buildings that once contained and protected them have been saved and rehabilitated. And as development pressures and urban sprawl continue to threaten historic buildings and landscapes, preservationists will be required to develop ever new and more sophisticated strategies for preserving the heritage of our rapidly changing society.

CONCLUSION

Since its humble origins in the early 19th century, historic preservation in the United States has evolved into a complicated and diverse social movement. A flourishing profession with an active field of academic study, historic preservation also has a firm basis in American jurisprudence and established uniform national standards. These standards determine what makes a property, landscape, or district historic and direct how historic sites, buildings, and other properties should be treated. Key players in the preservation movement today include the federal government, state and local governments, architecture and interior design firms, preservation consulting firms, and a slew of private advocacy organizations, large and small. Today, tens of thousands of historic sites, districts, and landscapes representing diverse historic resources have been conserved through the efforts of preservationists. These properties embody diverse architectural styles and building types, represent historic events from the distant and the recent past, and are associated with people from a wide range of ethnicities and socio-economic backgrounds.

The impact of historic preservation on the fields of architecture and interior design is steadily increasing as the number of historic districts grows and development in older neighborhoods at the centers of towns and within inner cities intensifies. With increasing awareness among clients and design professionals of the value of preserving the historic built environment, the field's influence will continue to grow.

Preservation enhances the livability of communities and increases their potential to attract tourist dollars. Preserving America's heritage is critical to maintaining our identity and our connection with past generations. In an era of architectural uniformity, of big box retail and massive commercial and housing developments, historic architecture and landscapes provide American communities with unique and irreplaceable sites that embody authentic local character and intrinsic value.

STUDY QUESTIONS

1. What were the motivations that prompted early preservationist Anne Pamela Cunningham to create the Mount Vernon Ladies Association to save the ancestral home of George Washington?

2. What influence did the strategies and methods of the Mount Vernon Ladies Association have on later American preservation efforts?

3. What is the 1906 Antiquities Act, and how did it impact historic preservation?

4. How might current preservationists criticize the methods used to restore historic Williamsburg and those used at Greenfield Village?

5. What aspects of the 1935 Historic Sites Act were significant in establishing the role of the federal government in historic preservation?

6. Over the history of historic preservation, what attitudes did architects and designers generally have about the field and how did those views change over time? What factors led to changes in these attitudes?

7. Name and define four major preservation initiatives mandated by the 1966 Historic Preservation Act.

8. In what ways does a heritage area differ from a local historic district?

9. In what ways has the scope of the field of historic preservation widened in recent decades? These include, economic, stylistic, social, and historical factors.

10. Do you think historic preservation has a significant role in the green design movement? Why or why not?

EXERCISE: IDENTIFY HISTORIC PROPERTY TYPES

Identify the historic property type for each example from the chapter (an example can represent two or more property types):

A) Building

B) Structure

C) Object

D) District

E) Site

F) Heritage Area

G) Outdoor Museum

1 _____ Mt. Vernon

2 _____ Yellowstone

3 _____ Hermitage

4 _____ Williamsburg

5 _____ Shiloh Battlefield

6 _____ Independence Hall

7 _____ Touro Synagogue

8 _____ Casa Grande

9 _____ Skansen

10 _____ *Vieux Carré*

11 _____ Greenfield Village

12 _____ The Battery

13 _____ Pennsylvania Station

14 _____ Illinois & Michigan Canal

15 _____ Madison Square Garden

16 _____ Path of Progress

17 _____ Lustron House

18 _____ Grand Central Terminal

Answers and explanations found in Instructor's Guide.

SOURCES

Advisory Council on Historic Preservation. "Federal Historic Preservation Case Law, 1966–1996." Accessed June 24, 2010. http://www.achp.gov/book/COVER1.html#.

———. 2002. "Executive Order No. 13007: Indian Sacred Sites." Accessed February 24, 2012. http://www.achp.gov/EO13007.html.

———. 2007. "The Preserve America Executive Order: Report to the President." Accessed February 24, 2012. http://www.achp.gov/pubs-eoreport.html.

———. 2008. "The Preserve America Program." Accessed November 27, 2013. http://www.preserveamerica.gov/docs/PA%20Overview%2010-29-13.pdf.

Appleton, William Sumner. 1941. "The Society for the Preservation of New England Antiquities and Its Work." *The Journal of the American Society of Architectural Historians* 1(3–4): 19–20.

British National Trust. "Who We Are: Our History." Accessed June 24, 2010. http://www.nationaltrust.org.uk/main/w-trust/w-thecharity/w-thecharity_our-past.htm.

Bucy, Carole Stanford. 2009. "Ladies Hermitage Association." Last modified Feb. 21, 2011. http://www.thehermitage.com/mansion-grounds/mansion/preservation.

Cooke, Edward S. 1987. *Draperies in Interior Decoration*. New York: W. W. Norton & Company.

Federal Preservation Institute. YEAR? "About the Federal Preservation Institute (FPI)." Accessed July 11, 2010. http://stage.historicpreservation.gov/About.aspx.

Finley, David E. 1965. *History of the National Trust for Historic Preservation 1947–1963*. Washington, DC: National Trust for Historic Preservation.

Hermitage, the Home of President Andrew Jackson. "Preservation." Accessed February 17, 2012. http://www.thehermitage.com/.

Historic Sites Act of 1935 [Public—No. 292—74th Congress] [S. 2073]. Accessed February 19, 2012. http://www.cr.nps.gov/history/online_books/unrau-williss/adhia7.htm.

Hosmer, Charles B., Jr. 1965. *Presence of the Past: A History of the Preservation Movement in the United States before Williamsburg*. New York: G. P. Putnam's Sons.

Historic New England. "Founder and History." Accessed June 20, 2010. http://www.historicnewengland.org/about-us/founder-and-history-1.

The Inflation Calculator. Accessed March 2, 2012. http://www.westegg.com/inflation/

Mires, Charlene. 2002. *Independence Hall in American Memory*. Philadelphia: University of Pennsylvania Press.

Morton, W. Brown, III. 1987. "What Do We Preserve and Why?" In *The American Mosaic: Preserving a Nation's Heritage*, edited by Robert E. Stipe and Antoinette J. Lee, 146–177. Baltimore: US/ICOMOS, J.D. Lucas Printing Company.

Mount Vernon Backgrounders. 2006. "The Formation of the Mount Vernon Ladies' Association and the Dramatic Rescue of George Washington's Estate." Accessed June 20, 2010. http://www.mountvernon.org/press/backgrounders/mvla.

National Park Service (NPS). 2005. "Survey of Historic Sites and Buildings." Accessed March 2, 2012. http://www.nps.gov/history/history/online_books/colonials-patriots/sitec35.htm.

———. "National Heritage Areas." Accessed June 21 2010. http://www.nps.gov/history/heritageareas/.

———. "National NAGPRA." Accessed April 26, 2012. http://www.nps.gov/nagpra/.

———. "Save America's Treasures Grant Program." Website updated October 25, 2013. http://www.nps.gov/history/hps/treasures/.

National Trust for Historic Preservation. 2003. "Save Our Heritage Press Release." Accessed June 24, 2010. http://www.saveourheritage.com/Library_Docs/SOH_Eleven_Release.pdf.

Plosky, Eric J. 2000. "The Fall and Rise of Pennsylvania Station; Changing Attitudes Toward Historic Preservation in New York City." Unpublished dissertation, Massachusetts Institute of Technology.

Preserve America. "Overview." Website updated December 7, 2012. http://www.preserveamerica.gov/overview.html.

Rothman, Hal. 1989. *Preserving Different Pasts: The American National Monuments*. Chicago (URBANA?): University of Illinois Press.

Route 66 Corridor Act [Public Law No. 106-45]. 1999. Accessed March 22, 2012. http://www.nps.gov/rt66/PublicLaw106-45.pdf.

Special Committee on Historic Preservation. 1966. *With Heritage So Rich: A Report of the Special Committee on Historic Preservation*. Washington, DC: Double Dot Press, Inc.

GOVERNMENT INVOLVEMENT IN PRESERVATION: THE FEDERAL AND STATE ROLES

2

OBJECTIVES

- Describe the many programs the federal government administers in historic preservation today.

- Explain how these programs operate and what impacts they have on historic resources.

- Outline the responsibilities the states have to help preserve our nation's heritage.

- Explain how governmental programs at both the federal and state levels impact the work of designers.

Despite the field's private origins, the federal government and the states have a significant role in preservation today. Governments often work in conjunction with private organizations and concerned individuals. In general, unlike in many countries such as Great Britain, the national and state governments do not dictate how historic properties are to be treated by private owners but form partnerships and programs aimed at encouraging and rewarding preservation.

FEDERAL INVOLVEMENT IN HISTORIC PRESERVATION

Federal involvement in historic preservation is extensive and has grown substantially since the passage of the Antiquities Act of 1906. As we saw in Chapter 1, the federal government did not take a significant role in historic preservation until the passage of the Historic Sites Act in 1935. The 1935 law declared for the first time that it was "a national policy to preserve for public use historic sites, buildings, and objects of national significance for the inspiration and benefit of the people of the United States" (Historic Sites Act 1935). The act also directed the Secretary of the Interior to, among other things, create a survey and a list of national historic landmarks, and help preserve buildings both in and out of federal ownership by making "cooperative agreements with States, municipal subdivisions, corporations, associations, or individuals . . . to protect, preserve, maintain, or operate . . . historic propert[ies] . . ." (Historic Sites Act 1935). The Historic Sites Act helped establish the basis and the language that would shape the development of the field of historic preservation as it is today.

NATIONAL HISTORIC PRESERVATION ACT OF 1966

As discussed in Chapter 1, despite the provisions of the Antiquities Act of 1906 and the Historic Sites Act of 1935, and the creation of a number of a number of local historic districts, the era between the 1930s and the 1960s was disastrous for America's historic neighborhoods, buildings, and landscapes. For this reason, Congress passed a stronger and much more comprehensive national historic preservation law in 1966. The National Historic Preservation Act of 1966 (NHPA) encourages the preservation of historic sites by directing federal agencies to "assume responsibility for considering historic resources in their activities" (Bell 1985). The act accomplishes this mostly through the creation of the National Register of Historic Places discussed in Chapter 4; the state historic preservation offices discussed later in this chapter; and grant and loan programs designed to provide funding to survey, study, acquire, restore, or rehabilitate properties listed or eligible to be listed on the National Register. The law also created the following programs and requirements:

The Advisory Council on Historic Preservation

One of the more significant programs created by the National Historic Preservation Act of 1966, the **Advisory Council on Historic Preservation** is a federal agency with 23 official members, 21 of which are appointed by the president. The council is dedicated to promoting the preservation of all types of historic properties across the nation, with its mission: "to promote the preservation, enhancement, and productive use of our nation's historic resources, and advise the president and Congress on national historic preservation policy" (Advisory Council on

Historic Preservation 2006). A small staff supports the Advisory Council, including a number of preservation architects and other professionals with design backgrounds. The council works to create public-private partnerships to promote preservation activities. To that end, it manages the Native American Program, which deals with preservation issues related to Indian tribes and Native Hawaiian organizations and provides assistance to individuals and organizations working to preserve, restore, and interpret Native American sites (Advisory Council on Historic Preservation 2006). In addition to these responsibilities, the Advisory Council has the last say in disputed reviews performed under Section 106 of the National Historic Preservation Act of 1966.

Section 106 Review

In theory, Section 106 gives the Advisory Council the right to comment on any project proposed within the entire United States and its possessions involving federal funds or requiring a federal permit. The law states, "the head of any Federal department or independent agency having authority to license any undertaking shall, prior to the approval of the expenditure of any Federal funds on the undertaking or prior to the issuance of any license, as the case may be, take into account the effect of the undertaking on any district, site, building, structure, or object that is included in or eligible for inclusion in the National Register. . . . [and] shall afford the Advisory Council on Historic Preservation . . . a reasonable opportunity to comment with regard to such undertaking" (NHPA of 1966). In practice, the law requires any entity contemplating a construction project using federal funds or requiring a federal permit to complete the Section 106 process, which consists of a number of defined steps.

Section 106 regulations involve only federal activities or "undertakings." The regulations define "federal undertakings" as activities funded in whole or in part by the federal government and those requiring a federal license or permit to proceed. Examples of federal undertakings include most road and highway projects because they usually use federal highway money, and even purely state-funded highway projects become federally licensed undertakings if they involve work on a bridge that passes over "waters of the United States," which includes all navigable waterways and many smaller streams. Any work involving waters of the United States requires a permit from the Army Corps of Engineers. Federal undertakings include any building rehabilitation, demolition, or alteration that uses any kind of federal grant or requires any kind of federal permit. This applies even to the construction of cell phone towers, because building one requires a license from the Federal Communications Commission. Most activities that involve architectural and or interior design are considered undertakings. However, projects not involving physical activities that have the potential to affect historic resources, such as federally funded studies or planning efforts, are not considered federal undertakings for purposes of Section 106 review.

Once it has been established a federal undertaking indeed exists, staff at the SHPO determine if the project actually has the potential to harm historic properties. By their nature, undertakings have little or no possibility of adversely affecting historic properties if the project's scope—such as with road resurfacing or replacing existing railroad track—is limited. If the SHPO, in conjunction with the agency proposing the undertaking, determines that the project has no potential to harm historic properties, the Section 106 process is complete and the project can go forward.

If, on the other hand, the SHPO determines that the undertaking is significant enough to possibly impact historic properties, the SHPO explores what effect it anticipates the undertaking may have within the project's **Area of Potential Effect** (APE). The APE is the geographical area in which a project has the potential to impact any historic property that may be present. For example, if a federally funded flood control project included a levee that would be clearly visible from a historic house, even though the levee did not require that the house be demolished, the historic house would be included in the project's APE. The levee might cut through the house's yard or make access difficult or simply spoil its historic integrity by altering its surroundings, and thus "adversely affect" the historic property. For large projects, such as major highways or dams, the APE may extend in all directions as far as 800 feet or more from the actual site of construction; whereas for small projects, such as installing a turning lane, the APE will only encompass the immediate project area.

Once the APE has been determined, people working for one of the agencies involved, or SHPO personnel, or in some cases, consultants who are trained architectural historians, will perform a survey of the project's entire APE, particularly if it is a large area. For small projects, often the people planning the project submit a form accompanied by some photographs to the SHPO, which will determine if any historic properties potentially harmed by the project are within the project's APE. In many cases, no historic properties will be found within the APE. If this occurs, the SHPO determines that "no historic properties are present" within the APE. This normally completes the 106 process, and the project proceeds.

However, if historic buildings, structures, or sites listed or eligible for listing on the National Register (see Chapter 4 for how this is determined) are found within the APE, then staff at the SHPO, who are often specially trained architects, will carefully examine and assess the potential impacts the project may have on the historic resources and will determine whether the undertaking will have "no effect," "no adverse effect," or an "adverse effect" on one or more of the historic resources located within the APE. If the SHPO determines there will be no effect, or no adverse effect, usually the 106 process is complete, and the project may proceed.

If the SHPO determines a project will have an adverse effect, the agency then negotiates methods to mitigate the alleged adverse effect in consultation with the SHPO, although in higher profile projects the Advisory Council may also become involved. Once an agreement is reached, a document called a **Memorandum of Agreement** (MOA) is drafted and signed by all involved parties. The MOA officially documents any agreement that all of the involved parties have come to. MOAs usually include measures the agency doing the undertaking will take to minimize the adverse effect(s). These measures are called **mitigation**. Mitigation ranges from the minimal—taking photographs of a doomed structure for archival purposes—to the extreme—halting work on the project altogether in order to preserve the threatened historic resource or resources. Some Section 106 reviews become very contentious and politicized, and a few even end up in court (see Chapter 5). Sometimes political pressure from concerned individuals motivates the agencies involved to avoid controversy and bad publicity by coming to some kind of agreement to resolve the issue, which can end up saving historic properties (King 2000).

If no memorandum of agreement can be reached among the interested parties and the SHPO, either side can appeal to the Advisory Council, which makes the final determination of effect. However, if the project's promoters and the Advisory Council cannot come to an agreement, then normally the project is allowed to move forward regardless of the harm it may do to historic properties. This may make the process seem pointless, but often by the time such an impasse has been reached, months or even years have gone by. The prospect of delays and bad publicity often motivates agencies to cooperate with the SHPO and make agreements acceptable to all parties.

Section 106 rarely stops a project dead; however, the process has the potential to reduce the adverse impact of federal projects on historic resources because it allows time for negotiations with concerned parties and gives time for practical alternatives to be devised. While Section 106 can act as a useful tool to force an agency to slow down a project and negotiate, preservationists

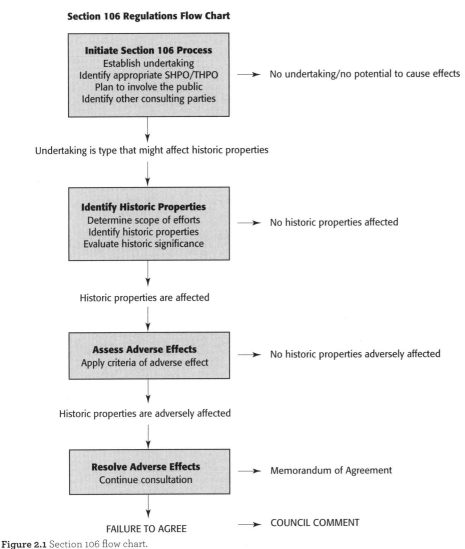

Section 106 Regulations Flow Chart

Initiate Section 106 Process
Establish undertaking
Identify appropriate SHPO/THPO
Plan to involve the public
Identify other consulting parties
→ No undertaking/no potential to cause effects

Undertaking is type that might affect historic properties

Identify Historic Properties
Determine scope of efforts
Identify historic properties
Evaluate historic significance
→ No historic properties affected

Historic properties are affected

Assess Adverse Effects
Apply criteria of adverse effect
→ No historic properties adversely affected

Historic properties are adversely affected

Resolve Adverse Effects
Continue consultation
→ Memorandum of Agreement

FAILURE TO AGREE → COUNCIL COMMENT

Figure 2.1 Section 106 flow chart.

cannot rely on such regulations alone, especially if the agency involved will not compromise. In some instances when a resource stands directly in the path of a project, photographic documentation of the resource followed by its demolition ends up being the only realistic mitigation. In general, though, the Section 106 process has reduced the negative impact of federal undertakings on historic properties.

Section 110: Additional Protection for National Historic Landmarks

Section 110 of the National Historic Preservation Act of 1966 stipulates, "Prior to the approval of any Federal undertaking [that] may directly and adversely affect any National Historic Landmark, the head of the responsible Federal agency shall, to the maximum extent possible, undertake such planning and actions as may be necessary to minimize harm to such landmark, and shall afford the Advisory Council on Historic Preservation a reasonable opportunity to comment on the undertaking" (NHPA of 1966). This language requires federal agencies to guard against federal money or oversight being used to damage National Historic Landmarks. It is more directive and perhaps more effective in protecting National Historic Landmarks from harm by federal activities than the more general review process required under Section 106. It is important, therefore, that professionals in the design fields working on or within a National Historic Landmark or in the vicinity of one be aware of the special federal protection to that property's integrity and its historic context provided by Section 110.

HISTORIC PROPERTIES AND THE NATIONAL TRANSPORTATION ACTS

In 1966, Congress passed the **National Transportation Act**, which was the first transportation law that addressed historic preservation (in section 4(f) discussed later in this chapter). In 1991, Congress created the Intermodal Surface Transportation Efficiency Act (ISTEA), and in 1998, it passed ISTEA's successor, the Transportation Equity Act for the 21st Century (TEA-21). In 2005, Congress replaced TEA-21 with the Safe, Accountable, Flexible, Efficient Transportation Equity Act (SAFETEA-LU). These laws, designed to provide federal funding for highways and other modes of transportation, such as city buses and commuter railroads, placed a new emphasis on quality of life and environmental issues; and included funding for transportation enhancement grants, which are administered by the Federal Highway Administration (FHWA). Among the twelve categories of activities approved for Enhancement Grants in TEA-21 were the "acquisition of scenic easements and scenic or historic sites, creating scenic or historic highway programs, historic preservation, and the rehabilitation and operation of historic transportation buildings, structures, and facilities" (Rails to Trails Conservancy 2010).

Enhancement Grants

Enhancement grants awarded under those categories have been used for such activities as the purchase of historic easements, rehabilitation of historic buildings, and adding landscaping around historic buildings and structures. The enhancement grant program has led to a great number of successful preservation projects. More than $7.1 billion in enhancement grants of all types was made available between 1992 and 2005, and over this same period more than $1.1 billion of that $7.1 billion was used for historical and archeological projects, constituting a significant investment in preservation (Advisory Council on Historic Preservation 2006).

In order to receive the grants, the design of any project must maintain the historic integrity of the historic resources involved (see Chapter 4). This program has provided millions of dollars for projects that employ architects, landscape architects, and interior designers who have a working understanding of historic preservation.

To be considered historic under the program, a property must be listed on the National Register. The property must also be transportation related (such as a historic rail station or highway rest stop) and be owned by nonprofits, municipalities, or other government entities, but not by private individuals or for-profit corporations. For enhancement money to be awarded, all work done on historic properties must be done in accordance with the Secretary of the Interior's Standards for Rehabilitation (see Chapter 10).

Technically, the transportation enhancement program is not a grant program but functions as a reimbursement program. In most states, 20 percent of the cost of a project must be provided by its local sponsor with the remaining 80 percent provided from Federal Highway Trust funds (Rails to Trails Conservancy 2010).

Section 4(f) of the National Transportation Act

Section 4(f) of the National Transportation Act, originally passed in 1966 and retained in the federal transportation statutes passed since then, was created to protect historic sites from demolition caused by transportation-related federal undertakings. Although 4(f) may seem redundant because of Section 106, it is actually a stronger law. Section 4(f) requires an agency, most often a state highway department using federal transportation funds, to explore all "feasible and prudent" options to "minimize harm" to a historic property if it is to be directly impacted by a highway project. As with Section 106, 4(f) defines a historic property as one listed or eligible for listing in the National Register. Section 4(f) also applies to projects impacting parks and wildlife refuges. While Section 106 is essentially advisory and only requires the agency or agencies involved to complete the required bureaucratic process, 4(f) directs the Federal Highway Administration (FHWA) or any other federal transportation agency involved (such as the Federal Aviation Administration) to prepare a meaningful "discussion of alternatives" for any project that will take land from a historic property. In this case, "take" means land directly associated with the historic property is actually condemned (seized under eminent domain) or otherwise acquired for direct use by the project.

Another form of "taking" a historic property under Section 4(f) is called *constructive use,* which means a project adversely impacts a property to such a degree the property can no longer be used for its historic or intended purpose. An example of constructive use would be if a limited access highway were to cut a historic farm in half such that the farmer could no longer utilize one half of his land because he would not be allowed to cross the highway to access it. If the Federal Highway Administration determines through Section 4(f) that a particular project will harm historic resources, the agency must make all "prudent and feasible" efforts to alter the project's design in order to avoid or at least minimize the adverse effect. This law has saved entire neighborhoods from destruction, such as in the 1971 legal case of *Citizens to Preserve Overton Park v. Volpe,* when Section 4(f) was used to force the builders of Interstate 40 to reroute the highway around Overton Park in a historic area of Memphis, Tennessee (Federal Highway Administration 2012).

THE NATIONAL PARK SERVICE AND HISTORIC PRESERVATION

The **National Park Service (NPS)**, which falls under the Secretary of the Interior, has a critical role in historic preservation in the United States. The NPS was founded in 1916 to manage and protect the national parks and national monuments. Although the Park Service did operate a few historic sites from the beginning, the agency did not take on a significant role in historic preservation until 1933, when a presidential Executive Order transferred 56 national monuments and historic military sites from other agencies to the NPS (NPS "History" 2010).

Two years later, the Historic Sites Act of 1935 gave the NPS much broader responsibilities regarding historic preservation. The NPS assumed the responsibility of creating an archive containing drawings, photographs, and descriptions of historic sites. The NPS was also charged with surveying historic areas around the nation and investigating, researching, acquiring, restoring, and managing historic sites. The agency was encouraged to enter into cooperative agreements with "states, municipal subdivisions, corporations, associations, or individuals . . . to protect, preserve, maintain, or operate any historic [sites]," and to erect and maintain historical markers to commemorate historic sites and events (Historic Sites Act of 1935). The 1935 act created the foundations of the vast role the NPS plays in historic preservation today. In the 1930s, the NPS started hiring historians and designers and soon developed an increasingly professionalized staff (Whisnant 2006).

After the passage of the Historic Preservation Act of 1966, the NPS became even more involved in preservation. In 1971, the Secretary of the Interior gave the NPS the responsibility of managing a major portion of the national historic preservation program, which the 1966 act had created (Hertfelder 1986, 136).

Today, the NPS administers a wide range of preservation programs, including the National Register of Historic Places, the American Battlefield Protection Program, Federal Agency Preservation Assistance Program, and the Federal Historic Preservation Tax Incentives. The NPS also runs the Technical Preservation Services for Historic Buildings, which provides technical assistance on the preservation of buildings and building materials; the Tribal Preservation Program, which assists Native American tribes in preserving their historic properties and cultural traditions; and the Certified Local Government Program, discussed later in the chapter. In 2000, the NPS also created the **Federal Preservation Institute**, which provides federal officials and other interested parties with training in subjects related to historic preservation (Federal Preservation Institute 2010).

In addition to the preservation programs listed, the NPS directly manages a wide range of significant historic sites (Figure 2.2). Currently, about 60 percent of the 391 park areas administered by the National Park Service emphasize history or prehistory (NPS, "National Park Service History" 2010).

Figure 2.2 National Park Service–administered site: carriage house at home of Franklin D. Roosevelt, National Historic Site, Hyde Park, New York. The NPS manages hundreds of diverse historic sites, many of which not only include the homes of historically significant individuals, but also associated historic landscapes and outbuildings. Source: Photograph by Peter B. Dedek, 2010.

FEDERAL TAX CREDITS FOR REHABILITATION OF HISTORIC STRUCTURES

The **Federal Historic Preservation Tax Incentives** is a federal program that has saved thousands of significant American historic buildings (Figure 2.3). The program is administered by the Department of Interior through the National Park Service, with the assistance of the Internal Revenue Service and the state historic preservation offices. Rather than just regulating the

Figure 2.3 1 Powell Street, San Francisco. Built in 1920 in the Renaissance revival style, this building was recently seismically retrofitted and rehabilitated by Gensler according to the *Secretary of the Interior's Standards*. Source: Photograph by Peter B. Dedek, 2009.

activities of building owners and the work of designers, the law provides financial incentives for preservation and the implementation of accepted preservation practices in commercial development projects. The program was intended to provide an incentive for rehabilitating historic buildings and does not apply to structures such as bridges, or objects such as ships.

Because of its vast scope and its emphasis on design, the Preservation Tax Incentives Program is the vehicle by which many architects and other design professionals become involved in historic preservation. Understanding basic preservation principles and how to apply the *Secretary of the Interior's Standards* (explained in Chapter 10) are necessary skills when working with tax act projects. In large cities, design firms often specialize in working with historic buildings and employ at least one design professional trained in historic preservation, often a historical architect. Such firms work on tax act projects on a regular basis. In some instances, architects and interior designers who are not familiar with historic preservation become involved with tax projects, either directly or tangentially, often providing them with a trial-by-fire education in historic preservation design.

Private owners of commercial (income producing) buildings listed on the National Register, and their partners and investors are eligible to use the Federal Historic Preservation Tax Incentives Program. This is one of the significant benefits of listing, which goes beyond the protections from federal undertakings provided by Section 106 and Section 4(f). Listing on the register makes owners of commercial properties eligible for a 20 percent federal tax credit if they rehabilitate their building in a historically sensitive manner according to the Secretary of the Interior's Standards for Rehabilitation. Using the federal tax credit can sometimes make the difference between a profitable venture and one that does not make a return for investors.

A tax credit is different from a tax deduction. A tax deduction reduces the amount of income subject to taxation during a given span of time, while a tax credit is taken directly from the amount of tax liability owed. For example, if a person who spends $100,000 rehabilitating a historic building is awarded the 20 percent tax credit, that person will be allowed to reduce any federal taxes owed by $20,000 or 20 percent of $100,000. If a person or company doesn't owe enough taxes to cover the credit in the year after the recently rehabilitated building is put into service, the credit can be taken over the subsequent five years.

The Federal Historic Preservation Tax Incentives Program was initiated in 1976, when Congress passed the Tax Reform Act, which Congress strengthened in 1978 by establishing the tax credit program. Originally, the tax credit incentives were enacted to counter elements of the tax code that favored demolition by making tearing old buildings down and replacing them with new construction more economically feasible from a tax perspective than rehabilitating existing ones. The 1978 program offered a 25 percent tax credit for the rehabilitation of historic buildings listed on the National Register.

This program has had a dramatic impact on American cities. According to the National Park Service, between 1978 and 2006, "the tax incentives have leveraged over $33 billion of private sector investment to preserve and rehabilitate over 32,000 historic properties, including the creation of nearly 185,000 housing units, of which over 75,000 are low- and moderate-income units" (NPS "Tax Incentives" 2010). Each year, around 1,200 tax act projects are proposed across the nation, and nearly the same number are completed each year, amounting to a capital investment in the area of $2.8 billion annually (Roberts 2007). Despite the success of the program, Congress, under political pressure to reform the tax code, lowered the tax credit in 1986 to a 20 percent credit and placed restrictions on what types of income were eligible for the credit by certain kinds of investors. Despite the percentage reduction, a great number of rehabilitation projects continue to be carried out under this program all across America.

The Two Types of Investment Tax Credits

There are currently two levels of tax credits included in the program: a 10 percent credit, which applies to the rehabilitation of nonresidential buildings constructed before 1936 that lack the historic integrity needed to be eligible for the National Register (Figure 2.4a) and a 20 percent tax credit designed for the rehabilitation of buildings listed or eligible to be listed on the National Register (Figure 2.4b). Both types of credits cannot be used on the same project. Also,

Figure 2.4a 10 Percent Tax Act candidate building, Storm King, New York. This apartment building was obviously built prior to 1936 but lacks historic integrity. Source: Photograph by Peter B. Dedek, 2011.

Figure 2.4b The Hibernia Bank Building in San Francisco by architect Albert Pissis, built in 1892, was one of the few buildings to survive the 1906 San Francisco earthquake largely intact. A 20 Percent Tax Act Candidate, the building is clearly historic. Source: Photograph by Peter B. Dedek, 2009.

any building listed on the National Register or one located within a National Register district is not eligible for the 10 percent tax credit. If an ineligible building is located within a National Register district, the owner has to apply to his or her state historic preservation office to have the building in question certified as being a "noncontributing" building within the district in order to be allowed to use the ten percent credit. This rule was enacted so the law would not encourage the destructive remodeling of intact historic buildings.

The basic application requirements for the both the 10 and the 20 percent credits are:

- The building has to be commercial or "depreciable," in that at least a portion of it must generate income for its owners and be used as an income producing property for at least five years after the rehabilitation has been completed.

- The work done to the building must be "substantial," meaning at least $5,000 will be spent on the rehabilitation and the cost of the rehabilitation in question must be higher than the pre-rehabilitation cost of the building minus the value of the land it is sited on. Normally, this requirement has to be met within two years for a project done in a single phase or within five years for a project constructed in multiple phases (in most cases, the amounts spent on tax act projects are in the hundreds of thousands or even millions of dollars).

- The building must be "depreciable" for tax purposes, which basically means it's a commercial building that produces income according to Internal Revenue Service (IRS) regulations.

The credit cannot be applied to owner-occupied residences unless at least part of the property is to be used for a paying commercial purpose, in which case only the cost of work done to commercial portion of the building will qualify for the credit. Types of buildings that typically qualify include hotels, apartment buildings, shopping centers, and office buildings—virtually any historic income producing property.

The 10 Percent Credit

For the 10 percent tax credit, the work done on the building does not have to be performed according to *Secretary of the Interior's Standards for Rehabilitation,* and the work is not reviewed by either the SHPO or the National Park Service. The only requirements are that at least 50 percent of the building's external walls extant before the work began must remain in place as external walls and at least 75 percent of the building's external walls extant prior to the work must remain in place as either external or internal walls, and at least 75 percent of the building's internal structural framework has to remain in place when the work is complete (EPA 2013). The 10 percent tax credit provision encourages developers to retain old buildings not eligible for the National Register due to a previous loss of integrity with the purpose of retaining the basic character of older neighborhoods and conserving building materials, making the 10 percent provision compatible with the green building movement (discussed in Chapter 13).

The 20 Percent Credit

In order to be considered for the 20 percent tax credit, a building must be deemed a **Certified Historic Structure,** which means it has been individually listed on the National Register or has been determined to be a "contributing" building located within a National Register district. If an applicant's building hasn't been listed and is not in a district, but the applicant believes the building may be historic, she or he can apply to the state historic preservation office for the state in which the building is located and apply for a determination of eligibility for individual listing in the National Register, which allows the application process for the tax credits to go forward while the building is being nominated and listed. Also, buildings included as "contributing" in a local historic district but not listed on the National Register qualify for the 20 percent credit.

For the 20 percent credit to be awarded, work on the project must meet the Secretary of the Interior's Standards for Rehabilitation (discussed in Chapter 10), rather than the *Secretary of the Interior's Standards for Restoration*. Because of their commercial nature, tax act projects are not required to be strict restorations but are rehabilitations, which allows for greater design flexibility. If a tax act project were done as a restoration, this would be allowed so long as, in the end, the property ends up being income producing. To be approved, tax act projects have to adhere to all ten of the standards, although minor variances are allowed in certain cases, and a degree of negotiation may take place among the project architects and designers, owners, SHPO staff, and possibly NPS staff during the review process. However, significant, character-defining exte-

rior features, such as porches, towers, and historic windows (if present), must be retained. As with most rehabilitations of historic buildings falling under some type of historic preservation regulations or guidelines, windows are a common point of contention in tax act projects. Many architects and developers are motivated to replace historic windows, which are usually made of wood or metal and have but one thickness of glass, with new multiglazed windows, which are usually easier to maintain and are sometimes more energy efficient. Regardless, historic windows are a significant feature of both the exterior and the interior and help define the historic quality of a building.

Another common point of conflict is roof additions. Generally, while inconspicuous additions to roofs are allowed in tax act projects, the kind of overpowering roof additions often favored by developers hungry for a maximum of rentable square footage can cause a project to be refused final approval (Figure 2.5).

In addition to significant characteristics on the exterior, the treatment of major historic features within a building's interior are also considered and reviewed in tax act projects. This is a departure from most governmental reviews of alterations to historic buildings, which are usually limited to protecting the exterior. In most tax act projects, the interior spaces that express the building's style, historic use, and major spatial relationships—such as major staircases, distinctive lobbies, decorated fireplaces, ornate floors,

Figure 2.5 Nonconforming roof addition. The recent rooftop addition overwhelms the scale of this turn-of-the-20th-century Romanesque revival building in San Francisco. Source: Photograph by Peter B. Dedek, 2009.

HISTORIC BLIND GIRLS' HOME BUILDING SERVING THE NEEDY WHILE RETAINING ITS HISTORIC INTEGRITY

Figure A Blind school home building. Source: Jeffrey A. Brambila, AIA.

From its construction in 1908 until 1966, this historic red-brick Georgian revival building in St. Louis, Missouri, provided a communal home for disadvantaged blind girls and women, allowing them to live independently and earn a living. A significant example of early 20th-century institutional architecture designed by architect J. Hal Lynch, the building originally had 50 sleeping rooms for its sight-impaired residents, a dining hall, and two communal living rooms. A small infirmary was added in the 1920s. After the Blind Girls' Home left the building in 1966, it became run-down and was eventually occupied by squatters.

In 2010, the building was restored to become the home of Places at Page, a facility designed to serve people with mental illnesses, many of whom have been homeless at some point in their lives. While the exterior of the building remained mostly intact since its construction, the interior had suffered insensitive remodeling, vandalism, and water damage. The $4.6 million rehabilitation, funded in part with tax credits from the National Park Service's Federal Historic Preservation Tax Incentives Program, repaired the damage inside and out and reconstructed many significant interior features (Allen 2011). On the exterior, damaged or missing bricks and terra cotta blocks were replaced or repaired. Inside, the historic appearance of the former lobby was restored, and "layers of drywall and paneling were removed to reveal a beautiful wood and tile fireplace, beamed ceiling, and grand staircases" (NPS "Featured Case Study" 2013). In addition, the former girls' dormitories were rehabilitated into 23 low-income apartments.

This project demonstrates that sensitively rehabilitated historic buildings can serve people and offer an enriched atmosphere inside and out. The historic facility once again offers support and care, allowing its residents to lead mostly independent lives.

Figure B Lobby before restoration. Source: Jeffrey A. Brambila, AIA.

Figure C Lobby after restoration. Source: Jeffrey A. Brambila, AIA.

and patterned ceilings—will need to be retained. For example, if a historic hotel had a large open lobby with a highly decorated grand stairway, after the renovation is complete, the lobby should stay open and the stairway should remain intact. Less significant spaces, such as offices on upper floors or storage rooms, can usually be altered and modernized as needed.

A common issue concerning historic interiors that often comes up in tax act projects is the retention of the interior plaster in buildings with load-bearing brick walls. Often architects and interior designers want to remove the plaster in old commercial buildings to expose the structural brick on the interior walls to give the interior a "historic" textural look (Figure 2.6). This type of treatment is often used in spaces such as restaurants and bars. However, in the view of SHPO and NPS project reviewers, if historic plaster is present at the beginning of the project, it should be still there at the end of the project. Removing plaster reduces the historic integrity of the interiors of historic commercial and residential buildings, particularly those from the 19th century, the vast majority of which originally had plastered walls in all but storage and attic spaces.

Generally, if a significant historic feature, such as interior plaster, is present when the application is first made, it must be retained; but if the feature has been removed prior to the application, it does not have to be reconstructed. However if there is evidence an applicant purposely removed any historic features or materials prior to applying for the credit with the intention of not having to preserve them in the course of the rehabilitation, the application may be denied. Also, in some cases, an applicant may be required to reconstruct a missing feature. In a case where an original front entrance was bricked in at some point, the project designs may

Figure 2.6 Brick exposed on a historic interior. Source: Photograph by Peter B. Dedek, 2011.

be required to unbrick the entrance and install a new door that looks like the door that existed there historically.

Architects and their clients work with three governmental agencies throughout the process required for the 20 percent credit: the SHPO, the National Park Service, and the IRS. Of these, designers and building owners work most closely with the State Historic Preservation Office. The SHPO serves as the first point of contact and provides technical assistance and application forms. The SHPO also determines if the building in question is listed on the National Register and guides the process of having it nominated and listed if need be.

The SHPO staff reviews the plans for the proposed tax act rehabilitation prior to construction to determine whether or not the project adheres to the Secretary of the Interior's Standards for Rehabilitation. If aspects of the project do not meet the standards, the SHPO staff advises the design team on needed alterations to make the project comply. The SHPO then advises the property owner when the plans do meet the standards and when building work can commence. As construction progresses, SHPO staff often make site visits and review any design changes that become necessary during the design development and construction phases. Finally, once construction is complete, the SHPO makes a recommendation to the NPS as to whether the finished project should be certified or not based on documentation, such as photographs of the building before and after the work is completed.

The National Park Service has the final say as to whether the project qualifies for the 20 percent tax credit, however the NPS seriously considers the recommendation already made by the SHPO. Once the NPS makes its determination, the agency forwards copies of all decisions to the IRS.

The Internal Revenue Service processes the tax credit documents and answers any questions concerning the legal and financial aspects of the Federal Historic Preservation Tax Incentives program. The IRS publishes a guide called the *Market Segment Specialization Program: Rehabilitation Tax Credit.* The IRS may audit taxpayers to make sure they are entitled to any tax credits they claimed on their tax returns (NPS "Tax Incentives" 2010).

Once a project has been approved, it is referred to as a "certified rehabilitation." Under this program, large historic warehouses, department stores, and factories are often converted into condominiums, apartments, and office buildings. These projects are fairly easy to spot because of their historical authenticity and integrity and their lack of insensitive nonhistoric features, such as major roof top additions and vinyl windows.

State Investment Tax Credit Programs

In addition to the Federal Historic Preservation Tax Incentives, at least 29 states have enacted their own tax incentive programs for historic preservation (Moe 2008). Most of these state programs are modeled on the federal program but offer credits against payment of state taxes rather than federal taxes.

NATIONAL HERITAGE AREAS

According to the NPS, which administers America's federal **National Heritage Areas,** "National Heritage Areas (NHAs) are designated by Congress as places where natural, cultural, and historic resources combine to form a cohesive, nationally important landscape." (NPS "Heritage

Areas" 2013). First initiated in 1984, National Heritage Areas are coordinated regional efforts to preserve historic resources related under a common theme. Generally, once a heritage area is designated, Congress allocates a limited amount of federal funding for a number of years to promote the project, which is a cooperative venture among local, state, and federal agencies, nonprofit groups, private enterprise, and interested individuals.

An example of a heritage area mentioned in Chapter 1, Congress designated the Southwestern Pennsylvania Industrial Heritage Route (Path of Progress) in 1988. The Path of Progress focuses on the three historic industries—railroading, mining, and steelworking—that helped shape the development of a nine-county region of southwestern Pennsylvania. The heritage area offers visitors a marked five-hundred-mile driving route that interprets and connects historic sites such as the Johnstown Flood Museum, the Cambria Steel Mills, Altoona's Horseshoe Curve (a significant railroading engineering feat), and the remains of the Allegheny Portage Railroad, an early route that combined canals and a type of cable railway to get freight and passengers across the mountains. The Path of Progress used both federal and private funds. Other heritage areas, which are located all over the United States, interpret and link historic sites with diverse historical themes such as the Civil War, the Mormon migration, and the life of Abraham Lincoln.

CERTIFIED LOCAL GOVERNMENT PROGRAM

The **Certified Local Government Program (CLG)** was created in 1980 and is administered by the SHPOs at the state level and the NPS at the federal level. Its purpose is to encourage local governments to participate in the national historic preservation program and to utilize national preservation standards, such as the Secretary of the Interior's Standards, in their decisions regarding historic properties. In addition, the CLG Program provides technical and financial assistance to strengthen local preservation programs (Synatschk 2012). Between 1985 and 2008, more than $40 million in grants were awarded to communities under the Certified Local Government program, and over 1,228 local governments across the United States currently participate in the program (NPS "CLG Program" 2010).

In order to qualify to apply to the NPS to become a Certified Local Government, municipalities must have established at least one local historic district established by a historic preservation ordinance, must maintain a preservation review commission that meets certain professional qualifications, have an active local historical survey program, and provide for public participation and input in local historic preservation activities and issues. CLG status enables a local government to receive technical assistance and small grants for preservation planning and public relations activities from their state's SHPO. It also allows the CLG review commission to review National Register nominations within its jurisdiction. According to the NPS website, CLGs use grants to:

produce historic theme or context studies, cultural resource inventories, assessments of properties to determine their eligibility for local and National Register of Historic Places designation, building reuse and feasibility studies, design guidelines and conservation ordinances, and publications to educate the public about the benefits of historic preservation (NPS "CLG Program" 2012).

SUMMARY OF FEDERAL ROLES

Despite the great harm 20th-century federal initiatives such as the urban renewal and interstate highways did, the federal government has also passed laws, created programs, and made initiatives that have promoted historic preservation. Starting in 1935 and then greatly strengthened in 1966, the federal leadership role in preserving America's historic resources continued to expand. The Preservation Tax Incentives Program of 1976, which continues to operate today, albeit reduced, further deepened the federal government's commitment to historic preservation. As described in Chapter 1, the federal government created Save America's Treasures in 1998 and in 2003, Preserve America, both of which continued the expansion of federal involvement in historic preservation. However, due to recent budget cuts, federal support of these initiatives has been suspended, and federal involvement in historic preservation may have reached a turning point.

By creating a sophisticated system of preservation partnerships among the federal, state, and local governments and also by working with private groups and individuals, the federal government has managed to build a preservation ethic in a nation that historically had little regard for its built heritage. Although the federal government leads the field, most preservation planning and activity actually takes place at the state and local levels, especially within the state historic preservation offices.

THE STATE ROLES IN HISTORIC PRESERVATION

The Historic Preservation Act of 1966 and the resulting federal regulations delegated many historic preservation responsibilities to the states. Today, state governments usually act as intermediaries between federal agencies and local governments, preservationists, and citizens. The participation of states in historic preservation is a result of the federalism laid out in the United States Constitution, which reserves many governmental powers and responsibilities to the states. By taking on many duties related to preservation, the states took a great burden off federal agencies, especially the Advisory Council for Historic Preservation and the National Park Service, after the passage of the National Historic Preservation Act of 1966.

STATE HISTORIC PRESERVATION OFFICES

In addition to the federal mandates it established, the National Historic Preservation Act of 1966 (NHPA) created historic preservation programs at the state level when it directed each state to appoint a state historic preservation officer. The goal of the 1966 act was not to create a monolithic federally administered program, but instead to create a decentralized system where the states carried out many of the preservation goals set out in the act. To accomplish this, the states created state historic preservation offices (SHPOs) to support the work of the state historic preservation officer in implementing elements of the national historic preservation program within his or her state. To help fund these offices, the SHPOs receive 50 percent of the total amount of money allocated by Congress to support the national historic preservation program. The responsibilities of the SHPOs were more clearly defined in federal law when the NHPA was amended in 1980 (Hertfelder 1987). In addition to promoting and regulating the preservation of historic buildings, structures, and objects, SHPOs also have archeology divisions that protect and sometimes excavate historic and prehistoric archeological sites within their states.

All 50 U.S. states and the District of Columbia have a SHPO, as do many U.S. territories, such as Puerto Rico and Guam. In addition, there are also currently 76 **tribal historic preservation officers** (THPOs), who assume the role of a state historic preservation officer within the tribal lands under their care. Although the SHPOs are state agencies and the THPOs are sponsored by individual tribes, their work is united under the federal umbrella of national programs such as the National Register of Historic Places, the Federal Historic Preservation Tax Incentives, and Section 106.

In addition to implementing federal programs, many SHPOs sponsor an array of state-based programs, such as providing state-funded preservation grants, maintaining state historic registers, and in some states, implementing state laws requiring review processes similar to Section 106 and Section 4(f) for state-funded projects. For example, the state of Florida requires a review of state-financed undertakings, which is almost identical to Section 106 at the federal level (Florida Statute, Title XVIII, Chapter 267, 267.061 Section 2b).

While all the SHPOs and the THPOs are currently active, some states have stronger preservation laws than others and have more involved SHPOs. The size of the SHPO usually depends on the size and population of the state it serves. For example, the Texas SHPO employs around 175 people, while the state of Wyoming's SHPO employs only about 20. The number of historic properties located within a given state might also be a factor. However, all states have a vast number of historic resources listed on, or eligible to be listed on, the National Register, and since under National Register guidelines properties normally become potentially historic when they turn 50 years old, more historic sites are emerging in every state and territory all of the time.

SHPOs are state agencies that often have different names and are organized differently depending on what state they represent. For example, in Texas the SHPO is called the Texas Historical Commission, while the name of North Dakota's SHPO is the State Historical Society of North Dakota. Some states place their SHPO under the authority of another state agency, while in other states the SHPO operates as an independent state agency. For example, the Tennessee Historical Commission is under the authority of the Tennessee Department of Environment and Conservation, while the Texas Historical Commission functions as an independent state agency.

Most SHPOs are overseen by a board of directors usually appointed by the state's governor. In addition, SHPOs also have a state review board made up of architects, archaeologists, and other professionals with expertise in historic preservation. The state review board has the duty of reviewing nominations made by applicants seeking to have a historic property or historic district located within the state listed on the National Register. Once it has reviewed a National Register nomination, the board makes its recommendation to the National Park Service.

The SHPOs play a very significant role in preservation at the state level, and most preservation activity that takes place in the United States involves the SHPOs in some way or another. The SHPO is often the point of contact for architects and other professionals who deal with historic properties. If one suspects a historic or potentially historic building or other type of property may be impacted by a given project, contacting the SHPO is always a good starting point. SHPO staff can determine whether the property is listed on the National Register or determine whether it is eligible to be listed, if need be. The SHPO can also determine what regulations a project may fall under and guide architects, interior designers, developers, and building owners toward grants and tax credits that might be available to restore, rehabilitate, or preserve a historic property.

Duties of State Historic Preservation Offices

SHPOs have a number of routine duties they generally perform in every state. The existence of federal programs and guidelines that apply to all states and territories helps to standardize the organization and the activities of all SHPOs and THPOs. The duties all SHPOs have in common include implementing the following federal programs:

- Reviewing properties being nominated for the National Register of Historic Places. In some cases and in some states, SHPO staff complete some or all of the actual nomination forms and submit them to the state review board for the applicant.

- Evaluating applications for and making funding decisions on federal historic preservation grants. At times when such grants exist, the point of contact for most federal preservation grants is the SHPO.

- Carrying out consultation with agencies, applicants, and concerned individuals involved in the Section 106 review process.

- Conducting National Register surveys of historic properties within the state. Some states, such as Delaware, have completed extensive historic resource surveys that cover the entire state, while others are continuing the process of obtaining a full survey.

- Reviewing federal Historic Preservation Investment Tax Credit projects within the state and guiding architects and building owners so they design tax act projects in accordance with the Secretary of the Interior's Standards for Rehabilitation and thus make them ultimately successful. The SHPO staff also make recommendations to the National Park Service as to whether completed Historic Preservation Investment Tax Credit projects should be certified or rejected.

- Providing technical assistance to design professionals and other individuals wishing to plan, fund, or implement preservation projects. This assistance can take the form of providing federal preservation publications, such as Preservation Briefs and the National Register Bulletins to the public, consulting with people individually, and making site visits to historic sites and preservation projects.

- Implementing the Certified Local Government (CLG) program. This involves helping local municipalities become CLGs and helping established CLGs reap the benefits of their CLG status.

- Overseeing required federal archeological reviews.

Most SHPOs also have duties associated with state and local programs. Since state laws vary, SHPOs located in some states and territories may not perform all of the following functions:

- Assisting municipal governments with local historic preservation programs, districts, and projects and assist in locating state and private funding for projects.

- Overseeing review and compliance under any state programs similar to Section 106 or Section 4(f).

- Managing state-owned historic sites. Some SHPOs directly operate historic museums and other historic sites located in their state.

- Enforcing historic easements and deed covenants within the state (these will be explained in Chapter 4).

- Running education programs for preservation and design professionals, archeologists, business people, and the public in general. These can take the form of classes, conferences, presentations at professional conferences, public tours, and informative visits to historic sites.

- Holding an annual conference and other public meetings. Some SHPOs hold an annual conference, for example the Texas Historical Commission hosts a conference each year for professionals and volunteers interested in historic preservation to assist preservationists achieve their goals.(THC "Annual Conference" 2013).

- Administering and awarding any state-funded grants for preservation projects. State grants can provide funds for preservation planning activities, such as creating tours of historic districts or educational programs for the owners of historic properties, or for brick-and-mortar projects, such as the rehabilitation of a local train station owned by a city or the restoration of a historic private residence. In some cases, state grants are used in conjunction with federal and private grants for the same project and are sometimes counted as matching grants. An example of a state-run preservation grant program, the Massachusetts Preservation Projects Fund, makes monies "available for the restoration, rehabilitation, stabilization, and documentation of historic and archaeological properties owned by municipalities or nonprofit organizations. Through the Massachusetts Preservation Projects Fund, 50 percent matching grants are available to qualifying properties listed on the State Register to ensure their physical preservation" (Massachusetts SHPO 2010).

- Implementing a state historic preservation program if one exists. Some states have developed individual state historic preservation programs to augment the national historic preservation program.

- Assisting the owners of historic properties affected by hurricanes, floods, earthquakes, or other natural disasters. For example, in 2006 the state of Louisiana received federal

Figure 2.7 Historic New Orleans double shotgun house damaged by Hurricane Katrina. Source: Photograph by Peter B. Dedek, 2007.

funding to create a grant program to repair historic buildings damaged by hurricanes Katrina and Rita (Figure 2.7).

- Maintaining and amending a state register of historic places if one exists. In many states, a property listed on the National Register is automatically listed on the state historic register as well.

- Carrying out special state historic preservation initiatives. An example of such an initiative is the Texas Historic Courthouse Preservation program. This program, which was initiated in 1999, has allocated over $255 million in state money to create matching grants to rehabilitate a significant number of Texas's 234 historic courthouses, many of which had fallen into disrepair and had become endangered by the late 1990s, using the *Secretary of the Interior's Standards for Rehabilitation* (THC "Courthouse Program" 2010) (Figure 2.8).

- Operating the Main Street program within the state in cooperation with the National Trust for Historic Preservation and local Main Street towns and cities.

- Assisting individuals and groups within local communities with preservation planning and rehabilitation, restoration, and interpretive projects. This is one of the most significant roles of the SHPOs.

Figure 2.8 Restored historic Texas courthouse, Lockhart, Texas. Source: Photograph by Peter B. Dedek, 2010.

STATE PRESERVATION RESPONSIBILITIES IN ADDITION TO SHPOS

In addition to operating the state historic preservation offices, states perform other functions related to preservation and restoration.

State Enabling Legislation for Local Historic Districts

Despite common misconceptions to the contrary, listing a property on the National Register does nothing to limit private activities. For example, a private landowner could list a house on the register one day and demolish it on the next, and break no laws and face no legal action. Since listing does not restrict private demolitions and alterations to historic buildings, structures, and sites, many municipalities have chosen to create local historic districts. In order to have the authority or "police power" to regulate changes to historic properties located within the district, the municipality requires legislation at the state level, which gives local governments the authority to create and enforce architectural design guidelines within historic districts. As described in Chapter 1, the first state to pass such legislation was South Carolina in 1931, followed by Louisiana in 1936.

Roles of Other State Agencies

State environmental agencies sometimes review projects that affect historic properties. Also, state agencies other than the SHPO often own and operate historic buildings, such as historic state houses and governors' mansions. Generally, state agencies in most states consult with the SHPO on issues relevant to the preservation and care of the historic sites in their care.

CONCLUSION

The National Historic Preservation Act of 1966 took advantage of the federalism of the American system of government when it delegated many preservation responsibilities under the national historic preservation program to the states. In so doing, it created a complicated yet flexible system that promotes historic preservation often without having to mandate it outright. The NHPA established a national framework of preservation standards, practices, and values that could be applied at the state and local levels, with the state historic preservation offices acting as the primary clearinghouses for preservation. By emphasizing encouragement and cooperation among various levels of government and private organizations and individuals rather than a purely top-down approach, the preservation movement has managed to avoid the kind of political polarization that has afflicted many other social and environmental pursuits.

STUDY QUESTIONS

1. What is the mission of the Advisory Council on Historic Preservation? Whom does it advise?

2. What classification of historic properties does Section 110 of the National Historic Preservation Act of 1966 (NHPA) protect? Why do you think Congress gave this particular type of historic property greater safeguards?

3. What is the provision that makes Section 4(f) more effective than Section 106 in controlling the harmful effects of highway projects on historic resources?

4. Which areas of the national historic preservation program do the National Park Service administer? Why do you think Congress chose the National Park Service to have such a significant role in historic preservation?

5. Describe the purpose of the Investment Tax Credit Program. In what ways does the purpose of the 10 percent and the 20 percent credit differ? How is this program likely to influence the work of architects and interior designers?

6. What is a National Heritage Area, and why do you think they were created? What advantages do National Heritage Areas have over preserving individual sites and historic districts?

7. Describe the Certified Local Government Program (CLG). What is it and what are its benefits to the National Historic Preservation Program and for the individual communities involved? How might a design professional be involved in a CLG?

8. Why do you think the NHPA created the position of State Historic Preservation Officer? What are the advantages of administering many preservation efforts at the state level rather than at the federal level?

9. List six major responsibilities that all state historic preservation offices have in common.

10. What are the responsibilities of the Division of Architecture at the Texas Historical Commission? How might these activities affect architects and interior designers?

EXERCISE: IDENTIFY ASPECTS OF FEDERAL AND STATE HISTORIC PRESERVATION PROGRAMS

Identify the federal or state preservation law or program associated with each term (in quotes) or duty listed in the right-hand column (some terms or duties can apply to two or more programs):

A) Federal Historic Preservation Tax Incentives

B) Section 106

C) Section 110

D) Section 4(f)

E) State Historic Preservation Offices

F) National Park Service

G) Advisory Council on Historic Preservation

1 _____ Manages state register of historic properties

2 _____ "Certified Historic Structure"

3 _____ "Mitigation"

4 _____ Manages Native American Program

5 _____ "Prudent and feasible"

6 _____ Protects National Historic Landmarks

7 _____ "Constructive use"

8 _____ Administers the American Battlefield Protection Program

9 _____ "Area of Potential Effect"

10 _____ Administers the National Register of Historic Places

11 _____ Conducts National Register surveys

12 _____ "Memorandum of Agreement"

13 _____ Operates the state Main Street program

14 _____ Reviews properties being nominated for the National Register of Historic Places

Answers and explanations found in Instructor's Guide.

SOURCES

Advisory Council on Historic Preservation. "Federal Financial Assistance Specifically for Historic Preservation—General." Accessed July 9, 2010. http://www.achp.gov/funding-general.html.

———. "Tribal Historic Preservation Officers." 2006. Accessed July 30, 2010; website updated September 24, 2013. http://www.achp.gov/thpo.html.

Allen, Michael R. 2010. "MDHC Approves Two Major North St. Louis Projects," Preservation Research Office. Accessed November 29, 2013. http://preservation-research.com/2010/08/mhdc-approves-two-major-north-st-louis-projects/.

Bell, Charlotte R. 1985. *Federal Historic Preservation Case Law: A Special Report.* Washington, DC: Advisory Council on Historic Preservation.

Editorial Board, 2010. "Home for Christmas: Blind Girls Show the Way in a New Century." *St. Louis Post Dispatch.* Accessed November 29, 2013. http://www.stltoday.com/news/opinion/columns/the-platform/home-for-christmas-blind-girls-show-the-way-in-a/article_8038b730-0eec-11e0-9dc8-00127992bc8b.html..

Environmental Protection Agency (EPA). "Federal Historic Preservation Tax Incentives for Brownfield Development." Accessed November 29, 2013. http://www.epa.gov/brownfields/tax/tax_guide.pdf.

Federal Highway Administration. "Highway History." Accessed April 6, 2012; website updated October 15, 2013. http://www.fhwa.dot.gov/infrastructure/50section4f.cfm.

Federal Preservation Institute (FPI). " The Federal Preservation Institute (FPI)." Accessed November 29, 2013. http://www.nps.gov/history/fpi/.

Florida Statute, Title XVIII, Chapter 267, 267.061 Section 2b. Historic properties; state policy, responsibilities, §2(a), "Compliance Review Section." Accessed November 29, 2013. http://www.flsenate.gov/Laws/Statutes/2012/267.061.

Hertfelder, Eric. 1987. "The National Park Service and Historic Preservation: Historic Preservation Beyond Smokey the Bear." *The Public Historian* 9, no. 2 (Spring): 135–142.

Historic Sites Act of 1935 (49 Stat. 666; 16 U.S.C. 461-467). Accessed April 6, 2012 http://www.cr.nps.gov/local-law/FHPL_histsites.pdf.

King, Thomas F. 2000. *Federal Planning and Historic Places: The Section 106 Process.* Walnut Creek, CA: Alta Mira Press.

Massachusetts State Historic Preservation Office. "Grants Division." Accessed July 15, 2010. http://www.sec.state.ma.us/mhc/mhchpp/grdhpp.htm.

Moe, Richard. Address delivered at the First Church of Christ, Scientists, Berkley, CA, March 27, 2008.

National Historic Preservation Act (NHPA) of 1966 (Public Law 89-665; 80 STAT.915; 16 U.S.C. 470) as amended through 1992. Accessed April 6, 2012. http://www.nps.gov/history/local-law/nhpa1966.htm.

National Park Service (NPS). "History." Accessed July 10, 2010; website updated October, 17, 2013. http://www.nps.gov/aboutus/history.htm.

———. "National Heritage Areas. What Are National Heritage Areas?" Accessed November 29, 2013. http://www.nps.gov/heritageareas/.

———. "National Park Service History." Accessed July 10, 2010. http://www.nps.gov/history/history/hisnps_NEW.htm.

———. "About the Federal Tax Incentives for Historic Preservation." Accessed July 9, 2010. http://www.nps.gov/tps/tax-incentives.htm.

———. "Certified Local Government Program." Accessed July 11, 2010. http://www.nps.gov/history/hps/clg/index.htm.

———. "Certified Local Government Program." Accessed April 13, 2012. http://www.nps.gov/history/hps/clg/become_clg.html.

———. "Featured Case Study: Blind Girl's Home: Institutional Building Continues to Serve Those in Need." Technical Preservation Service. Accessed November 29, 2013. http://www.nps.gov/tps/tax-incentives/case-studies.htm#blind-girls.

Rails to Trails Conservancy. "Transportation Enhancement Activities," Accessed July 19, 2010; website updated October 25, 2013. http://www.fhwa.dot.gov/environment/te/teas.htm.

Roberts, Tristan. 2007. "Historic Preservation and Green Building: A Lasting Relationship." *Environmental Building News,* January.

Synatschk, Matt (State Coordinator, Certified Local Government Program, Community Heritage Development Division, Texas Historical Commission). 2012. Personal communication.

Texas Historical Commission (THC). "Courthouse Program." Accessed November 29, 2013. http://ftp.thc.state.tx.us/courthouses/chdefault.shtml

———. "Annual Historic Preservation Conference." Accessed November 29, 2013. http://ftp.thc.state.tx.us/annualconference/cofdefault.shtml.

———. "Divisions." Accessed July 14, 2010. http://ftp.thc.state.tx.us/aboutus/abtdiv.shtml.

———. "THC Fact Sheet." Accessed April 20, 2012. http://ftp.thc.state.tx.us/faqs/faqpdfs/THC_FctSht_04_12.pdf.

Whisnant, Anne Mitchel. 2006. *Super-Scenic Motorway: A Blue Ridge Parkway History.* Chapel Hill: University of North Carolina Press.

3

LOCAL GOVERNMENT
AND THE PRIVATE SECTOR
IN PRESERVATION PLANNING
AND DESIGN

OBJECTIVES

- Describe preservation as practiced at the local level by municipal governments, advocacy groups, and individuals.

- Explain how local historic districts are created and regulated.

- Outline how preservation on the local level impacts designers who work with historic buildings.

- Discuss how private organizations contribute to the preservation movement on the national, regional, state, and local levels.

Figure 3.1. Advocates are the driving force of the preservation movement. Source: Photograph by Peter B. Dedek, 2011.

As with politics, all preservation is local. Despite significant federal guidance and the involvement of state historic preservation offices (SHPOs), applied preservation work—such as rehabilitations, establishment and enforcement of historic districts, architectural surveys, and the operation of history museums—actually happens within America's communities, and it wouldn't take place at all without the support of private groups and individual Americans (Figure 3.1). With the exception of federally owned historic sites, federal involvement in historic preservation is usually advisory, and state governments act mostly to guide, encourage, occasionally regulate, and sometimes help finance local preservation efforts. Federal historic preservation programs often aim to foster local and private partnerships within a federal framework. Federal initiatives, such as the Certified Local Government Program and the National Register of Historic Places, are geared toward empowering individuals and communities to take charge of the preservation of their historic resources.

LOCAL PRESERVATION ACTIVITIES

Preservation at the local level often involves voluntary preservation, such as when a homeowner lovingly restores her or his historic house or when a community historical society or preservation nonprofit obtains and preserves a historic building. Local preservation activities also include activism, such as public opposition to projects that would harm historic properties, which may result in public protests or in court cases. Planning and marketing, such as coordinating landowners and businesses in historic downtowns through the National Trust's Main Street program, are also aspects of local preservation. Local preservation can also be obligatory and enforced by law: one of the most significant and effective components of historic preservation in the United States is the local historic district, which regulates private construction, rehabilitations, and demolitions.

LOCAL GOVERNMENTS AND PRESERVATION

Municipal governments are responsible for creating, approving, and enforcing design guidelines for local historic districts and local historic landmarks. With local districts and landmarks, private owners of contributing or individually designated historic buildings must apply to the municipality's historic preservation commission or architectural review board for permission to begin work before they can make significant changes to the exteriors, and in some instances to the interiors, of their buildings. Because they require architectural design review and control, local districts are probably the most significant element in protecting historic properties in the United States. Although National Register listing does offer some protection against federally funded or licensed activities (as described in Chapter 2), it does not restrict private actions.

Local Historic Districts

In the decades since the first local historic district was created in Charleston, South Carolina, in 1931, similar districts have been established in cities and towns across the nation. Today, more than 2,300 historic preservation commissions conduct routine design reviews for proposed changes to buildings and landscapes in local districts in the United States (NPS 2012).

Local historic districts protect a specific geographical area of a city or town where there is a concentration of historic resources, such as buildings and structures, which possess a distinct character. A local historic district generally contains at least two or more historic buildings or structures, although historic districts vary in size and can include thousands of properties. A district must occupy a distinct physical location that has clear boundaries outlined on a map. The historic buildings or structures located within that geographical area must constitute a majority of the buildings or structures present there. A historic property is generally one that is listed or eligible for listing on the National Register of Historic places (see Chapter 4). Historic properties are considered "**contributing**" to the district, and nonhistoric buildings located within the district are classified as "**noncontributing**." If a district contains one hundred buildings, for example, at least 51 of those buildings should be considered "contributing." In some local districts, a property may considered contributing even if by itself it would not be significant or intact enough to be listed individually on the register, because the property contributes to the higher historic value of the district as a whole.

In both National Register and local historic districts, the historic properties located within usually have a common historical theme or share a combination of themes. Their primary connection might be nothing more than a general association with the development of a particular city or town. The district may contain properties that represent a wide range of different periods and styles. For example, the New Orleans French Quarter has the Ursuline Convent (1745), a building from the French period of the early 1700s, many buildings from the Spanish period,

1762–1803, and hundreds of buildings from throughout the 19th and early 20th centuries in styles as diverse as Italianate, Greek revival, and Arts and Crafts, all of which are considered contributing to the same district. Despite their diversity in age and style, these buildings are all related to the unique history and cultural development of that particular neighborhood over the course of almost three centuries and the history of the city of New Orleans as a whole.

In other cases, historic districts contain contributing buildings that are more closely associated with a particular historic period or event, such as a Victorian suburban housing development, where all of the houses in the district were built by a particular developer between, say, 1860 and 1870, or a district of buildings and structures associated with a particular industry, such as a complex of early 20th-century steel mills and the company housing associated with them.

Often the areas that eventually become historic districts were originally preserved inadvertently. In some cases, as with the French Quarter, there was little development pressure for demolition and new building in the district because the area was a relatively low-income neighborhood in the early 20th century, which didn't inspire much interest from developers. In other cases, as with the Battery in Charleston, prior to being designated as a historic district, the area was a stable, mostly high-income area that the residents and business owners preserved themselves until national companies started building gas stations and other modern intrusions there in the 1920s. However, preserving a historic area over the long term without some kind of government-enforced architectural controls is all but impossible. Most historic areas that have not been preserved as local historic districts have suffered from destructive forces such as neglect and demolition. To see this one need only travel to the downtowns of most American cities and witness the many parking lots and incompatible recent architecture that have replaced most of the historic buildings (Figure 3.2).

Why Local Historic Districts Are Created

The destruction of historic areas can happen for a number of reasons. If a low-income historic area remains unprotected by being designated as a local historic district, it could fall victim to developers looking for cheap land to build factories, shopping centers, new housing, or the like. Or the low-income area may be "discovered" in a process called **gentrification**, where artists and other "urban homesteaders" who are attracted by the unique aesthetic qualities and location of the area move in. Urban pioneers are usually followed by higher-income professionals, who end up driving out many of the original residents by increasing demand, which inflates area rents and real estate prices. This motivates landowners to sell out to developers who often plan to demolish the old buildings that made the area interesting and special to begin with. Developers often replace the historic architecture with new buildings, such as high-rise condominiums that provide a higher economic return. While local historic districts can protect historic buildings in an area, it is important to note that creating local historic districts doesn't necessarily slow or stop gentrification. Preservationists and municipal governments have to look to other urban planning tools, such as providing subsidized housing or rent control, if they wish to maintain diversity and allow low- and moderate-income residents to remain living in gentrifying neighborhoods.

Figure 3.2. Parking lot in the historic heart of Austin, Texas. Source: Photograph by Peter B. Dedek, 2010.

In cases where there is no gentrification and an unprotected historic neighborhood remains low income, seeing no reason to pay for maintenance, the owners of historic buildings located in low income areas sometimes opt to defer maintenance and even allow demolition by neglect to take place. **Demolition by neglect** occurs when building owners purposely or inadvertently allow buildings to deteriorate to the point that it is no longer feasible to rehabilitate them (Figure 3.3). If buildings are not maintained for too long a time, they usually become undesirable places to live or work and eventually become unsafe. If enough buildings in an area are allowed to fall vacant, entire neighborhoods become subject to vandalism and arson.

Figure 3.3 Demolition by neglect: historic railway station in Newburgh, New York. Source: Photograph by Peter B. Dedek, 2009.

Figure 3.4. Missing tooth syndrome in downtown San Francisco. Source: Photograph by Peter B. Dedek, 2008.

If too many buildings become derelict or are destroyed by fire or demolition, a historic neighborhood becomes increasingly fractured. As buildings are lost and become empty lots or are replaced by incompatible buildings and land uses such as gas stations and car lots, the neighborhood ceases to look or feel historic and loses its sense of unity and identity. The condition where buildings are removed and their sites left empty, breaking the historic spatial arrangement of the streets, the blocks, and the rows of buildings, is sometimes referred to as the **missing tooth syndrome** (Figure 3.4). This process has occurred in many American cities in the early 21st century, especially in midwestern cities, such as Detroit, where thousands of potentially historic buildings have been destroyed.

Upper-income historic areas can also become endangered without local protection. High-rent areas and those located in or near historic downtowns often fall victim to intense development pressure. Under the concept of **highest and best use**, land is supposed to be used for the purpose that provides the greatest economic return. Landowners and developers often push for the demolition of the old and less profitable in order to replace it with the new and more lucrative (Figure 3.5). This is true even when the main reason an area became desirable in the first place is because of the special character of the historic buildings and significant landscapes found there. While there is nothing wrong with people desiring to profit from real estate, without an established, enforceable local historic district, many formerly stable and economically viable historic areas self-destruct as more and more old buildings are either replaced with new ones or altered

Figure 3.5. "Highest and best use." Source: Photograph by Peter B. Dedek, 2010.

beyond recognition, causing a loss of all unique historical character and feeling. This hurts the neighborhood as a whole and can lower land values and actually reduce the overall profitability of the area over time. Eventually, many prosperous yet unprotected historic neighborhoods become disjointed and lose their critical mass and are no longer identifiable as historic at all.

Neglect and new construction are not the only threats to historic areas. Unprotected downtowns often end up having many of their historic buildings torn down and replaced by parking lots. In a car-centered culture such as the United States, renting parking spaces can be a very profitable business, and developers purchase historic downtown buildings, demolish them, make parking lots where they once stood, and wait for property values to rise over time while they receive a consistent return from a parking lot business. This simple money-making strategy has destroyed countless urban historic buildings. In addition, many businesses and institutions—such as banks, hospitals, universities, and churches—buy and demolish neighboring buildings to provide parking for their customers or employees, students, or members. The problem is that the surrounding community suffers as its historic areas lose vibrancy, urban density, and beauty. In many American cities, once prosperous downtown areas became virtual wastelands by the 1970s because of demolitions and poorly planned development, and many have yet to recover.

The ethic behind local historic districts is that, although the profits that some landowners might potentially make from their investments may be reduced because they are not allowed to demolish or significantly alter the historic buildings in their possession, having a functioning historic district preserves the overall economic health of the district. This benefits all of the landowners, because the area retains the positive qualities that attract people to it and will keep the neighborhood or business district viable in the long term. Also, historic districts become an asset to a whole town or city and can become an asset to the region as well, because people, including tourists, who don't live or work in the district themselves may still travel there to enjoy its unique qualities.

The distinctive buildings and structures, such as monuments and bridges, and landscapes, such as parks and boulevards, that historic districts contain possess decorative motifs, materials, massing, and urban spatial relationships that are unique and irreplaceable (Figure 3.6). Modern development tends to be uniform, and areas constructed within the last fifty or so years are often automobile-oriented and lack the architectural interest and human scale that many historic areas embody. New buildings often lack the interest, diversity, and details of historic buildings and tend not to support a neighborhood atmosphere. Many historic buildings house small businesses, such as specialty shops and family-owned restaurants, that are accessible directly from the sidewalk, providing a **permeable membrane** that allows direct access into the buildings from sidewalks and squares. Newer buildings tend to greet the street with an impermeable membrane of blank walls, plate glass windows, and locked doors, especially at night. New development also can be geographically and culturally generic—in that a big-box shopping center located in Seattle, Washington, may look much like one located in Providence, Rhode Island—whereas historic

Figure 3.6. Sixth Street historic district in Austin, Texas. Source: Photograph by Peter B. Dedek, 2011.

areas tend to be unique to the region where they were built because of the use of local building materials, regional building techniques, and greater architectural adaptation to local climate and geography, especially in neighborhoods that date from the 1800s or earlier.

Historic buildings inspire memories and have features that illustrate local history, culture, and craftsmanship. Perhaps the most common justification for creating local historic districts is that old places connect us with the past and help to preserve local and regional character. Historic areas create a sense of place where stories of the past can be told in an environment that illustrates them, where people can gain an experiential understanding of the environments where people of past generations also lived and worked. Also, historic landmarks within districts help to orient us in the urban or rural landscape and allow people to experience a **sense of place**. Geographer and essayist J. B. Jackson describes a sense of place: "It is place, permanent position in both the social and topographical sense, that gives us our identity" (1984). Most great cities are known for their historic landmarks and their established neighborhoods. Paris with its Eiffel Tower and Arc de Triomphe, and Washington, D.C., with its Capitol Building and the Washington Monument are obvious examples, but historic landmarks, such as county courthouses, historic theaters, old churches, and historic monuments give character and a sense of place to countless cities and towns. Landmarks and historic neighborhoods help to orient and inspire both locals and visitors and can become the focus of local, state, or national identity and pride (Figure 3.7). Famous historic landmarks, such as the Empire State Building, the

Figure 3.7. Old San Francisco Mint, 1874, Alfred B. Mullet, architect. Source: Photograph by Peter B. Dedek, 2008.

old San Francisco Mint, the Statue of Liberty, and Independence Hall fulfill this function at the national level.

Since people from all over America take vacations to major cities in America such as New York, San Francisco, New Orleans, and Boston in order to spend time in historic places, it only makes sense that the special historic sites closer to home for all Americans should be preserved as well.

Local districts are created in order to legally protect historic or contributing landmarks and other historic properties located within the district's borders from potentially destructive public or private undertakings, and to protect the general historic character of the district and the municipality as a whole by controlling intrusive and inappropriate development and harmful alterations to individual buildings.

How to Create Local Historic Districts

Municipal governments create local historic districts through the zoning authority granted them by the states. In some states, county governments have zoning authority and can also create local historic districts. Establishing a local historic district requires that a municipal or county government creates and approves a preservation ordinance, which is legislation that outlines how historic resources will be identified, documented, and preserved. Once a preservation ordinance is in place, a historic preservation commission must be set up to identify resources, establish district boundaries, and regulate construction projects within any local historic districts under its jurisdiction. These commissions are usually made up of residents of the municipality or county, the majority of which have a special interest in and knowledge of disciplines associated with historic preservation, such as history, the building trades, architecture, interior design, law, and archaeology.

The ordinance, which creates and defines the location of local historic districts, is a historic "overlay zone" similar to a municipal zoning law and is backed by state-enabling legislation. For example, in North Carolina, a state statute allows for the establishment of historic districts by municipalities and also provides the legal basis for enforcement of preservation standards and guidelines within those districts. All 50 states have passed some form of enabling legislation for historic districts. While differences exist in the exact process by which local historic districts are established from state to state, the process is relatively consistent nationwide.

Once an area is surveyed, the local historic preservation commission, usually working with staff from the SHPO and local preservation advocates, determines whether a potential district exists there, and if so, boundaries are established and an ordinance creates the district. Before the ordinance can be passed, however, the commission generally contacts all property owners within the proposed district to inform them of the plans to create a district in their neighborhood and to explain what responsibilities property owners would have after the historic district has been enacted. Public hearings and meetings are held to air the concerns of residents and business owners within the proposed district and from surrounding areas within the community. At times, a district may be created over the objections of a minority of the property owners within its bounds, but it is crucial and legally necessary that the public is given a say.

The commissions' powers include making districts within their jurisdictions and reviewing applications from owners of contributing properties who plan to make changes to their properties. If a commission approves any proposed changes, it will issue a **certificate of appropriateness** to the owner, which will allow him or her to obtain a building permit, which is required before any work is allowed to begin. The commission or its designee (the police in some locations) may check up as the work goes forward to ensure that the owner or contractor performs it according to the plans submitted to the commission. In addition to overseeing alterations and additions to historic properties and regulating new construction within historic districts, local historic preservation commissions may also inventory and survey historic properties, conduct public education programs, accept and manage state and federal grants, pursue court cases to preserve historic properties, acquire and manage historic properties, and hold preservation easements (discussed later in this chapter).

In addition to planning and implementing new districts, local historical commissions can designate existing National Register districts as local historic districts. Completing this process affords the historic resources within a National Register district the same protection as local districts provide. Starting with a National Register district is a more streamlined process than planning a local district from scratch, because the surveys and determinations of contributing structures have already been completed. In some locales, municipalities pass ordinances that designate all existing National Register districts within their jurisdiction as local historic districts. This requires significant public participation, because of the limits on demolition and alteration on the part of property owners that the local districts require.

Because landowners and other concerned individuals sometimes challenge the authority of local preservation commissions to limit demolitions and alterations within districts, local preservation ordinances must be written carefully and need to contain specific legal safeguards. Most local preservation ordinances are based on national model ordinances, copies of which are available from the SHPOs. According to Heritage Preservation Services of the National Park Service, a preservation ordinance should include the following:

- A clear statement of purpose.

- Definitions of terms used in the ordinance.

- The process for establishing a preservation commission and a specific discussion of its powers and duties.

- Criteria and procedures for designating and removing designation of historic buildings and districts.

- Identification and a clear definition of actions that are reviewable by the commission within the district, such as new construction, alterations to historic buildings, moving buildings, and changing landscape features. Also, the ordinance needs to spell out what areas of properties are reviewable. It should indicate if the ordinance covers only street facades, or all exterior walls, and if it protects any historic interiors or specific elements thereof or alterations to secondary buildings.

- Specific criteria and procedures for the systematic and consistent review of all reviewable actions within the district.

- A definition of the legal authority of the commission's decisions, whether it be advisory or binding.

- Provisions for economic hardship. In some cases, the ordinance can make exceptions for individual building owners who have difficulty complying with the district's design guidelines due to limited finances.

- Clear and affirmative maintenance and demolition by neglect provisions. Some ordinances make demolition by neglect an offense punishable by fines or even the seizure of a historic property through eminent domain.

- Procedures for appeals to the decisions of the commission. Under the United States Constitution, all laws must have appropriate provisions for appeals and due process.

- Enforcement provisions and procedures. The ordinance has to define the process of how its architectural controls will be enforced.

- A concise set of design guidelines based on the *Secretary of the Interior's Standards of Rehabilitation* (explained in Chapter 10). The ordinance must spell out exactly what architectural guidelines all property owners in the district who own contributing buildings need to abide by (Reap and Hill 2007).

The scope and content of these provisions will be guided and limited by the language of the state enabling legislation of the state in which the district is located. For example, the North Carolina enabling legislation does not allow for the regulation of changes to the interiors of historic buildings within local historic districts created within the state, therefore no preservation ordinance implemented within that state can contain language protecting historic interiors within historic districts.

All local preservation ordinances must comply with any applicable federal, state, and local laws. Also, to avoid being challenged and possibly overturned in a court of law, the ordinance needs to treat all people fairly and equally, provide adequate due process, and be flexible enough to allow the properties within it to be used in some practical manner and give their owners an adequate place to live in the case of residences or a reasonable economic return in the case of commercial buildings (legal challenges to preservation laws are discussed in Chapter 5).

Conservation Districts

Conservation districts are created in a manner similar to historic districts, but their regulations are not as stringent. Areas designated as conservation districts are often not considered as historically significant as regular historic districts. They may have a lower concentration of historic structures but still have a distinct character worth preserving. For example, a community may want to protect a neighborhood of small 1950s ranch houses with fairly large lots and many trees from having its houses replaced by much larger contemporary dwellings, without desiring strict architectural controls for alterations to the existing houses. Established to maintain a general feeling of a residential area without focusing on architectural details, conservation districts mainly prohibit demolition or construction of incompatible buildings in order to maintain the general character of a neighborhood.

Local Historic Landmarks

Some local historic preservation ordinances allow for the designation of individual local historic landmarks, which may or may not be listed on the National Register. Landmark status is given in order to protect individual historic buildings or structures or objects, especially those located outside of local historic districts. **Local historic landmarks** may have national, state, or local historical significance or a combination thereof (Figure 3.8). As with local historic

Figure 3.8. Pasadena City Hall, built in Pasadena, California, in 1927 in the Renaissance revival style. The building received an extensive renovation in 2004 and was modified to better withstand earthquakes. Source: Photograph by Peter B. Dedek, 2009.

districts, owners must apply for a certificate of appropriateness before they can make significant alterations to their landmark property. Landmark designation often acts as an honor or distinction for homeowners and can function as a marketing tool for businesses, such as bed and breakfasts or restaurants, located within historic landmark buildings.

As with contributing resources inside local historic districts, local landmarks have much greater protection than properties that are listed on the National Register but have no local designations. In some places, local landmarks have greater protections and benefits for their owners than do contributing properties in a local historic district. For example, in North Carolina communities, the owners of landmarks qualify for a 50 percent reduction in their property taxes, while the owners of contributing properties in a local historic district do not. To encourage owners to preserve their landmark, "recapture penalties" may be enforced against an owner who demolishes the property or otherwise seriously harms its historic integrity. If this happens, the owner will have to repay any back taxes not collected because of the landmark designation. Also in North Carolina, the historic interiors of local landmarks can receive legal protection with the owner's consent at the time of designation, which, as we have seen, is not true for contributing properties in a local historic district.

PROTECTING HISTORIC INTERIORS

The interiors of historic buildings are significant and distinctive elements of the built environment that people interact with directly, yet, nationwide, historic interiors receive little legal protection (Figure 3.9). For example, in the French Quarter, one of the nation's most restrictive local historic districts, only elements of historic buildings that "come in contact with outside air" receive legal protection. This preserves areas such as porches and courtyards, but developers can treat interiors as they wish. One unfortunate result of this is that in the early 2000s, the

Figure 3.9. Interior of Osterley Park, an English mansion designed by neoclassical architect Robert Adam, in 1767 in London, England. Significant interiors define the character and people's experience of historic buildings but are often not preserved except in highly significant properties, such as house museums. Source: Photograph by Peter B. Dedek, 2013.

distinctive and historic interior of a bar on Bourbon Street called the Old Absinthe House Bar (Figure 3.10a), was gutted and its unique 19th-century interior replaced with a generic and sterile 21st century daiquiri shop (Figure 3.10b).

Although the interior is where people connect most with a building, interiors have been traditionally neglected in historic preservation, especially within historic districts. The following language, taken from the Commission on Chicago Landmarks is typical: "Landmark qualities are defined by the Commission as significant historical or architectural features. In the case

Figure 3.10a. Preserved exterior of Old Absinthe House in the French Quarter of New Orleans, circa 1830. Source: Photograph by Peter B. Dedek, 2010.

Figure 3.10b. Ruined interior of Old Absinthe House, circa 1830. The original interior had a 19th-century bar complete with the original absinthe dispensers. Source: Photograph by Peter B. Dedek, 2010.

of landmark districts, these features are confined to the exterior aspects of the property" (Commission on Chicago Landmarks 2009). Under the Jacksonville, Florida, local historical ordinance, "A Certificate of Appropriateness will not be required for any interior alterations" (City of Jacksonville 2010).

Despite the general bias against protecting interiors, the interiors of individual historic landmarks are considered worthy of protection in some instances. For example, even though interiors are not regulated in historic districts in Chicago, historic features of some large buildings in that city are "landmarked [sic] inside and out" (Commission on Chicago Landmarks 2009). For example, the lobby and the auditorium of the historic landmark Chicago Theater are regulated.

In addition to occasional protection of the interiors of historic landmarks, other protections exist. For example, some historical organizations offer grants specifically for the restoration of interiors, such as the Cynthia Woods Mitchell Fund for Historic Interiors, which provides grants ranging from $2,500 to $10,000 for nonprofit organizations and public agencies for the preservation, restoration, and interpretation of significant historic interiors across the nation (National Trust 2012). Another significant protection for interiors, the Federal Historic Preservation Tax Incentives Program requires that particularly significant historic interiors and features, such as lobbies and main staircases, must be considered and are normally retained in the process of a certified rehabilitation. However, despite these exceptions, historic interiors remain among the most vulnerable historic resources. Part of the reason for this is that interiors are often seen as private and that granting them legal protection is a violation of the owner's rights. For example, the Supreme Court of Massachusetts ruled in 1990 that the legal protection of the interior of Boston's Church of the Immaculate Conception was inappropriate because government intrusion in the interior was "invasive" (see Chapter 5). The historic interiors of private houses are even less likely to be regulated than those of churches. Generally, the more accessible a historic interior is to the public, the more likely it is to be protected.

THE SIGNIFICANCE OF PRIVATE PRESERVATION ORGANIZATIONS AND INITIATIVES

The vast majority of historic properties in the United States are privately owned, making most preservation activity private. As we saw in Chapter 1, preservation in the United States started mainly as a private endeavor, and private organizations such as the National Trust for Historic Preservation and local preservation groups still often take the lead. In addition to the National Trust, many regional preservation organizations, such as Historic New England and the Preservation League of New York State, support preservation activities within their geographical areas of interest, as do city preservation organizations such as the San Antonio Conservation Society and the Preservation Resource Center of New Orleans.

NATIONAL TRUST FOR HISTORIC PRESERVATION

As described in Chapter 1, the National Trust for Historic Preservation was established as a public-private venture in 1949 but has operated as an independent private nonprofit since the 1990s. The purpose of the National Trust is to provide "leadership, education, and advocacy to save America's diverse historic places and revitalize communities," (National Trust 2012). Along with the National Park Service and the Advisory Council on Historic Preservation, which are federal agencies, the National Trust helps lead and guide the field of historic preservation in the United States at the national level. The National Trust engages in a range of activities including:

- Publishing its "America's 11 Most Endangered Historic Properties." Each year the trust identifies 11 historic resources, including buildings, districts, landscapes, and even entire states (in 1993 the trust listed the entire state of Vermont as endangered due to proposed "big box" retail development there), which it considers to be particularly in danger of being harmed, neglected, or destroyed. The list, which the trust publicizes widely, acts as an appeal for the preservation of the listed places and has helped secure interest and money to aid in their preservation.

- Operating 29 diverse historic sites including the Acoma Sky City in Acoma Pueblo, New Mexico, and Montpelier, President James Madison's home in Orange, Virginia, and architect Phillip Johnson's Glass House. In this way, the National Trust takes a direct role in preserving historic properties.

- Maintaining a list of Historic Hotels of America, which are operating hotels that have historic significance. Hotels use this designation as a marketing tool, which if successful, tends to encourage the hotel to make an effort to preserve the hotel property because its historic nature has become a selling point.

- Operating the National Trust Community Investment Corporation, which is a for-profit subsidiary of the National Trust that makes investments in real estate projects using federal historic tax credits and other historic preservation incentives.

- Publishing its widely circulated periodical *Preservation Magazine.*

- Providing technical and legal assistance and training to aid in preservation research, advocacy, and practice nationally.

- Lobbying to retain and create preservation-friendly programs and laws at the national, state, and local levels.

- Holding an annual conference.

- Operating the Preservation Green Lab, a green building initiative.

- Managing the Main Street Program (discussed below).

These activities help to garner public support for preservation and allocate limited resources.

THE MAIN STREET PROGRAM

Concerned that many downtown areas in villages and small cities in the United States were deteriorating in the late 1970s and that a great number of historic downtown buildings were being demolished or insensitively remodeled, the National Trust created a pilot program to explore possible design improvements and methods of economic revitalization that would

Figure 3.11. Circa 1970 slipcover over a late-19th-century façade. Note contrast with rehabilitated building next door. Source: Photograph by Peter B. Dedek, 2011.

promote the rehabilitation and sympathetic reuse of historic downtowns. Since its inception in 1980, the Main Street Center has created individual **Main Street programs** in over 2,000 communities, helping to transform many downtowns from mostly vacant, unpleasant areas into busy, attractive places. From the 1950s through the 1970s, building owners demolished many historic downtown buildings or covered them with new "modern" facades often made of sheet metal. Preservationists refer to these false fronts as "slipcovers." One of the activities of the Main Street program has been to remove these architectural modifications and return the buildings to their original, historic appearance (Figure 3.11). Interestingly, however, some slipcovers are now considered historic in themselves because they are now over 50 years old and are sometimes being preserved.

The Main Street Center seeks to better organize businesses located in historic downtown areas, promote downtown areas to consumers, assist in the redesign of streetscapes in historic downtowns in order to retain or even recreate their historic nature and qualities, and to help economically restructure historic commercial areas to make them more competitive and successful. According to its official website, the Main Street Center has served "as the nation's clearinghouse for information, technical assistance, research, and advocacy . . . [and] educated and empowered thousands of individuals and local organizations to lead the revitalization of their downtowns and neighborhood commercial districts" (National Trust 2007). The mission of the Main Street program is primarily a business strategy for enterprises located in town and city centers, but it has a preservation component and has undoubtedly led to the preservation of many historic buildings that would have otherwise been lost.

REGIONAL AND STATE HISTORICAL ORGANIZATIONS AND NONPROFITS

Some regions and states have private, nonprofit historical associations. These organizations use a variety of strategies to promote preservation within their given region or state. Most are **501(c) (3) charitable nonprofit organizations**, charitable groups that "must not be organized or operated for the benefit of private interests, and no . . . net earnings may inure to the benefit of any private shareholder or individual" (IRS 2012). Regional and state historical associations offer preservation tools, such as grant and loan programs and educational workshops, and perform many of the same functions as the National Trust but are focused on a single state or region.

Significant examples of such groups include Preservation Pennsylvania, Maine Preservation, Historic New England, the Indiana Landmarks, and the Florida Trust for Historic Preservation.

The Florida Trust for Historic Preservation was founded in 1978 to "promote the preservation of the architectural, historical and archaeological heritage of Florida through advocacy, education and historic property stewardship" (Florida Trust 2012). The Florida Trust does many of the same things as the National Trust, such as lobbying for preservation and providing training for preservationists, partners with the National Trust, and even publishes an annual list of the eleven most endangered historic sites in Florida. In an era of reduced government spending and involvement in historic preservation, regional and state organizations will become increasingly important.

LOCAL HISTORICAL SOCIETIES

Many cities, counties, and towns also have private, nonprofit historical associations. These organizations concentrate on a very specific geographical area. Members often have a direct connection with, and intimate knowledge of the history and historic resources within a particular city, town, or county. Members also have close connections with local preservationists and potential donors, making this kind of organization particularly effective. An example of such an organization is the San Antonio Conservation Society in San Antonio, Texas, which is one of the oldest local preservation organizations in the country. Founded by 17 women in 1924, the San Antonio Conservation Society hosts a number of programs similar to those offered by the Preservation Resource Center. The San Antonio Conservation Society also offers direct grants for preservation projects, and raises a portion of its funding by running the large annual Fiesta San Antonio street fair, which features local food, music, and crafts in a historic area of San Antonio. Active conservation societies focus resources and activism and are often successful in changing local attitudes and practices.

Another example of a local private preservation organization is the Preservation Resource Center (PRC) of New Orleans founded in 1974 with the purpose of promoting "the preservation, restoration, and revitalization of New Orleans' historic architecture and neighborhoods" (PRC 2012). The PRC seeks to protect "New Orleans' historic architecture by expanding the constituency that understands the economic, cultural, and aesthetic importance of historic preservation, and by involving citizens in preservation projects," utilizing its approximately 50 full and part-time staff and a budget of over $6 million (PRC 2012). A PRC program called Operation Comeback helps individuals purchase and rehabilitate vacant historic properties. The PRC also provides low cost loans and maintains a historic preservation revolving fund (explained later in this chapter). Already one of the most active local preservation organizations in the country, the PRC increased its budget, staff, and activities after Hurricane Katrina flooded the city in 2005.

GRASSROOTS PRESERVATION: TOOLS AND ACTIVISM

In order for preservation to work, it has to have public support. The best way to preserve is through voluntary, even enthusiastic participation by landowners, officials, business people, and the public in general. Knowing this, preservation advocates have sought to make historic preservation part of the American culture.

In addition to advocacy, a variety of preservation tools exist that do not involve government funding or restrictive regulations. These include preservation easements and revolving funds (explained next), and outright purchase of resources for the purpose of preservation.

PRESERVATION EASEMENTS

Preservation easements and covenants are legal agreements in which a property owner donates or sells an aspect or a number of aspects of his or her property rights to another entity, usually a local government or private preservation organization. Restrictions written into the deed require that the present owner and all future owners preserve specified features of the historic property. An easement can require the preservation of only a building's street façade or can be written to require the protection any historic features on a building's exterior or interior or even to preserve its context, such as outbuildings or gardens and surrounding landscapes. Since an easement becomes incorporated into the deed, it is transferred from owner to owner whenever a property is sold, thus protecting the resource even if future owners would prefer to demolish or alter it against the stipulations of the easement. However, with the exception of the preservation restrictions spelled out in the covenants, the property owner keeps the right to full use of the property.

The easement is an enforceable private contract that can overrule or go further than local historic district regulations, and unlike ordinances and laws, which can be changed or rescinded, the easement remains in force regardless of public policy or politics. Although permanently embedded in the deed, the easement must be overseen and enforced by an outside agency or a property owner might choose to ignore it and not suffer any ramifications. This is why preservation easements are granted to organizations, such as the National Trust for Historic Preservation, municipal preservation commissions, or private preservation nonprofits, which are given the responsibility of checking up on the property every so often to ensure that it is being maintained and preserved. If an owner is found to be breaking the terms of the easement, the organization holding the easement may file suit to force compliance. In most cases, before making alterations to the property that might have the potential of impacting any parts of the property covered by the easement, the property owner is required to submit plans to the body holding the easement and gain its approval of the proposed changes before proceeding with construction.

The property owner who originally granted the preservation easement and all future owners are eligible for special tax deductions in many jurisdictions. The reasoning behind this is that when a landowner donates a permanent conservation easement to a charitable or governmental organization it often reduces the value of the property since certain kinds of potentially profitable development are restricted by the easement. The landowner deducts this reduction in value caused by the easement, which is the difference between the fair market value of the property without the restrictions and the fair market value with the restrictions in place, from federal and, in some states, state income taxes. Because they are private contracts that protect specific properties and do not depend on government regulation, easements are an important tool in historic preservation.

REVOLVING FUNDS

Revolving funds help generate financing for preservation and restoration work. To create a revolving fund, a preservation organization amasses a sum of money through donations or grants or by other means and uses it to build up an initial pool of money. The organization then lends the money to borrowers who use it to purchase or to restore historic properties. As the borrowers repay their loans, usually with interest, the money goes back into the fund, and the organization lends the money out again to other buyers who use the money to save additional historic properties. As long as the loans are repaid, the process can go on indefinitely.

Sometimes, a preservation organization will use a revolving fund to purchase endangered historic buildings and then resell them with protective easements to new owners who will rehabilitate them, which preserves the building and quickly replenishes the fund allowing for the purchase and protection of additional properties.

PRESERVATION ACTIVISM

Sometimes purely voluntary preservation does not work. Property owners, governmental agencies, and the like are sometimes determined to harm historic properties in order to achieve their goals. The most common justification is that the retention of a historic property stands in the way of making a profit for the property owner or owners. In other cases, a historic property may stand in the path of a project deemed to be in the public interest. In instances such as these preservationists often have to use political and legal tools to try to stop or alter a project. Short of direct confrontation, sometimes negotiations will produce an acceptable compromise.

PRESERVATION ADVOCACY

Methods of preservation advocacy include creating historical tours to inspire appreciation of historic properties and districts; publishing literature, such as preservation newsletters and letters to the editor; holding and attending meetings and speaking out for the preservation of specific landmarks or districts; creating educational programs for professionals such as architects, interior designers, contractors, and the general public; organizing neighborhoods to promote the creation of historic districts and support other preservation measures; and lobbying at the federal, state, and local level for legislation and governmental policies that require and or encourage preservation. Advocacy makes up a significant portion of the activities of historic preservationists.

Opposition to Demolitions and Other Projects That Harm Historic Properties

Opposition to projects that are harmful to historic properties can take many forms. Sometimes, preservationists are relatively disorganized and limit their activities to individual actions, such as writing letters and making phone calls, while in other cases the resistance can be sustained and highly organized. While the popular image of preservation activists has them throwing themselves in front of bulldozers, most preservation battles take place in city council chambers, meeting halls, and courtrooms. Sometimes the controversy is minor and easily resolved; however, many preservation battles can be drawn out for years.

In the case of the Riverfront Expressway, preservationists won the day, however, in many cases they did not, such as the effort to save Pennsylvania Station in described in Chapter 1.

THE SECOND BATTLE OF NEW ORLEANS

An example of an extended battle to preserve the integrity of an entire historic district is called "the Second Battle of New Orleans." This extensive political and public relations effort to save the French Quarter historic district from encroachment by a highway began in the 1960s when a group of local activists voiced their opposition to a proposed riverfront expressway (Interstate 310) that would have divided the famed French Quarter from the Mississippi River. The riverfront expressway was to be a busy, six-lane elevated highway that would have passed within yards of many 19th century landmarks within the French Quarter, including the old Greek revival style United States Mint (1835) by architect William Strickland and the Café du Monde, which is located in a historic French Market building (circa 1813) (Figure 3A). Construction of the highway would have blocked the entire historic district, including Jackson Square and the St. Louis Cathedral, from the river and damaged the district's historic integrity with off-ramps, vibrations, noise, and visual obstruction.

In 1946, Robert Moses, the sometimes controversial New York City city planner, had proposed the construction of a riverfront

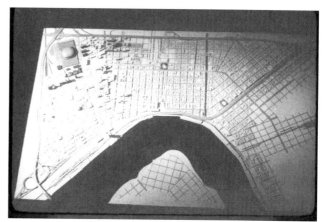

Figure 3A A model of the proposed expressway route. The rectangular French Quarter at the center would have been divided from the river and flooded with noise and auto exhaust by the proposed highway. Source: New Orleans Virtual Archive.

highway for New Orleans in a transportation plan he created for the city. In the early 1960s, the city government and many other key players in Louisiana revived the idea and began to work to make the expressway a reality. At first, even the Vieux Carré Commission (the city agency entrusted with the protection of the French Quarter) supported the project, but at the urging of a determined and growing group of local activists based in the French Quarter allied with other area preservationists, the commission changed its position in 1963. Despite this increasing opposition, under pressure from a number of influential Louisiana officials, the Federal Highway

Figure 3B Jackson Square, French Quarter, New Orleans. Had the Riverfront Expressway been constructed, this picture would have been taken from the elevated westbound lane of a major highway. Source: Photograph by Peter B. Dedek, 2013.

Administration promoted the project and agreed to fund it in 1964.

In response to the increasing likelihood the expressway would soon be built, the project's opponents, with the help of the Secretary of the Interior, tried to have the French Quarter declared a national historic landmark, which the city council rejected. As the battle was still going on, the 1966 Historic Preservation Act and Section 4(f) of the National Transportation Act were passed. By the late 1960s, the New Orleans City Council, the City Planning Commission, the Board of Port Commissioners, the Orleans Levee Board, and the Public Belt Railroad had all approved the project (Weingroff 2005).

Expressway opponents persevered, however, and filed suit to force the project to go through the newly created Section 106 and Section 4(f) reviews in 1967, which helped slow the project down. It wasn't until 1969 after the Nixon Administration took power that John A. Volpe, the new Secretary of Transportation, who, ironically, was a former highway contractor, decided to cancel the project. Volpe cited his reasons for withdrawing funding for the project:

A careful review of the highway proposal and the positions of various interests convinced me that the public benefits from the proposed highway would not be enough to warrant damaging the treasured French Quarter. . . . The Riverfront Expressway would have separated the French Quarter from its Mississippi River levee and waterfront" (Weingroff 2005).

This was the first time in American history a major highway project was cancelled due to public opposition related to historic preservation. The only portion of the project that was built was a vast tunnel under the old city convention center, which had been paid for with state funds and is currently used as an underground valet parking garage by the casino that now occupies the site.

CONCLUSION

Preservation in the United States is truly a collaborative effort with the federal government and the National Trust for Historic Preservation coordinating the efforts of, and creating partnerships with state, local, and private entities. The public-private, national-local nature of preservation in the United States has created a remarkably flexible and effective system for protecting historic recourses given that land use controls in America tend to be weak especially at the national and state levels, compared to those in Europe and many other developed regions of the world. Most preservation is enforced at the local level, making preservation truly a grass roots movement.

STUDY QUESTIONS

1. What kinds of construction, demolition, and rehabilitation are regulated in National Register districts?

2. If an owner of a historic building located inside a historic district desires to make significant changes to that building, what are the basic steps of the required process?

3. Describe three common reasons that the integrity of historic areas within cities is lost.

4. Describe the process of gentrification of a historic area. Why do many neighborhood advocates often oppose it? What effects might gentrification have on the preservation of a neighborhood?

5. What is demolition by neglect? Why would a building owner purposely allow it to happen? How might it pose a threat to property values and even public safety?

6. What is a sense of place, and why is it important to historic preservation?

7. Would you describe historic interiors as being well protected in the United States? Why or why not?

8. How do preservation easements benefit a building's preservation? Why do you think a building owner would sell or donate one?

9. What is a revolving fund and how does it promote preservation?

10. Describe the preservation battle sometimes called the Second Battle of New Orleans. What preservation laws, organizations, and tools did it end up involving?

EXERCISE: CONCISE DEFINITIONS

Define the following terms taken from the chapter in 12 words or less.

1. Local historic district _____

2. Contributing property _____

3. Noncontributing property _____

4. Gentrification _____

5. Demolition by neglect _____

6. Missing tooth syndrome _____

7. Permeable membrane _____

8. Sense of place _____

9. Certificate of appropriateness _____

10. Conservation districts _____

11. Local landmarks _____

12. 501(c)(3) charitable nonprofit organization _____

13. Preservation easement _____

14. Revolving fund _____

Answers and explanations found in Instructor's Guide.

SOURCES

City of Jacksonville Florida. "Regulatory Boards and Commissions." Accessed July 21, 2010. http://www.jaxjazzfest.org/NR/exeres/12BC12CB-1264-49CC-B126-9FB7815A119E.htm?NRMODE=Unpublished. http://www.coj.net/departments/planning-and-development/community-planning-division/default/tools-for-local-preservation-springfield.aspx

Commission on Chicago Landmarks. 2009. "The Commission on Chicago Landmarks designation process and criteria; how landmarking and its tax incentives could affect you, and the differences from National Registry. Renovation, Home Improvement, Decorating." Accessed November 29, 2013. http://www.hydepark.org/historicpres/landmarkscrit.htm.

Florida Trust for Historic Preservation. "About the Trust." Accessed May 11, 2012. http://www.floridatrust.org/about-the-trust/overview.

Internal Revenue Service (IRS). "Exemption Requirements 501(c)(3) organizations." Accessed May 11, 2012. http://www.irs.gov/Charities-%26-Non-Profits/Charitable-Organizations/Exemption-Requirements-Section-501%28c%29%283%29-Organizations.

Jackson, J. B. 1984. *Discovering the Vernacular Landscape.* New Haven, CT: Yale University Press.

National Park Service (NPS). "Working on the Past with Local Historic Districts." Accessed May 11, 2012. http://www.nps.gov/tps/education/workingonthepast/index.htm.

National Trust for Historic Preservation. 2007. "Main Street, Revitalizing your Commercial District." Accessed November 29, 2013. http://publicwatchdog.org/wp-content/uploads/2007/11/0240_001.pdf.

——. "Cynthia Woods Mitchell Fund for Historic Interiors: Guidelines & Eligibility." Accessed May 23, 2012. http://www.preservationnation.org/resources/find-funding/special-funds/cynthia-woods-mitchell.html#.UpkDhCfxDjE.

Preservation Resource Center (PRC). "PRC Mission." Accessed May 11, 2012. http://www.prcno.org/aboutprc/mission.php.

Reap, James K., and Melvin B. Hill, Jr. 2007. "Law and the Historic Preservation Commission: What Every Member Should Know." *Cultural Resources Partnership Notes.* Washington, DC: Heritage Preservation Services, National Park Service, U.S. Department of the Interior. Accessed August 16, 2010. http://www.nps.gov/history/hps/pad/partnership/index.htm.

Weingroff, Richard, F. 2006. "The Second Battle of New Orleans—Vieux Carré Riverfront Expressway (I-310)." Accessed July 17, 2010. http://www.fhwa.dot.gov/infrastructure/neworleans.htm.

HOW HISTORIC PROPERTIES ARE IDENTIFIED: EVALUATING, RESEARCHING AND DOCUMENTING HISTORIC PROPERTIES

OBJECTIVES

- Explain the standards that must be met for a property to be considered historic.

- Explain the concepts and process involved in determining eligibility for the National Register and listing a historic property on the register.

- List and explain the National Register Criteria.

- List and explain the National Register Criteria Considerations.

- Describe the National Historic Landmark program.

- Describe the steps of researching and documenting a historic building.

- Describe the best practices and the process of surveying and examining a historic building that is about to be restored or renovated.

- Outline the main methods of documenting and recording historic buildings and their significant features.

- Outline and discuss the variety of historical records and other resources, both primary and secondary, available to researchers when studying the history, style, and significance of an old building.

Before beginning to practice historic preservation, designers must understand the many factors that are used to determine whether a property should be considered historic. While some properties are obviously historic, such as a well-preserved Georgian farmhouse from the 1700s (Figure 4.1a), the status of others, such as a rundown motel from the 1930s, may not be so clear (Figure 4.1b). Fortunately, a national set of standards exists to determine if a property is, indeed, historic. In the United States, that guide is the National Register of Historic Places.

Figure 4.1a Derby House, Salem, Massachusetts, built in 1764. Source: Library of Congress, Prints and Photographs Division, Washington, DC, 20540 USA. http://hdl.loc.gov/loc.pnp/hhh.ma0158. Historic American Buildings Survey. HABS MASS,5-SAL,30-4.

Figure 4.1b Hall's Cabins, an early tourist court in Monongahela, Pennsylvania, circa 1930. Source: From Peter B. Dedek collection.

So what factors make a property historic? The short answer is that a historic building, structure, site, district, or object in the United States:

- Is normally at least 50 years old,

- Has a documented association with a historic event or with a notable person, or

- Has architectural merit as an example of a distinctive historic style of architecture or as the work of an accomplished designer.

Although this definition already sounds complicated, it is only the beginning. Determining whether a property is historic can be quite a challenge, and multiple factors must be taken into account. In the simplest sense, a property or district that is listed on the National Register of Historic Places (see Chapter 1) or has been determined eligible to be listed on the register is considered to be "historic" for purposes of most federal, state, and local historic preservation programs. A property is placed on the National Register thorough a nomination process.

After the passage of the National Historic Preservation Act, which created the National Register of Historic Places, the National Park Service developed a specific set of standards called the National Register Criteria to determine whether a property is eligible for the National Register. Before studying the National Register Criteria, it is important to understand what types of properties can be deemed historic and be listed on the National Register.

BASIC TYPES OF HISTORIC PROPERTIES

The pursuit of historic preservation involves many kinds of historic properties, including historic buildings, structures, sites, districts, and objects (see Chapter 1 for a description of each type). It is possible, under certain circumstances, to list "objects" on the National Register. For example, the historic steamboat the *Delta Queen*—built in 1927 at Stockton, California, and now based on the Mississippi River in New Orleans— is listed on the National Register (Figure 4.2).

DETERMINING ELIGIBILITY AND LISTING PROPERTIES ON THE NATIONAL REGISTER OF HISTORIC PLACES

Created by the 1966 Historic Preservation Act, the National Register of Historic Places currently contains over 81,000 "districts, sites, buildings, structures, and objects significant in our prehistory and history," representing over 1.4 million individual historic resources (NPS "National Register:

Figure 4.2 Delta Queen. "Objects" such as this historic sternwheel steamboat are sometimes listed on the National Register. Source: Courtesy of Delta Queen Steamboat Company, National Park Service.

About Us" 2012). The National Register was intended to act as a record of historic properties of national, state, and local significance "in American history, architecture, archaeology, engineering, and culture" that is "maintained and expanded by the National Park Service on behalf of the secretary of the interior" (Andrus 1990, i).

THE NATIONAL REGISTER PROCESS

Before properties can be listed on the National Register, they have to be researched and documented and presented in a National Register nomination. Each listed property must go through the nomination process. To accomplish this, preservationists assemble information about the property including detailed data such as a researched history, date of construction and designer, if known, photographic documentation, including historic photos or other period illustrations, if available, and a "statement of significance." The term **significance** in historic preservation means the factors that make a property historic, such as association with a historic event or a famous person or possessing distinctive architecture. Significance is often measured in terms of the property's historical context, such as its relationship with the development of a community, a particular industry, or a social movement. A statement of significance is a narrative that outlines the reasons why a given property or district is historic and thus "significant."

Nominating a property for listing on the National Register is an extensive process that involves a good deal of research and documentation. Sometimes the property's owner or owners prepare nominations, while in other cases (especially in certain states such as Louisiana) personnel from the State Historic Preservation Office (SHPO) prepare them. In other instances, professional historians and historic preservation consultants prepare nominations. In any case, under federal law, whoever nominates a historic property has to obtain the permission of the owner or owners of the property.

The National Park Service publishes a series of informational booklets called **National Register Bulletins** to guide individuals writing National Register nominations and completing the National Register nomination form. However, even with the availability of National Register Bulletins and other government publications, preparing the National Register form still requires a good understanding of the National Register Criteria and historic architecture and an ability to conduct, assemble, and present credible historical research.

Once nominated, properties are not automatically listed on the National Register. The petitioner must submit the nomination to the SHPO of the state in which the property is located and then present the nomination to a statewide review board, often with assistance from the SHPO. The state board, which is usually made up of professionals in fields related to preservation, such as architects, historians, architectural historians, cultural geographers, archaeologists, historic preservation specialists, and the like, evaluates the qualities of the nominated property and makes a recommendation. Based on the information contained in the nomination, the state review board either deems a property "eligible" for the National Register or "not eligible." Regardless of its decision, the board forwards its recommendation to the state historic preservation office, which forwards it to the National Park Service. An NPS official, the Keeper of the National Register, along with his or her staff, makes the final decision and officially maintains the National Register.

To make its recommendation, a state historic preservation board evaluates the property type that a nomination should fall into (building, structure, site, property, or district), examines the "historical context" of the property, decides the National Register Criterion for which the building is significant (A, B, C, or D, to be discussed in this chapter), and applies a set of criteria considerations (discussed in this chapter) as established by the National Park Service. Once the process is complete, the nominations of listed properties are archived at the SHPO of the state where the property is located. Another important factor in the nomination process is the historical integrity of a given property (discussed later).

HISTORICAL CONTEXTS

To be eligible to be listed on the National Register, a property must be representative of "a significant part of the history, architecture, archaeology, engineering, or culture of an area," (Andrus 1990, 7). A property must also have an authentic association with history and or historic architecture at the local, state, or national level. The area of significance, a property's connection to wider historic events, noteworthy people, its surroundings, or architectural trends is called the property's **historical context**. For example, the historical context of a building can be very specific, such as in the case of the Robie House, designed by Frank Lloyd Wright, located on the University of Chicago campus in Chicago, Illinois (1908), or Wright's Hanna House in Palo Alto, California (1936), where the house would be considered significant as the work of an architect of international importance. The wider historical context for such houses includes the life and work of Frank Lloyd Wright, who designed 532 constructed buildings of which more than 400 still exist. An even broader context of Wright's buildings would be the Arts and Crafts movement and Japanese architecture in the case of the Robie House and Wright's organic interpretation of modern design embodied in the Hanna House.

In other cases, the historical context of a property can be quite general, such as with a house that was used as a safe haven in the Underground Railroad before the Civil War. In this case, the historical context of the house is the institution of slavery in America and the organized effort to assist individual slaves trying to escape its cruelties. Even if the house was not the site of a specific, documented individual historical event, it has significance as having played a small part in a much larger picture.

The National Park Service defines historic contexts as "those patterns, themes, or trends in history by which a specific occurrence, property, or site is understood and its meaning (and ultimately its significance) within prehistory or history is made clear." (Andrus 1990, 7) In other words, a historic context is the larger historical trend or pattern with which a given property was directly associated. For example, the context of an old stone, pyramidal iron furnace near Johnstown, Pennsylvania, would be connected to the development of the iron industry in southwestern Pennsylvania in the 19th century in the wider context of the general industrial history of in the region. The historic context of the furnace would include the clear-cutting of millions of trees to make charcoal used to melt iron ore in the furnaces, the creation of canals, and, later, railroads to transport firewood, ore, and finished pig iron. Other structures associated with the industry—such as mines, and associated buildings, such as the large, stylish mansions that the owners of iron furnaces often built—would also comprise the historic context of the furnace.

A sizable group of buildings and structures can be associated with a single context, and a single building can be associated with more than one historic context. For example, a mansion built by a 19th-century iron master might have been designed by a well-known architect. This is true for the Baker Mansion in Altoona, Pennsylvania, a stone Greek revival house built in 1849, designed by Baltimore architect Robert Cary Long, Jr. (Figure 4.3). Its history places the mansion in at least two historic contexts, the development of the iron industry and the work of Robert Cary Long, Jr. In addition, the historic context of a building can be related to its embodiment of a distinctive architectural style. Therefore the historical context of the Baker Mansion also includes its distinctive Greek revival style of architecture.

As we have seen, there are many types of historical contexts. In order to be considered as being relevant to a property's eligibility for the National Register, the context and the property itself must be clearly associated with actual historical events and trends. This must be determined through scholarly research. However, increasingly certain historic contexts, especially at the national and state levels, have already been established by former National Register nominations. These can be used as precedents for future nominations. In fact, a specific type of National Register nomination called the Multiple Property Documentation Form can be used to document broad historic contexts for use in future National Register nominations. In addition, contexts are associated with one or more areas of significance. An **area of significance** is the overall theme into which a context falls. Examples of commonly used areas of significance include such diverse themes as: agriculture, architecture, commerce, education, the heritage of a particular ethnic group, exploration and settlement, industry, military history, religion, and transportation. Any of these areas of significance can be used to develop the historic context of a property at the local, state, or national level, or a combination of them. When determining historic contexts, it is very important to place them within the correct historical time frame, or "period of significance."

Figure 4.3 Baker Mansion, Altoona, Pennsylvania, built in 1849. Source: Library of Congress, Prints and Photographs Division, Washington, DC, 20540 USA. http://hdl.loc.gov/loc.pnp/hhh.pa3044. Historic American Buildings Survey, HABS PA,7-ALTO,162-1.

PERIODS OF SIGNIFICANCE

Historic contexts are related to specific periods in history, so when a property is associated with a particular context, the period of that context and the property's association with it determines the property's **period of significance**. In the example of the Baker mansion, the proprietor, Elias Baker, built the house in 1849, and it functioned as the headquarters of his iron plantation until his death in 1864. This places the period of significance of the house in the context of the iron industry in southwestern Pennsylvania from 1849 to Baker's death in 1864.

Two of the most significant factors in determining whether a property should be listed on the National Register are its historic context or contexts and its period of historical significance. In order to determine whether or not a given historic property represents a particular historic context and period of significance, its association with that context has to be established through sound research. To help accomplish this, the National Register "Criteria of Evaluation" are used.

THE NATIONAL REGISTER CRITERIA FOR EVALUATION

The National Park Service created the **National Register Criteria for Evaluation**, which are four distinct classifications under which a property may be deemed eligible for the National Register—historic events, noteworthy people, distinctive architecture, and archeology. In some cases, a single property may be eligible under more than one of these criteria.

Criterion A: By Association with Historic Events

Some historic properties are considered historic because they are associated with events in history. An example of such a property is the Alamo in San Antonio, Texas (Figure 4.4). Originally named Misión San Antonio de Valero, a Spanish Catholic Mission built in 1724 and abandoned

Figure 4.4 The Alamo, San Antonio, Texas. Source: Library of Congress, Prints and Photographs Division, Washington, DC, 20540 USA. http://hdl.loc.gov/loc .pnp/hhh.tx0035. Historic American Buildings Survey, HABS TX-318.

in the early 1800s, the site was little more than a ruin at the time the battle of the Alamo was fought in 1836, during the Texas Revolution. Since the Alamo building and grounds were the site of the battle, they are clearly associated with this historic event and with the Texas Revolution as a whole, which, of course, has both state and national significance.

For an event to qualify under Criterion A, it must have local, statewide, or national significance, and that historic significance has to be established through scholarly research using dependable sources. Also, the event should have had a general impact on history at the local, state, or national level, rather than impacting only a limited group of people. For example, a property with significance limited to events associated with a particular family's genealogy will usually not qualify the property for the National Register under Criterion A, unless the events surrounding that family had a significant impact on others. In addition, the impact of specific historic events should fit into one or more established areas of significance, such as industrial history or the settlement of the West.

To qualify for listing under Criterion A, a given building or structure must have had direct association with the historic event in question. It can't just have been located nearby but not been actually involved in the event, nor can it be located on the site where the event had already taken place before the building itself was constructed. In that case, the site and any earlier features located on it might still be eligible under Criterion A, but the building itself would not. Most properties listed on the register under Criterion A contain structures or buildings directly associated with the event in question, such as a bridge that was used by troops during a Civil War battle or an old union hall where a historic strike was planned. Also, a property will not be eligible if its association with a given event is speculative: the event and the property's connection with it must be clearly documented with historical evidence such as narratives, period documents, photographs, oral histories, or a combination thereof. A building where the hanging of a well-known outlaw was rumored to have taken place would not be considered eligible under Criterion A unless those rumors are substantiated with dependable historical documentation.

Events for which a property may be deemed eligible for the National Register can be a specific, single event such as the Battle of the Alamo or be associated with more general historical contexts and areas of significance, such as the development of railroading in America. In the second case, the specific events that took place on the site may not have been historic in themselves, but because of their association with a broader historic context consisting of many related events, which taken together had a significant impact on local, state, and or national history. For example, the Harriet Barber House in Richland County, South Carolina, was listed on the National Register in 1986, because the site was purchased by Samuel Barber, a former slave, under a program designed to provide land for ex-slaves. In this case, the property is associated with slavery and Reconstruction in South Carolina and no specific event of particular notoriety has to have happened on the particular site for it to be listed under Criterion A.

Criterion B: By Association with Historic People

Properties eligible for the National Register under Criterion B are those associated with "individuals whose activities are demonstrably important within a local, state, or national historic context" (Andrus 1990, 14). In other words, the property must have a clear association with a person or group of people who made documented contributions to history at the local, state, or national level. In some cases, the people may be very well-known, such as Martin Luther King, Jr., or may be relatively unknown except within a local area, such as a particularly successful banker who made significant contributions to the development of a small Midwestern town. The person for whom a site is significant can sometimes be more infamous than famous, such as with Redcliffe, a Greek revival plantation in South Carolina (Figure 4.5), which is known for its association with U.S. Senator John Henry Hammond, who coined the phrase "cotton is king" and was a strong advocate of slavery and secession in the years leading up to the Civil War.

It is important that a National Register nomination clearly demonstrates that the individual or an association of individuals in question made genuine contributions to history and that the property in question has an authentic connection with that person or group. As with Criterion A, any assertions made about the historical associations and significance of a property nominated under Criterion B must be supported with historical evidence and competent academic research. Many historic sites are eligible under both Criteria A and B. An example is the Alamo in San Antonio, Texas, which is significant because of the Battle of the Alamo in 1836 and also because of its association with historically significant people who fought there, such as Davy Crockett and Antonio López de Santa Anna.

In most cases, any building or structure nominated under Criterion B should have been associated with the actual life and work of the person involved and not have been merely

Figure 4.5 Redcliffe Plantation. Source: Courtesy of SCPRT/Photo by Perry Baker.

constructed to commemorate his or her contributions to history. For example, the house in Gettysburg, Pennsylvania, where President Lincoln stayed on November 19, 1863 and put the finishing touches on the Gettysburg Address would be eligible under Criterion B for association with Lincoln, while a monument built to commemorate Lincoln's visit to Gettysburg would probably not.

In addition, a property should have a direct association with the notable person or people at a time when they were engaged in the activity or activities that made them important to history. Generally speaking, birthplaces and childhood homes are not eligible under Criterion B, while places where the individuals in question lived and worked as productive adults are. The property may be associated with a pivotal event in a person's career, such as the aforementioned house in Gettysburg, or it may be a place where the person lived or worked over an extended period, such as Springwood, the home of Franklin D. Roosevelt in Hyde Park, New York (Figure 4.6). In some cases, if no properties exist that are related to a noteworthy person's adult, productive life, properties related to his or her childhood or later years may be deemed eligible for lack of a more significant site.

In the last several decades, the scope of what constitutes a contribution to history has been broadened both in terms of the National Register and the discipline of history as a whole. While in the past the contributions of members of the elite were the focus of most historical research and National Register nominations, now the contributions of individuals from diverse religious or ethnic backgrounds such as small businessmen, labor leaders, migrants, and leaders in the civil rights movement of the 1950s and 1960s have been widely studied and recognized as well. Today, a building is just as likely to be nominated for its association with an activist such as Monteith Simkins (1899–1992)—who was an African-American leader in health reform and equal rights and lobbied for an anti-lynching bill and protested police brutality in Columbia, South Carolina (SHPO 2007)—as a building associated with an industrialist or politician.

Figure 4.6 Springwood, home of Franklin Delano Roosevelt, Hyde Park, New York. Source: Library of Congress, Prints and Photographs Division, Washington, D.C. 20540 USA. http://hdl.loc.gov/loc.pnp/hhh.ny1240. Historic American Buildings Survey, HABS NY-4355.

This increasing inclusiveness in the field of historic preservation has helped rescue it from the cultural-centric elitism that once dominated the field.

Because the National Register is concerned with history and not with current events, in most cases, properties associated with living people are not eligible under Criterion B. Also, properties designed by significant architects, interior designers, and builders are usually eligible under Criterion C, Architecture, rather than Criterion B.

Criterion C: Significance Due to Architecture

The most used of the four National Register Criteria is Criterion C: Architecture. The reason for this is that in many instances significance in architecture is the easiest case to make to list a property. To establish a building or structure as being significant for architecture, all a petitioner usually needs to do is to document the age, condition, and general history of a building, photograph its façades and significant interior spaces, record its distinctive features, and present this information in a National Register nomination. This is often simpler than researching a property's association with historic events or people. In addition, a great number of historic buildings that contribute to the American landscape have no known association with significant events or notable people.

Despite its being nominated for architecture, whether a building or other type of property is historic does not depend on how pretty or ugly it is. While many historic buildings and structures are very aesthetically pleasing and even fancy, some buildings deemed historic for their architecture, such as a small house made of bargeboard located near the Mississippi River or an antebellum slave cabin located on an old plantation (Figure 4.7), may appear quite bland to many people. But these buildings represent rare and historically important building types that are often at least as significant as obvious architectural landmarks such as a Victorian mansion. Preservationists measure architectural value by uniqueness in design and construction, connections to history and people, and a sense of historic authenticity, not whether a property is particularly stunning in appearance. Although historic places can elicit a lot of emotion, preservation is actually a rather academic pursuit that seeks to promote objective methodologies and authentic perspectives.

In order to list a property under Criterion C, a petitioner must demonstrate that the property qualifies for at least one of the following reasons:

Figure 4.7 Former Slave Cabin, Chicora Wood Plantation, Georgetown, South Carolina. Source: Library of Congress, Prints and Photographs Division, Washington, D.C. 20540 USA. http://hdl.loc.gov/loc.pnp/hhh.sc0539. Historic American Buildings Survey, HABS SC-482-F.

- Has "distinctive characteristics of a type, style, or method of construction,"

- Is "the work of a famous builder, designer, or architect," or

- Has "high artistic value." A building may possess just one of these factors and still be eligible, but most historic buildings exhibit a combination of them (McClelland 1977).

Figure 4.8 Shotgun house, New Orleans. Source: Photograph by Peter B. Dedek, 2011.

To have "distinctive characteristics of a type, style, or method of construction," a building has to represent a particular mode of historic design. It may be of a certain **type**, meaning that it belongs to a class of buildings with a particular form or function in common (McClelland 1977). An example of a type of architecture is a Southern shotgun house. Shotgun houses are long, thin residences with African and West Indian influences built approximately between 1840 and 1940 in the American South, particularly along the Gulf Coast. In shotgun houses, the rooms are lined up one after the other single file from front to back with no hallways (Figure 4.8). The term comes from the idea that supposedly one could shoot a shotgun through the length of the house without hitting any walls, because the rooms and the exterior and interior doors are aligned in a straight line from front to back. Shotgun houses constitute a type of architecture and not a style. The reason for this is that examples of these long, skinny houses can be found in a number of styles, such as colonial revival, Italianate, or craftsman, depending on what decorative features they exhibit on their façades, such as columns and brackets. The log cabin is another example of a building type.

A building eligible under Criterion C may also embody a certain historic style. Styles are distinct decorative systems that are applied to both the exteriors and interiors of buildings. Styles may also influence the overall form a building takes in addition to determining its decorative motifs. Most historical styles have been given names and represent the fashion of specific periods in history. Examples include Greek revival, a style based on Greek temple architecture that was used from around 1820 to the 1880s, and Italianate, a style used from around 1830 to the 1880s that was based on the architecture of Italian villas from the Renaissance. Another style that is quickly becoming historic is modernism, which was founded largely on the design concepts developed at the Bauhaus school in Germany in the 1920s and used in the United States from around 1930 to the 1980s. If a building represents a strong example of one of these or one of many other historic styles, it may be eligible for inclusion in the National Register under Criterion C.

A building may also qualify for the register because it represents a distinctive method of construction used during a given time or in a specific place or by a certain group of people. For example, an adobe pueblo with mud brick walls, a stucco exterior, large wooden beams called *vigas,* and wooden waterspouts called *canales,* built in New Mexico using both Native American and possibly some Spanish architectural precedents represents a distinctive method

Figure 4.9 Carson Pirie, Scott, & Company Building, Chicago, Illinois, designed by Louis Sullivan in 1899. The invention of the steel frame structural system allowed for tall buildings with large, flexible interior spaces and big plate-glass windows, even on the lower floors. Source: Library of Congress, Prints and Photographs Division, Washington, DC, 20540 USA. http://hdl.loc.gov/loc.pnp/hhh.il0067. Historic American Buildings Survey, HABS IL-1064.

of construction. Another example of a distinctive method of construction are the early iron-framed skyscrapers of cities such as Chicago and New York designed by pioneers of modern structure, such as Louis Sullivan (Figure 4.9).

A building may also qualify for the National Register because it is the "the work of a famous builder, designer or architect." This category is quite straightforward. Buildings designed by architects or builders with local, state, or national recognition are often eligible under Criterion C solely for this reason. Examples include most buildings designed by well-known architects, such as Frank Lloyd Wright, Louis Sullivan, and Mies van der Rohe, although a building's designer doesn't have to be as famous as these architects to be eligible. It is possible some buildings designed by a famous architect may not be eligible; however, the reason would usually involve its having a lack of "integrity," an important factor that impacts National Register eligibility, which will be discussed in the next section.

And finally, a building may be eligible for the National Register if it has "high artistic value." This means a property displays the attributes of a particular design style or architectural concept very distinctively. For example, a city park from the turn of the 20th century might be deemed eligible because of high artistic value if it expresses the concepts of the City Beautiful Movement. This urban renewal ideal emphasized the creation of formal urban parks and classically-inspired monumental buildings based on the ideals of the French Beaux-Arts style that emerged in the 1890s and had a significant impact on the planning of many American

Figure 4.10 United States Capitol and Lincoln Memorial. Source: Library of Congress Prints and Photographs Division Washington, DC, 20540 USA. http://hdl.loc.gov/loc.pnp/pp.print. Reproduction number LC-DIG-highsm-16008.

cities. City Beautiful parks were designed using a clear central axis and classical proportion with a strong sense of symmetry and order and were often adorned with neoclassical monuments, such as in the National Mall in Washington, D.C. (Figure 4.10).

Criterion D: Archeology

Criterion D is reserved for properties that have yielded or may be likely to yield important archeological information related to history or prehistory. A site does not necessarily have to have any standing historic structures on it to qualify under this criterion. An example of such a site is the African Burial Ground National Landmark in lower Manhattan, which contains the remains of hundreds of African Americans buried there during the late seventeenth and 18th centuries. Since this book focuses on architecture, Criterion D is beyond its scope.

REQUIREMENTS FOR ELIGIBILITY FOR ARCHITECTURE

In addition to meeting one or more of the National Register Criteria, a building or structure or a collection of buildings and or structures that constitute a property must have some degree of historical integrity. In fact, whether or not a property possesses integrity is one of the most discussed and critical issues addressed when determining whether properties are eligible for the National Register.

Historic integrity is the degree to which a property has retained its original historic features. To have integrity, a building has to look similar to the way it did when it was constructed or at least resemble the way it looked during its period of historical significance (the era during which the historic event, notable person, or distinctive architecture existed that makes the building historic). For example, the historic gas station in Figure 4.11 has a high level of historic integrity. This site, located in a small Texas city, has retained the look and features of a classic mid-20th-century service station in its original context and even fairly early gas pumps.

In another example, Victorian Queen Anne–style houses, built from about the 1870s to the 1890s, typically have towers, porches with wooden "gingerbread" posts and railings, steep roofs, decorative clapboard and wooden shingle siding, dormers, bay windows, and tall chimneys (Blumenson 1977, 63). If an example of this style retains all or most of these features, it probably has a high degree of integrity. However, if the gingerbread posts have been replaced with wrought-iron from the 1970s, a standing-seam metal roof and vinyl siding have been added, the chimneys and dormers removed, and the windows replaced, the house no longer possesses enough integrity to be eligible for the National Register or be considered historic at all, even if the house has documented associations with significant historical events or people.

Without integrity, a building simply has ceased to be what it once was. The ultimate insult to integrity, of course, is demolition. In some cases, character-defining features, such as those listed above can be reintroduced to a point (by removing the vinyl siding or reconstructing a

Figure 4.11 Circa 1940, Service Station, Gonzales, Texas. Source: Photograph by Peter B. Dedek, 2009.

lost porch, for example) and a building can regain some of its integrity, but this can be tricky, because all changes have to be made based on sound historical evidence on the historical appearance of the building (such as old photographs) (Figure 4.12).

According to the National Park Service, to have integrity, a building must possess physical characteristics that fall into seven categories: location, design, setting, materials, workmanship, feeling, and association (Andrus 1990, 44).

Figure 4.12a Historic Photo Service Station, Columbus, Texas, circa 1920. Source: From Peter B. Dedek collection.

Figure 4.12b Same Service Station, Columbus, Texas, 2012, as a Hardware Store. Although the building retains little of its original character it is easily identified by the stenciling on the front corner column. Source: Photograph by Peter B. Dedek, 2012.

LOCATION

In most cases, an eligible building cannot have been moved from its original location unless it is nominated because of a historical event that took place when the building occupied its present location even though it was not its original one, a rare circumstance. In unusual cases, a building that has been moved can be eligible, but the building usually has to possess an extraordinary level of historic significance. The reason most moved buildings are not eligible is that the location of a building is an integral aspect of its character and context. It is difficult to understand a building's development over time or appreciate its historical significance without witnessing it with its original setting and surroundings (Figure 4.13).

DESIGN

Design refers to the features that make a historic building or historic district distinctive. One of the main reasons to preserve historic buildings and their contexts at all is that they exhibit distinctive and often obsolete features that are both interesting and informative and can offer contemporary observers an experiential window of insight into the past. Therefore, to be considered historic, a building or group of buildings needs to have retained a majority of the original design features that make them distinctive and representative of a particular type, style, method of construction, or a combination of these. To determine this, architectural historians often look to see whether character-defining features remain. **Character-defining features** include such elements as historic porches, windows, rooflines, decoration, and in the case of districts, historic blocks and street configurations. Without retaining the significant features

Figure 4.13 This historic school in Fort Stockton, Texas, was moved from its original location and has lost its original context: note modern concrete foundation and stairs. Source: Photograph by Peter B. Dedek, 2010.

Figure 4.14 The once-historic house in New Paltz, New York (left) was a Victorian house in the Italianate style. The house originally had ornate posts on its porch, decorative brackets along the rooflines, wooden siding, and articulated windows. Now, with the possible exception of its chimney, all that is evident is its original massing and overall proportions. Defining characteristics, such as historic porches, wooden siding, decorative elements, and original windows define a building's historic integrity. The house probably looked similar to the house pictured on the right, which possesses greater historic integrity, before it was remodeled. Source: Photographs by Peter B. Dedek, 2010.

that their architects or builders envisioned, buildings lose their ability to inspire and educate, such as with Figure 4.14.

SETTING

Setting is related to location and refers to a building's immediate physical surroundings, its context. To determine how a building's setting impacts its integrity, one should compare its surroundings during its period of historical significance to those of today. A building does not have to be moved to lose its context. Contexts can also be lost because of insensitive additions on or near the site. Road and highway construction often impacts a building's setting in an adverse manner, because road widening can rob houses of their front yards, and highway construction can take their backyards or split them away from their traditional neighborhoods. The addition of major highways can impact buildings so drastically as to make them into isolated relics that are difficult to inhabit or use effectively.

Different types of buildings have different types of historic settings that are appropriate to them. A farmhouse suddenly surrounded by apartment houses loses its setting and thus much of its integrity, while an urban row house would lose integrity if the houses adjacent to it were demolished. Many large historic houses are surrounded by gardens that, if removed, reduce the houses' integrity. The setting of a historic building can consist of natural features such as trees and hills as well as human-built features. Not all changes to setting have a significant effect on a building or district's integrity, but those that drastically impact the basic character of a property and its character-defining elements do. A common insult to the integrity of historic buildings is modern-looking and overwhelmingly unsympathetic additions.

MATERIALS

A major aspect of any building, both on its exterior and its interior, is the materials used in its construction. It is important to preserve the materials with which a building was constructed, especially visible surface materials. Building materials help to define the character of a building. When an architect chooses brick, for example, that material communicates the building's character, indicating attributes such as permanence, strength, and tradition, and if the brick were to be removed or covered up, the character of the building and the messages it communicates would be significantly altered. In addition, many historic building materials, such as old growth timbers, wide-plank floors, and aged stone and brick, are virtually irreplaceable today (Figure 4.15). These materials, which have unique textures and finishes, add to the intrinsic value of historic architecture and can be appreciated by most anyone.

WORKMANSHIP

One of the most valuable and often irreplaceable aspects of historic buildings is workmanship. Many details found inside and outside historic buildings display the skill, craftsmanship, and artistry of long-dead artisans, which would be difficult or impossible to replicate today. In a modern technological world in which we are surrounded by machine-made objects, experiencing historic craftsmanship creates an authentic link to the past. Many elements of historic buildings are handmade and very personalized. For example, it is possible to see the impressions of the fingers of slaves who made the bricks of some historic Southern plantation houses or to witness the individual scratches made by chisels on the limestone blocks of 18th- and 19th-century townhouses.

Figure 4.15 These historic cypress floor planks located in an old railroad freight station are nearly a foot wide and are essentially irreplaceable today. Source: Photograph by Peter B. Dedek, 2012.

FEELING

One of the most abstract concepts in the field of preservation is feeling. **Feeling** refers to a property's ability to communicate its period of historical significance and to remain unique to the time in which it was created or the time when it hosted famous events or people. In a sense, feeling sums up all of the other categories. If the building's location, design, setting, materials, and workmanship have been preserved, then the historic feeling will follow. This category can act as an overall gauge of a property's integrity: does a place feel historic to people who visit it? When people explore a site, are they inspired by its sense of history and its unique atmosphere?

ASSOCIATION

Association refers to a property's documented or observable links to the past. As stated earlier, for a building or site to be eligible because of its connection with historical events or notable people, it has to have a direct physical and documented link with the event or person for which it is considered significant. The place where a historic happening occurred must be sufficiently intact to communicate the relationship between the event or person and the place as it exists today. For example, a historical marker stating a certain historic event took place in a house that once stood where a parking garage now stands clearly lacks association. The house is gone, its setting long destroyed, and all that is left is the idea something happened on that particular piece of real estate. A historic property that retains its association is the Gettysburg Battlefield. One can stand in many areas in the park and witness landscapes with the same topography and natural and man-made features that directly influenced the fighting that took place there more than a century and a half ago.

THE NATIONAL REGISTER CRITERIA CONSIDERATIONS

In addition to the Criteria for Evaluation, the National Park Service created a number of additional guidelines called the **Criteria Considerations**. These describe types of properties generally considered not eligible for the register, but that may be eligible under extraordinary circumstances. According to the Criteria for Evaluation, the following types of properties are usually not eligible for or are "excluded" from the National Register:

- Religious buildings

- Buildings that have been moved

- Birthplaces or graves of historical figures

- Cemeteries

- Reconstructed buildings

- Monuments, buildings, and structures that achieved their significance less than 50 years before the time the National Register nomination is made

These exclusions were created so that the National Register program would not be flooded with a flurry of nominations for common sites, such as family graves, local churches, and celebratory monuments. Like most aspects of National Register eligibility, the criteria considerations require explanation.

RELIGIOUS PROPERTIES

Although normally excluded from listing on the National Register under the criteria considerations, a religious building that has architectural or historical significance in addition to its role as a center of religious worship may be eligible. For example, a church that is a good example of the Greek revival style and possesses a high level of integrity would be likely to be eligible under Criterion C for its architecture. An example of a listed religious building is the Touro Synagogue, built in the Georgian style in 1763, in Newport, Rhode Island, mentioned in Chapter 1. It is the oldest synagogue extant in America and also played a role in the Revolutionary War. Since the Touro Synagogue's historical significance goes beyond its religious role, and the building itself has a high level of architectural interest and integrity, the building is easily historic enough to be included on the National Register despite the criteria consideration against religious properties (Figure 4.16).

BUILDINGS THAT HAVE BEEN MOVED

When historic buildings are moved from their original location, they lose historic integrity because their original location and setting has been destroyed, and their historical

Figure 4.16b Touro Synagogue interior. Source: Library of Congress, Prints and Photographs Division, Washington, DC, 20540 USA. http://hdl. loc.gov/loc.pnp/hhh.ri0083. Historic American Buildings Survey, HABS RI-278.

Figure 4.16a Touro Synagogue built in the Georgian style in 1763, in Newport, Rhode Island. Source: Library of Congress, Prints and Photographs Division, Washington, DC, 20540 USA. http://hdl.loc.gov/loc. pnp/hhh.ri0083. Historic American Buildings Survey, HABS RI-278.

context is often completely lost. However, in certain cases, when a moved building is the only property associated with a particular event or person or represents a very rare style or method of construction, it may be eligible despite its having been moved.

BIRTHPLACES AND GRAVES

Sites of birth and burial and associated monuments are normally ineligible for the National Register because they usually have little direct association with the life and work of the individual born or buried there. Also, there are also so many of these sites, that if they were included, listing on the National Register would lose much of its meaning. Occasionally a birthplace or grave can be listed in the National Register if there are no alternative sites associated with a particular individual of significant historical importance or if the memorial itself has somehow gained historical significance in its own right.

CEMETERIES

For the same reasons individual graves are usually ineligible, entire cemeteries are excluded as well. If a cemetery is particularly distinctive for the design of its monuments or the manner in which the monuments were arranged, it may be eligible. An example of a cemetery listed for architecture (Criterion C) and for its role in the development of landscape architecture, specifically the design of garden cemeteries and public parks (Criterion A) is Laurel Hill Cemetery, begun in 1836 in Philadelphia, Pennsylvania (Figure 4.17). In addition, as with religious properties, if the cemetery itself has historical associations beyond its role as a cemetery, such as being the site of a battle, it may also be eligible.

Figure 4.17 Laurel Hill Cemetery, Philadelphia, Pennsylvania, 1836. Although a cemetery, Laurel Hill was listed as a National Historic Landmark in 1998, primarily because of its significance in the development of American landscape architecture. Source: Photograph by Peter B. Dedek, 2013.

RECONSTRUCTED BUILDINGS

Buildings that are not actually historic but are complete reconstructions of lost architecture are generally ineligible for inclusion on the National Register due to their inherent lack of authenticity and association. If a significant part of original building, such as its outer walls and roof, still exists, the building is normally not considered a reconstruction. Therefore, if the interior of a historic building was lost and is reconstructed based sound historic evidence, the building will not be considered a reconstruction.

As with graves and birthplaces, however, if there is no other site associated with a particular person or historical event, a reconstructed building may be eligible if it was constructed using sound historical evidence and according to a restorative master plan. The successful listing of a reconstructed building is very rare, however. Because of the common difficulty of finding enough documentation and the complexities of recreating historic materials and workmanship, reconstructed buildings often mimic originals in ways that never existed historically. In addition, regardless of the accuracy of the reconstruction, a rebuilt structure can never be truly authentic.

PROPERTIES THAT GAINED HISTORIC SIGNIFICANCE LESS THAN FIFTY YEARS BEFORE BEING NOMINATED

Generally, properties less than 50 years old are not eligible for the National Register. In addition, older places that achieved historical significance less than 50 years ago are also usually not eligible. For example, a building where a series of meetings during which significant decisions were made by notable people occurring a mere 20 years ago normally won't be eligible until 30 years from now, that is, 50 years after the event took place—even though the building itself may be more than 50 years old. Exceptions do exist: for example, sites having national significance, such as the Apollo Mission Control Center near Houston, Texas. It was listed in 1985 as a National Historic Landmark even though the site was not nearly 50 years old at the time (NPS "Apollo" 2013) (Figure 4.18). Also, many sites associated with Martin Luther King, Jr. and

Figure 4.18 Mission Control, Houston, Texas. Source: NASA.

other significant leaders in the civil rights movement were listed on the National Register much sooner than 50 years after the events that made them historic occurred.

NATIONAL HISTORIC LANDMARKS

Sites possessing significance in the history of the United States as a whole are considered National Historic Landmarks (Figure 4.19). **National Historic Landmarks** are also listed on the National Register but enjoy added status. Approximately 2,500 National Historic Landmarks are listed across the nation, constituting less than 3 percent of all properties listed on the National Register. In a practical sense, national landmarks are treated in a similar manner afforded all properties listed on the National Register and even properties that have not been listed but have only been determined to be eligible for the register. The main difference between the treatment of a property listed on the register and one listed as a National Historic Landmark is psychological. However, once a property is designated a National Historic Landmark, "the National Park Service commits to assist in the preservation of these irreplaceable properties through the National Historic Landmarks Assistance Initiative," which "promotes the preservation of National Historic Landmarks through technical assistance to their stewards, owners, managers, and friends groups." The initiative also assists in the "education of the general public about the importance of National Historic Landmarks" (NPS "Initiative" 2010). National landmarks

Figure 4.19 The White House is one of the best known National Historic Landmarks. Source: Library of Congress, Prints and Photographs Division, Washington, D.C. 20540 USA. http://hdl.loc.gov/loc.pnp/hhh.ri0083. Historic American Buildings Survey. Survey number HABS DC-37.

receive a higher degree of recognition and are afforded a limited amount of additional federal protections, such as periodic access to voluntary inspections by NPS preservation experts, than regularly listed properties. As with all properties listed on the National Register, privately owned National Historic Landmarks have no legal protection from purely private activities.

METHODS OF RESEARCHING AND DOCUMENTING BUILDINGS

When researching a historic property to create a National Register nomination or to have it designated as a local landmark or as contributing to a local historic district, it is always best to start with the easiest research methods first. These include asking the current owner what he or she knows about the building, doing an Internet search on the property, and checking with the State Historic Preservation office to see if an individual National Register nomination or other historical documentation exists for the building or if it is already located within a designated historic district. Then, using any information derived from these primary steps, it's best to proceed as needed with more time-consuming research methods.

These basic steps of researching and documenting buildings should be implemented in roughly the following order:

- Photographing the building's major façades and significant interior spaces to create an easy to use and permanent record of the building in its current condition. Good pictures may be used to look for clues that will help in the investigation. Pictures can shared with architectural historians to determine the building's style and its approximate age.

- Asking the owner and neighbors for any information they might have before doing archival research. **Archival research** is the act of investigating written sources, such as those found in archives and libraries.

- Searching secondary sources. **Secondary sources** are written information already gathered and interpreted by other researchers about the building (its history, style, and methods of construction) and its context (site, neighborhood, and region). Examples of secondary sources include books and articles on local history, National Register nominations, books, or articles on architectural styles or about a certain building type.

- Searching primary sources. **Primary sources** are documents dating from the historical era being studied. Examples include historic photographs, old letters, period newspaper articles, and original documents such as building contracts and architectural plans.

- Performing a thorough survey of the building's exterior, interior, and utility spaces to identify the historic construction methods, design features, decorative motifs, and materials existing in the building. Before any work begins, the location, properties, and condition of all building elements should be identified and documented. Media used for this include photographs, as-built architectural plans, video, and written descriptions (see Chapter 11 for more on surveying historic buildings).

- Collecting the information derived from the previous steps, organizing it, and examining it in order to identify the building's age (see Chapter 9), its style, its history, and to better assess its condition.

- Before any work rehabilitation begins, stabilize any elements that are threatened by natural or manmade dangers (see Chapter 11). For example, if a roof leak has been identified, have the roof repaired immediately instead of waiting for a larger rehabilitation project to begin.

SOURCES AVAILABLE TO RESEARCH HISTORIC PROPERTIES

Fortunately, researching historic properties can often be much faster and easier than it was before the Internet due to the profusion of indexed information available online. However, finding historical documents for specific buildings can still be difficult, because records for the vast majority of everyday buildings have been lost or may have never existed at all. In addition, some buildings have been so altered from their historic condition that a great deal of research and physical investigation is needed to determine what their original character may have been (Figure 4.20). To

Figure 4.20. Some historic buildings are so altered that a great deal of physical investigation and historical research is required to even begin planning their rehabilitation. Source: Photograph by Peter B. Dedek, 2012.

complicate matters even further, often an individual piece of evidence—such as an undated photograph or a footprint on an insurance map—is not enough to prove anything, and several types of historical evidence must be used together to produce an accurate history for a building and be useful to a designer. For example, if an elderly neighbor relates that the house next door used to have a fancy porch that was torn off a few decades ago, for this information to be both verified and useful in reconstructing the historic porch as part of a restoration, at least one historic photograph or drawing must be found, and the building itself should be examined for any physical remnants of the porch that may exist, such as an outline in old paint or nail holes.

There are a number of potential sources of information about historic buildings available to researchers, all of which should be explored in the course of studying a property's history.

ORAL SOURCES

Speaking to individuals either informally or interviewing them is a quick and enjoyable way of gathering information about a historic building. People often know facts that were never written about or otherwise recorded, and individuals associated with a site might even possess relevant letters, pictures, or other evidence and be willing to share it.

Building Owner(s), Former Owner(s)

As stated earlier, begin with the owner or former owners. Often they will have a lot of knowledge about the building, which can save a lot of research time, or at least they will be able to provide ideas that can point a researcher in the right direction. Most people are interested in any historic property they own, and as a researcher, you can agree to share the information you discover in the course of your study with the owner as a way of thanking her or him for taking the time to talk with you.

Occupants and Neighbors

Ask anyone who might be familiar with the building what they know about it. Often when talking to someone directly associated with the building, such as the current owner, the researcher can ask if she or he knows of anyone else who might also have knowledge of the site. Older people who live or work in the area and have for a long time may remember the building from decades past and provide valuable information that may not be available from any other source.

Architect or Architecture Firm

If a building was designed by a known architect or builder and the architect can be identified, it is possible, depending on the age of the building, that the architect might be alive and could be interviewed. At the very least, the architect's firm may still exist. If so, they may have information about the project and possibly even architectural plans. If there are any known contractors, they may also be able to provide information.

SECONDARY WRITTEN AND GRAPHIC SOURCES

Secondary written sources, such as articles, books, and other published documents, often allow a researcher to gain a broad understanding of a site and its context. Such sources also allow researchers to use and build on primary research others have already done, which saves time and work.

Websites

A good place to start is to type keywords pertaining to your building (addresses, names of previous owners, names of businesses once housed there, etc.) into an Internet search engine, which can often yield instant results and save a lot of time. Examples of many of the resource types (such as books, articles, and maps) have been published on Internet sites and are easily accessible. Therefore, before engaging in other methods of archival research such as visiting a library, it's always wise to try a simple search of the Internet first. If too many sites but none pertaining to a particular building come up, narrow the search by placing key phrases in quotation marks. If no relevant sites appear, use more general search words. Sometimes the Internet will yield little useful information. In this case, databases at local libraries and historical societies may provide information not available on the Internet as a whole.

National Register Nominations

If a building is over 50 years old and has some degree of historical significance, one of the first research steps should be to check to see if it has been listed on the National Register. This can be done by contacting the State Historic Preservation Office (SHPO) for the state where the building is located; in some states the listings are accessible from the SHPO website. National Register listings can also be accessed on the National Park Service website; however the NPS provides only summaries, and the full National Register file usually has to be found at the SHPO. If an individual National Register listing is found, then a good deal of research has already been done, especially if the nomination was written after the 1970s. Nominations normally contain information such as the historic name of the building, its owners, address and legal description, its date of construction, its style and period, information on the condition of the building at the time the nomination was written, a statement of historical significance, photographs, and, sometimes, architectural plans. Even if the building was not listed individually on the National Register, but is located within a National Register district, the district National Register nomination will provide valuable information about the building and its historical context.

Books and Articles

Books can include nonfiction written by local authors that might contain information about the building you are researching, its builders, its occupants, its historical context, or all four. Books such as genealogies, bibliographies, travel books, and local histories may yield information about specific buildings. Books on American architectural history can provide contextual and stylistic information about the building in question.

NATIONAL REGISTER OF HISTORIC PLACES PROPERTY: JACK KEROUAC HOUSE, ORLANDO, FLORIDA

Jack Kerouac house, Orlando, Florida. Source: © ALLAN HUGHES / Alamy.

The Jack Kerouac House, a one-story, vernacular craftsman-style bungalow, dating from the early 20th century, located in Orlando, Florida, was listed on the National Register in 2013 for national significance under Criterion B (association with historically-significant people) for its connection with author Jack Kerouac (1922–1969), who lived and wrote in the house in 1957 and 1958 (NPS "Kerouac" 2013). Kerouac rented the house because he could write there, and his mother could be near her family. While living in this house, Kerouac, an American author and a founder of the Beat Generation, became famous for the publication of his bestselling novel, *On the Road*. Kerouac made the final edits of this, his seminal novel, while living in the Orlando house. He also wrote another novel, *The Dharma Bums*, here and a play called *The Beat Generation*. A cultural phenomenon that emerged in the United States after World War II, the Beat Generation rejected materialism and experimented with drugs, free sexuality, and Eastern religions. "The Beats esteemed self-reliance and self-expression, and honored street hustlers and making a living by one's wits. The definers of the Beat Generation, and its greatest manifestation, were a small group of writers, and their published poetry and novels" (NPS "Nomination" 2013).

The best location to find books of local interest is at libraries in the area. However, Internet searches of databases of the collections of more distant libraries—such as the Library of Congress—or merchandising sites—such as Amazon.com—can also yield titles of interest. Many books have also been published on the Internet and are available there, sometimes free of charge.

Articles may be found in library collections or on the Internet, or in magazines, newsletters, and journals. As libraries and archives continually digitize and index more of their collections, relevant articles are becoming easier and easier to locate.

Theses and Dissertations

Academic theses can provide specific and credible information if their subjects involve the history of the area where a building is located, people associated with the site, the type or style of the building, or even its architect(s) or builder(s). Internet searches using key words associated with a given site can often yield lists of relevant titles of theses and dissertations and can sometimes locate an easily accessible digital copy of the entire work.

Vintage Newspapers

Although print newspapers are currently disappearing across the country, many still exist, including a lot of weekly small town tabloids that focus on local news. Because of the increasing dominance of the Internet as a source of news, many newspapers have been replaced by websites. However, in the past, thousands of local newspapers were in operation, and some of them have been archived. This can be of benefit to someone researching a site in a location that has or had such a newspaper as it increases the chance the building has been mentioned, either recently or during its period of historical significance. Unless the building is particularly historic, it probably will not have been the subject of an article, unless some significant event, tragic or not, took place there. Local papers often documented events that occurred in or near a historic building, such as fires, grand openings, and weddings. Often vintage newspapers yield more information about historic sites than contemporary newspapers do, and they are generally considered primary sources. Historically, local newspapers reported on a lot of happenings, such as social events, that would probably be considered insignificant today. Computerized indexes searchable by key words may be available for a given newspaper in a local historical society or library, making the data much more accessible. Many old newspapers were recorded on reels of microfilm, which requires a lot of painstaking, often nauseating searching reel by reel, unless the microfilm files have been indexed for key words. Fortunately, digital files, such as PDF documents, are gradually replacing microfilm.

Commercial Histories

Commercial histories have been written about local areas for well over a century. They are especially common for communities in New England and the Midwest but can be found all over the country. Sometimes they told the history of a community and sometimes a county. They were written by authors whose main motivation was profit, and they sometimes bent the facts to suit the wishes, delusions, or pretensions of their paying clients, who were usually members of the local elite seeking to aggrandize their particular roles and those of their families in local history. Therefore, the information contained in such volumes should always be crosschecked using other sources. Despite this, commercial histories do often contain important genealogical information—detailed accounts of the development of local businesses and institutions—some of which may have been housed in or near the building of interest. Commercial histories can also contain useful photographs of historic sites and related streetscapes. These books were often published in small numbers and may only be available at local historical societies, libraries, or in private collections.

DOCUMENTARY SOURCES: PRIMARY

Primary documents, such as historic photographs, letters, and governmental records often provide the hard evidence needed to understand a site and to restore it to its historic condition. Primary documents can sometimes be found on the Internet or featured as examples in books, but they are more often discovered moldering on shelves or in filing cabinets in archives and attics or in dusty corners.

Historic Photographs

Among the most valuable and useful historic resources for researching and documenting historic buildings, historic photographs are particularly important because they can be used as the basis to clearly understand the design of historic features and rooms. Photographic evidence can be used to accurately repair or replicate lost historic architectural features during rehabilitations and restorations. Photographs can also clearly document changes to a building over time, both to its interior and exterior. Most old photos show the exterior of buildings and were often not taken to memorialize or document the building itself but to record an event or depict people (Figure 4.21).

Historic photographs can be found in books, such as local and commercial histories, in files or drawers in archives or libraries, in the possession of people whose families or businesses were associated with the historic site, and even sometimes hidden within the buildings themselves in places such as attics and under floorboards. National Register nomination files often contain historic photographs that other researchers have found.

Figure 4.21. Historic photographs can tell a lot about the history of a building. This 1970s picture reveals that this late-19th-century house was moved from its original location. Source: Photograph by Peter B. Dedek, 2013.

Identifying the age of old photographs isn't always easy, but there are clues that can help. One indicator is the type of photograph it is. Early, solid type photographs called daguerreotypes, ambrotypes, and tintypes, were made from around 1839 to the 1890s. **Daguerreotypes,** the first type of commercially made photograph, were etched on a copper sheet plated with silver. Daguerreotypes are rare, as only one copy was made of each image, and they can be identified by their copper backing and silvery sheen. They were made until about 1870.

The **ambrotype** was printed on a sheet of glass and is easily identified because of the glass and the fact they have a black paper backing. Patented in 1854, ambrotypes were produced until the 1880s or so. A more common historic photograph was the **tintype**, which was used up until about 1900. These are similar to ambrotypes but have a sheet metal backing.

Early paper-backed photographs were produced from the late 1800s, and examples are black and white and printed on thick cardstock. Some buildings were portrayed on **stereographs** as well, which featured two identical photographs mounted over a cardboard backing to create the illusion of a three dimensional scene when seen through a viewer designed for the purpose. These date from around 1851 to the 1930s.

Although color photographs were invented in the 1800s, they did not come into wide use until the middle of the 20th century. The majority of historic photographs of buildings a researcher is likely to encounter are black-and-white photographs printed on photograph paper that date from around 1890 to 1950.

Another way to discern the approximate date of historic photographs is to examine any fashions people in the photograph are wearing or technology visible in the picture, such as different models of automobiles. For example, a black-and-white photograph printed on paper with boxy black cars and electric lights suggests the 1920s, while a picture on sheet metal with a view of formally dressed people in a buggy suggests the mid- to late-1800s. Further study, such as researching specific car models through the years or individual fashion trends can narrow the age of the photograph to within a decade or so. An even more accurate date can sometimes be found if the photograph depicts a specific historic event that can be identified and documented. For particularly old and revered buildings, historic paintings or copies thereof are sometimes available. They can be used and evaluated in a manner similar to old photographs.

Old Business Literature and Advertisements

Historic advertisements that may pertain to a historic building can sometimes be found in old newspapers and local magazines, in brochures, or on posters. While few such items have survived, they may sometimes be found in archives, local libraries, or in the possession of individuals. They can yield valuable information, such as vintage pictures of a building or of its context, or provide information about a business located in or near the building.

City Directories

City directories are books, similar to phone books, that were published lists of the addresses of residents and businesses in communities ranging from small towns to large cities. The directories were first published in the late 1700s and were used widely across the nation throughout the 1800s and 1900s. Held in many local libraries and historical archives, these collections of books can provide valuable information about who lived at a particular address, how long that address has existed, and what types of businesses may have been located within a given building.

City Lithographs

In the late 1800s and early 1900s, a number of companies made, printed, and sold bird's-eye-view maps of entire towns and cities that depicted streets, natural features such as rivers and hills, and even included small, three-dimensional images of individual buildings. A close look at one of these images can often reveal the approximate design of a particular building at the time the map was made. While these maps can be helpful, they were often somewhat cursory and even speculative, making the images found on them more suggestive than factual. They can, however, be used to back up and substantiate information from other sources. They also indicate the urban and geographical context surrounding a building at a specific period in history.

Local Maps

Archives and libraries often have collections of historic maps of particular localities. Historic maps could be very detailed, often indicating the locations of buildings, sometimes even showing the basic footprints of structures present at the time they were created. And, like city lithographs, they can also show natural and man-made aspects of a landscape, such as diverted creeks or removed railroad tracks, that might have been significantly altered or may have disappeared since the map was made.

Sanborn Insurance Maps

First made in 1867, Sanborn maps were created by the Sanborn Insurance Company, headquartered in Boston, to document the buildings in cities and towns where the company issued fire insurance policies. The maps showed the basic footprints of buildings and any additions, and often depicted a building's basic materials (using color-coded hues for different types of materials or through handwritten notes). Some early Sanborn maps even included detailed elevations of buildings, done in watercolor. The maps are a valuable resource because they are often the only specific historical information available on a particular building showing its overall design at a given time as well as its location.

The Sanborn map records, located at an archive or in a library or found on a website, will usually be a series of maps of the same area created at different dates. If Sanborn maps depicting the site of interest exist from a number of different decades, this can reveal valuable information about how the site evolved over time, as changes in footprints, materials, and additions can be chronicled.

Unpublished Documents

Census records The United States has performed a nationwide census of its citizens every ten years since 1790. Census records are usually used by genealogists studying family histories. However, if the location of a particular individual or family is relevant to better understanding the history of a building, these records can be valuable to historical designers and preservationists. In the decades after 1850, the census not only included the names and location of the head of household and the number of family members and others in the household as it had before this time; it also included the names and ages of all members of the household, the value of the family's home or farm if they owned one, and sometimes the occupation and income of the head of household as well. Census information can shed light on the character and economic status of a building's occupants and also provide the approximate value of a given property at a specific time. In recent years, many of the census records from various decades have been digitized and indexed. Some databases require a fee for access, however, the entire 1880 Census, the 1940 Census, and parts of the census from other years are available from the Church of Latter-Day Saints at familysearch.org, free of charge.

Chain of title   A chain of title is a list designed to track real property ownership consisting of real estate deeds in a succession of owners of a specific property over time. These documents are usually found in city hall or county courthouse records, but they can also be found and searched on the Internet in some jurisdictions. They are very important, because unless the names of a property's historic owners are known, other records such as wills, letters, census data, newspaper articles, and biographies will usually not be found. Deeds also sometimes mention occupations of buyers and sellers.

In order to research a chain of title, one needs the address of the property of interest in order to access the appropriate county's real estate website, or visit the courthouse itself if the records for that county have not been digitized, to find the latest recorded deed book and page number, which will indicate the current owner. Then the researcher needs to enter the deed book and page number into a computer or look it up manually. Each deed page has the deed book and page number of the former deed listing on it, providing access to the next deed back in the chain of title. The successive deed should include the deed book and page number of the previous deed, leading the researcher back in time. As this process is repeated, earlier and earlier deeds are found all the way back to the first deed recorded.

Historic deeds may indicate changes in property lines as land was subdivided and also reveal jumps in tax assessments, which can indicate instances where buildings were constructed or added to significantly. The deeds show who owned a building when, which allows for searches on the owners, often revealing more information about a given site.

Tax and land records   The usefulness of these records varies from place to place. Some records are very specific about the properties a particular person owned, while in other places and times they only indicate the total tax liability of an individual taxpayer. Tax and land records can be used to support, or in some cases refute, evidence found in other sources.

Records of lawsuits   Legal records can be useful if a given property was ever the subject of a lawsuit. Many lawsuit records are now computer indexed by municipal and county offices and archives (Kyvig and Marty 2000).

HABS/HAER records   As described in Chapter 1, Congress created the Historic American Building Survey (HABS) in 1933 to employ out-of-work architects, photographers, and historians during the Great Depression. Since then, over 35,000 historic sites have been documented with photographs and measured drawings under the HABS program and the HAER (Historic American Engineering Survey) program started in 1969. Today, the records are available online from the Library of Congress as a searchable database.* These records offer a great deal of information and can be a valuable resource if a building of interest was ever recorded. HABS records include descriptions, photographs from different eras, and sometimes even architectural plans and building elevations.

CONCLUSION

As we have seen, researching a historic property and determining what constitutes a historic building can be quite complicated. However the system established for the National Register by the National Park Service has proved to be quite effective and workable over the decades since it was established. Within every state historic preservation office and in many other governmental agencies and private consulting firms and in communities nationwide, citizens, preservationists, and design professionals use the National Register standards to determine whether properties are to be treated as historic. A working knowledge of the guidelines outlined in this chapter enables anyone working with existing buildings to be able to identify which ones may be historic and to begin to understand what activities might possibly harm them.

*The database can be found at http://memory.loc.gov/ammem/collections/habs_haer/.

ELIGIBLE FOR THE NATIONAL REGISTER OR NOT?

Use the following key to indicate whether each property shown is likely to be eligible for inclusion in the National Register. If so, which of the criteria may apply? If not, why not?

(criteria considerations? lack of integrity?)

1) Eligible	2) Not eligible	3) Criterion A	4) Criterion B
5) Criterion C	6) Criterion D	7) Criteria Consideration: write it in.	

A. _____   E. _____   H. _____   K. _____

B. _____   F. _____   I. _____   L. _____

C. _____   G. _____   J. _____   M. _____

D. _____

Answers and explanations found in Instructor's Guide.

SOURCES

Andrus, Patrick W. 1990. "National Register Bulletin: How to Apply the National Register Criteria for Evaluation." 15. Washington, DC: National Park Service, National Register Branch, Interagency Resources Division. Revised 1991.

Blumenson, John J.-G. 1977. *Identifying American Architecture: A Pictorial Guide to Styles and Terms 1600–1945,* 2nd edition. New York: W.W. Norton & Company.

California Office of Historic Preservation. 2003. "Historic Structure Report Format." Accessed October 11, 2012. http://ohp.parks.ca.gov/pages/1069/files/historic%20structure%20report%20format.pdf.

Kyvig, David E., and Myron A. Marty. 2000. *Nearby History: Exploring the Past Around You,* 2nd edition. Nashville, TN: The American Association for State and Local History.

McClelland, Linda F. 1977. "National Register Bulletin: How to Complete the National Register Registration Form." Number 16A. Washington, DC: National Park Service, National Register Branch, Interagency Resources Division. Revised 1986 and 1991.

National Park Service (NPS). 2010. "What is the National Historic Landmarks Assistance Initiative?" Accessed August 28, 2010. http://www.landmarkwatch.org/resourcePages/landmarkProgram.html.

———. 2011. "National Register of Historic Places Program: About Us." Accessed March 12, 2012. http://www.nps.gov/nr/about.htm.

———. YEAR? "National Register of Historic Places Program: Research." Accessed June 19, 2010. http://www.nps.gov/nr/research/index.htm.

———. 2013. "National Historic Landmarks Program: Apollo Mission Control Center," Accessed November 29, 2013. http://tps.cr.nps.gov/nhl/detail.cfm?ResourceId=1932&ResourceType=Building

———. 2013. "National Register of Historic Places Program: Jack Kerouac House." Accessed September 17, 2013. http://www.cr.nps.gov/nr/feature/weekly_features/13_02_15_Kerouac.htm.

———. 2013. "National Register of Historic Places Nomination: Jack Kerouac House." Accessed September 17, 2013. http://www.cr.nps.gov/nr/feature/weekly_features/2013/FL_12001254.pdf.

State Historic Preservation Office of South Carolina. 2007. "African American Places in South Carolina." *Department of Archives & History.* March.

HISTORIC PRESERVATION LAW

5

OBJECTIVES

- Outline the major legal issues that have been raised when American preservation laws and regulations are challenged.

- Discuss the interpretation and enforcement of preservation law.

- Outline ways that designers can encourage good preservation practices to avoid having themselves or their clients enter into conflicts with historic preservation commissions and other agencies and avoid court cases.

- Cite examples of various significant court cases involving historic preservation to illustrate relevant legal issues.

When push comes to shove, law is the ultimate foundation of historic preservation. While it would be ideal if everyone preserved America's heritage happily and willingly, inevitably some people will see preserving historic properties as counter to their economic interests and will seek to skirt, ignore, or defy preservation laws and standards. Unfortunately, it sometimes becomes necessary to go to court to compel individuals to preserve legally protected properties. It is important for architects and designers to realize that beyond being an ethic, ideal, or a luxury, historic preservation can be a matter of complying with the law. When historic resources are involved, the destruction or insensitive treatment of a building can expose landowners and professionals to lawsuits and civil penalties.

At some point in their careers, many designers and architects will work on projects involving historic buildings. With increasing numbers of buildings becoming designated as historic and with hundreds of historic buildings being renovated each year using federal and state tax incentives, an understanding of historic preservation rules and laws helps design professionals serve their clients better. The best practice is to identify and address potential preservation issues before they become legal issues.

As described in previous chapters, preservation laws exist at the federal, state, and local levels. Some of these laws, such as the federal law that created the National Trust for Historic Preservation in 1949, simply encourage preservation without requiring it; others, such as the Historic Sites Act of 1935, direct governmental officials to perform certain tasks that encourage preservation; still others, such as Section 4(f) of the Department of Transportation Act, require government agencies and anyone funded or licensed by them to make preserving historic sites a priority; and finally other preservation laws, such as the state-enabling legislation that gives local historical architectural review commissions police power, require private landowners of historic properties to obey preservation guidelines or face the consequences. As one might expect, this final category has created the greatest number of lawsuits, although federal regulations, such as Section 4(f) and Section 106 have been the subject of legal action as well.

Before describing the major issues that surface in preservation cases, it is helpful to outline some relevant legal terms.

PRESERVATION LAW TERMS

DEFENDANT

The **defendant** is the party (person, corporation, or governmental entity) whose actions (or lack of action) have caused someone else to sue them. The defendant is the party that is being sued. For example, a landowner may sue a municipality in order to demolish a historic building in violation of the historic preservation standards of a local historic district, making the municipality the defendant in the case.

PLAINTIFF

The **plaintiff** is the party that starts the lawsuit. A plaintiff must claim that he, she, or the entity involved was somehow injured or otherwise negatively affected by the defendant's actions or lack thereof. For example, the landowner mentioned in the previous example, the plaintiff, may claim that the municipality, the defendant, is causing economic harm by not allowing the demolition to go forward.

REMEDY

The **remedy** is the action or payment the plaintiff is seeking. In order to sue, a plaintiff needs to have a certain goal in mind. What will the defendant be required to do if he or she loses the case? To even file a lawsuit, the plaintiff has to clearly state some desired outcome wanted from the defendant to make a court case relevant, although once the suit commences, a court can add additional remedies or delete remedies that the plaintiff originally had in mind. A municipality forcing a landowner to rehabilitate a house that is located in a historic district rather than allowing the landowner to demolish it is an example of a remedy in a preservation case. In general law, cash settlements are the most common remedy.

TAKINGS

A **taking** occurs when a governmental entity confiscates someone's property without compensation. This is the central issue of the property rights movement and is a critical element in many historic preservation cases as well. The concept is based on the clause in the Fifth Amendment of the U.S. Constitution that prohibits the government from seizing a person's property without paying "just compensation." Property rights advocates argue that any time a government regulation, such as the rules enforced by a historic district, limits the owner's use of that property in a manner that costs him or her money, it constitutes a "**regulatory taking[1]**" because the government does not provide money to the landowner to make up the supposed loss. Many historic preservation cases involve this issue, and as we will see, over the past century or so American courts have created a series of legal precedents that establish what actually constitutes a regulatory taking in the United States.

POLICE POWER

Police power is the right of government to compel citizens to act or to force them not to act in certain ways. Local historic district architectural controls constitute a type of police power because they use the law and the courts to require citizens to preserve their properties. The justification usually given for using police power to promote preservation is that while preserving historic properties may curtail the economic opportunities of certain individuals, historic preservation serves the general good by maintaining properties and districts that create a better quality of life and economic development (as in the case of heritage tourism) for the community as a whole.

STANDING

Standing is the right to sue in court. In order to file a lawsuit a plaintiff must prove standing. Legal standing requires that a plaintiff can allege that an injury to a personal interest that is within the zone of interests protected by local, state, or federal statute (law) has occurred and that somehow the defendant is responsible. For example, if a homeowner tries to tear down his house located in a local historic district, the city may sue him to prevent the demolition, claiming that its interests (the social and economic benefits provided to the community by having an intact historic district located within its boundaries) are being threatened by the demolition. The city can cite the local preservation ordinance as the law that protects its interests and that the homeowner is violating. Standing requires that the party suing has some real interest in the issue, for example, people cannot challenge the constitutionality of a law if they can't demonstrate that they are being or may be personally impacted or harmed by that law. Standards as to who has and who does not have standing in legal cases vary by state. If a court determines that a potential plaintiff lacks standing, it will dismiss the case.

JURISDICTION

Jurisdiction is the area (geographical or governmental) where a legal body (such as a court) or a political entity (such as a city council) possesses the authority to deal with legal matters. To have jurisdiction a court must have authority over the parties involved as well as the subject matter. In historic preservation, jurisdiction usually exists because a given case involves a given property or properties located within a certain political territory, be that a city, state or the United States or the case involves certain agencies, such as the Department of Transportation or the National Park Service. A court must have jurisdiction, that is, it must have authority over the defendants and the plaintiffs, to hear a case. For example, in a case concerning Section 106, a federal court would have jurisdiction because Section 106 cases always involve federal agencies or bodies acting with federal monies or authority (in the form of federal licenses).

LACHES

This is a legal term which refers to the timeliness of a case. In some cases, plaintiffs are barred from maintaining a lawsuit if they have unreasonably delayed bringing action and this delay may cause prejudice to defendants if the suit were allowed to go forward. In environmental cases such as historic preservation, defendants have a very difficult time trying to prove laches. An example would be if acting as the plaintiff, a city waited ten years to sue a landowner for demolition by neglect, the owner may claim laches because the allegation of demolition by neglect may be harder to defend against now than if the city had sued after only five years. Such a strategy may or may not work.

RIPENESS

Before a court case is ripe, a plaintiff must try using all administrative remedies (other possible legal means) before resorting to a lawsuit. If he or she has not, the case might be deemed not "ripe" for consideration in a court, and the plaintiff may be required to go through alternate administrative procedures instead of suing. For example, a landowner who is seeking to demolish a property located within a local historic district can't sue in court if he or she has not already applied to the district's architectural review board and been refused permission to demolish the building and then exhausted any other available administrative procedures or appeals (Law.com 2013). Ripeness is a common issue in historic preservation cases.

MOOTNESS

When a lawsuit is deemed frivolous or otherwise unnecessary (such as when the conflict at hand has already been resolved) during preliminary examinations, it is considered moot. This would be true in a Section 106 case in which federal involvement had ceased before the case made its way to court (Bell 1985, 21).

BUNDLE OF RIGHTS

The **bundle of rights** is the many-faceted set of rights that a landowner may possess. These include the right to develop, to extract minerals, to demolish buildings, to build tall buildings (sometimes called "air rights"), and to occupy a property. In some cases, a landowner does not possess all of these rights. He or she might give away or sell certain rights, or some of the rights within the bundle may be removed by law, such as by a zoning ordinance that prohibits certain kinds of development. In some cases, when a landowner buys a property some of the rights don't convey with it. This is very common in the case of mineral rights under tracts of land, which are often held by mining or oil companies. Preservation easements written into a deed take away the right to demolish or significantly alter a historic property, thus reducing the bundle of rights that a landowner possesses.

DEMOLITION BY NEGLECT

When a property owner deliberately allows a historic property to become severely deteriorated by not maintaining or repairing it, possibly allowing a building to decay to the extent that rehabilitation is no longer feasible, it is called demolition by neglect (see Chapter 6). Property owners may use demolition by neglect to circumvent historic preservation laws and ordinances (National Trust for Historic Preservation 1999).

FEDERAL CONSTITUTIONAL PRESERVATION ISSUES: PRIVATE PROPERTY RIGHTS

In the course of the history of preservation cases in the United States, a number of Constitutional issues have been raised when plaintiffs and defendants have alleged that preservation laws and their enforcement has violated their constitutional rights.

REGULATORY TAKINGS

The most common of these is the "takings" issue. The Fifth Amendment requires that the government not deprive citizens "of life, liberty, or property, without due process of law; nor shall private property be taken for public use, without just compensation," and the 14th Amendment extends this requirement to state governments. The wording was originally intended to prevent governments from seizing property outright and using it for public purposes (such as building a road across someone's farm) without paying the owner the approximate value of the land or other property so used. In 1922, however, the concept of a "regulatory taking" was created in the United States

Supreme Court case, *Pennsylvania Coal v. Mahon*. In that case, the Supreme Court held that if a government regulation goes "too far," it will be considered a regulatory taking, requiring the payment of just compensation to the affected landowner. The court did not specify exactly what "too far" meant. Mahon owned and resided on a property in Pennsylvania that was located above a coal mine. An aggressive form of mining that included the removal of all the coal including supporting "pillars" beneath Mahon's land was causing his property to subside, and he sued to stop the mining. The Pennsylvania Coal Company claimed that since Mahon only owned the surface rights to his land, he had no right to sue, despite a Pennsylvania law forbidding subsidence unless the land was owned outright by the mining company. In a decision that seems unthinkable today, the high court ruled that because Mahon had only the surface rights, the mining company could continue mining under his land using any method it wanted. In this case, the court introduced the concept of regulatory takings when the justices in the majority wrote "if regulation goes too far it will be recognized as a taking" (*Pennsylvania Coal Co. v. Mahon* 1922).

The takings issue came up again in 1987 in a case involving property rights, but not historic preservation directly, in the Supreme Court case *First English Lutheran Church v. County of Los Angeles.* Los Angeles County had denied the church the right to build on a property it owned due to brush fire regulations. The church sued, and the case eventually made its way to the Supreme Court.

The high court ruled that the county actually did owe the church "just compensation" due to a regulatory taking, because in denying of any kind of development at all on the property owned by the church, the county made the property all but worthless. The court ruled that the county's regulation went too far because it did not permit a "reasonable use." This case helped to define what "too far," the term the Supreme Court had used back in 1922, actually meant. The case acted as a warning to governmental regulators, including the writers of historic district ordinances, that if they wrote their laws so that they did not allow property owners any return on their land or buildings, their laws may be deemed unconstitutional.

In 1992 another property rights case involving takings, *Lucas v. South Carolina Coastal Council,* made it to the Supreme Court. In 1986, Lucas purchased some residential lots on a South Carolina barrier island, intending to build single family houses similar to others located nearby. When he bought them, Lucas's lots were not subject to the state's coastal zone building permit requirements. However, in 1988 the state legislature enacted the Beachfront Management Act, which prohibited Lucas from building any permanent habitable structures on his land. The South Carolina Coastal Council denied Lucas a permit to build houses on his beachfront property because they claimed the area was vulnerable to storms and located on environmentally sensitive coastal dunes. He filed suit, contending that the complete ban on all construction deprived him of any "economically viable use" of his property and therefore was a "taking" without just compensation under the Fifth Amendment (Kayden 2011).

The court ruled that since the South Carolina Coastal Council deprived the landowner any economic use of his land, the denial of the permits did constitute a regulatory taking. In the end, the state of South Carolina was forced to buy the lots from Lucas at fair market value (*Lucas v. South Carolina Coastal Council* 1992). This case was yet another confirmation that if a regulation makes a property essentially worthless and does not allow a "reasonable return" on private property, it is probably unconstitutional.

In the 1994 case *Dolan v. City of Tigard,* the U.S. Supreme Court added to this by ruling that local governments must make an "individualized determination" that its land use regulations are "related both in nature and extent to the impact" of the regulation, and there must be a "rough proportionality" between any burden placed on private property owners and the "benefit" the regulation provides to the public (Phelan 1994). This means that a municipal government may have to justify a preservation law by demonstrating that its public benefits outweigh the potential economic harm it may cause to landowners.

Fifth Amendment issues could pertain to a preservation case where an owner of a historic building, such as an old railroad hotel located in a historic district in a depressed area, can find no businesses or other renters. In such a case, the building's owner might successfully argue using the takings clause that she can find no reasonable return from her land so long as the building is left standing and therefore must be allowed to tear it down.

ZONING

Historic preservation law is a branch or perhaps a subset of environmental law, because they share many of the same legal issues and basis in law. However, preservation law is also closely associated with zoning. In 1926, the Supreme Court heard another case where a concept similar to regulatory takings was alleged. In this case, the plaintiff, a real estate company, argued that a regulation deprived it of the value of its property without due process, in violation of the 14th Amendment.

This case involved zoning, which was a new concept at the time. New York City had created the first zoning ordinance in 1916. Zoning is a type of land use regulation that allows local governments to control the development of land within their jurisdictions by regulating how individual properties located within different "zones" may be used. Writers of zoning laws map out areas within a jurisdiction in which residential, industrial, recreational, or commercial activities may or may not take place. For example, a certain type of residential zone might allow only single-family detached houses and not duplexes or apartment complexes. Generally, zoning focuses on property uses that cannot be permitted in a particular area. For example, a factory cannot be located in an area zoned R-1 for single-family residences, but normally a single-family residence can be located in an area designated for industrial uses. The assumption is that landowners usually wouldn't desire to locate near industrial or commercial areas anyway.

In the 1926 case of *Village of Euclid v. Ambler Realty Co.*, the Ambler Company sued the Village of Euclid, Ohio, to try to force it to repeal its zoning ordinance and comprehensive zoning plan of 1922. Ambler owned land in the village that it sought to develop and claimed that the zoning ordinance prevented development of its land for industrial purposes and thereby reduced its value from "$10,000 an acre to $2,500 an acre," which, in its view, meant that the zoning regulation had deprived the company of its property by taking three-fourths of the value of its land. (*Village of Euclid v. Ambler Realty Co.* 1926).

The court upheld the village's zoning law (by a narrow margin), because the village had a rational and comprehensive plan that applied to everyone, and its laws did not prohibit a "reasonable use" of the land, that is, one which provides a fair profit. Comparing zoning ordinances with the then well-established nuisance laws, the court stated that due to the increasing complexities of urban life, restrictions on use of private land were acceptable. This meant that a landowner was not always entitled to the highest and best use of his or her land. This case turned out to be very important to historic preservation, because the case established zoning as a legitimate use of police power, and in the United States, historic districts are essentially a type of zoning.

LEGALITY OF LOCAL HISTORIC REGULATIONS TESTED

The possibility that a local preservation ordinance might create a regulatory taking was tested directly in *Maher v. the City of New Orleans* in federal court in 1975, when a property owner who desired to tear down a bungalow located in the Vieux Carré (French Quarter) historic district in order to build an apartment house on the lot appealed to federal district court. Maher asserted that by not allowing him to redevelop his land, the City of New Orleans had taken the value of his property in violation of his Fifth Amendment rights (one can only wonder if the amount of money he stood to make by developing a single lot could possibly match what he probably spent in legal fees through a number of appeals). The court ruled that the plaintiff had not demonstrated that the ordinance had "so diminished the property value as to leave Maher, in effect, nothing . . . that commercial rental [of the existing property] could not provide a reasonable rate of return . . ." (*Maher v. the City of New Orleans* 1975). The reasoning of the Fifth Circuit court in *Maher* proved to be very important to the most significant preservation case testing the constitutionality of preservation regulations, *Penn Central Trans. Co. v. City of New York* of 1978.

The takings issue resurfaced in the *Penn Central* case. In this case, which reached the United States Supreme Court, the Penn Central Railroad planned to build a 55-story tower above the historic Grand Central Terminal in New York City (see Chapter 1, Figure 1.12). The historic building had been designated a local Historic Landmark by the New York City Landmarks Commission (HDLC). Penn Central had opposed the designation. The railroad applied for a certificate of appropriateness for the construction project, and the HDLC denied the permit on the grounds that the tower would adversely effect the historic and aesthetic nature of the Beaux-Arts style terminal. Penn Central went to court arguing that denial of a building permit constituted a taking "without just compensation," or a regulatory taking of its development rights.

The high court ruled in a 6–3 vote that the City of New York had a right to deny the permit, and the city's preservation ordinance did not constitute a taking. The case is important because it established that municipal authorities can protect properties based on aesthetic concerns, that aesthetics and history are considered to be public goods worthy of being protected under the law. Also, as in the earlier *Maher* case, the court limited the takings argument to a "reasonable use," meaning that if a landowner continues to have an economic return on its property, a regulation that may prevent an even better return does not constitute a taking. Penn Central was allowed to sell its development rights to a nearby landowner, which had been limited by building height restrictions. Also, importantly, the City of New York won, in part, because it had a comprehensive landmarks plan, which was well written and applied to all owners of historic buildings equally. In the *Penn Central* case, the Supreme Court affirmed that in some cases at least, police power can be used to protect the aesthetic qualities of a city. The majority position stated, ". . . this Court has recognized, in a number of settings, that States and cities may enact land-use restrictions or controls to enhance the quality of life by preserving the character and desirable aesthetic features of a city . . ." (*Penn Central Transportation Company v. New York City* 1978).

RELIGIOUS PROPERTIES AND PRESERVATION

Under the First Amendment of the United States Constitution, religious organizations are given the right of free exercise of religion: governments must remain neutral toward religion, and laws cannot promote or inhibit religious activities. In recent decades, some religious groups have taken this to mean that they and the historic properties that they own should not be subject to the same historical regulations that apply to secular properties. The basic argument is that government regulation of the treatment of historic religious buildings is tantamount to government regulation of the religious activities associated with the building.

A significant case relating to the issue of the regulation of historic religious buildings is the 1990 case *St. Bartholomew's Church v. City of New York*.

Only months after the St. Bartholomew decision, the United States Supreme Court weighed in on the issue in *Employment Division of Oregon v. Smith*, when the Court characterized

PRESERVATION AND RELIGIOUS FREEDOM
ST. BARTHOLOMEW'S CHURCH V. CITY OF NEW YORK

Bartholomew's Church, a large historic urban church designed by Bertram Goodhue in 1919, is an exceptional example of the Byzantine revival style. In 1967, the City of New York designated the site as a local historic landmark, which the church leaders had opposed. In the 1980s, the church's leadership proposed demolishing the church's community house, built in 1928 (Figure 5.1A) and located adjacent to the church building itself, and replacing it with a 59-story glass-clad skyscraper in order to create income for the church, which they claimed had lost congregation members and needed additional income to "carry on and expand the ministerial and charitable activities that are central to its religious mission" (Ross 2005, 42). The Landmarks Commission refused to allow the demolition, based on the church's landmark status. The city argued that the tower would impede the historic integrity and destroy the historic context of the property, with one commissioner saying the project was "nothing so much as a noble work of man about to be crushed beneath a gargantuan ice cube tray" (Tyler 2000, 89). The St. Bartholomew's proposal must have reminded members of the Landmark Commission of Penn Central's scheme for Grand Central Terminal from less than a decade earlier.

St. Bartholomew's Church. The community house is to the left. Source: Photograph by Peter B. Dedek, 2011.

After an extended battle with the city in which the church lowered its proposed tower to forty-seven stories in an attempt at mitigation and applied for a "hardship exception," the city still refused, and the church sued in 1986, claiming that preventing the proposed demolition would constitute governmental interference with its right to practice of religion freely as guaranteed by the First Amendment and the takings clause of the Fifth Amendment. The U.S. District Court for the Southern District of New York disagreed and upheld the Landmark Commission's refusal to allow the project to go forward, stating that the landmark designation "creates no more than an incidental burden on the practice of religion" (Miller 2008).

preservation ordinances as "'neutral laws of general application' because they are not specifically intended to interfere with religious practice. They apply to all historic sites that meet their criteria, regardless of whether the site has a religious connection" (Miller 2008). Reacting to the Smith case, Congress passed the Religious Freedom Restoration Act (RFRA) in 1993, which required governments to accommodate religious conduct unless they could prove that, "it had a 'compelling interest' to justify a law or regulation and the law was the 'least restrictive means' to achieving its compelling interest" (Miller 2008).

The constitutionality of the RFRA was soon tested in *Flores v. City of Boerne,* a case in which a Catholic church applied for a building permit to enlarge its church building, a mission-style church deemed a contributing resource in Boerne, Texas's local historic district. The City of Boerne denied the permit because the alteration would adversely impact the historic integrity of the building. The church filed a lawsuit in U.S. District Court in Texas believing that the City's denial of the building permit violated RFRA. When the case reached the Supreme Court, the high court declared RFRA unconstitutional as a violation of the constitutional doctrine of "separation of powers." Since that time, Congress passed the Religious Land Use and Institutionalized Persons Act of 2000, which targets the impact of land use regulations on religious organizations (Religious Freedom Library 2013).

The *St. Bartholomew* and *Boerne* decisions have certainly not settled the issue of whether preservation laws violate religious freedom. Since the *Boerne* decision, at least 13 states have passed state laws similar to the RFRA, which may be upheld in the courts, because states are allowed to pass laws that grant a higher level of protection to individual rights than those provided under the United States Constitution (Reap and Hill 2007). Besides the passage of laws attempting to exempt religious groups from land use regulations, some courts have ruled against preservation on this issue. For example, as we saw in Chapter 3, the Supreme Judicial Court of Massachusetts ruled in 1990 that the Boston Landmark Commission's designation and legal protection of the interior of the Church of the Immaculate Conception violated the constitution of Massachusetts. The court stated that the regulation of the church's interior was inappropriate: "The government intrusion here is substantially more invasive, reaching into the church's actual worship space" (Ross 2005, 38). The Massachusetts court did have the opinion that regulating the outside of the church was acceptable, but it allowed the church to convert its main worship space, a highly significant interior, into offices.

This issue of whether or not preservation regulations restrict religious freedoms is bound to continue be a point of contention. Those seeking to alter or rehabilitate historic religious buildings will be impacted by future court rulings on this volatile issue.

MAKING A FEDERAL CASE:
TESTING PRESERVATION LAWS

In addition to court cases challenging local preservation ordinances, many cases have been filed concerning compliance with federal historic preservation laws. While most federal laws on preservation do not require or mandate that private landowners or even governmental entities preserve historic sites, laws such as Section 106 require that under certain conditions, a bureaucratic process—in this case Section 106 review—must take place before historic properties are impacted by federal undertakings.

ENFORCEMENT OF SECTION 106

Federal preservation laws tend to emphasize that the Section 106 process is completed as required over what the end results are. Therefore, the goal of the plaintiffs in most cases concerning Section 106 is to attempt to postpone a project until the Section 106 process has been properly completed in order to allow more time for negotiations. Since in order for a Section 106 review to be triggered, a federal undertaking must exist in which either federal money or a federal permit is involved, many cases involve determining if a given project or portion of a project was actually a federal undertaking in the first place. For example, in *Thompson v. Fugate* (1972), the Department of Transportation proposed building a small segment of an interstate beltway system around Richmond, Virginia, through the edge of Tuckahoe Plantation, a National Historic Landmark listed on the National Register of Historic Places. Although the majority of the beltway had been funded by federal money, this particular segment was not (this was evidently an attempt to circumvent having to perform federal reviews on the segment that passed through the National Landmark property).

The United States Court of Appeals for the Fourth Circuit held that the beltway, including the segment, should be taken as a whole as a federally assisted undertaking, and the short segment passing through plaintiffs' land could not be broken off from the whole, therefore, the whole project fell under the requirements of Section 106 and Section 4(f). The court also rejected the argument that construction had progressed too far to enforce these statutes and that the statutes applied to all unfinished segments of the project. The court halted the highway project until the defendants fully complied with Section 106 and Section 4(f) (Bell 1985).

In another case that dealt with the issue of what constitutes a federal undertaking under Section 106, *Fill the Pool Committee v. Village of Johnson City*, a group of preservationists sued in 1983 to stop the village of Johnson City, New York, from demolishing the C. Fred Johnson swimming pool, a large and unusual concrete above-ground public swimming facility built in the early 20th century. The pool and its surrounding park, originally constructed and operated by the Endicott Johnson Corporation (a local producer of footwear), were bought by the village of Johnson City in 1968, partly using National Park Service (NPS) money under its Land and Water Conservation Fund. The grant contract required the village to obtain NPS consent before making any changes in the use or ownership of the pool or park. The pool became run-down and had begun to leak, and the city closed it in 1972. When the village decided to demolish the pool, plaintiffs requested that NPS determine whether the pool was eligible for the National Register of Historic Places. Soon, the village closed the entire park, and the state historic preservation office determined that the pool was eligible for the National Register. Nevertheless, the village began to demolish the pool. Shortly after the court had issued an order to halt demolition, the National Park Service concurred with the state's eligibility determination.

The court determined that Section 106 applied and that the grant contract provision requiring NPS approval for changes in the use of the park constituted "continuing Federal involvement" and that the demolition constituted an "undertaking." The court held that the village of Johnson City violated Section 106 and temporality restrained the demolition (Bell 1985).

Years later, in 1983 (the pool had been closed and sitting in the park unused and partly demolished for 11 years), the parties returned to court on motions to dissolve the preliminary injunction. Because the village had, by that time, complied with Section 106 review requirements, the court lifted the injunction and the pool was demolished, most likely after being documented with photographs in the manner of HABS.

The two preceding cases are typical of preservation litigation regarding Section 106 compliance. In many Section 106 cases, the plaintiff alleges that for some reason the defendant did not complete the Section 106 process or did not complete it properly and tries to halt a project until the process is complete. The major benefit of cases such as these is that the litigation and possible court orders to delay demolition or postpone the construction of a potentially harmful undertaking give the parties involved time to negotiate and provides time for more voices to be heard. In some instances, the process saves the historic resource, though in many cases, as in the case of the C. Fred Johnson swimming pool, the resource is lost regardless.

FEDERAL CASES: SECTION 4(F)

Most plaintiffs in cases involving federal regulations are asserting that the proper procedures were not followed by the defendant in the case. Section 4(f) of the Department of Transportation Act of 1966 is somewhat of an exception because it mandates that federally funded or licensed transportation projects avoid harming historic sites so long as the measures needed to avoid such harm are "prudent and feasible."

Probably the most important federal case regarding Section 4(f) is *Citizens to Preserve Overton Park v. Volpe,* mentioned in Chapter 2. This case was heard by the United States Supreme Court in 1971 just five years after the Department of Transportation Act of 1966, which contained Section 4(f), was passed. It tested the enforcement of the clause "feasible and prudent alternative." If such an alternative existed, could the Department of Transportation (DOT) be compelled to avoid running highways through historic sites, parks, or wildlife refuges?

A local citizen's organization and two national environmental groups sued to overturn the U.S. Department of Transportation's decision to route interstate highway 40 through Overton Park in Memphis, Tennessee. During the late 1950s and 1960s, DOTs had viewed parks as desirable paths for new highways, however, Section 4(f) seemed to have been designed to counter this trend. The plaintiffs used this new legal tool to try to force the DOT to change its proposed alignment of the new highway.

In 1971, the Supreme Court upheld the "prudent and feasible" clause and directed the DOT to study other alternatives. Writing the majority opinion, Justice Marshall wrote,

> These statutes prohibit the Secretary of Transportation from authorizing the use of federal funds to finance the construction of highways through public parks if a "feasible and prudent" alternative route exists. If no such route is available, the statutes allow him to approve construction through parks only if there has been "all possible planning to minimize harm" to the park (*Citizens to Preserve Overton Park v. Volpe* 1971).

Soon thereafter, Transportation Secretary John Volpe withdrew his decision, and motorists driving westbound on Interstate 40 toward Memphis today will encounter a curve where the highway sharply banks to the right. This is where the highway begins the "prudent and feasible" route that avoids Overton Park.

The Overton Park case is significant to preservation because it set a precedent that DOTs were subject to Section 4(f) and would be required to seriously study alternatives to directly impacting historic sites as well as parks. Because of this case, Section 4(f) became one of very few federal laws that actually requires preservation. In some cases, however, the courts have found that Section 4(f) does not apply.

In *Nashvillians Against I-440 v. Lewis,* heard by a United States District Court in 1981, the plaintiffs opposed the construction of a proposed interstate bypass, I-440, through and around Nashville, Tennessee, on the grounds that its route would come dangerously close to several National Register historic districts. Section 106 review had taken place and the Tennessee DOT had determined a finding of "no adverse effect" to the districts due to the new highway. The plaintiffs demanded that the DOT perform further studies to comply with Section 4(f) regulations, arguing that the project would impact the "constructive use" of buildings within the districts. The plaintiffs first claimed that the act of constructing the highway, such as blasting, might damage the districts, but the court rejected this argument. The plaintiffs then argued that the Belmont Hills historic district was threatened, but the court ruled that the needed Section 106 review, Memorandum of Agreements, Section 4(f) review, and Environmental Impact Statements had been properly completed (Bell 1985).

PRESERVATION CASES INVOLVING *TOUT ENSEMBLE*

In 1941, the Louisiana Supreme Court heard *City of New Orleans v. Pergament.* In this case, Mr. Pergament who owned a gas station located within the French Quarter historic district had erected a large sign in front of his establishment without permission from the Vieux Carré Commission. The commission sued to have the sign taken down. Pergament argued that since his gas station was not historic, he should not be subject to the historic regulations.

The Louisiana Supreme Court ruled that, despite its nonhistoric and nonarchitecturally significant nature, the business was located within the district, and Pergament was subject to its rules because his sign would reduce the overall historic integrity and feeling of the area. Using the phrase "*tout ensemble,*" French for "taken together," the court forwarded the idea that a historic district should be seen as a whole and that modern intrusions can ruin its total character, even if they do not directly impact a historic building. In its ruling, the Louisiana Supreme Court wrote, "The purpose of the ordinance is not only to preserve the old buildings themselves, but to preserve the antiquity of the whole French and Spanish quarter, the *tout ensemble,* so to speak, by defending this relic against iconoclasm or vandalism. Preventing or prohibiting eyesores in such a locality is within the police power and within the scope of this municipal ordinance" (*City of New Orleans v. Pergament* 1941). The *Pergament* case has been frequently cited by courts in other jurisdictions.

A concept similar to *tout ensemble* was applied by another state court in 1981 in *Faulkner v. Town of Chestertown,* in which the Maryland Court of Appeals held that a plaintiff's structure located in Chestertown's local historic district was subject to its restrictions, even though the building itself was not considered as contributing to the district, because it had no architectural or historical significance. The Maryland court affirmed the lower court's decree ordering that the owner remove siding that had been installed without a certificate of appropriateness (*Faulkner v. Town of Chestertown* 1981).

CASES INVOLVING DEMOLITION BY NEGLECT WITHIN LOCAL HISTORIC DISTRICTS

In *Maher v. the City of New Orleans,* the United States Court of Appeals for the Fifth District stated:

> Once it has been determined that the purpose of the Vieux Carré legislation is a proper one, upkeep of the buildings appears reasonably necessary to the accomplishment of the goals of the ordinance. . . . The fact that an owner may incidentally be required to make out-of-pocket expenditures in order to remain in compliance with an ordinance does not per se render that ordinance a taking (1975).

The court upheld the requirement to keep historic buildings in good repair, in part, because letting a building deteriorate, especially within an urban setting, is an issue of public safety (Figure 5.1).

A common defense that landowners use in demolition by neglect cases is that they are experiencing economic hardship. While in some cases this may be the case, it often is more a matter of the owner's priorities than in their ability to pay to keep a building in their possession safe. A case that addresses this issue is *Harris v. Parker,* 1985, in which a court in Virginia

Figure 5.1a. Demolition by neglect not only destroys the character of a historic district, it also can pose a threat to public safety due to the threat of fire, pests, and collapse. Source: Photograph by Peter B. Dedek, 2012.

Figure 5.1b. Fortunately, demolition by neglect cases can be resolved and even severely damaged buildings restored. Source: Photograph by Peter B. Dedek, 2011.

ordered the owner to carry out repairs in compliance with the affirmative maintenance requirements in Smithville, Virginia's ordinance. Another case is *Buttnick v. City of Seattle*, 1986, where a court in Washington State ruled that a historic commission requiring an owner to replace a defective parapet on a historic building did not cause unreasonable economic hardship. Also, in 1994 the Washington, D.C., Court of Appeals in *District of Columbia Preservation League v. Department of Consumer and Regulatory Affairs* reversed approval of the demolition of a historic landmark in dilapidated condition caused by the owner's own lack of action because the demolition permit was unauthorized under the district's preservation act (National Trust for Historic Preservation 1999).

CONCLUSION

The issues surrounding preservation law are complicated and touch on many of the fundamental tenets of American law, especially those concerning property rights. Preservation law involves other significant and often controversial issues such as environmental protection, architectural aesthetics, city planning, and religious freedom. These issues and the multiple layers of governmental regulation involved make preservation cases particularly onerous. For the most part, the courts have supported preservation laws at all levels of government; however, actions of antipreservation forces such as the property rights movement, which opposes virtually all land use regulations, have sought to undermine the legal basis for historic preservation.

For example, at the prompting of property rights advocates, Oregon voters approved a state initiative called Measure 37 in 2004. Measure 37 essentially designated all potential losses on the part of property owners due to land use and environmental regulations as regulatory takings, forcing governments to either pay landowners compensation for economic losses due to regulations or to waive the regulation. However, the measure was challenged in court, and limits were placed on the requirements of Measure 37 in 2007 with the passage of Measure 49, which scaled back many provisions of the earlier law (Reap and Hill 2004; Oregon 2011). Similar attempts have been attempted in other states with limited success, so far. In 2006, measures similar to Oregon's Measure 37 were put to voters in six states, and they were rejected everywhere except in Arizona. In addition, courts have thrown out similar laws in other states.

Despite limited efforts to enact new property rights laws, the legal precedents set by the *Penn Central* case are still basically intact, with only minor modifications established by rulings in cases such as *Lucas* and *Dolan*. The future of preservation law and practice depends on whether state and federal courts continue to use the precedents described in this chapter, or if jurists decide to set new precedents that contradict the existing understanding of what constitutes a regulatory taking and how preservation laws and land use regulations should be interpreted and enforced.

In addition to the legal issues discussed in this chapter, the application of preservation law relies on the existence of standard rules regarding the treatment of historic properties and universal guidelines that regulate preservation design. In the United States, these are the *Secretary of the Interior's Standards,* which are discussed in Chapter 10.

STUDY QUESTIONS

1. What is a regulatory taking? Describe why it is relevant to historic preservation.

2. Can property owners always do what they like with their property? What is a bundle of rights and what are some of the factors may limit property rights?

3. What is zoning and how is it related to historic preservation?

4. Describe the Penn Central case. Why is it so important?

5. How might religious freedom impact preservation? Is it important for religious organizations to have the right to circumvent preservation laws? Why or why not? Use the cases described in this chapter to support your arguments.

6. How does the intent and the enforcement of Section 106 differ from that of Section 4(f)?

7. What is *tout ensemble* and why is it important for the preservation of the character of historic districts?

8. What is demolition by neglect and how might a municipality regulate to try to prevent it?

9. What are the basic arguments of the property rights movement? How do preservationists counter these arguments?

10. What are the main reasons that plaintiffs usually challenge preservation laws?

EXERCISE: LEGAL DISCUSSION PROBLEM: READ AND ADDRESS THE QUESTIONS

Situation: You own a vacant, dilapidated six-story railroad hotel located in Paducah, Kansas, a very depressed town which had more than 2,000 residents in 1970 but has fewer than 500 now, which you inherited from your grandpa Clyde McCoy, the family railroad tycoon. The building was built in 1915 in the Beaux-Arts style and is basically structurally sound. The exterior features are intact, although some windows and interior elements have been damaged. The tracks are long gone, and the area is very economically depressed. All of the buildings on the square are vacant except the art deco courthouse and PJ's Guns & Pawn on the opposite corner of State Hwy 000. Over a period of years, you have tried several businesses in the building, all of which failed miserably. You can't rent the building out or sell it, and now teenagers are breaking in and setting fires and taking drugs in it. You've boarded it up, but to no avail. They keep breaking in, and your lawyer has recommended that you demolish it immediately to avoid lawsuits. Now, an oil company has offered to buy the lot from you for a nice sum, provided the building has been removed, because they want its corner lot for a gas station and convenience store. You applied for a demolition permit from the local architectural review board, because your building is in Paducah's historic district. The board has refused your petition and is now requiring you to stabilize the building or face fines.

1. What arguments might you use in court to procure a demolition permit?

2. What past landmark court cases involving property rights and historic preservation and "regulatory takings" might you use to support your cause?

3. What court cases would the local review board use to support its case?

4. Explain the legal options and arguments you have as a landowner and also explain the legal options and arguments that the local architectural review board can use to save the building.

5. Finally, which party do you think is most justified by legal precedent and why?

Answers and explanations found in Instructor's Guide.

SOURCES

Bell, Charlotte. 1985. *Federal Historic Preservation Case Law, A Special Report.* Washington, DC: Advisory Council on Historic Preservation.

Citizens to Preserve Overton Park v. Volpe, 401 U.S. 402 (1971).

City of New Orleans v. Pergament, 5 So. 2d 129 (La. 1941).

Faulkner v. Town of Chestertown, Md A2d (No 122, April 30, 1981).

Kayden, Jerald S. 2011. "Historic Preservation and the New Takings Cases: Landmarks Preserved." *Fordham Environmental Law Review* 6(3).

Law.com. "Legal Dictionary." accessed November 29, 2013. http://dictionary.law.com/Default.aspx?selected=1864.

Lucas v. South Carolina Coastal Council, (91-453), 505 U.S. 1003 (1992).

Maher v. the City of New Orleans, 516F.2d 1051 (5th Cir, 1975).

Miller, Anita P. 2008. "Grassroots Historic Preservation." New Mexico Historic Preservation Division. Accessed June 26, 2010. http://www.nmheritage.org/wp/wp-content/uploads/2011/11/Grassroots-Historic-Preservation.pdf.

National Trust for Historic Preservation. 1999. "Preservation Law Reporter." Accessed June 27, 2010. http://www.rhdc.org/sites/default/files/NHTP_DemoByNeglect.pdf.

Oregon Department of Land Conservation and Development. 2011. "Ballot Measures 37 (2004) and 49 (2007) Outcomes and Effects." accessed May 29, 2012. http://www.oregon.gov/LCD/docs/publications/m49_2011-01-31.pdf?ga=t

Penn Central Transportation Company v. New York City, 438 U.S. 104 (1978).

Pennsylvania Coal Co. v. Mahon, 260 U.S. 393, 415 (1922).

Phelan, Marilyn. 1994. "Current Status of Historical Preservation Law in Regulatory Takings Jurisprudence: Has the Lucas Missile Dismantled Preservation Programs?" *Fordham Environmental Law Journal* 785 (1994–1995).

Reap, James K., and Melvin B. Hill, Jr. 2007. "Law and the Historic Preservation Commission: What Every Member Should Know." *Cultural Resource Partnership Notes.* Washington, DC: Heritage Preservation Services, National Park Service, U.S. Department of the Interior. Accessed August 16, 2010. http://www.nps.gov/history/hps/pad/partnership/index.htm.

Religious Freedom Library, "*City of Boerne v. Flores.*" Accessed November 29, 2013. http://religiousfreedom.lib.virginia.edu/court/boerne_v_flores.html

Ross, Andie. 2005 "Historic Preservation: First Amendment Considerations." Master's Thesis, University of Pennsylvania.

Tyler, Norman. 2000. *Historic Preservation: An Introduction to its History, Principles, and Practice.* New York: W.W. Norton & Company.

Village of Euclid v. Ambler Realty Co., 272 U.S. 365 (1926).

FROM DEMOLITION TO PRESERVATION: DIVERGENT APPROACHES TO MANAGING AND REHABILITATING HISTORIC BUILDINGS

OBJECTIVES

- Discuss the overall strategies of managing and modifying historic buildings and interiors for continued use.

- Using examples and illustrations, the chapter defines and evaluates options that building owners and designers have when working with historic architecture ranging from the most destructive, demolition, to the most benign, preservation.

- The chapter examines each major preservation category of treatment, such as rehabilitation, and also destructive practices, such as remodeling and outlines its effects on historic buildings.

- Understand, identify, and implement the strategy that best preserves historical integrity while keeping a building useful and economically viable.

Buildings change and evolve along with the people who occupy, manage, and rehabilitate them. Without deliberate preservation, more often than not, buildings are altered beyond recognition through time and successive uses due to decay, remodeling, or demolition (Brand 1994). There is no neutral treatment of a historic building. Everything done or not done and every change in use has the potential to impact a building's historic integrity and its future viability. Lack of action can have as much impact as action. In fact, one of the most harmful things for a historic building is to be left unoccupied. Abandoned buildings become subject to decay because there is no one present to notice a roof leak or to remove a destructive animal. Vacant buildings are also more subject to being burned down, vandalized, or looted for architectural antiques. They are demolished more frequently than occupied buildings because justifying the preservation of an abandoned building is often more difficult than defending a building in use. Abandoned buildings also offer no economic return and are often legal liabilities because people can get hurt in them and sue the owner.

Despite their inherent changeability, if preserved and cared for, historic buildings can continue to function in a recognizable form for decades or even centuries. Historic preservation is an active process involving the routine interaction between people and the built environment. In order to keep historic buildings and structures viable, decisions by those who own, manage, or occupy them have to be made as to their use, maintenance, and possible alterations and updates. In order to work effectively with historic buildings, designers should be aware of the possible ways historic buildings can be treated and know how each affects a building's historic integrity.

The possible treatments of historic buildings fall into a number of categories. They are described in this chapter from the most drastic and destructive to the most conservative and preservation-oriented: demolition, reconstruction, remodeling, "façadism," moving buildings, rehabilitation, restoration, and preservation. Of these, reconstruction, façadism, rehabilitation, and restoration involve the most design and are of particular interest to architects and interior designers.

DEMOLITION

There are two types of demolition: passive and active. Passive means doing essentially nothing. Generally, when a building or structure is left without maintenance, protection, or efforts to stabilize it, it will eventually decay and will often do so more quickly than one might expect (Figure 6.1). Of course active demolition usually involves purposeful destruction by people, however, natural disaster and fire can also actively wreck architecture.

PASSIVE: DEMOLITION BY NEGLECT

Often "natural" decay is aided by a number of human factors, including vandalism, arson, accidental fires lit by squatters, vibrations from motor vehicles or trains, and even acts of war or terrorism. Neglected historic buildings are more likely to fall victim to natural threats, such as fires started by lightning, water intrusion, earthquakes, wind damage, storm surges, plants growing on them, mold, and invasive animals such as rats, raccoons, pigeons, and termites, than

Figure 6.1. Demolition by neglect: abandoned. An important landmark of Chicago's rich African-American heritage constructed in 1887, Unity Hall was designated a Chicago Landmark in 1998. The building is also listed on the National Register of Historic Places. Unity Hall was threatened with demolition by neglect in 2012. Source: © Darris Lee Harris.

well-maintained ones. In order to survive and remain viable, buildings require a lot of effort and care, and the older the building, the more this tends to be true.

Sometimes passive demolition is unintentional. The ownership of the building might be in dispute, such as when it is unclear who inherited a property and a kind of real estate custody battle, which could go on for years or even decades, is underway. In other instances, buildings may be difficult or impossible to keep in use in any economically feasible manner, because their original function has become obsolete, such as an isolated water-powered mill, a coastal military fortification, a historic bridge that has been bypassed, or a hotel built to house railroad passengers in a town that no longer has passenger trains. Unless creative new uses can be found to make such structures worth maintaining, they may be lost.

Perhaps the economy of an entire area may make buildings difficult to keep in service. Many towns on the Great Plains, for example, have lost economic viability due to changes in farming technology and various macroeconomic trends, leaving entire towns practically abandoned. One such town is Paducah, Texas, which at this writing had a 20 percent occupancy rate in its downtown courthouse square area. At its height in 1950, the town's population stood 2,952 but had declined to only 1,186 in 2010, a 60 percent reduction (Texas State Historical Association

2013). Farther north, the city of Detroit has seen abandonment of buildings on a massive scale. Finding new life for buildings in hard-hit areas is a difficult challenge that requires a lot of effort, resources, and innovation.

Sometimes passive demolition is intentional. A situation where owners of buildings purposely let them decay is called demolition by neglect (Figure 6.2). Sometimes owners allow historic buildings to decay because they want to get rid of them. This usually occurs when a building has been designated as being historic or is located within a local historic district that does not allow active demolition. If the owner wants to build on the lot the building occupies, or simply doesn't want to pay for a historic building's upkeep, it may be more feasible to just do nothing and allow the building to either just crumble or be burned down or otherwise vandalized until the owner can go to the preservation authority and argue that there is no possible way to save what's left of the building and that the only viable option is to demolish it.

Preservationists, however, are wise to this underhanded strategy. In some places, owners have been fined for demolition by neglect and forced to maintain the building, sell it, or donate it to some individual or organization with the means and the will to preserve it. Cities such as Washington, D.C., and New York City have ordinances that subject owners of landmark buildings and buildings contributing to local historic districts who attempt to demolish them by neglect to fines and other legal action if they do not sell or repair them. In New York, penalties for demolition by neglect can be as high as $5,000 a day, and in Washington, D. C. the city can obtain a court order to enter a landmark building and unilaterally make any repairs needed to stabilize it and then charge the cost to the building's owner (Martin 2007). The reason demolition by neglect is illegal in many jurisdictions is not only to save historic architecture, but also because dilapidated buildings can pose a hazard to public health because they can provide habitat for pests, such as rats and pigeons, cause fires, and even collapse into the street possibly striking cars or people.

Figure 6.2. This abandoned house in New Orleans's French Quarter has fallen victim to demolition by neglect aided by vandalism. Source: Photograph by Peter B. Dedek, 2010.

ACTIVE DEMOLITION

Active demolition is the focus of many preservation battles, and like demolition by neglect, a number of reluctant historic building owners elect to demolish their historic buildings on the sly, such as on Saturday night or Sunday morning, and either hope they won't be fined or sued or simply get caught and pay the fines, which are sometimes less expensive from a purely economic point of view than keeping the building. To prevent this, preservation laws need to levy strong enough penalties so that demolition will not be a financially viable option. In any case, demolition is costly and not environmentally friendly. The environmental costs of demolition are discussed in Chapter 13. Some owners of potentially historic buildings demolish them proactively because they believe the building will soon be designated as historic and believe the designation will limit their rights as property owners. This is called **anticipatory demolition**, and is also illegal.

RECONSTRUCTION

If a historic building has been demolished or otherwise destroyed in the past, sometimes those who want to interpret the site for visitors want to reconstruction it. **Reconstruction** is the total rebuilding of a historic building or complex of related structures that once existed on a given site. Some reconstructions are done shortly after the historic building or structure has been lost, such as when a historic building has become so structurally unsound that it has to be taken apart and rebuilt. In these cases, distinctive architectural elements taken from the original building can be used in the reconstructed version, allowing it a greater degree of authenticity than a reconstruction made of totally new materials. For example, the corner building housing the Le Petit Theatre Du Vieux Carré in the French Quarter of New Orleans was rebuilt in 1963 based on the historic design (Figure 6.3).

Reconstructions come in many degrees of quality from a preservation standpoint. Generally, the more thoroughly the original building to be reconstructed is researched and documented with drawings, photographs, and descriptions, the more accurate and hence desirable the reconstruction is likely to be in the eyes of preservationists. Primary historical evidence

Figure 6.3. Le Petit Theatre Du Vieux Carré in the French Quarter of New Orleans was rebuilt in 1963 but is indistinguishable from the original. Source: Photograph by Peter B. Dedek, 2009.

of what the original building looked like and how it was constructed should be applied to the design of the new building as much as possible. However, this comes with one important caveat: the reconstruction must always be clearly presented to the public as a reconstruction and not as the original. Also, if elements from the original building are included, it must be made clear, through design or interpretation or both, which elements are historic and which are modern, such as with the reconstructed Roman tomb in Cordova, Spain, shown in Figure 6.4.

Sometimes reconstruction is conceptual, such as the reconstruction of Benjamin Franklin's house in Philadelphia by Philadelphia architect Robert Venturi, which is a painted steel frame that simply outlines the volume that his house once occupied. The benefit of this kind of reconstruction is that it communicates the impression of the lost building but can never be confused with actual historic architecture. On the other hand, when the National Park Service rebuilt the Indian quarters at the San Jose Mission in San Antonio, it created visual confusion. Although NPS presents the structure as a reconstruction, it is difficult to imagine the site without the 20th-century additions because they are so massive and imposing, leaving the area as much NPS speculation as actual Spanish colonial (Figure 6.5).

A more historically accurate design for reconstruction might have been to indicate in some visual manner which materials are original and which are historic on the walls while defining their historic form. Perhaps the new material could be a lighter stone leaving the original elements looking different, similar to the example of the Roman tomb in Cordova, Spain. This would allow visitors to easily understand which aspects of the site have been rebuilt. An alternative would have been to avoid reconstruction all together and to interpret the site as it was. In some cases, the reconstruction may be virtual, such as allowing visitors to a historic site see digital images or perhaps projections or even holograms that illustrate its historic appearance. The advantage of virtual reconstruction is that it does not disturb the actual site, leaving it undamaged.

Figure 6.4. Reconstructed Roman tomb in Cordova, Spain. Only a small percentage of the material is original; however, the designers used brick as the new material to clearly distinguish the original from the reconstructed elements. Reconstructions often give tourists something to look at. Source: Photograph by Peter B. Dedek, 2008.

Figure 6.5. Stone walls surrounding the Indian quarters at the San Jose Mission in San Antonio, Texas, built in the 1930s. The reconstructed walls and buildings make it difficult to discern what is historic Spanish colonial and what is historic National Park Service, but does provide a spectacle for visitors. Source: Photograph by Peter B. Dedek, 2008.

Reconstruction is essentially an educational tool, but preservationists tend to see it as a last resort. When the original resource has been lost or can't be viably preserved, reconstruction can be a meaningful tool to recreate the character and feeling of a historic place; however, many reconstructions are either too heavy-handed or not based enough on solid research to be useful and can actually damage the historic integrity of a site and destroy significant archeological evidence. This happened to the ancient site of the Tower of Babel in Iraq when Saddam Hussein irresponsibly destroyed most of the archeological ruins and any information they may have yielded by attempting to rebuild the temple. Oftentimes, not enough archeological or historical evidence exists to make an authentic reconstruction possible. In those instances, it is best to leave the site alone and interpret the authentic ruins as they are. It is always important to use the preservation ideal of reversibility when reconstructing so that any new work won't negatively impact the site.

REMODELING

To remodel means to modernize or to remake. Remodeling activity seeks to physically alter a building in order to have it look more up-to-date and possibly function in a more modern way. This is usually achieved by replacing historic windows, tearing off porches, covering the exterior with new siding materials, gutting and replacing interiors, altering roof lines, and replacing historic doors with new glass or metal ones (Figure 6.6). Not a preservation activity, the only good thing to be said about remodeling from a preservation perspective is that it can save a historic building by at least keeping it occupied and maintained. Unfortunately, though, by its very nature, remodeling is antithetical to preservation. Short of demolition, remodeling is probably

Figure 6.6. This formerly 2nd Empire-style house, built in the late 19th century in upstate New York, has been remodeled beyond recognition, with only its Mansard roof and brackets revealing its true identity. Source: Photograph by Peter B. Dedek, 2007.

the worst thing one can do to a historic building. Often the changes done in remodels are not reversible, and significant historic features are removed and either sold off to salvage yards or hauled off to the landfill. While, as stated earlier, historic buildings evolve and change over time, remodeling can make a historic building almost unrecognizable as being historic.

Of course, the more historic and architecturally distinctive the building, the more potential damage remodeling can do to it. Remodeling also harms a building to a greater degree if, before the work is done, the building started out having historical integrity, because buildings with a high level of historic integrity have more to lose.

Most of the time remodeling is done out of apathy or ignorance. From the 1950s through the 1970s, remodeling was probably the most common treatment to the historic buildings that were not demolished. During these decades, in which the modernist mentality of "newer is better" prevailed, aluminum or vinyl siding was added, pesky old ornate porches torn off, intricate 19th-century storefronts hacked up and covered over with decorative aluminum panels or some such (Figure 6.7), picture windows installed to replace those old-fashioned wooden double-hung types, and old paneled doors replaced with clean, modern flush doors, sometimes with three small windows arranged at an angle above the knob. Historic interiors suffered the most, with many being removed entirely, leaving many still impressive historic buildings with utterly bland, characterless interiors that in no way match the exterior. The remodeling mentality implies that the owner would actually prefer to have a nice new building, but alas can't afford one and so will attempt to make the old building look as modern as possible.

Since the early 1980s, a trend of what can be called "unremodeling" has taken place all across America. With unremodeling, the modernistic elements added to historic buildings in the recent past have been removed and the original appearance restored or recreated as best as possible (Figure 6.8).

Figure 6.7. This early-20th-century commercial building's historic storefront was replaced in the mid-20th century with something more up-to-date, to the detriment of the historic district in Lockhart, Texas, in which it is located. Preservationists refer to these false fronts as "slipcovers." Source: Photograph by Peter B. Dedek, 2009.

Figure 6.8. Across America for the past several decades, fancy brickwork and ornate storefronts have again been seeing the light of day. The Hairpin Lofts, a formerly vacant 1929 commercial flatiron building was purchased by the City of Chicago in 2007 and restored, a process that involved reproducing a number of missing decorative elements. Originally the building housed the Hump Hair Pin Manufacturing Company. Sources: Left: Courtesy of Landmarks Illinois; Right: Patsy McEnroe Photography.

MOVING HISTORIC BUILDINGS

Moving buildings is often a last resort, a way to at least salvage something when a structure and its site are otherwise doomed because the land is destined for development. As a form of large-scale recycling, the practice has some environmental merit, but again, from a preservation point of view, the practice is inferior to preserving a building at its historic location. Moving a building almost always destroys its eligibility to be included on the National Register of Historic Places, because relocation removes and detaches it from its historical context. A historic building doesn't exist in a vacuum: in order to be interpreted properly, it must be viewed and understood within its surrounding environment, which usually includes its relationship with elements such as outbuildings, sidewalks, trees, views, roads, and gardens. Without these and other environmental cues, the historic nature of a building is often difficult to understand or appreciate (Figure 6.9).

Figure 6.9. This 19th-century school is being removed from its original site. The Colburn School building was moved to make way for new town library in Westwood, Massachusetts. Moving buildings robs them of their historical context. Source: Boston Globe via Getty Images.

Perhaps the biggest problem with moving buildings is how common the practice is. On a month-long National Endowment for the Humanities Institute on preserving the African American history of South Carolina, the author saw so many historic buildings recently moved or about to be trucked to a different location all across the state that it became a joke among the participants: "the great building migration." While moving buildings is preferable to demolition, it shouldn't be seen as the best preservation option, and those interested in preserving the historic character of communities should fight the practice and insist that buildings remain in their native locations whenever possible. It's too easy for developers to just say that they'll pay to move historic buildings out of their path and continue to build big box shopping centers and gas stations in historic areas as historic landmarks are shuttled off to the periphery. Preservation isn't just about buildings: it's about neighborhoods and communities and landscapes.

FAÇADISM

An unfortunate compromise sometimes reached between preservationists and developers is called **façadism**, when only the historic street façade is retained with just a thin strip behind it, while the rest of the building is demolished and replaced with a totally new structure. The idea is that the "look" of the historic building from the street can be preserved while leaving the developer free to do what he or she wanted to do all along—build an essentially new and usually larger building on the site. In the vast majority of cases, the end result is a kind of parody where the context and character of what's left of the historic building, now reduced to a kind of architectural taxidermy, is isolated and usually overwhelmed by a new building constructed behind and sometimes growing up above or around it (Figures 6.10a and 6.10b). The reason the old façade usually becomes dwarfed by the new construction is that most of the time the reason the developer wanted to

Figure 6.10a. The Texas Theater in San Antonio, disfigured in the late 1980s. A bolder, more honest design choice would have been to remove the historic façade and create a genuinely modern building. Source: Photograph by Peter B. Dedek, 2008.

Figure 6.10b. The historic Hearst building located at 959 8th Avenue in New York City was designed by architect Joseph Urban and completed in 1928. The original building was initially designed to function as the base for a proposed skyscraper, but the tower was not constructed because of the Great Depression. The new 46-story tower, designed by architect Norman Foster, was completed in 2006. The historic landmark building's original cast stone facade was retained in the project, but little else. The New York Landmarks commission approved this project; however, recalling Breuer's 1970s Grand Central Terminal proposal, one can ask if this project preserved the historic art deco–inspired building which had existed as a six-story building on the site for almost 80 years. Source: Arcaid Images / Alamy.

demolish the historic building in the first place was because of a desire to put a building on the site that provides more rentable space (Figure 6.11). If a developer did not want more square footage, the original building probably would have been retained. In most cases, neither the scale nor the materials of the new building match the old façade, and the effect can be rather bizarre

Figure 6.11. This once charming art deco building in San Francisco has been wedged in by concrete monoliths and suffers for lack of context. Source: Photograph by Peter B. Dedek, 2008.

Figure 6.12. This Beaux-Arts post office in New Orleans was cut short and most of its mass replaced by a new addition, giving the effect of a failed scientific experiment. Source: Photograph by Peter B. Dedek, 2009.

(Figure 6.12). This practice is not considered to be a proper form of preservation because it does not retain the integrity or even most of the physical existence of the historic building. "A façade does not a building make," one might say. The practice isolates the historic façade from its surroundings, alienates it from the building's massing, and destroys all or most of its historic interior.

REHABILITATION

Rehabilitation is the most common accepted preservation treatment. When the use of a building is being changed from one function to another, the process of altering the building to suit its new function is called "adaptive use," a phrase some preservationists prefer to "adaptive reuse" because that phrase contains a redundancy. Rehabilitation involves the careful alteration of a historic building in order to make it viable for a contemporary use without remodeling it. This means that after the work is completed, the building will still be easily recognizable as historic and will retain most, if not all, of its key character-defining elements. A character-defining element is a feature that makes a building look historic (see Chapter 4) (Figure 6.13).

Character-defining elements are the aspects of a building that allow us to identify it as being from a particular era, architectural style, or as the work of a particular designer. Examples include the mansard roof of a Second Empire house from the 1870s, the columned temple-front of a Greek revival bank from the 1830s, the spiraling staircase in a federal-style mansion from the 1810s, the streamlined sign of an art deco movie theater from the 1930s, the gingerbread brackets of a Queen Anne house from the 1880s, or the plate-glass strip windows of a Bauhaus-inspired factory building from the 1920s.

Character-defining features should be the focus of good rehabilitation work. In rehabilitation, minor aspects of the building such as bathrooms, kitchens, attic rooms, closets, and rear additions are often altered and updated as needed, while the character-defining features and spaces are retained, restored, and maintained or replaced with an identical substitute if too deteriorated to simply repair. In rehabilitations, functional features such as bathrooms and kitchens are normally updated and are often modern in appearance once the work is finished. Generally, such spaces are not considered to be character-defining or significant enough to warrant preservation, and the need for modern function prevails.

Most rehabilitations in the United States are performed using the Secretary of the Interior's Standards of Rehabilitation as a guide. The Secretary of the Interior's Standards will be discussed in detail in Chapter 10. These national standards help to advise architects, interior designers, contractors, and building owners on what actions to take and what not to do while rehabilitating a historic building. Adherence to the standards is required when the rehabilitation is being done with the goal of obtaining a tax credit under the federal Investment Tax Credit Program, and the standards are also employed by many state preservation grant programs and by many local historic district architectural review boards.

The goal of rehabilitation is to balance historic integrity with modern function and current building codes. One of the most common aspects of rehabilitation is to bring a building up to code, which is often a difficult balancing act.

Figure 6.13. The Seagram Building in New York City, designed by Mies van der Rohe and Phillip Johnson and built in 1958. Its character-defining features include its flat rooflines, repetitive plate glass windows, horizontal banding, and vertical I-beam exterior decoration. When evaluating character-defining features, the period and style of the building must be well understood. Source: Photograph by Peter B. Dedek, 2011.

For example, many Texas courthouses have grand open staircases, often made of wood, that connect the first and upper floors. These distinctive staircases break modern fire codes, because the openness that makes them so impressive can promote the spread of a fire. The staircases are major character-defining elements of the courthouses, and to enclose them would drastically impact the historic nature and the beauty of major interior spaces. Compromises, such as retaining the staircases as open while installing fire suppression systems (such as a sprinkler system), are sometimes made to satisfy the need for historic integrity while protecting public safety.

Rehabilitation projects usually involve the updating of plumbing, HVAC, and electrical systems. These updates don't only save energy and protect the public safety, they also help protect the building itself, because two of the most significant threats to historic buildings are electrical fires and leaking plumbing. If implemented carefully, these updates rarely hurt the integrity of the building.

A more challenging problem is the need to bring historic buildings in compliance with the Americans with Disabilities Act (ADA) and other handicapped accessibility regulations. Although the ADA has special provisions for historic buildings, even these modified standards are often difficult to reconcile with historic features such as staircases, narrow doorways, and historic flooring. Accessibility issues in historic buildings will be presented in Chapter 12.

As stated in Chapter 3, the focus of most design reviews of rehabilitation projects, be they federal Investment Tax Act project reviews or in local historic district design reviews, tend to focus on changes to the exterior of buildings. Although there are over 1,800 regulated historic districts in the United States (Silver 2004), in general, interior elements are protected by historic ordinances in the United States in only a handful of districts. A 2007 study revealed that although 14 of 20 American cities studied had provisions protecting historic interiors, they overwhelmingly protected only interiors within individually landmarked buildings, which constitute a small fraction of the number of historic buildings within those cities that contribute to historic districts (Preservation Alliance 2007). Since interiors are the aspect of a building that people interact with the most, they will hopefully gain more attention and protection in the future (Figure 6.14).

Figure 6.14. Intact historic interiors such as this one in the old U.S. Mint in San Francisco contribute greatly to a building's integrity. Source: Photograph by Peter B. Dedek, 2008.

RESTORATION

Restoration is the activity that most people associate with historic preservation. Unlike rehabilitation, the focus is not on reuse, but on taking a building and its grounds back to the way they appeared during a particular period in its history. For example, Mount Vernon, the home of George Washington, has been carefully restored to its "appearance in 1799 in the last year of Washington's life" (Mount Vernon Ladies Association 2010). This means that any alterations made to the house or its immediate surroundings added by subsequent occupants have been removed, and any objects or features known through research to have existed there in 1799 have been reintroduced wherever possible.

The period (or sometimes periods) that are the focus of a restoration project is a property's period of historical significance, usually the time the building was constructed, or the time when the person or people for whom the property is famous occupied or used the site, or the time in which a significant historic event took place there. The criteria of historical significance used for the National Register of Historic Places, as discussed in Chapter 4, are used when determining the period of significance for a property.

The act of restoration is a meticulous process that should always be based on extensive historical research and, in some cases, archeological investigation. Often restorations involve some kind of reconstruction, even if it's just the remanufacture of a bracket, column, fabric, or wallpaper, because few old buildings look exactly the way they did during an earlier period (Figure 6.15).

Figure 6.15. The Mills Mansion near Rhinebeck, New York, remodeled in 1896 by the architectural firm McKim, Mead, and White, was undergoing restoration when this photo was taken. The façade to the left is finished. Note missing modillions on the front façade. Source: Photograph by Peter B. Dedek, 2008.

Restoration is often the most appropriate treatment for buildings that are destined to become museums (Figure 6.16). Because the exacting nature of the restorative process does not allow for a lot of flexibility of function, most users would find a restored building difficult to occupy, however even many restored buildings have cleverly hidden modern kitchens, bathrooms, and mechanical systems, such as air conditioning, electricity, and central heat.

Although before the 1980s strict restoration to a certain period was the norm for many historic sites and even for whole towns such as Williamsburg, Virginia, the practice has come under some criticism in recent decades. The reason for this is that preservationists have recognized that buildings evolve over time and may have significance in more than a single period. A prime example is Colonial Williamsburg. As described in Chapter 1, when its historic areas were restored from 1926 through the 1950s, buildings built after 1800 were torn down to assure that the area would have a "colonial" appearance. Yes, Williamsburg did regain much of its superficial colonial appearance, but many significant early buildings were lost in the process, forever preventing visitors from experiencing the evolution of the town in the 19th century and beyond.

The approach to restoration today tends to be more inclusive than in the past. Often, later additions and changes to historic properties that do not particularly impact the historic quality of the rest of the property are retained and simply interpreted to visitors as being from an era other than the period that most of the elements of the property reflect. In addition, the significance of properties was often quite narrowly defined in the past. For example, the restoration

Figure 6.16. Formal parlor of the Herman-Grima House, a federal-style urban mansion built in 1831 in New Orleans, Louisiana. In the early 1970s, the house was meticulously restored to its appearance from the late 1800s after functioning as a rooming house for women for many decades. The purpose of most interior restorations is as exhibits that provide a window into the past. Source: Photograph by Peter B. Dedek, 2013, courtesy Herman-Grima House.

and interpretation of Southern plantations usually focused on the "big house" and those who occupied it. Today many sites seek to interpret the lives and material culture of not only of the main house and its owners, but of other buildings on the site (if any still exist) and the people who lived and worked in them (Figure 6.17). Today, the few buildings where slaves lived that still survive are often viewed as being at least as valuable to the visitor experience as the main house (Figure 6.18). This shift in attitude reflects a wider understanding of history and who contributed to the development of any given historic site.

Figure 6.17. Original slave cabin circa 1860 at Redcliffe House, South Carolina. Such buildings are rare and have a very high degree of historical significance. Source: Photograph by Peter B. Dedek, 2007.

Figure 6.18. Kitchen at the Herman-Grima House. Enslaved workers spent their days working in this kitchen. A significant part of the story of the site, restored spaces such as this provide visitors with a more accurate portrait of 19th-century life. Photograph by Peter B. Dedek, 2007.

PRESERVATION

Preservation is the best treatment for a historic building. Essentially, **preservation** means that a building continues to function for decades and perhaps even centuries without ever falling into disrepair or being substantially altered in any way. The process of preservation is one of careful stewardship. It is possible for a property that has been restored to then be preserved for the rest of its existence (Figure 6.19). The term "conservation," which means essentially the same thing, is used more commonly in non-American English-speaking countries, such as England and Canada.

Preservation isn't as passive as it may sound. Whoever manages a given historic property must make numerous decisions about its maintenance and function. These decisions often impact the historical integrity and can affect the continued survival of the structures. Therefore, even to just preserve a property, guidelines such as the *Secretary of the Interior's Standards* are often needed. Preservation involves the implementation of sound maintenance practices and gradual upgrades as needed to assure that a restoration or rehabilitation will never be necessary. The principles used are essentially the same as those used in restoration, except that less activity occurs.

Figure 6.19. Springwood, Franklin Roosevelt's family house in Hyde Park, New York. FDR's residence has been faithfully preserved and, with the exception of a fire that damaged the house in 1982, has been maintained since its inception, first by the Roosevelts and later by the National Park Service. Source: Photograph by Peter B. Dedek, 2007.

DRAYTON HALL: AN AUTHENTICALLY PRESERVED HISTORIC PLANTATION HOUSE

Figure 6A. Drayton Hall. Source: Photograph by Peter B. Dedek, 2007.

An excellent example of a building in the state of preservation is Drayton Hall, a rare Georgian style plantation house built for John Drayton (1715–1779) in 1738 along the Ashley River, about 15 miles northwest of Charleston in the South Carolina Lowcountry. Operated by the National Trust for Historic Preservation, Drayton Hall is a National Historic Landmark and is probably the oldest plantation house open to the public.

The house was owned by the Drayton family, who ran an indigo and rice plantation there for seven generations. The main house is nearly in its original condition, although the outbuildings that once flanked it did not survive. In 1886, an earthquake destroyed the laundry house, and in 1893 a hurricane demolished the kitchen. The slave quarters were also lost. The family never modernized or significantly altered the main dwelling, offering a unique opportunity for visitors to see what the house was like centuries ago. Today, the interior has no furniture, and the rooms have not been repainted in modern times. The National Trust maintains the nearly empty structure to inspire the imaginations of the public as it surveys its vacant neoclassical interior without the distraction of modern attempts to recreate period furniture and interior decorations (Drayton Hall 2010).

Light-handed preservation methods, such as those employed by Drayton Hall, add a sense of authenticity and meaning to a site.

Figure 6B. Drayton Hall interior. Source: Photograph by Peter B. Dedek, 2007.

Buildings being preserved often continue in their original function, such as a 1920s movie house that still shows movies or a historic hotel that still accepts guests (Figure 6.20). In some cases, managers of museums located in historic buildings can employ the preservation stratagem as well.

Figure 6.20. Lobby of the El Rancho Hotel, Gallup, New Mexico, built in 1936 on historic Route 66. The hotel, which attracted a number of famous actors making western films in the area in 1950s and 1960s, has operated as a hotel almost continuously since its construction and was listed on the National Register in 1988. The two-story lobby has been preserved and, with its original design and historic materials and finishes, embodies the building's unique character. Source: Photograph by Peter B. Dedek, 2011.

CONCLUSION

The appropriate treatment of historic buildings and their contexts varies by the type of property involved and by its intended contemporary use. While a large art deco downtown warehouse dating from the 1930s probably doesn't warrant meticulous restoration, it may very well be a good candidate for rehabilitation and adaptive use into lofts or some other economically viable purpose. For such a building, no option other than rehabilitation may be advisable. Demolition, be it by neglect or the wrecking ball, would diminish the historic quality of the area and would be bad for the environment (see Chapter 13 for a discussion of the environmental impact of historic preservation). Remodeling, while probably preferable to demolition, would still reduce the historical integrity of the area. Moving a large warehouse isn't viable, and preservation may not allow the building to be of any practical use unless it can continue in its original warehouse function.

In certain cases, demolition may even be the appropriate or at least the only viable option, for example, if the aforementioned warehouse had serious structural defects, it may simply not be feasible to rehabilitate it. Demolition ends up being a last resort in other cases as well, such as when a building stands in the way of a vital project, or when a building has been so damaged by fire as to be unsalvageable. In other cases, smaller historic buildings can be moved if, despite the best efforts of preservationists, their fate is sealed otherwise. Remodeling, however, is almost never necessary for a building that is historic, as a sensitive rehabilitation is, in virtually all cases, a better option. However in rare cases where an old building has lost its integrity and can barely be deemed historic at all, because it has lost most all of its once defining characteristics due to prior alterations, remodeling it into something more contextual to the neighborhood might be warranted.

Historic preservation is not an exact science. It combines the very diverse pursuits of history, architectural design, urban planning, business, social welfare, environmentalism, and real estate development. As a multidisciplinary field, preservation usually involves the cooperative interaction of many people and decisions are often based on compromise. Because of this, rigid preservation fundamentals may be impractical in some real-life situations. Designers who are willing to listen to the views and needs of others while still desiring to preserve the historically significant characteristics of historic buildings and their interiors often can find workable solutions and appropriate treatment strategies for historic properties.

STUDY QUESTIONS

1. Which of the building treatments described in the chapter would be most appropriate for a house museum? Why?

2. Why do preservationists tend to frown on reconstructing historic buildings?

3. What kinds of threats are unoccupied historic buildings often subjected to?

4. Describe anticipatory demolition. What would motivate a building owner to do such a thing?

5. Why does moving historic buildings reduce their historic integrity?

6. In what ways does rehabilitation differ from remodeling?

7. Give three examples of major character-defining features found on the building pictured in Figure 6.19 of this chapter.

8. Would the strategies to restore Mount Vernon be useful when rehabilitating an early-20th-century warehouse into condominiums? Why or why not?

9. Why is it important to preserve and restore historic slave quarters?

10. What are the advantages of the preservation strategies used at Drayton Hall? What may be some disadvantages for visitors of the largely unaltered and unfurnished house?

Label each of the images as an example of one of the approaches listed. One picture may represent more than one possible treatment or condition: work to eliminate the treatments or conditions that appear not to be possible for a given building and list the ones that are possible):

1) Demolition by neglect	2) Reconstruction	3) Remodeling	4) Façadism
5) Moved building	6) Rehabilitation	7) Restoration	8) Preservation

A. _____   E. _____   I. _____   L. _____

B. _____   F. _____   J. _____   M. _____

C. _____   G. _____   K. _____   N. _____

D. _____   H. _____

Answers and explanations found in Instructor's Guide.

SOURCES

Brand, Stewart. 1994. *How Buildings Learn: What Happens After They're Built*. New York: Viking.

Drayton Hall. "This Is More than a House." Accessed June 11, 2010. http://www.draytonhall.org/.

Martin, Anna. 2007. "Demolition by Neglect: Repairing Buildings by Repairing Legislation." Historic Preservation Seminar. Accessed September 4, 2010. http://lsr.nellco.org/cgi/viewcontent.cgi?article=1016&context=georgetown/hpps.

Mount Vernon Ladies Association. "History of Mount Vernon." Accessed June 11, 2010. http://www.mountvernon.org/learn/explore_mv/index.cfm/ss/27/.

Preservation Alliance for Greater Philadelphia. 2007 "Protecting Historic Interiors: A Survey of Preservation Practices and Their Implications for Philadelphia." Accessed February 1, 2010. http://www.preservationalliance.com/publications/InteriorsFINAL.pdf.

Silver, Sass. 2004. "Not Brick by Brick: Development of Interior Landmark Designation Policies in Washington, D.C." Student Paper, Georgetown Law Center. Accessed January 30, 2010. http://scholarship.law.georgetown.edu/cgi/viewcontent.cgi?article=1014&context=hpps_papers.

Texas State Historical Association, 2013. "Handbook of Texas: Paducah, TX." Accessed November 29, 2013. http://www.tshaonline.org/handbook/online/articles/hjp01.

A SURVEY OF HISTORIC BUILDING MATERIALS

OBJECTIVES

- Describe the basic properties and preservation issues of common structural and finish materials used on the exteriors and interiors of historic buildings.

- Define compressive and tensile strength of materials.

- Focus on historic building materials used in the United States prior to about 1950.

This chapter introduces the basic structural considerations and aesthetic applications of a selection of common historic building materials. Designers working with historic structures should begin with an understanding of the properties of the materials they will be working with and know the overall principles and techniques needed for their appropriate treatments.

The materials used in buildings constructed before the Second World War tend to be more natural and sometimes more fragile than those used in contemporary buildings. For example, prior to about 1900, historic brick and mortar were softer than the brick and mortar used today. Rather than specifying the concrete, glass, and steel often used today, early designers selected more natural materials, such as stone and wood. Prewar architecture also usually had more intricate detailing and decoration than recent buildings, and ornamental detail is easy to damage with harsh or heavy-handed repairs or high pressure and mechanical cleaning techniques. The general approach to treating historic building materials should emphasize gentleness, care, and an ability to respectfully adapt them to contemporary function wherever possible.

COMPRESSIVE AND TENSILE STRENGTH

Understanding the relative strength of building materials is fundamental to effectively preserving them. Designers use specific building materials for particular applications based, at least in part, on their inherent strengths and weaknesses. All building materials possess two basic types of strength: compressive and tensile. Materials with great compressive strength are commonly used to support the weight of buildings and their contents, while materials with tensile strength are used to bridge openings and span over spaces. Building materials with little of either type of strength, if used at all, are more likely to have purely decorative applications or, as in the case of plaster, must be held up by another, stronger material.

COMPRESSIVE STRENGTH

Compressive strength is the ability of a given material to resist force or weight that presses directly down on it, as when stone blocks are piled up: the stone at the bottom will have to resist greater compressive stress than the blocks above. Some materials have more compressive strength than others. Granite has a tremendous amount of compressive strength, while adobe (dried, unfired mud) has far less. Granite can withstand a vast amount of crushing force, while adobe will break apart much sooner.

TENSILE STRENGTH

Tensile strength is how well a given material will hold up when being sheared. This means that force is being applied to a material at a point where it has little or no support directly under the point of pressure, for example, weight pressing down on the middle of a beam that spans a room and is supported only at its ends. Tensile strength is also tested when a force presses on the side, not the top of a wall. Some materials have more tensile strength than others. While stone has a great deal of compressive strength, it does not have so much tensile strength. If a stone header (lintel) over a window is overloaded with weight, the stone is likely to crack. A pencil is an object that has a lot of compressive strength but not much tensile strength: if one sets a pencil on a solid surface and pushes directly down on it (applying a crushing force), it will take a lot of force to crush or break it, but if one takes a pencil in two hands and snaps it sideways (applying a shearing force), it will break easily. Steel, on the other hand, has both high compressive and high tensile strength.

COMMON STRUCTURAL AND EXTERIOR HISTORIC BUILDING MATERIALS

Structural architectural materials and those intended for exterior use include masonry, such as stone, brick, concrete, adobe and terra-cotta, and also wood and metals. Whether masonry or not, each material has unique relative strengths and weaknesses and were specified in buildings to address specific needs for structural integrity and sometimes aesthetic effect and attractiveness.

MASONRY

Consisting of heavy materials derived from the earth usually with good compressive strength, masonry was historically used for load-bearing, relatively permanent construction. The first masonry used in prehistoric times was probably unfired clay (adobe), followed by fired clay blocks (brick), and stone. Concrete and terra-cotta tile were also used in ancient times, particularly by the ancient Romans, and both are still used today. If well-engineered, masonry construction can last for centuries. However, even concrete and stone can fall victim to destructive forces, such as erosion, settling, and vandalism, and must be actively preserved.

ADOBE

Probably the first masonry material, **adobe**, is sun-dried clay. Adobe was used all over the world for many thousands of years because it is easily found and extracted and requires little processing. The early Native Americans of the American Southwest constructed their adobe walls as unified clay structures, but after the arrival of the Spanish in the American Southwest in the 1500s, adobe was molded into bricks that usually consisted of clay and sand, with grass or straw acting as a strengthener, as had been done in Europe and the near East (Figure 7.1). Adobe, often combined with stone construction, was used for thousand of years and continued to be common in the American Southwest well into the 1800s. The material is still employed today in the Southwest and in other parts of the world, such as relatively arid parts of South America and Asia. Adobe is used primarily in arid regions all over the world because it is vulnerable to water damage.

Figure 7.1. This deteriorating structure at Taos Pueblo in Taos, New Mexico, shows the original adobe block and adobe stucco construction. Source: Photograph by Peter B. Dedek, 2010.

Adobe Walls

Adobe bricks are laid up on as walls and mortared together with mud. Because it is a soft, unfired material with very little tensile strength and limited compressive strength, walls made of adobe are thick and usually have narrow door and window openings, with wooden lintels to provide the tensile strength needed to support the weight above them. The material has excellent thermal qualities and provides good acoustical separation between rooms and from the outside.

A protective layer of stucco made of a similar material but with more straw added to strengthen it is applied to cover the adobe bricks. The stucco is then sometimes finished with a whitewash made up of pulverized gypsum and clay suspended in water. In the 19th century, lime plaster was sometimes used to stucco over adobe, and in the 20th century, cement-based stucco was often applied over adobe walls.

Adobe Floors

In addition to being used to construct walls, adobe has also been used on floors. The adobe was laid directly on the earth and then compressed, leveled, and smoothed off to create a fairly solid and smooth surface. Traditionally, adobe floors were coated with oils, plant extracts, and even animal blood to harden the surface and make it smooth. Today adobe floors are often preserved using commercially available water-repellent sealers.

Adobe Roofs

In particularly arid regions, such as Arizona, even the roofs of many early buildings were made of adobe supported by a structure of beams and wood lath. Historic adobe roofs tended to be nearly flat, with short parapet walls built on all sides of them. The adobe roof was supported by log beams, called **vigas**, that were set into the upper section of the adobe walls with their ends sometimes projecting through (Figure 7.2). Smaller logs or other available natural materials such as sticks or leaves were then layered above the vigas to create a platform for the adobe roofing, which was caked on above. The roofs did slope slightly to allow rain to trickle off and out through hollowed logs called **canales**, which projected through the parapet walls and directed the flowing rain water out away from the walls of the building. As adobe buildings were remodeled and retrofitted, later occupants often replaced their flat adobe roofs, which needed to be regularly maintained and recoated with stucco, with slanting constructions surfaced with more waterproof materials, such as roofing tile, asphalt, or metal.

Adobe Preservation Issues

Historic adobe requires a great deal of maintenance because it is vulnerable to erosion due to wind and water, infestation by insects and rodents, intrusion by the roots of trees and shrubs, cracking and settling because of its weight and lack of tensile strength, and expansion and contraction with changes in relative humidity and temperature. If adobe is not repaired periodically (at least once a year in many places) and re-stuccoed, and if plants are not kept from growing in it, the material will simply erode away (Figure 7.3). The maintenance, care, and repair of adobe usually requires the involvement of experts, but one of the fundamental rules is to always repair adobe with new materials that are as close in composition to the original historic material as possible (Patterson and Look 1978).

FIRED BRICK

Brick, a common masonry material in historic buildings, is essentially rectangular blocks of fired clay mixed with sand to increase its dimensional stability. In ancient times, bricks evolved from adobe bricks, which were molded and dried in the sun. The Mesopotamians and later

Figure 7.2. Taos Pueblo in Taos, New Mexico, adobe construction with vigas and canales. Source: Photograph by Peter B. Dedek, 2010.

Figure 7.3. In this deteriorated structure at Taos Pueblo in Taos, New Mexico, the original adobe block and adobe stucco construction has melted away due to a lack of maintenance. Source: Photograph by Peter B. Dedek, 2010.

the ancient Romans began to fire their building bricks in rudimentary kilns at far lower temperatures than today's bricks. In America, bricks were used in the Dutch settlement of New Amsterdam (later New York) in the early 1600s and were also fired on-site for use in buildings in Jamestown, Virginia, after 1610. Brick was also made in other colonial settlements where usable clay deposits could be found (Weaver 1993, 99).

Historically, brick was much softer than contemporary brick. The size of individual bricks was not standardized from one building to another. Prior to the late 1800s, most bricks were molded by hand and fired at the building site in makeshift kilns. Such kilns cooked the outside of the brick at higher temperatures than the core, as some of the heat did not penetrate to the inside, making the outside of the bricks harder. In the latter half of the 19th century in America, mills began to produce harder, more evenly colored, and smooth-pressed bricks in standard sizes, but they were still soft by today's standards because the clay was not vitrified like the clay used in bricks today.

Clay is vitrified by being heated to high temperatures, normally from about 1000 to 1500 degrees Celsius. During the **vitrification** process, the brick becomes less porous and smaller in volume, and its strength and resistance to water increases (Al-Amaireh 2009). The clays used in historic bricks were not as processed as those of today, causing inconsistencies and occasional defects that sometimes weakened them. Because of their lack of density and their inherent flaws, historic bricks are quite porous and absorb water readily.

Brick Load-Bearing Walls and Foundations

Bricks are used for their compressive strength, their fire resistance, their resistance to pests such as termites, and their immunity to rot. Most bricks in buildings from the early 20th century and before were incorporated into heavy, load-bearing walls, which were several layers thick and were usually held together with lime-based mortars. Masons laid up historic brick in a variety of patterns, called "bonds." These patterns combined layers of bricks laid with their long sides parallel to the wall called **stretchers**, with occasional layers of bricks set down perpendicular to the direction of the wall called **headers**. Using a combination of courses with stretchers and headers strengthened the structure of the wall.

The various types of bonds used in historic buildings have names, such as **Flemish bond**, which has stretchers and headers alternating with one another within each course (Figure 7.4); **English bond**, which has alternating courses consisting of all stretchers and all headers; and **American common bond**, which has all header courses separated by five or so all-stretcher courses. The **English Cross** or **Dutch bond** has alternating courses of headers and stretchers, and the **stack bond** has courses of all stretchers that do not overlap from course to course. Today, bricks rarely support the weight of a building and are used as a durable siding called "brick veneer" and are

Figure 7.4. Flemish bond, which has stretchers and headers alternating with one another within each course. The presence of this bond indicates that a building was probably built before the late 1800s. Source: Photograph by Peter B. Dedek, 2011.

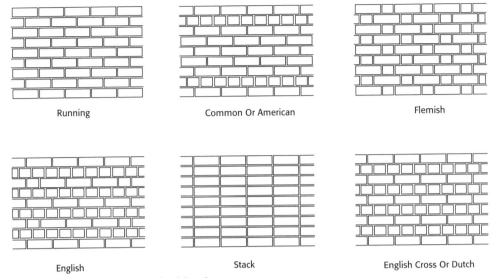

| Running | Common Or American | Flemish |
| English | Stack | English Cross Or Dutch |

Figure 7.5. Six of the most common brick bond types.

laid up on the very exterior of the wall in **running bond**, which is just one brick thick using only alternating courses of stretchers (Figure7.5).

In addition to being used in walls, bricks have been used historically to support the bases of buildings as foundations. Bricks usually made up either basement walls or piers, which were anchored into the ground and supported a wooden structure above. In the 1800s, the outer surface of brick foundation walls that were below ground were usually sealed with cement coatings. After 1900, such walls were usually sealed with tar instead. These layers helped keep ground and surface water from damaging the brick and flooding the cellar. If these protective coatings fail, they need to be replaced with a modern waterproof sealant also applied to the outside of the brick basement wall below grade.

Brick Preservation Issues

Because they are so porous, historic bricks tend to deteriorate if exposed to excessive water or moisture. Moisture can erode brick or cause it to break apart due to freeze-thaw cycles where water enters the brick and then freezes in cold weather, such as when temperatures drop below freezing at night. When water freezes inside a brick, it expands and can cause the face of the brick to crack and break off in a process called **spalling** (Figure 7.6). Water can also wash away the historic mortar, which usually was made up of a soft combination of lime and sand until the

Figure 7.6. A spalling brick wall damaged by water intrusion. About the only remedy for this is to find and stop the source of the water and rebuild the wall. Source: Photograph by Peter B. Dedek, 2010.

late 19th century. **Lime** is a fine, white powder that is manufactured by grinding up limestone or oyster shells and firing the resulting grit at high temperature in a kiln.

Since historic bricks have low tensile strength, they may crack if the foundations beneath them settle or subside significantly (see Chapter 8). If a brick wall is heavily damaged, it often must be torn down and rebuilt, which is a complicated and expensive process. Because the colors and textures of old bricks were not uniform, it is difficult to match the color of a historic brick wall using new or even salvaged bricks. Also, the replacement brick has to be the exact size and shape of the original, which can be difficult because previous to about 1900, brick sizes varied. Bricks can be custom produced to match historic material, but the per-brick cost is high, particularly if ordered in amounts of fewer than 20,000 (Stahl 1984). If possible during the reconstruction of a wall, damaged bricks are sometimes reversed so that their undamaged sides now face outward, restoring the wall's original appearance and integrity without having to match new brick with the original.

It is always the best practice to maintain and care for historic brick walls to avoid having to rebuild them. Methods of doing this include ensuring that walls are not exposed to flowing water, such as spillage from broken gutters, and that water is not allowed to pool against brick walls and soak into them. Also, unpainted brick should normally not be painted because paint alters the historic character of the brick and is often impossible to remove without seriously damaging the material. Brick mortar should be properly repointed with the appropriate mortar when the existing becomes deteriorated (see Chapter 8 for a discussion of mortars and repointing). When defects are found in the walls of historic brick buildings, the building's structure should be evaluated by an architect or engineer to ensure the building is safe and sound.

STONE

Stone has been used in important buildings since prehistoric times. When they desired to build substantial and permanent temples, tombs, and monuments, the Egyptians and the Greeks converted from wood to stone. When ancient peoples built in stone, they often mimicked earlier construction techniques used in wooden structures. For example, the Egyptians carved stone columns, which mimicked earlier columns made of bundled palm logs, and the Greeks designed stone Doric temples with decorative features, such as triglyphs, that mimicked the ends of large beams used in the timber frame construction of earlier wooden temples.

As with brick, stone was employed historically to construct thick, load-bearing walls and foundations. Stone was also used as a thin surface material or veneer and for decorative elements on historic buildings, such as gargoyles and grotesques, carved reliefs and ornate cornices. In early building projects, most stone was quarried close to the building site, but when steam-powered ships and locomotives were developed in the mid-19th century, specialty stone such as Vermont granite and Ohio sandstone, even Italian marble, began to be shipped over long distances. The use of stone for building varies by region depending on whether stone was available locally at the time the building was constructed, and if so, what types of stone were available to be collected or quarried near the site or shipped in. In parts of New York and New England, stone was common and found on or close to the surface and was used extensively, while in New Orleans and Florida and in many other coastal areas, little or no local building stone was available at all. Because of the difficulty and complexity of construction, stone was used for relatively permanent buildings.

All stone, including all building stone, falls into one of three categories: igneous, sedimentary, or metamorphic. **Igneous stone**, such as granite and basalt, was created deep in the earth directly by volcanic activity. It tends to be hard and durable (although not always). **Sedimentary stone**, such as sandstone and limestone, was created when silt or sand or fossils or a combination thereof settled in layers that gradually compressed and hardened into stone. Sedimentary stone is common in building and tends to be softer than most igneous rock. **Metamorphic stone**, such as marble and slate, was created when already existing rock was subjected to extreme heat and pressure and "metamorphosed" into a new stone deep underground. In building, these stones, especially marble, are often used in decorative applications.

Each variety of building stone has different qualities and preferred uses. Some common types of building stone are:

Granite

Granite, the hardest of all stone used in building, is an igneous rock that comes in various colors including white, red, pink, tan, and black. Granite has strong resistance to erosion from rain and wind and can last for thousands of years. For example, the Great Pyramids of Egypt, which have survived over 4,600 years, were constructed of granite blocks. Granite does not have bedding but can have small defects that can weaken the stone's integrity in places. Historically, granite was used for structural elements, such as walls and foundations, and at times for decorative elements, such as veneers, sculptures, and monuments. But the artistic detail on granite is usually fairly crude because the stone is difficult to carve. Today, sheets of granite are cut, often using diamond-headed tools or lasers, and polished and used as decorative veneers both on the exteriors and interiors of buildings. The stone is also popular for kitchen countertops.

Sandstone

Sandstone is a relatively hard sedimentary rock that comes in various colors including tan, pink, and brown. The brown version is referred to as "brownstone." Sandstone can be found in most parts of the world and is very common as a building stone. As a sedimentary rock formed from the accumulation and eventual hardening of layer upon layer of sands and silts, sandstone has layers, or bedding. Sandstone was used to construct the foundations and walls of many historic buildings, and some sandstone elements were carved and used as decorative elements.

Limestone

Limestone is a relatively soft, easily worked sedimentary stone that comes in a number of colors including white, grey, and red but is usually white or tan. Formed from the accumulation and compression of fossilized shells and other organic materials, limestone is soft and can erode

Figure 7.7. This granite column on the Texas state capitol has a carved limestone capital. Source: Photograph by Peter B. Dedek, 2008.

easily when exposed to environmental forces, such as acid rain and freezing water. Limestone is very common and was used in a great number of historic buildings for structural elements, such as walls and piers. The stone was also commonly used for decorative motifs as it is easily carved (Figure 7.7).

Travertine

Travertine forms in springs and waterfalls over millions of years, in hot springs most commonly. While travertine is being created, hot or cold water passes through existing limestone beds, leeches calcium and other minerals from the limestone, and carries it to the surface where the water evaporates, depositing calcium crystals in successive layers. As the layers form, they trap organic matter, such as plants, which then rots out leaving irregular holes and impressions in the resulting stone. Coming in colors including tan, orange, and green, travertine can be very decorative. The stone is also hard and was used in ancient Rome and in the Italian Renaissance for columns and in load-bearing walls as well as for veneers. Recently, it has been mostly used as a decorative face stone in high-end interiors. Travertine finishes were particularly favored in the art deco–style architecture of the 1920s and 1930s.

Marble

Marble, like travertine, forms from limestone, but in a very different process. Also like travertine, it was sometimes used to construct entire buildings, such as certain ancient Greek temples, but the stone was and is still used mostly as a veneer on both exteriors and interiors. **Marble** is a metamorphic stone created when limestone is subjected to heat and pressure underground. The heat and pressure cause the limestone's texture and composition to change in a process called crystallization. Impurities present in the limestone during the crystallization process alter the mineral composition of the marble. Because there is such a wide range of possible impurities, marble comes in a vast array of sometimes bright and striking colors often with a number of different hues or tones mixed in one slab. More than 250 colors of marble have been found in the United States alone. Marble is used mainly as a decorative face stone on building exteriors and interiors and for sculpture and tombstones. It is relatively soft and easy to carve and can be damaged by exposure to the weather, particularly in wet and cold climates. Marble was a favored material in neoclassical architecture because it was used so often by the ancient Greeks and Romans and during the Italian Renaissance.

Like marble, slate forms metamorphically. When shale, a sedimentary rock, undergoes tremendous heat and pressure, it transforms the clay present in the shale into mica and chlorite, altering the properties of the stone. Slate is bedded in very thin, brittle layers and is often used where uniform flat plates of stone are required, such as in roofing and floor tiles. It usually comes in grey or dark grey and, because of its hardness, resists weather well.

Stone in Load-Bearing Walls and Foundations

In many historic buildings, the type of stones used to build foundations and walls were natural, roundish stones, or flat, naturalistic field stones that were mortared together. This is called **rubble masonry construction** (Figure 7.8). Stone squared-off and carved into blocks called **ashlar masonry construction** was often used to construct more substantial and ornate buildings (Figure 7.9). Prior to the industrial revolution (around 1840 in America), ashlar construction was very expensive because of the difficult and time-consuming process of cutting stone by hand and the difficulty and expense of shipping it to a building site. In most cases, especially in North America, masons used some type of mortar between the stones in both kinds of stone construction. Before the 20th century, most mortar was lime based, whereas after 1900 harder Portland cement-based mortars were increasingly used.

Until the turn of the 20th century, most buildings constructed in places where stone was readily available were constructed on wide footings of stacked flat stones laid out in trenches with rubble stone foundations built directly on top of them. Brick, wood, or stone walls were then constructed above the rubble foundations (Shopsin 1986).

Some walls were built entirely of solid stone, while many had brick load-bearing walls behind with stone facings or veneers, especially after 1850. In many 19th- and early-20th-century buildings, stone was used for decorative elements, such as lintels, pediments, and cornices on otherwise brick buildings.

Figure 7.8. Rubble stone walls are constructed with natural stones mortared together. Source: Photograph by Peter B. Dedek, 2008.

Figure 7.9. Ashlar stone construction uses stones that have been squared off into blocks, which are then laid up and usually mortared together. This stone has been "rusticated" by beveling the blocks at the seams to accentuate them and create texture. Source: Photograph by Peter B. Dedek, 2008.

Because sedimentary stone formed over time from layers of sediment, it has **bedding**, meaning that layers within—which in some ways resemble wood grain—run in a particular direction. When building a wall, masons usually lay the stone so that the bedding is horizontal and thus perpendicular to the direction of the loads they must bear from the weight of stones and other building elements above. In some cases, however, masons laid stone so that the bedding planes were perpendicular to the ground and parallel to the exposed face of the stone. This is called face bedding, and it often has led to decay as the weaker grain of the stone peels away and flakes off layer by layer over time. Although face bedding is considered an inferior method of building with stone, it was practiced fairly commonly. Face bedding allows water seeping down from above to soak into the layers of stone in a wall, exposing the stone to erosion and further damage due to freeze-thaw cycles. Face bedding was often used in the brownstones (row houses) that were popular in Northeastern cities, especially in New York, between around 1850 and 1900. The softness of the brownstone itself combined with the use of face bedding has caused many conservation issues in these otherwise impressive historic buildings (Friedman 2010).

All types of stone have tiny pores that allow them to absorb water. Some stone, such as limestone and sandstone, absorb water fairly easily, while others, such as granite and slate, are relatively water-resistant. Stonework can be damaged by environmental factors such as acid rain, oxidizing metal elements such as tie rod ends, bronze fittings, and iron balconies (Shopsin 1986). Sometimes special sealants can be used to stop stone from absorbing water, however the best practice is to prevent water from pouring over or pooling on the stone to begin with (see Chapter 8). As with brick, matching new stone to historic stone is difficult because many of the old quarries are closed, and because as stone ages it can change in color as it gains a patina due to weather, pollution, and sunlight.

CONCRETE

Concrete is an artificial compound material made up of sand, gravel, and cement, which has a great deal of compressive strength but, if not reinforced, not so much tensile strength. Before the invention of Portland cement, cement was usually a mixture of lime and clay, sometimes combined with other materials, such as sand. Due to chemical reactions among the ingredients, cement hardens once its components, which have been made wet and mixed together, begin to set. **Hydraulic cement**, which can dry while damp and can even set up when submerged under water in some applications, was first invented by the ancient Romans around 200 BC when they mixed slaked lime with pozzolana, a volcanic ash found near Mount Vesuvius.

Well-mixed and cured concrete can grow harder and harder as it cures over time. The dome of the Pantheon, made of Roman concrete in 125 AD, still stands today. After the fall of the Roman Empire in around 600 AD, the technology of making concrete was lost until the 1400s, and hydraulic cement was not reinvented until 1756, when John Smeaton, a British engineer, reformulated it. In 1824, Joseph Aspdin invented Portland cement, which is made from a mixture of clay and limestone that is crushed and fired in a kiln at temperatures of up to 1500 degrees Celsius. Portland makes a much harder concrete than other cements and was used widely by the 20th century.

A French lawyer demonstrated that concrete could be reinforced with iron rods called **rebar** when he exhibited a boat that he had made of reinforced concrete at the Paris Exhibition of 1855. Reinforcement allows concrete to not only have great compressive strength but gives it significant tensile strength as well, making it much more versatile than plain concrete. In the United States, Ernest Ransome experimented with constructing sidewalks and bridges using reinforced concrete in the 1880s and successfully built factories using the material in the 1890s. In addition to its tensile strength, the material's main advantage is its resistance to damage from fire. Along with Portland cement, reinforced concrete came into common use in the 20th century (Weaver 1993).

Concrete can be used essentially in any situation where the use of stone or brick would be appropriate, because, unlike stone, it is a malleable material; it is poured wet into forms and can be molded into many shapes, giving the material many uses and making for greater flexibility in architectural design. With the invention of reinforced concrete, the uses for concrete increased dramatically.

Concrete in Load-Bearing Walls and Foundations

Modern reinforced concrete is much stronger than historic concrete, which was prone to crumbling. Before reinforced concrete, concrete walls cracked if there was any settling beneath the building, and it was not often used for foundations; because of its tensile strength, reinforced concrete is now nearly universally used for foundations. In the early- and mid-19th century, builders experimented with concrete or "hydraulic lime" as a material for constructing foundations and walls, and examples exist, but its use did not become widespread until the 20th century. As more and more 20th-century buildings become historic, studying and implementing methods of conserving historic reinforced concrete will become increasingly important.

Cast Stone

Cast stone, also called "artificial stone," is actually unreinforced concrete formed into blocks designed to mimic ashlar stone. It was used as a cheap alternative to authentic stone in the late 19th (after about 1865) and early 20th centuries (Figure 7.10). Builders used cast stone in

Figure 7.10. This historic late-19th-century train station was constructed of cast stone. Source: Photograph by Peter B. Dedek, 2012.

situations where natural stone could be employed, such as for constructing load-bearing walls, and forming decorative elements such as lintels, arches, and cornices; however where the material was used for lintels, usually the actual load was borne by a concealed iron or steel beam or by a brick arch. Because it could be molded into nearly any shape and formulated to simulate a wide variety of stone colors, cast stone was used extensively for carved elements, reliefs, and sculptures in ornate buildings in the late 1800s and early 1900s. The material was particularly useful in buildings with highly decorated styles, such as the Renaissance revival and art deco. Unfortunately, cast stone did not always have the strength and durability of authentic stone and often has been subject to decay. The material can be fairly easily identified by observing the unnatural uniformity of the blocks used in walls.

Concrete Preservation Issues

Concrete is a durable material; however it, like any masonry, it can fall victim to damage from settling and erosion, and particularly from being exposed to water. Older concrete is generally more subject to damage than modern concrete. Aggregates such as cinders and crushed brick used in some early concretes absorb water and made the material weak when exposed to moisture. All concrete can soak up some water and can be damaged by it, particularly when absorbed water freezes and expands. In some cases, the historic concrete was not mixed correctly in the first place, causing it to decay prematurely. Major signs of concrete damage include cracking, spalling, bending or sagging, stains, erosion, and corrosion (Coney 1986).

Reinforced concrete can become particularly vulnerable if the rebar was inserted too close to the surface. If the surface of the concrete becomes saturated with water, the concrete may absorb the water, and this can cause the metal rebar to rust inside the concrete. When iron or steel rusts, it expands, which causes the concrete to crack and spall, often exposing the rebar, which makes it rust further, increasing the damage to the concrete structure (Figure 7.11).

Figure 7.11. This concrete pier has been damaged due to water intrusion rusting the rebar and spalling off the concrete. Source: Photograph by Peter B. Dedek, 2008.

ARCHITECTURAL TERRA-COTTA

Architectural terra-cotta is a relatively soft blend of fired clays. In the United States, terra-cotta was commonly used in the late 19th and early 20th centuries to construct and decorate buildings. Ancient in origin, terra-cotta was used by the Egyptians, Mesopotamians, Greeks, and Romans. Use of the material faded away in Europe during the middle ages but reemerged in the Renaissance. The material, which usually comes in the form of glazed tile, continued to be used throughout the Islamic world and in parts of Asia throughout the middle ages.

Terra-Cotta in Load-Bearing Walls and Veneers

Terra-cotta can act both as a structural material to construct walls and as an ornamental material to decorate the exteriors and interiors of buildings. Terra-cotta employed for structural purposes was usually cast in hollow blocks with an open side and reinforced with internal strengtheners called web- bing, which increased the material's compressive load-bearing capacity without significantly increas- ing its weight. As a structural material, terra-cotta was cheap, strong, relatively light, and fire resistant.

Figure 7.12. Hollow terra-cotta blocks were used in the ear- ly 20th century to build inexpensive, load-bearing walls for small buildings. They were also used for non-load-bearing interior walls. Source: Photograph by Peter B. Dedek, 2008.

Terra-cotta blocks were used extensively in the United States during the late 19th and early 20th centuries for sheathing or "cladding" the steel frames of early skyscrapers and to construct the cores of interior and exterior walls (Figure 7.12). Terra-cotta provided fire protection and insu- lation for steel beams that would be likely to bend and possibly collapse if exposed directly to intense heat.

Terra-cotta was also used as a veneer to sheath and decorate the outsides of buildings, including those of many early skyscrapers. Some terra-cotta used on exteriors was unglazed, but it proved difficult to clean, so glaze was often applied to the surface by the end of the 19th cen- tury (Figure 7.13). Glaze not only made the terra-cotta easier to clean, it also allowed architects

Figure 7.13. Glazed terra-cotta was widely used as an exterior material in the late 19th and early 20th centuries. Although decorative and attractive, the mate- rial has often fallen prey to cracking and water intrusion, especially in harsh climates, and can pose serious challenges to preservationists. Source: Photograph by Peter B. Dedek, 2008.

to use the strong, naturalistic colors that had become popular in the late Victorian era with the introduction of the Arts and Crafts, Art Nouveau, and Beaux-Arts styles and in the early 20th century with the popularity of the Art Deco style (Figure 7.14). Because it can be cast in molds and fired in large quantities fairly inexpensively, terra-cotta allows for a great deal of design flexibility and for the inclusion of decorative detail, which would be very expensive if similar finishes were carved in stone or wood. Like cast stone, terra-cotta can be employed to simulate carved stone. At times, glazed terra-cotta on a historic building's façade looks so much like stone that it has been mistaken for it.

Terra-Cotta Preservation Issues

Despite its advantages, terra-cotta poses a number of significant conservation issues. Terra-cotta used on building exteriors has failed in many instances. Terra-cotta blocks used in some types of cladding systems in historic skyscrapers have spalled, requiring significant repairs or even replacement. Exposure to water is a significant cause of damage to the material. The clay body of terra-cotta is quite soft and porous and will absorb water if exposed to it. If, for instance, because of a leaking gutter or a design defect in the roof or eaves, water runs down or into a wall clad in terra-cotta tiles, it may seep into cracks between the tiles. If this happens, water will soak into the clay, making it expand. This can have a number of deleterious effects. One is that since the glaze doesn't expand along with the clay, expansion will often crack the clay causing "crazing," which isn't a major problem in itself, except that continued expansions and contractions

Figure 7.14. Glazed terra-cotta was ideal for the geometric patterns used on Art Deco architecture as seen here on the historic S & W Cafeteria built in 1929 in Asheville, North Carolina. Source: Photograph by Peter B. Dedek, 2008.

can begin to create deeper cracks in the clay as well, possibly making it break over time. Sometimes water can well up behind the glaze and pop the glaze surface off. This is much more likely if the water absorbed by the clay body freezes and expands.

Another result of terra-cotta expanding due to water is that the clay body may expand too much for the space where it was installed, which can cause bulging, cracking, and spalling when the tiles push against each other and the brackets that hold them on or against the mortar between them. Sometimes this can even cause tiles to break up and fall off or to lose their glazed faces. Once lost, historic terra-cotta elements are nearly impossible to repair and difficult to replace. Terra-cotta is also quite brittle and will break when put under stress when elements of a building settle.

Sometimes the metal anchors that hold terra-cotta onto the exteriors of historic buildings rust and fail, causing the tiles to loosen or fall off, which can even become a danger to people passing below a tall building's façades. Unfortunately, it is difficult to detect failing anchoring until visible damage to the tiles has already occurred. Architectural terra-cotta needs to be inspected on a regular basis, and the key to preserving it is to ensure that water and freeze-thaw does not penetrate a terra-cotta system (Tiller 1979).

NONMASONRY HISTORIC BUILDING MATERIALS

The nonmasonry historic building materials to be discussed here are wood, metals, and glass. Although none are considered masonry, the three types of materials are very different from each other. Most wood is lighter and less permanent than masonry, while metal is more permanent and heavier, as is glass. While masonry tends to have a good deal of compressive strength and not as much tensile strength (with the exception of reinforced concrete), nonmasonry materials (wood and metal) have both compressive and tensile strength, while most glass is dense but brittle.

WOOD

Wood was probably the first material used in building and continues to be a common architectural material in both structural and decorative applications. The material is used for nearly every kind of architectural element, such as joists, posts, walls, roofs, siding, flooring, doors, windows, and shutters. Wood has been favored in building because of its abundance, its strength both in compression and tension, its lightness, and its ease of working. In the English colonies along North America's Atlantic coast and in other heavily wooded areas, wood was plentiful and was available as a building material as a by-product of the clearing of forests for farm fields. However extensive clearing of forests eventually made wood less abundant in many regions.

Many historic buildings built before the 1940s in America are made almost entirely of wood, especially residences. Even historic buildings from the 19th and early 20th centuries with brick or stone walls usually have significant wooden elements, such as beams, posts, roofs, and floors. The conservation of wood is very significant for historic preservation in America.

Wood used in buildings comes in many varieties and from many species of trees. There are two basic classifications of wood: **hardwoods**, which generally come from deciduous trees (those that drop their leaves in the winter) and **softwoods**, which come from conifers, commonly known as pine trees. Although hardwoods are not always denser or stronger than softwoods (balsa wood, for example, the soft and light wood used in architectural models, is technically a hardwood, and cypress, a durable and dense wood that resists rot, is technically a softwood), most softwoods, such as southern pine, are lighter and softer than most hardwoods, such as oak. Softwoods were more commonly used in architecture, while hardwoods were more often used in furniture construction, although hardwoods were also used in interior applications, such as staircases, trim, and flooring. The varieties of wood found in historic buildings often depended on what species of trees were available locally. This is particularly true before railroads arrived to a particular locale. Oak is a typical hardwood used in interiors.

Wood in Load-Bearing Walls and Structures

Wood is both a structural and a finish material. Before around 1850, most buildings in the United States were built using timber frame structures. **Timber-frame buildings** are constructed out of heavy posts and beams that are normally joined together with mortise and tenon construction in which **tenons** (squared-off chiseled projections) are joined with **mortises** (squared-off chiseled holes) and pegged together (Figure 7.15). Before wire nails were made available in the early 20th century, more expensive square or cut nails were needed, making timber framing more economically viable than it would be in the 20th century, when cheap wire nails became available. Also, as forests were cut down in the mid-1800s for lumber and other purposes, such as fuel for iron furnaces, the resource became increasingly scarce.

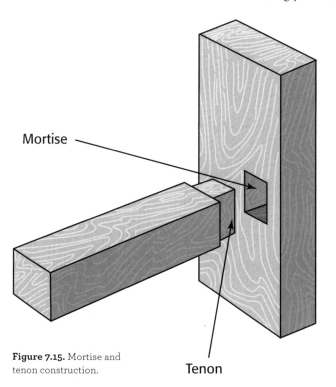

Mortise

Tenon

Figure 7.15. Mortise and tenon construction.

In the mid-1800s, in part because of the rising cost of wood, most American builders began constructing buildings using long rough-cut two-by-fours and two-by-sixes along with wider boards used as beams held together by nails in a system called **balloon framing** (Figure 7.16). In the late 19th century, most builders converted to stud-frame construction, which is still used today. In **stud-frame construction**, also called **platform framing**, each successive story of a building is constructed separately using shorter studs and posts, rather than the tall vertical studs that extend up two or more floors used in balloon framing. Structural boards are planed smooth today but were mostly left rough cut until the mid-20th century. Planed wood has smaller dimensions than historic rough cut boards, for example, a modern two-by-four is actually only 1½ by 3½ inches.

Wood was also used for finish material, such as pine for millwork and paneled walls (historically, paneled wooden walls were made of the solid wood used in old Georgian farm houses, not photo-grain Masonite paneling of modern ranch houses) and hardwood for floors. Interior applications of wood will be discussed later in this chapter.

Wood Preservation Issues

The conservation of wood focuses on two main areas, structural integrity and aesthetic appearance. Each involves different methods, but the most important thing for the conservator to keep in mind is to find the source of the damage and not to just treat symptoms.

Both hardwoods and softwoods are porous and vulnerable to damage from water intrusion, rot, and insects. Wood also expands and contracts with changes in humidity and temperature across its grain (but very little along the length of the grain, meaning that the width of a board can change but not its length). Changes in wood due to humidity can cause the structures of buildings to shift over time as boards expand and contract and sometimes buckle and warp over time and become damaged (Figure 7.17). Fortunately, because much of the wood used in historic

Figure 7.16. Balloon framing like this was used mainly in the late 19th century. Source: Photograph by Peter B. Dedek, 2012.

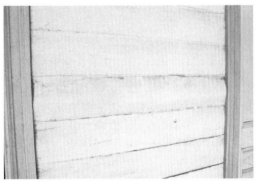

Figure 7.17. This wood on the exterior of a house built in 1839 has buckled due to over a century and a half of expansion and contraction due to hot and humid Texas weather conditions. Source: Photograph by Peter B. Dedek, 2012.

buildings (at least those built before 1900) was from old growth forests, it tends to be denser and more durable than the wood used in building today.

Preservationists often deal with historic wooden elements that are in various states of deterioration. The best way to prevent deterioration is to keep wood dry by keeping puddles, flowing water, and excessive humidity away. Moisture is the mortal enemy of wood. However, wood is also vulnerable to fire, especially wood in historic buildings, which tends to have a low moisture content when sheltered from the elements. Wood can also become damaged due to defects in the wood itself, such as knots; abrasion from foot traffic in the case of floors; being chewed or eaten by animals such as rats, termites, and carpenter ants; photodegradation from exposure to sunlight; and thermal degradation due to exposure to high temperatures over time, and also from weathering from wind, dust, and sand (Weaver 1993). These and other threats to wood will be discussed further in Chapter 8. Despite wood's vulnerabilities, well-maintained wooden structures can last for centuries.

METALS

Metals have been used in historic architecture as structural support, roofing, decorative elements, and even entire façades. Metal's high compressive and tensile strength, durability, and the fact that metal architectural components can be industrially mass-produced are factors that have made use of the material in building widespread since the late 19th century.

Wrought and Cast Iron

Wrought or "worked" **iron** is formed into rods and pounded by a blacksmith into bars, which can be twisted or hammered into various shapes. The hammering and working process helps to strengthen the metal by dispelling the carbon contained within the metal. **Cast iron,** on the other hand, is refined iron ore that is melted and poured into molds to create diverse shapes. While cast iron can be molded into a wide variety of forms, it is high in carbon and is generally more brittle and weak than wrought iron. Both types of iron were extensively used in historic architecture in America.

Like terra-cotta, wrought iron was used both as a structural material and as decorative one in historic buildings. In the middle of the 19th century, the iron truss was invented, which could be used in place of wooden trusses or masonry arches. One of the first major applications of using iron trusses in architecture was London's Crystal Palace, designed by Joseph Paxton in 1851. This giant structure, which housed an international exposition and covered eighteen acres, had a frame made of iron with cast iron columns and wrought iron trusses. Wrought iron, which is more flexible and has more tensile strength than cast iron, was also used as pins and tie rods to hold blocks of masonry together in a variety of 19th-century buildings and later as rebar in concrete.

Since wrought iron is worked and can be bent or hammered into shapes and welded, it was used in a lot of ornamental iron work, especially in the railings of balconies, porches, and staircases. It is easily identifiable by its iron strips often worked by hand into delicate patterns (Figure 7.18). As an architectural material, wrought iron is very durable and is usually only damaged by rust as the result of being exposed to excess moisture and not being painted or if it is damaged by powerful forces, such as being struck by a vehicle or by falling trees during a storm.

Cast iron was used for both structural and decorative purposes as well. Because of its great compressive strength, cast iron was employed to create nonflammable columns as early as the late 1700s in England and applied in the same function by the 1820s in the United States. By the 1840s, cast iron was being used for entire storefronts and building façades and soon thereafter, builders began experimenting with entire structural cast iron frames for buildings. Strong and able to be molded in many shapes, cast iron could be molded to mimic all kinds of decorative masonry while requiring much less on-site labor to construct, because it consisted of industrially produced interchangeable parts that were manufactured in large amounts and shipped to a site. The material was also marketed as being fireproof, although it tended to twist under extreme heat, causing buildings to collapse.

Cast iron was also molded into intricate railings and other decorative elements that were used widely during the 19th century and the beginning of the 20th. Examples can still be found on the interiors and exteriors of historic buildings across America. The French Quarter in New Orleans is famous for the wide use of wrought and cast iron on its buildings. Cast iron was also used in the 19th century for fences and gates, lampposts, outdoor furniture, and even in the production of iron gravestones and entire mausoleums (Figure 7.19).

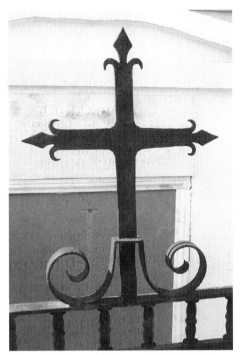

Figure 7.18. A wrought-iron cross in St. Louis Cemetery Number One, New Orleans. Source: Photograph by Peter B. Dedek, 2012.

Figure 7.19. An intricate cast-iron fence in St. Louis Cemetery Number One, New Orleans. Source: Photograph by Peter B. Dedek, 2012.

The main threat to cast iron is from rusting, which can occur in unprotected cast iron at humidity levels of over 65 percent, which is not uncommon in the eastern, midwestern, and south-central states. Also, a deterioration process called **galvanic corrosion** can occur when cast or wrought iron has been welded or otherwise connected with nonferrous metals, such as lead and copper, and is then exposed to moisture. The joining of the metals causes an electrochemical reaction that deteriorates the iron. Exposure to polluted air, acid rain, and saltwater can also damage iron, especially if they enter stress cracks (Waite 1991).

To protect iron, it should be cleaned if rusted. Unlike other historic building materials, iron can be sandblasted so long as the iron elements are removed from the building before being cleaned. Then the metal needs to be properly primed and painted. Even painted iron needs to be protected from direct and consistent contact with standing or flowing water.

Nonferris Metals in Historic Architecture

Copper and copper alloys such as bronze and brass were also used in historic architecture. Copper was sometimes made into roofing sheets, which would oxidize creating a green coating that protects the copper from further oxidation. Copper makes good roofing, but it expands and contracts due to changes in temperature and must be installed in ways using expansion joints that compensate for this, or the metal will become damaged by ripping or buckling. Copper was also used for architectural elements besides roofing, including gutters, dormers, flashing, cornices, hardware, vents, and wall tiles.

Except for sheet roofing, brass and bronze can be used for many of the same elements in buildings as copper. Brass, an alloy of copper and zinc, and bronze, an alloy of copper and tin, were used for ornamental elements, such as railings and flagpoles, where strength and resistance to corrosion due to environmental factors such as marine air and acidic rain were required. Although harder than copper, both metals are soft compared to iron and should not be sandblasted.

Additional nonferrous metals that can be found on historic building façades and interiors are aluminum, tin (as a coating over iron or steel sheets and gutters), and lead.

GLASS

Early glass was a combination of silica and soda ash heated to high temperatures. Glass used for historic windows often contained silica sand, soda ash, lime, and perhaps a small amount of alumina-silicate and salt cake all heated up to a temperature of over 1,500 degrees Celsius. Although the Ancient Egyptians and Mesopotamians made glass beads and tableware, the ancient Romans were the first to produce glass windows sometime before 79 AD (glass windows were unearthed at Pompeii, which was destroyed in 79 AD). Roman windowpanes were small and thick and not very transparent, but they did let in light.

Clear glass was used in the early middle ages, and stained glass was installed extensively in medieval cathedrals in the 1100s. Although expensive and only somewhat transparent, windowpanes were found in many Renaissance-era buildings often held in place with lead dividers. In 1688, the French developed a method of making flat glass panels that were polished smooth, mainly for the production of mirrors, but the panes made with this process were very expensive. This is the reason that Louis XIV's Hall of Mirrors at Versailles was such an extravagant display of wealth.

Until around 1800, glass panes were usually expensive, thick, small, handmade, and full of bubbles. Most early panes had a "crown" of thicker glass at their centers, which was a product of how early panes were produced: by pouring out a circular glass plate, allowing it to cool, and then cutting the plate into one or more rectangular panes. This is the reason that many older panes are thicker at the bottom than at the top. A common explanation for this is that hardened glass flows down with gravity over long periods of time like a liquid, but this is a misconception.

After 1800, glass panes slowly grew larger, less flawed, and less expensive. In fact, if a building still retains its original windows, one can loosely determine its date of construction by the size and type of window panes it has (see Chapter 9). Originally used almost exclusively for windows and sometimes for mirrors, glass became a more versatile architectural material in the late 19th century, when it was specified for skylights as well as windows. In the late 19th century, glass manufacturers created large plate-glass windows, and structural glass block in the 20th. Glass panels were used to cover storefronts and even entire exterior walls in the modern "glass box" skyscrapers of the 1950s through the 1970s.

Glass Preservation Issues

Although brittle and easily broken, glass is actually very durable if not put under shearing stress and can last thousands of years. It is not subject to water damage or erosion from wind except in extreme conditions. The greatest danger to historic glass is the specter of window replacement (Figure 7.20). Another danger to glass comes from flying debris due to storms or destruction by vandals.

When twisting or shearing pressure is exerted on a pane through the window sash (the wooden or metal frame directly around the glass), the glass may crack or break. This can occur if a building is settling in a way that makes a window no longer square, or when the lintel above a window gives way and puts stress on the sash and the glass held in place by it. Cracks in glass

Figure 7.20. These modern replacement windows reduce the historic integrity of this early-20th-century building. Source: Photograph by Peter B. Dedek, 2008.

panes are often a clue that the window opening is being stressed by instability from underneath, above, or within the surrounding wall. To protect glass from this danger, the causes of the structural deficiency creating the pressure have to be addressed. Also, in order to protect historic glass, the windows in all unoccupied buildings should be boarded up. Boarding windows also protects the interior from exposure to weather, vandals, and pests.

STUCCO

Stucco is a plaster-like material that is applied to the exteriors of buildings to both beautify and protect them. Stucco on historic buildings was usually not applied for a decorative purpose, but to protect the structural building materials underneath, such as when stucco covers adobe. The soft brick used in the early 19th century and before often did not hold up in wet and humid climates and was sometimes stuccoed during the initial construction or at a later time to protect the brick from rain, atmospheric humidity, or flowing or pooled water. Therefore, a great deal of historical research on a building should be done before removing historic stucco. Anyone considering taking off stucco should determine if it was present during the building's period of historical significance. If so, the protective coating should be preserved and repaired if necessary rather than being removed or completely replaced.

Stucco has been a common building material since prehistoric times and was used extensively in the ancient world to protect and beautify buildings made of mud bricks (which constituted the vast majority of houses, markets, and other types of buildings in Egypt, Greece, and Rome). In the New World, the Pueblo Indians also used stucco to protect their adobe structures. Stucco has been in use ever since and is particularly associated in America with the Spanish Colonial and Spanish Colonial Revival styles, but was used on buildings in other styles as well, such as on modern art deco- and Bauhaus-inspired buildings. In some cases, as with many buildings designed in the Greek Revival style from the 1820s to the 1860s, stucco was applied to brick walls and then scored or painted to make the material imitate stone blocks. Sometimes, stucco was applied to a wall using some form of lath to help attach it to the wall.

Until the late 19th century, stucco was primarily a lime-based mixture often combined with sand and sometimes horsehair or straw as a binder. Most stucco mixtures used hydrated or "slaked" lime, and stucco walls were often whitewashed. After the late 19th century, Portland cement was added to make the stucco harder and more durable. Portland stucco could also be applied over a wider variety of materials, including wood.

Stucco Preservation Issues

As with restoring or replacing historic mortar, Portland-based stucco should never be used to make repairs to or to replace historic lime-based stucco. Being harder and less resilient, the Portland will not expand and contract with the historic materials that it is attached to and will likely detach from the surface to which it was applied and eventually fall off. Any new stucco used to repair or replace historic stucco should have a formula comparable to that of the original and should be applied by a professional plasterer. Historic stucco also breathes and allows water from inside the wall to evaporate and therefore should not be given highly water-resistant sealants. Instead, the sealant should be one that resists some water, but also is porous enough to allow for evaporation from within (Grimmer 1990).

COMMON HISTORIC INTERIOR FINISH MATERIALS

Many of the materials used in exteriors can also be found in historic interiors. However, interior elements tend to be more refined, intricate, and vulnerable to water. The treatment and conservation of interiors of buildings in good condition involves less need to protect from the elements, but more precautions from wear and damage due to use by people.

WOOD IN INTERIORS

Wood is present in nearly all historic interiors. Irreplaceable old-growth lumber with a tight grain was often used in historic interiors. It is also important to preserve the fine craftsmanship often evident in the wooden elements found in historic interiors.

Wooden Walls

Wood was used in wall paneling from the colonial period to the present and is a common flooring material. Most historic trim and interior features, such as staircases and fireplace mantels, were also made of wood, which is usually painted or varnished. In walls, softwoods were usually the preferred material, although hardwood was sometimes used where it was abundant. Before plywood was invented in the 20th century, walls that were finished in wood or had wooden wainscot often had pieces of wood artfully fit together as Georgian paneling or notched together as bead or tongue-and-groove boards (Figure 7.21). Doors were also often paneled. In less sophisticated 19th-century interiors, interior walls were sometimes made of plain wooden planks laid horizontally and then covered with wall cloth, which was sometimes painted. Tongue-and-groove boards, invented in the 1800s to reduce buckling, were used as a wainscot

Figure 7.21. Classic Georgian paneling from Drayton Hall built in 1738 near Charleston, South Carolina. Source: Photograph by Peter B. Dedek, 2007.

and wall finish in less expensive buildings and in utilitarian areas such as kitchens, halls, attics, bathrooms, and in public areas, such as railroad station waiting rooms. The boards were either stained or painted (Shopsin 1986).

Wooden Trim

Historic wood trim was designed and installed for both aesthetic and functional reasons. Moldings hide gaps and imperfections around openings in walls, and baseboard protects wall materials, such as plaster, from being struck by feet and furniture. Chair rails, picture rails, and wainscot also protect plaster from damage as well as being attractive (Figure 7.22). Wooden cornices (molding where the walls intersect with the ceiling) also hide imperfections and can give a room a sense of unity and grandeur. The proportions and décor of the wooden trim often determine the style of an interior.

Wooden Floors

In residential and many commercial interiors built before the mid-1800s, most floors were pine, and generally, the older the building, the wider the floor planks. The reason floor planks were wider before the late 1800s is most of the wood being harvested came from old-growth trees with wide trunks. Other types of wood were common in areas where they could be found in abundance. For example, poplar flooring was common in the Midwest from an early date. However, hardwoods, such as hickory, chestnut, and walnut, were increasingly used for flooring after 1870. Sometimes, carpenters installed new hardwood floors over earlier floors. Hardwood floors after the 1880s sometimes had intricate industrially produced patterned parquetry, the designs of which were based on the handmade parquet floors dating from the French baroque period of the 1600s and 1700s.

Figure 7.22. This music room at the French Legation house, built in 1839 in Austin, Texas, shows the aesthetic and practical aspects of wooden trim and wainscot. Source: Photograph by Peter B. Dedek, 2012.

Wood used in interiors can be vulnerable to insects, rot due to water intrusion, mold, and also to wear from touching and use by people. It helps if the conservator can identify the wood species used in a given historic interior. Some species, such as many softwoods, are more prone to decay and require more urgent action than wood that is more dense and moisture resistant, such as many hardwoods like maple. Wood identification in historic environments can be difficult, however, because historic stains and other finishes can mask identifying attributes such as the grain type.

Often rotten or severely damaged wood elements have to be replaced. They should be replaced with new wood as close as possible to the original in species and design. When matching unpainted wood, use the same species wherever possible. Usually historic woodwork is not found in the standard sizes used today and must be custom cut. Ornate molding either has to be custom fabricated or reproduced using another material such as fiberglass, which is lighter and less expensive; but of course such trim must be painted to simulate the appearance of the historic trim and cannot be used if the historic trim has a natural finish.

Wooden floors, particularly those made of softwoods, are subject to wear and staining. It is important that they not be sanded harshly; in cases of early floors, they should not be sanded at all, but should be sealed with a protective coating and shielded from excessive foot traffic, especially in house museums and other interiors open to the public. Hardwood floors can withstand more sanding than pine, but they should be sanded by experts as do-it-yourselfers can easily gouge the surface with an electric sander. Severely damaged wood floors or those with failing subflooring or joists sometimes have to be removed and reinstalled or encapsulated by being covered by new flooring, which should always be removable without damaging the original floor. If a specific area of a floor is damaged, sometimes matching flooring can be removed from a secondary space, such as an attic or a closet and used to make excellent repairs in visible areas.

PLASTER

Plaster is similar to stucco, but rather than being an exterior finish, it's used to cover interior walls and ceilings in order to provide a paintable, durable interior surface that can be applied to a wide variety of structural wall materials and can even be used to make walls that are angled or curved in creative ways. Like stucco, plaster has been in use since prehistoric times all over the world, and also like historic stucco, lime was a primary ingredient. Until the late 19th century, plasterers used a combination of lime, sand, animal hair, and water to compose plaster. The animal hair was used as a binder, similar to how straw is used in adobe. Around 1900, gypsum, a common mineral that dissolves easily in water, was introduced as an alternate plastering material. Gypsum gained favor because it sets up more quickly than lime and has a harder surface. Another reason gypsum replaced lime is lime plaster dried very slowly and could even take as long as a full year to dry completely, while gypsum plaster usually dries in around two weeks. Plaster is normally held in place by some sort of backing material, called lath.

Types of Lath

Lime plaster was sometimes applied directly to an interior surface of brick or stone, but in wooden buildings (and in many masonry buildings as well) lath had to be used. **Lath** is a material that plasterers attach to the interior surface of a wall to provide a rough surface for the wet plaster to attach onto. There are three basic types of historic lath:

- **Wood lath**, which consists of narrow strips of rough wood that are nailed to the studs or joists (Figure 7.23). With wooden lath, wet plaster is pressed against the wooden strips with a trowel, causing beads or "keys" of plaster to ooze between the boards and harden on the lath's back side, helping to hold the plaster onto the wall or ceiling. Wooden lath was used well into the early 20th century.

- **Metal lath**, which came into use in the late 19th century and is still used today, consists of a metal grid or screen that is attached to the wall. It creates a stronger bond because it holds a greater density of plaster keys than wood lath. Since it comes in sheets, metal lath is easier to install and is stronger than wooden lath as well. It is also highly fire resistant. Its one disadvantage is that it will rust if exposed to moisture and can sometimes fail because of excessive rusting.

- **Rock lath** came into use after 1900 and was used extensively after 1930. Rock lath comes in the form of sheets made up of compressed gypsum board faced with paper. Rock lath sheets are nailed to the wall. Some types are textured to key the plaster, and all provide a firm backing to the plaster and are the forerunner of contemporary plaster board or wallboard.

Types and Characteristics of Plaster Wall Treatments

Traditionally, plaster was applied in two and sometimes three coats. The first coat, called the **scratch coat**, formed the bulk of the plaster. The **finish coat**, which was usually only about one-eighth of an inch thick, provided a smooth surface.

Many historic interiors, especially inside Victorian-era and Renaissance-revival buildings, contain decorative plaster. Decorative plaster is often reinforced and molded into ornate shapes. Some can be simple plaster forms that mimic wooden or stone trim or cornices, while other plasterwork takes the form of ornate medallions in ceilings and fancy coffers, thick moldings, columns and pilasters, and interior sculpture designed to impress (Figure 7.24). By the late 1800s, many decorative plaster features were manufactured off-site and attached to the plaster walls in the building.

Plaster Preservation Issues

Water is, as one might guess, a major cause of damage to historic plaster, whether decorative or not (Figure 7.25). Gypsum plaster is actually more sensitive to water than lime plaster, and for this reason, gypsum plaster cannot

Figure 7.23. Wooden lath, such as this, holds the plaster to the wall. Rough-cut studs support the lath. Source: Photograph by Peter B. Dedek, 2007.

Figure 7.24. Handcrafted plaster medallion at Drayton Hall near Charleston, South Carolina. Source: Photograph by Peter B. Dedek, 2007.

Figure 7.25. Once lath is exposed to moisture, it can quickly lose its structural integrity. Source: Photograph by Peter B. Dedek, 2007.

be applied directly to the insides of masonry walls without the use of lath and some kind of moisture barrier. Historic plaster is also vulnerable to even minor settling of a building, which can make it easily crack or buckle. Vibrations from traffic, construction activity, or earth tremors, or failure of the lath behind it can also damage plaster, especially ornamental plaster (Figure 7.26). In some instances historic plaster fails because of poor workmanship, such as if it was applied to thinly or did not cure properly.

As with stucco, any new plaster used to repair historic plaster needs to match the composition of the historic material. All repairs should be done by qualified plasterers with guidance by a preservation architect, experienced interior designer, or a preservation specialist (MacDonald 1989).

Figure 7.26. This ornamental plaster cornice is buckling due to settling in the walls of the building. A brittle material, plaster cannot withstand much stress without cracking or buckling and can be a good indicator of structural problems. Source: Photograph by Peter B. Dedek, 2008.

PRESSED METAL CEILINGS

Pressed metal ceilings were a common treatment in many commercial and in some residential buildings from around 1885 to the 1920s. Often called "tin" ceilings, they were actually sheet steel squares sometimes coated with tin but more often just painted. The square metal sheets were pressed in a machine and embossed with attractive motifs that created regular, repetitive patterns, and modular geometry. They often were installed using matching metal cornices and medallions also made of pressed metal. Their use originally resulted from the imposition of fire codes, because metal was seen as being fire resistant, but they became popular because of their decorative quality. Metal ceilings had the look of molded plaster, but were far less expensive, were easy to install, and were not as subject as plaster to cracking and other damage. In their heyday, over 40 companies produced the ceiling panels in a wide variety of designs, and they were installed in interiors across the United States and Canada. The metal panels were also occasionally used on walls, particularly as decorative wainscot.

Pressed Metal Preservation Issues

When pressed metal is damaged, rust resulting from water intrusion from leaking roofs or plumbing or holes cut in them during upgrades to ventilation, heating, lighting, and other changes done to the building over time are usually the causes.

Dents can often be hammered out, and small holes can be repaired by attaching metal or fiberglass patches, however severely corroded or otherwise damaged panels must be replaced. Fortunately, the tiles are relatively easy to replace, because many of the dies originally used to produce individual panels historically still exist and are being used to make replacements available that match the originals exactly. If no dies exist for a particular pattern, the sheets can be custom produced based on the design of an intact existing panel, but this is more expensive.

CERAMIC TILE

Historically, tile was installed primarily on floors, but it can be found on walls mainly in bathrooms and kitchens. Historic tile was also used in the interior design of formal spaces, such as for wainscoting and flooring in foyers and lobbies and on fireplace hearths and fireplace facings. Much of the tile found in old interiors is terra-cotta similar to that used in exterior applications, but smaller and thinner. Other interior tile is of a vitrified, glazed variety.

Although earlier examples exist, such as tile used during the English Colonial period for fireproof hearths for fireplaces in the eastern U.S. and tile used by Spanish colonists in the Southwest, much of the tile found in historic American interiors dates from between about 1865 and the 1930s. Tile was first mass-produced in the 1860s, making it cheaper and more available than earlier. Most tile used before the 1880s was dull-finish encaustic tile that came mostly in earthy browns but also in reds, greens, and blues. Glazed earthenware tile, often with strong naturalistic colors and printed or relief designs and pictures, became popular during the late Victorian era and can be found frequently in the craftsman style interiors of the early 1900s (Seale 1979). Glazed and unglazed terra-cotta tiles were also used extensively in Spanish Colonial Revival–style interiors in the early and mid-20th century.

Around 1890, pictorial mosaics with small tiles and inlaid marble ornamentation became popular due to the rise of the Renaissance revival and Beaux-Arts styles for high-end residential and public buildings. Mosaic patterns and pictures decorated the floors, walls, inside domes, and vaulted ceilings of many mansions, churches, theatres, major railroad stations, and government buildings. These artistic works are character-defining interior features that are very important to preserve.

Tile Preservation Issues

When the wall or floor structure behind tile and mosaics has been maintained and is sound, the finish material is often easy to keep clean and properly grouted. Unfortunately, since tiles, especially those in bathrooms and kitchens, are often exposed to destructive factors such as moisture and impacts, the material behind them can break down. Other causes, such as a building shifting or leaks in roofs or walls can damage the backing of tile and make the tiles fall off or crack or spall in place. Before tile is repaired the source of moisture, settling, or anything else that is damaging the tile should be investigated, discovered, and rectified. Replacing historic tile is nearly impossible unless the replacement tiles are custom reproduced, which is very expensive, often making it necessary to either remove the damaged tile completely or preserve it in place in a less than perfect condition.

PAINT

Invented in prehistory, paint remains the most common finish on building exteriors and interiors. Paint is made up of a **pigment**, which provides the color; a **liquid vehicle**, which allows the paint to be spread thinly over a surface; and a **binder**, a glue-like substance that holds the compound together and helps it stick to and grip the surface to which it is applied. Throughout the ages, the ingredients that perform these functions have gradually changed. In the ancient world, many colors such as blacks, browns, and reds were widely available, because the pigments needed to manufacture those colors were cheap and easily obtained. For other colors, such as blue and yellow, semiprecious stones were often ground up and used for the pigment, making those hues of paint scarce and expensive. As early as 200 AD in Rome, white paint was manufactured using white lead.

During the Renaissance and in the centuries that followed, paint technology developed and pigments for new colors, such as cobalt blue, crimson lake, indigo blue, and Prussian blue, became available. Paint for buildings, however, remained vulnerable to weather, and individual painters mixed their own colors, which makes exact historic colors difficult to replicate, although modern paint-matching technologies are rectifying this problem.

This changed when the resealing paint can was invented in 1877, allowing paint to be easily stored and manufactured on a large scale. Paint manufacturers invented the first washable paint called "Charleton white" in the 1870s. To sell more paint, paint companies produced a wider range of colors. The availability of additional colors led many economically advantaged homeowners to use multicolor paint schemes on their fancy Victorian era houses in the last decades of the 19th century. Despite advances in making whites brighter and making paint more durable, lead remained a key ingredient of paint until as late as 1978. It is amazing that lead was used in paint and gasoline into the 1970s given that the ancient Roman architect Vitruvius noted that lead was harmful in the first century BC, and in the 1860s lead poisoning was described as "painter's colic" (Virginia Department of Historical Resources 1993).

Dealing with lead paint is a serious issue in historic buildings. Any building built before 1940 certainly contains lead paint, and any building constructed up to 1978, when such paint was finally banned by a federal regulation, may well contain lead paint. Generally, if lead paint remains undisturbed its potential harmfulness is limited. However, when lead paint, particularly in interiors, becomes disturbed it can poison humans and animals. Lead, which builds up in the human body over time, causes a variety of health problems and is a serious health issue, particularly in young children. When lead paint peels and flakes it can leave tiny chips that can be tracked around and even makes dust that can become airborne and be breathed in. Renovation work can cause lead paint to get into the environment, and when lead paint has been scraped off or has peeled off over time on the exteriors of buildings, it can contaminate nearby soils and poison children or anyone else who comes in close contact with the soil.

In some cases, lead paint must be removed to make a historic building safe to inhabit, but normally it can be **encapsulated**, which means that the old paint is left in place and sealed over. Sometimes all that is necessary is that the old paint be painted over with a coat of new paint. When lead paint is removed, it should be done by specialists with experience in safe lead paint removal.

Paint Preservation Issues

Paint is one of the aspects of a building that requires the most frequent replacement. After six to eight years, most paint applied to an exterior, even quality oil-based paint, usually breaks down and has to be scraped off and replaced. Buildings need to be repainted regularly, because a healthy coat of paint helps impede water penetration. Keeping paint fresh also helps maintain a good appearance for historic buildings, and keeping them looking vibrant is an important factor in helping inspire people to be enthusiastic about preserving them.

As with so many historic materials and finishes, water intrusion causes paint to fail, as well as damaging the substrate material, such as wood or plaster behind it. Flaking paint, particularly if accompanied by stains, can be the first indication of a significant water issue in a historic interior (Figure 7.27).

Removing loose or peeling paint is a vital part of the process of repainting. Scraping paint is a painstaking and expensive process, and care should be taken not to use harsh means of removal on historic architecture. Torches used to remove paint have accidentally ignited wood within the walls of historic buildings and burned them down, and the use of rotary brushes and sanders to remove paint can seriously damage old wood and masonry.

Often during restorations and rehabilitations, buildings are restored to their original colors. Since color photographs did not exist when many historic buildings were constructed, the best way to find out what the historic colors were is to perform historical paint analysis. When this is done, an area of paint should be found in a well-sheltered area of the exterior and a chip of paint should be removed. This chip is then cut at a very acute angle with a razor blade. This should reveal a rainbow-like spectrum of all the coats of paint that have been applied to the building over time, at least those that weren't totally scraped off. The chip can then be examined in a

Figure 7.27. This paint is being forced from the ceiling and walls by water intrusion, probably due to a roof leak. Source: Photograph by Peter B. Dedek, 2007.

microscope. Chemical tests for early paint colors are also available. This should be done on several areas of the building's exterior, and the chips should be compared. New paint can be mixed from one of the previous coats if it's clearly discernable. Keep in mind, however, that the very first coat may have been a primer coat.

WALLPAPER

In the late 1400s, French kings commissioned scenes to be painted on rolls of paper or cloth, which would be set against walls, but would not be permanently attached and could be moved along with the king when he traveled. The widespread use of wallpaper was not possible until the invention of printing and the industrial processes required to make printed paper in large quantities. Jean-Michel Papillon, a French engraver who made repeating block-printed designs for wallpaper in 1675, invented wallpaper as we know it, and soon wallpaper printed by wood block or stencil or a combination thereof became available across Europe.

Wallpaper was often used as a cheap alternative to tapestries, silk wall cloth, or wooden paneling. The art on some early wallpapers employed an illusion called **trompe l'oeil**, a method of rendering that attempts to make a two-dimensional painting or print look three-dimensional, thus "tricking" the eye. Some wallpaper had textured, "flocked" designs created to mimic more expensive damask and cut-velvet wall hangings. In the 18th century, most wallpaper was printed in France, although significant amounts were also produced in China and in England (Mapes 1997). Although it started out as handmade printed sheets, wallpaper began to be made industrially in rolls in the late 1700s.

A printing machine for the mass production of wallpaper was patented in 1839 in England. Rather than requiring a canvas backing, the new wallpaper could be glued directly to plaster. As supplies increased, prices dropped, allowing a wider range of people to purchase it. The Victorian era was characterized by dense decoration, and wallpaper became very colorful and ornate and was used in many rooms in middle-class houses. In Victorian houses, wallpaper with elaborate designs was even sometimes applied to ceilings.

In the second half of the 19th century, members of the budding Arts and Crafts movement led by William Morris reacted against the decorative excesses of the Victorian era. Morris wanted to restore simplicity of design and craftsmanship. When designing his own, now-famous wallpapers, Morris used naturalistic colors and natural motifs, such as vines and flowers. As time passed, the style and the colors, patterns, and motifs used on wallpaper evolved with changing fashions, and by the early 20th century, both modern and traditional patterns were available on wallpaper. Wallpaper technology also evolved. Vinyl wallpaper went on the market in 1947, and prepasted wallpaper appeared in the 1950s (Krasner-Khait 2001).

Early wallpaper was often hung on canvas using stretchers, which divided the paper from the wall behind it. Other installations used various kinds of liners that were applied between the wall and the paper, although some wallpaper was applied directly to the plaster or wood plank wall itself. Sometimes, old wallpaper was not stripped before new wallpaper was installed, and the walls of older historic buildings can have as many as ten or more layers of wallpaper on a single wall. If analyzed, these layers can be used to document the decorative changes that have been made to the building over time.

Wallpaper Preservation Issues

Historic wallpaper can deteriorate due to external or inherent factors. The condition of the paper alone should not only be considered, but also the condition of the adhesives that bind the paper to the wall, and the well-being of the plaster or other wall material beneath the paper is also important. Various components of the papered wall may respond differently to changes in the humidity and temperature of air in a room. This can result in the paper expanding and contracting at a greater rate than the materials beneath, possibly causing the paper to tear or buckle. When wallpapers go through seasonal variations of cold and heat, dry and moist air, they tend to deteriorate more quickly. Heating in winter will dry the paper out, making it contract, and the higher humidity of summer can make it expand and possibly bubble up from the wall. The advent and widespread use of central air conditioning and well-regulated heating systems have helped preserve wallpaper and other interior finishes in historic interiors, because they help keep the interior temperature and relative humidity more consistent throughout the year.

Wallpaper is often the first material to show damage when walls shift due to a building settling or when water leaks on or seeps into walls. Settling often tears the wallpaper, and leaks and moisture can stain it or cause it to become unstuck from the wall or damage the liner behind it. Moisture can also promote the growth of mold, and can cause the wallpaper and its adhesives to weaken. Salts in the form of efflorescence (see Chapter 8) can also build up behind wallpaper and endanger it.

Exposure to sunlight is another common external cause of damage, which can fade a wallpaper's patterns and colors over time. Because prolonged exposure to sunlight can fade wallpaper, many managers of historic buildings keep draperies at least partly closed, and sometimes install light filters in windows that screen out the ultraviolet light that causes much of the deterioration. Damage to historic wallpapers can also come from being touched by human hands, which contain harmful oils and dirt. Graffiti, misguided attempts at cleaning, scratches caused by furniture being moved, and holes made in walls for stoves, lights, and other interior fixtures can also damage historic wallpaper.

Defects in the materials and methods used in the manufacture of wallpaper historically can also cause it to fail over time. After the 1850s, acidic paper made from wood pulp, which eventually yellows and crumbles, was often used for wallpaper. In cases where such inferior paper was used, the wallpaper may become so deteriorated that in the course of a building restoration, it will have to be documented, removed, and replaced with a reproduction based on the original design. Since long-term product testing was not done on historic wallpaper, sometimes the historic inks fade or starch and animal glues used to hang the wallpaper shrink or dissipate or are eaten by insects (Mapes 1997).

The care of historic wallpaper should be undertaken by an experienced conservator. Where the damage isn't significant and is limited to small areas, the wallpaper repairs can be carried out **in situ** (in place), while in others, where the damage is more extensive, the wallpaper sometimes has to be removed, restored in a lab, and reinstalled. Despite its being one of the most fragile architectural fabrics, a great deal of historic wallpaper from many eras has survived to this day. Wallpaper is a significant aspect of a historic interior and, if present, should be preserved and kept in its original location if at all possible. If the wallpaper in a room is too severely damaged to preserve, samples of it should be kept as a historical record and in case someone ever desires to reproduce and reinstall it in the future.

ASBESTOS

Asbestos, an inorganic fiber now known to be very hazardous, was used as a fireproof building material from the beginning of the 20th century until the 1970s. Asbestos shingles and siding began to be produced after 1900 and became popular. Both asbestos shingles and siding were advertised for their strength and resistance to fire and were manufactured using a combination of asbestos and Portland cement. Asbestos roof tiles usually came in gray and often looked much like slate but were cheaper. Because dyes could be added to the mix, asbestos shingles also came in a variety of colors including "Indian red." Asbestos siding often looks something like painted cedar shakes (NPS 2010).

Although it is brittle and requires periodic repairs, asbestos roofing and siding is long lasting. Many historic buildings still wear it today, and it does not necessarily have to be removed. The danger from asbestos, particularly asbestos that has been combined with cement, only comes when it is disturbed and the asbestos fibers have the opportunity to enter the air where they can be breathed in and cause lung cancer, asbestosis, and other diseases. If asbestos shingles are to be removed, the work must be done by specialists familiar with this hazardous material, and the shingles themselves have to be disposed of as hazardous material.

Asbestos can be found in other parts of buildings, including heating systems where it occurs in the coatings on steam and air duct pipes leading out of furnaces, and in cement sheets and other insulation used around old furnaces. The material can also be found in old resilient floor tiles, such as those made of vinyl asbestos, and in some asphalt tiles; even in the backing of vinyl-sheet flooring, in floor tile adhesives, in a finish material that was sprayed on interior walls and ceilings, and in wall patches and joint compounds. Asbestos is generally grey in color and has a fibrous texture. Care should always be taken not to disturb these materials, and removing them can constitute a significant portion of the cost of rehabilitating a historic building. However, with the use of the proper methods of removal and or encapsulation, asbestos can be effectively dealt with, and the presence of asbestos should never be used as an excuse to demolish a historic building, especially given the fact that the material must also be properly disposed of in the course of a demolition.

MARTIN MITCHELL MANSION RESTORATION, NAPERVILLE, ILLINOIS

The 2003 restoration of the Martin Mitchell Mansion, a 12-room brick Victorian house, was based on extensive research presented in a historic structure report completed by an architectural firm in 1999. In 1883, George Martin II commissioned the mansion, which the Martin family called "Pinecraig." Illinois architect James Mulvey designed the house in a style referred to as "Victorian eclectic," because its limestone and brick exterior exhibits features from a number of different Victorian house styles. The mansion, which was listed on the National Register 1975, is now part of a 13-acre living history museum called the Naper Settlement, located in a suburb west of

Figure 7A. Martin Mitchell Mansion after restoration. Source: Naperville Heritage Society.

Chicago. The Naper Settlement planned and raised funds for the project, which was carried out by a restoration team including historians, curators, local volunteers, contractors, conservators, and a historical architect (Vogell 2001).

The $2.8 million renovation was completed in 2004. The Naper Settlement worked to restore the exterior and interior of the mansion to the way it appeared between 1890 and 1903. The house's porch was restored and its slate roof replaced. The exterior was cleaned and the walls resurfaced with a mixture of sand and limestone, called "parge," which matches the original exterior finish. Paint analysis was done on the exterior to determine what color the house probably was in the late 1800s, and that color was recreated and applied. The hardware on the exterior doors was removed, restored, and reinstalled (Penick 2003).

The first floor rooms have 12-foot ceilings with walls covered mostly in wallpaper. During the restoration, workers scraped off layers of wallpaper and looked under rugs for evidence of historic decorative materials dating from the restoration period. Historic artifacts, including antique light fixtures and a brass vase, were found in the house's attic during the renovation and placed back in their original locations based on evidence from old photographs. Two inventories dating from 1889 and 1937 were used to identify the contents of the interior during those periods, and three historic photographs of the interior, including one that showed how three draperies with lace curtains hung in the formal parlor, informed the curators how the interior looked historically. They also used period catalogs to cross-reference their findings with typical finishes, furnishings, and treatments of the period. The floral carpet in the parlor was preserved, and new plumbing was designed to accommodate historically accurate bathroom fixtures (McCammon 2003).

Throughout the significant rooms, fragments of historic wallpaper were used to reproduce identical paper. The blue wallpaper in the second floor sitting room was original to the period, and paper conservators Chris Young and Jodie Lee Utter restored it in place, using small sponges, electric erasers, and paintbrushes. The room's paper is flowery with a blue background, and topped with an original coordinating frieze and ceiling paper. Finding intact original early-20th-century wallpaper schemes such as this is rare, because wallpaper and other interior finishes were often harmed or destroyed by environmental factors, such as light, water, and smoke, and were usually changed as fashions evolved over time. Another complication is that wallpaper from this period is particularly fragile, because it was made of wood pulp rather than from rag fibers used in earlier wallpapers. In addition, areas of the plaster wall had been damaged, making it necessary to repair the plaster and have matching reproduced wallpaper applied in those areas (Stevens 2003).

The restored property is used to show visitors how the Martin family and similar people lived at the turn of the 20th century in Illinois.

Figure 7B. Livingroom. Source: Naperville Heritage Society.

Figure 7C. Wallpaper restoration. Source: Naperville Heritage Society.

CONCLUSION

Historic building materials have a many diverse properties, but most all of them have one thing in common: they are fragile when put under stress or exposed to the elements and may require a lot of attention and care. With the exception of glass, virtually all historic building materials can be damaged by water. Understanding the unique properties of historic building materials is a significant specialization within the field of historic preservation and historic architecture. The next chapter will outline common threats to historic materials and buildings.

STUDY QUESTIONS

1. Explain the difference between compressive and tensile strength, citing examples of materials that possess a lot of one, both, or neither.

2. Given that adobe has little compressive or tensile strength, why was it used?

3. What advantages do fired bricks have over adobe?

4. Explain how igneous, sedimentary, or metamorphic stone is formed and describe the basic qualities of each as building stone.

5. Why was the invention of reinforced concrete so important?

6. What is cast stone made of and how was it used? Why did designers sometimes specify cast stone instead of authentic stone?

7. What were some of the reasons that designers used wooden trim in interiors?

8. What is the purpose of lath in historic plaster? What are the three main types of lath?

9. It is not easy to match historic brick, wood, stone, and tile with new material. What are some of the reasons finding identical replacements for these historic elements is so difficult?

10. What is the single greatest environmental threat to historic building materials such as brick, stone, wood, adobe, plaster, and iron? Why?

VISUAL QUIZ

Name the primary historic material in the following eight images:

A _____   B _____   C _____   D _____

E _____   F _____   G _____   H _____

Answers and explanations found in Instructor's Guide.

SOURCES

Al-Amaireh, Mazen N. 2009. "Production of Fire–Clay Refractory Bricks from Local Materials." *European Journal of Scientific Research* 386–392. Accessed June 27, 2012. http://connection.ebscohost.com/c/articles/38123821/production-fire-clay-refractory-bricks-from-local-materials

Coney, William B. 1986. "Preservation of Historic Concrete: Problems and General Approaches." Preservation Brief 15. Washington DC: National Park Service.

Friedman, Donald. 2010. *Historical Building Construction: Design, Materials, and Technology.* Second edition. New York: W.W. Norton & Company.

Grimmer, Anne. 1990. "The Preservation and Repair of Historic Stucco." Preservation Brief 22. Washington, DC: National Park Service.

Krasner-Khait, Barbara. 2001. "The Development of Wallcoverings." *History Magazine,* October/November.

McCammon, Sarah. "Naperville Renovations are Finished," 2003. *Daily Herald* (Arlington Heights, IL), November 20.

MacDonald, Mary Lee. 1989. "Repairing Historic Flat Plaster, Walls, and Ceilings." Preservation Brief 21. Washington, DC: National Park Service.

Mapes, Phillipa. 1997. "Historic Wallpaper Conservation." Accessed August 7, 2010. http://www.buildingconservation.com/articles/wallpap/wallpap.htm

National Park Service (NPS). "From Asbestos to Zinc: Roofing in Historic Buildings." Accessed August 7, 2010. http://www.nps.gov/history/hps/TPS/roofingexhibit/introduction.htm

Penick, Stephanie. 2003. "Mansion's Restoration Provides History Lesson." *Daily Herald* (Arlington Heights, IL), November 18.

Seale, William. 1979. *Recreating the Historic House Interior.* Nashville: American Association for State and Local History.

Shopson, William C., 1986. *Restoring Old Buildings for Contemporary Uses: An American Sourcebook for Architects and Preservationists.* New York: Whitney Library of Design.

Stahl, Frederick A. 1984. *A Guide to the Maintenance, Repair, and Alteration of Historic Buildings.* New York: Van Nostrand Reinhold Company.

Stevens, Susan. 2003. "Eye for Detail a Must for Restoring Mitchel Wallpaper," 2003. *Daily Herald* (Arlington Heights, IL), April 24.

Tiller, de Teel Patterson. 1979. "The Preservation of Historic Glazed Architectural Terra-Cotta," Preservation Brief 7. Washington, DC: National Park Service.

Tiller, de Teel Patterson, and David W. Look. 1978. "Preservation of Adobe Buildings," Preservation Brief 5. Washington, DC: National Park Service.

Virginia Department of Historical Resources. 1993. "Lead Paint." Accessed August 6, 2010. http://www.dhr.virginia.gov/pdf_files/LeadPaint1.PDF

Vogell, Heather. 2001. "Aid for Museum Restoration." *Chicago Tribune Business,* June 24,

Waite, John G. 1991. "The Maintenance and Repair of Architectural Cast Iron." Preservation Brief 27. Washington, DC: National Park Service.

Weaver, Martin, 1993. *Conserving Buildings: Guide to Techniques and Materials.* New York: John Wiley & Sons, Inc.

COMMON THREATS
TO HISTORIC BUILDINGS

OBJECTIVES

- Outline the significant natural threats, such as fires, floods, earth-quakes, and pests to historic buildings.

- Outline and describe the significant man-made threats, such as vandalism, improper repairs and cleaning, and pollution to historic buildings.

- Address methods of identifying and rectifying damage to various aspects of the exteriors and interiors of historic buildings from both natural and artificial sources.

Figure 8.1. Interior of the Pantheon, Rome, built 120 AD.
Source: Photograph by Peter B. Dedek, 2012.

Well-constructed, properly maintained historic buildings can last for hundreds or even thousands of years. The Pantheon in Rome, once a pagan temple and now a church, has been in nearly constant use for almost 2000 years (Figure 8.1). And although the Taos Pueblo in the mountains of New Mexico is made mostly of adobe, which is soft and subject to erosion, the buildings have been occupied since the 1100s.

Despite the potential longevity of historic architecture, many threats to older buildings exist, both from natural forces and human interventions. Destructive forces, such as rain and wind, insects and rodents, fire, and the wrecking ball, can threaten historic buildings when they do not receive adequate maintenance and protection. The natural materials used to construct older historic buildings are more porous and often more frail than reinforced or synthetic materials, such as reinforced concrete and plastics commonly used in newer buildings. Before significant rehabilitation work begins on a historic building, a thorough inspection of both its exterior and interior is usually performed by a team that may include structural engineers, architects, preservation specialists, and interior designers. During such an inspection, the team examines and evaluates the condition and structural integrity of critical elements such as the building's roof, foundation, walls, floors, and ceilings. When damage is found, the inspectors investigate to discover the cause of the problem. This chapter describes a number of natural and man-made threats to historic buildings and introduces methods of identifying and managing them.

NATURAL THREATS TO HISTORIC BUILDINGS

Natural forces constantly erode and reshape the landscape. Mountains built through volcanic and tectonic activity eventually erode due to the force of wind and water, and events such as earthquakes and floods periodically reshape the features of the land. By building levees, roads, canals, and shelter, humans try to stabilize and control the vast power of nature. Maintaining the built environment takes a great deal of ongoing effort. Plants, animals, and the elements will damage and reclaim buildings if given the opportunity. The foundations, walls, and roofs of historic buildings can easily fall prey to a wide range of natural forces.

SETTLING

Buildings can sink and lean because the ground beneath them is not always stable. Soil types and rock formations vary greatly from place to place, and sometimes they subside over time, endangering a building's foundation. The likelihood of subsidence primarily depends on the type of soil beneath a building and the presence or the lack of stable soils, stone and bedrock, and water. At times, a building will sink or shift as a whole unit, but usually the subsidence or compression of the soils beneath a building's foundation will be uneven, causing sections or parts of the building to settle to a greater degree and at different rates than others, causing a destructive subsidence called **differential settling** (Figure 8.2). With differential settling, damage occurs because walls may start to crack or lean, and parts of a building may split away from the rest (Figure 8.3). Walls often tip and even collapse because the foundation beneath is giving way, leaving holes, gaps, and fissures. It is not uncommon for a porch to lean out and separate from the rest of a building because the foundation beneath it was not as heavily constructed as the foundation under the rest of the building. Additions may also break away from the main building for the same reason.

To last and remain sound, a building's foundation needs to be anchored either to bedrock or set in stable soil. This requires specific types of foundation design and engineering depending on where the building is located. For example, the soil beneath New Orleans is exceptionally deep and spongy. In that city, one has to drill down over a hundred feet to hit bedrock. When trains or heavy trucks go by, the ground near the tracks or street actually shakes. This happens because the earth beneath southeast Louisiana is made up of loamy sediment brought down and deposited by the Mississippi River only a few thousand years ago, which is very recent in terms of geological time. Therefore, while many large newer buildings rest on piers

Figure 8.2. When severe, differential settling can destroy the walls of a building, especially ones made of brick or stone, neither of which is as flexible or resilient to tensile stresses as wood. Source: Photograph by Peter B. Dedek, 2008.

Figure 8.3. Without a secure foundation, buildings or parts of buildings can float on top of the soil beneath as it expands and contracts due to changes in moisture content and temperature, often causing wall and floor cracks that widen and shrink causing increasing damage to all elements of the building over time. Source: Photograph by Peter B. Dedek, 2012.

driven deep into the ground, the foundations of most historic buildings were constructed on loamy dirt, which expands when wet or flooded and contracts when dry, making some kind of movement beneath older buildings nearly inevitable. Under normal conditions, if the foundations were set deep with significant masonry footings and the building was solidly constructed, this settling and shifting doesn't cause significant damage. However, if severe expansion or contraction takes place due to a flood or a drought, the soil beneath may not expand or contract evenly, causing differential settling and possible damage even if the building was stable previously.

The situation is very different many other areas of the country. The soils in the Nashville area of Middle Tennessee are very thin, and usually one finds limestone bedrock only a few feet beneath the surface, making constructing a solid building foundation there a much easier process than doing so in New Orleans or other places with deep soils. In Middle Tennessee, the footings or piers can usually be set right on top of solid bedrock, making the possibility of subsequent settling much less likely. So generally, in areas of the country with thick, clay soils that are prone to expansion and contraction or sandy soils that are prone to being washed away, differential settling is a more common problem than in regions with bedrock close to the surface and those with more stable soil types.

The signs of settling include significant cracks in masonry walls, sloping floors, and walls that are no longer plumb. **Plumb** means the wall is perpendicular to the ground, or straight up and down. The presence of cracks in a building does not always indicate that the building is in danger of serious damage or collapse, and cracks sometimes result from vibrations or failing lintels over openings in a wall or from additional causes that are not a result of settling.

Once a building has been inspected and symptoms of settling, such as cracking, walls out of plumb or sagging floors, ceilings, or rooflines have been identified, an engineer should be consulted. A structural engineer is required to properly diagnose the causes of and to correct differential settling. Common mitigation measures in cases where settling is a threat to a building include digging out under the existing structure to install deep concrete piers or piles underneath it, underpinning where wide holes are excavated under the historic foundation and masses of concrete are poured in to support it, and consolidation where chemicals are pumped into soils beneath a building in order to solidify and harden them. Measures to control water flow adjacent to and beneath the foundation are also often required.

CRACKING

Cracks in buildings can result from either compressive or tensile loads (the meaning of compressive and tensile stresses is explained in the previous chapter). Cracks can result from any stresses, such as from differential settling. Masonry tends to crack when subjected to shearing forces because it has relatively little tensile strength, whereas wood tends to bend under stress unless it is very brittle or otherwise damaged, or the force is sustained and excessive. Cracks caused by compressive crushing (usually due to differential settling) tend to be relatively vertical and parallel to the direction of the stress, while cracks caused by tensile shearing (usually due to very severe differential settling or earthquakes or other vibrations) tend to run diagonally

Figure 8.4. Step cracking such as this in brick, stone, or concrete block is a sign of structural instability that often requires the attention of a structural engineer. Source: Photograph by Peter B. Dedek, 2008.

in the wall. In walls that are made of blocks of stone or bricks, step cracking (Figure 8.4) tends to occur, which is usually an indicator of significant structural issues in a building.

Not all cracks indicate a serious problem; sometimes they simply mean that some shifting has occurred and that the masonry is merely adjusting to it. The speed at which a crack is widening can be a good indicator of how serious the problem is. If a crack forms very slowly, it is probably relatively benign, whereas if it opens quickly and keeps expanding, this indicates that conditions are changing rapidly and further action is probably required to prevent damage to the architectural fabric.

A simple device called a *crack monitor* can help determine how fast a crack is moving. It is made of two pieces of Plexiglas with grids etched or drawn on each. The pieces of Plexiglas and the grids on them are overlapped over the crack with one piece of Plexiglas attached to the wall on one side of the crack and the other attached to the other side of the crack (Figure 8.5). As the crack widens or narrows, its movements can be tracked over time by comparing how points on the grids that once lined up have ceased to be aligned, and measurements of how much worse a crack is becoming can be recoded and then analyzed by a structural engineer to determine what corrective action, if any, must be taken. If a crack widens measurably in a matter of days or weeks then a serious structural problem may be present, while if the width of a crack changes little over weeks or months, then it is more likely that no serious problem exists.

There are many methods of addressing cracks in historic buildings. The specific method depends on the cause and the severity of the cracks. Solutions include repairing or replacing a failing lintel, foundation repair, roof repair, and mitigation of the causes of some kinds of cracks, such as reducing moisture to limit the swelling and contraction of porous building materials, such as brick, or porous soils beneath the foundation. In all but minor instances of cracking, a structural engineer should be consulted.

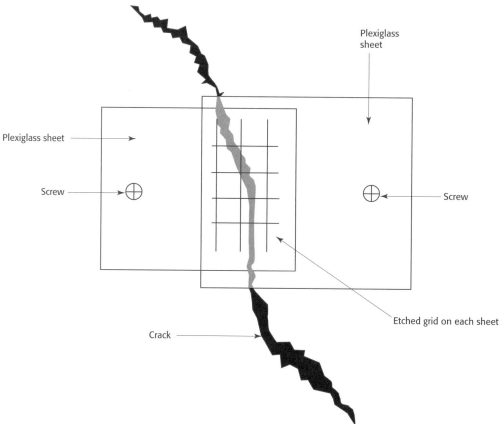

Figure 8.5. Crack gauge. This innovation is a simple, inexpensive method of evaluating the seriousness of cracks in masonry, stucco, or plaster.

WATER DAMAGE AND EFFLORESCENCE

Water posses the most dangerous threat to historic buildings. Much of the damage done to buildings over time is caused by water in one way or another, whether it is leaking in through roofs, seeping into walls, or even seeping up from the ground through foundations in a process called "rising damp."

Efflorescence is a powder or stain, usually whitish in color, that collects on the surface of masonry as the result of water intrusion (Figure 8.6). It can be found on the exterior or on the interior, although interior wall materials, such as plaster or wood, sometimes conceal it. Efflorescence actually consists of minerals from within the wall itself that have been loosened and washed out and up to the surface by water that has penetrated into the wall from one or more sources. As moisture evaporates on the surface, it leaves the minerals behind to gather on the surface and eventually become visible. Efflorescence is evidence that, by one means or another, water is seeping through the structure of a building and is weakening it. If left unchecked, the

problem may lead to failure of the wall. Efflorescence does not only affect walls; it can also occur in ceilings constructed of vaulted brick or stone or even in roofs made of concrete.

The source of the offending water may be difficult to find: water intrusion can happen due to many causes, such as a roof leak, which can result from a leak in flashing around a chimney or a parapet wall; from water penetrating a wall directly because of defects in the wall that allow water to collect; from water flowing or pooling around a building; or from a broken gutter or leaking or sweating plumbing. The water itself can arrive in the form of rain, snow, groundwater, pipe water, and even water suspended in the air as vapor that condenses on the surface of a wall. Water can penetrate and damage buildings in the following ways:

Roof Leaks

Roof leaks are a common path for water to enter a building. Without a waterproof roof, a building will not survive for long (Figure 8.7). In a building with evidence of water intrusion, the roof system is the first aspect that should be checked and evaluated for leakage. Defects or deterioration in roofing of various types provide many opportunities for leaks. Flat roofs

Figure 8.7. Without a waterproof roof, a building deteriorates rapidly. Source: Photograph by Peter B. Dedek, 2012.

are particularly vulnerable because they rely on drains, which can become plugged up without frequent maintenance. Slanted roofs, such as gabled roofs and hipped roofs, are easier to maintain, especially in wet climates, because their shape naturally sheds water. However, all but the simplest roofs have some kind of flashing around elements such as chimneys and vents that are vulnerable to leaks and need to be inspected on a regular basis, especially since damaging leaks into attics sometimes go undetected for long periods of time. Leaves and branches should also be cleared from roofs. While inspecting roofs, however, one should be careful, because walking or even crawling on some types of roofing material can damage them, especially if the roof is made of ceramic tile, slate, or asbestos tile. Ladders can be used to inspect many roof surfaces, and binoculars can help an inspector spot problems from the ground, from a ladder, or from a nearby building or structure.

Most roofs, such as those covered in asphalt shingles, need to be to be replaced every 20 years or so; however slate, metal, and tile roofs can last up to a century or even longer. Eventually though, due to erosion from rain and possibly snow and ice, breakdown due to ultraviolet light from the sun, and friction from wind and possibly the branches of nearby trees, any roof will have to be replaced. In historic buildings, a deteriorated roof should normally be replaced with the same material that was present historically, or if this isn't possible, by an alternate material similar in appearance to the original. Shifting caused by settling due to soil subsidence or internal structural problems can also compromise a roof. Water leaking from above due to a roof leak can cause a tremendous amount of damage to interior materials, such as plaster and finished wood in a short time, and leakage invites destructive factors such as termites, wood rot, and mold.

Mitigation measures include replacing a deteriorated roof, and the decking beneath it if needed, and reflashing around peaks, valleys, vents, and chimneys, sealing cracks, and breaks.

Damaged Gutters

Broken or clogged gutters can cause a lot of damage by allowing water to drain against the walls and penetrate through them into a building. Gutters are a very important element of any roof system and should be installed on nearly all historic buildings, especially in wet climates, even if they did not exist historically (although gutters either have to be well-concealed or not installed at all to maintain the historic integrity of some very old or highly historic buildings). Gutters, which are usually made of aluminum (although historically they were usually of iron or even wood), direct water away from the walls and foundation that would otherwise pond on the ground near a building if allowed to fall freely over the eaves. Gutters should remove water to a single location far enough from the building and downhill from it so that water does not flow back to the building's foundation. Preferably, gutter water should discharge directly into a municipal drainage system or be collected into cisterns for irrigation and household uses. However, if the roof is sheathed in asphalt, the water should be filtered before it enters the cistern, because asphalt shingles can introduce grit and possibly leached chemicals to the captured water. Water that ponds or flows around foundations can damage a building by washing away soils beside and under its foundation causing settling by seeping into the walls and foundation walls, introducing potentially destructive dampness into the building.

The gutters themselves should be installed so that water drains down them properly and doesn't pool within the gutters and possibly flow over the sides, defeating the point of installing gutters in the first place. Improperly installed gutters can also encourage the buildup of debris from leaves, branches, moss, and lichens. Clogged gutters and downspouts can lead to water flooding off the gutters and pouring over and damaging walls sometimes making the situation worse than if there were no gutters at all. Broken gutters and downspouts can lead to a number of serious water problems in buildings (Figure 8.8). Installing quality gutter systems and maintaining them is one of the most important aspects of the maintenance and preservation of historic buildings.

Figure 8.8. Broken gutter downspouts like this one invite water to seep into and damage walls and foundations. Water splashing up from broken downspouts can also damage masonry and wood. Source: Photograph by Peter B. Dedek, 2008.

Water Intrusion through Walls

Water intrusion through walls can not only be caused by malfunctioning or broken gutters but also by deteriorated flashing, peeling paint, cracked stucco, or deteriorated mortar in bricks or stone. The goal is to make walls water resistant by not allowing gaps, cracks, or deteriorated joints to invite water inside. Peeling paint can allow water into a wall, and the presence of peeling paint can also be an indicator that unwanted water entering by some another means is already present in a wall. While it is important to make walls relatively water resistant, it is also important not to totally seal the outside of a wall in order to make it completely waterproof, because this will not allow the wall to breathe. It is inevitable, particularly in historic masonry buildings, that some water will find its way into a given wall, and sealing the wall with a waterproof sealant traps any water present within the wall material, not allowing it to evaporate once it reaches the exterior surface. Trapped water can dissolve building materials from the inside over time and can freeze in cold weather, which often damages the wall surface because water expands as it freezes.

Rising Damp

When water wicks into wall material from below in a process similar to when water soaks up into a cotton swab or a wash cloth that has been partially dipped in water, it is called **rising damp**. The fibers in wood, brick, adobe, stone, and even concrete can draw water up, defying

Figure 8.9. Rising damp slowly erodes masonry walls and causes paint to flake off and often seeps through the wall and damages the interior wall finishes within. Source: Photograph by Peter B. Dedek, 2011.

gravity (Figure 8.9). As water wicks through a porous building material, it tends to dissipate and evaporate, usually leaving the lower section of a wall wetter than the upper section. With rising damp, sealing the wall with a water resistant sealer can actually make the problem worse by trapping the water within, where it can damage the wall material more than it would have if it had been allowed to evaporate on the surface. Rising damp is most common in older buildings, because the materials used to construct them were often more organic and softer than those used in more recent buildings, and fewer moisture barriers were used.

Remedies for rising damp include making sure water from rain or other sources does not pool or splash against a wall by installing gutters and grading the ground outside the wall such that the water drains away. If this doesn't work or isn't possible, the next-least-intrusive method of addressing the problem is to identify the source of the water and to direct it away from the wall by installing **French drains** (ditches filled with gravel containing perforated pipes that carry water away) or **footer drains** (perforated drainage pipes that run underground below the level of the basement or footer wall and drain water out to a location downhill or to a sump pump). If the problem still persists, installing moisture barriers (layers of rubber-like synthetic material) placed within the wall just above the foundation may be necessary. Adding moisture barriers to stop the rising damp is often complicated and expensive because it requires that sections of a masonry wall be taken down to the foundation, the barrier added, and the wall rebuilt.

Water Vapor

Water vapor from interior rooms sometimes makes its way into the walls of buildings. When the weather is cold, warmer air from within a heated building has the ability to hold more water in vapor form than the colder outside air can. If a wall does not possess a properly-installed **vapor barrier** between the interior plaster or wallboard and the interior structure of the wall (where the insulation would go in a stud-frame building) becomes water-laden, warm air from

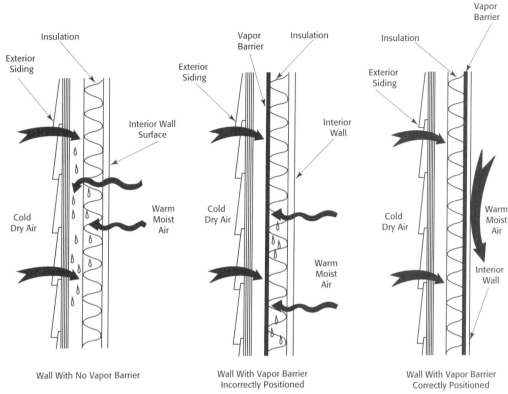

Figure 8.10. Vapor barriers and water condensation.

the interior can penetrate the wall. When it hits the cold inner surface of the outside of the wall, water vapor will condense and moisten the interior of the wall (Figure 8.10). Over time, this moisture can do a great deal of damage if it goes unnoticed. Water condensing inside a timber-frame or stud-frame wall can moisten insulation, making it cease to insulate, cause rot, encourage the growth of mold, and invite infestation by termites and other harmful insects.

The remedy is to install vapor barriers where possible or to otherwise seal the inside surface of the outer walls against airflow. As with most waterproofing efforts, sealing the outside of walls can make the problem worse because this doesn't allow water to escape by evaporation on the exterior.

INFESTATION BY PESTS

This section provides a general guide to a number of common pests that can endanger historic buildings. Once a potential threat has been detected or suspected, professionals trained in pest control need to be brought in to make a clear diagnosis and to correct the problem. Only after the source of any damage has been removed, including the conditions that allowed the pest to enter the building in the first place, should permanent repairs to the damage itself be performed. A number of common pests can damage historic buildings.

Termites in the United States come in two basic varieties, wet wood termites and dry wood termites. Both varieties eat wood and can be very destructive to historic buildings by literally gobbling away the wooden structures.

Wet wood termites are the most common in North America and include subterranean native termites, found in most parts of the United States, and the invasive **Formosan termites**, which originated in China and can be found in the South, mostly in coastal areas, and in Hawaii (Figure 8.11). Both varieties require moisture to infest buildings and both live in nests outside, usually located underground. The main way to detect subterranean native termites is by finding the mud tubes that they build, which will be wet if the insects are active.

Termites tend to swarm in the spring, which is another way of detecting their presence. Otherwise, termites are difficult to detect until damage to wood is visible or found by jabbing suspect

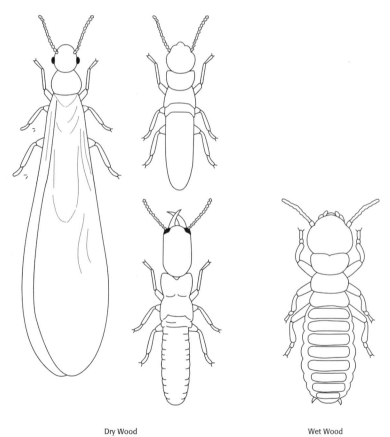

Dry Wood   Wet Wood

Figure 8.11. Dry and wet wood termites.

timbers with a knife or screwdriver to see if they have been hollowed inside. Native termites eat wood rather slowly but still need to be controlled by professional exterminators once detected because they will cause great damage over a number of seasons.

The primary method of defending against wet wood termites is to prevent water and moisture from entering a building and saturating its wooden components. Another defense is to keep soil and vegetation from touching any wood elements of a building, because wet wood termites need to travel through the moist earthen tunnels that they construct to connect their nests with their source of food, which, unfortunately is the building. In natural settings, these insects help the environment by breaking down fallen logs and helping transition the material into returning to the soil, but because they have such an appetite for wood, they can be very destructive to architecture.

Formosan termites operate in a similar manner to subterranean native termites except that sometimes their nests are located aboveground, and their colonies tend to be much larger. Formosans can also fly and swarm in massive numbers, usually in the spring when they are establishing new nests, making them more mobile and pestilent than subterranean native termites. They also eat more wood and can do a tremendous amount of damage in a matter of months. Formosan termites are most often found in southern regions, such as Florida and the Gulf Coast.

Dry wood termites are less common in the United States than the wet wood varieties. Rather than living in nests underground, these termites reside within the affected wood itself. They occur along the coast of the Southeast, in the deep South, in the lower Southwest, and along the California coast, and are usually detected when small holes become visible in the wood or when their fecal pellets, which have distinct ridges and are about 1/25th of an inch long, are discovered near the infested wood. Once evidence of any kind of termite is detected, professional exterminators need to be called in.

Carpenter Ants

Carpenter ants live in most parts of the United States, because they are resistant to the cold (Figure 8.12). Like wet wood termites, **carpenter ants** prefer moist timber, which is readily accessible from the soil, but unlike termites, carpenter ants do not eat the wood itself but destroy the material by chewing through it and building tunnels in order to nest in it. They tend to be darker in color than termites. Warning signs of infestation include swarms of winged ants emerging from wood in the spring and a slight rustling sound emanating from within wooden parts of a building. They may also leave droppings and sawdust. As with termites, the best defense is to keep a building dry and to keep vegetation from brushing against the sides of a building. Once detected, the ants' nest or nests must be destroyed by a professional exterminator.

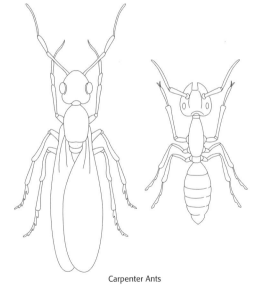

Carpenter Ants

Figure 8.12. Carpenter ants.

Powderpost beetles make small holes in usually unfinished wood, such as wall studs and other framing elements, but they also sometimes infest wood planks. These small insects leave small piles of a fine, flourlike sawdust near or beneath the holes they make, which they drill to create nests. Over time, the holes weaken the structural integrity of wood. Like termites and carpenter ants, powderpost beetles prefer to attack wood that is moist and usually operate in out-of-the-way areas, such as crawlspaces and attics. Preventing infestation involves ventilating crawlspaces and attics and not bringing wood inside that has been stored outside for long periods. The damage occurs slowly, but mediation should be performed if the visible holes continue to produce sawdust over time, and as with other damaging insects, they should be addressed by professionals.

Boring Bees

Carpenter or **boring bees** are a variety of large bee that look something like a bumblebee. They make their nests by boring large (1/2 inch in diameter) holes into wood. Several species can be found in most parts of the United States, and they prefer wood that is weathered and unpainted, so painting and treating wood helps defend against them. The damage they do can be quick, but it usually takes multiple attacks to significantly weaken a wooden post, beam, or plank. The holes they cause can invite moisture and other pests and should be plugged with a wooden dowel covered in glue. A sign of the presence of boring bees is the often annoying humming sound they make as they are drilling into wood. Common insect sprays will usually kill them.

Rodents

Rodents and raccoons can enter and reside within historic buildings and do significant damage in the process. They usually find their way into attics, crawlspaces, and basements, although raccoons have been known to open screen doors and walk right into living spaces looking for food or water. The usual way the presence of rodents and other animals in a building is revealed is when people hear them scurrying through walls and attics or see or smell damage due to their chewing, defecating, and urinating. This is one of the many reasons that it is important to keep historic buildings occupied. Without people present on a regular basis, rodents and other intruders can operate for long periods without detection or interference and can cause damage and contamination. A mouse, for example produces about 70 droppings a day and a large amount of urine (General Health District 2012).

Animals, such as rats and mice, can chew straight through wires. When a rat gnaws, it exerts up to 24,000 pounds per square inch (Winston 1999). When its teeth cut through wires and electrical insulation, this chewing can cause short circuits and fires. Also, the urine and feces of animals living inside buildings damage walls, add moisture that invites other problems, such as mold and rot, and can make buildings difficult or impossible to inhabit because of stains and foul smells. Mice and rats also carry a number of diseases, such as meningitis, leptospirosis, and hantavirus, some of which can be deadly. Preventive measures include removing potential food and water sources and sealing potential paths of access. When discovered, some animals, such as raccoons, can be humanely trapped and relocated, while rats and mice are usually killed with poison or traps.

Pigeons

Pigeons are common in cities and towns all over the world, including North America. The species originated in Asia and the Middle East and was transported from Europe to America by early settlers who used them as livestock. Some escaped, and their decedents have thrived ever since. Pigeons love to nest and roost on historic buildings, which often have architectural details, such as horizontal belt courses, hood moldings, and decorative cornices that provide excellent nesting sites and habitats (Figure 8.13). Unfortunately, pigeons are very destructive to historic buildings and their occupants. Their feces create an acid compound that deteriorates building materials, especially paint, asphalt, limestone, and steel. Pigeons produce a lot of feces—a single feral pigeon excretes between 22 and 26 pounds of waste annually—and pigeons are very social animals (Jones 2007). The birds also build nests in places where they break apart and plug gutters and drains, leading to water pooling on roofs, overflowing gutters, and other water problems.

The most significant danger from pigeons comes from their potential to carry disease. Pigeons help transmit more than 40 human diseases including meningitis, salmonella, and tuberculosis. Pigeon droppings, which cover everything in the vicinity of places where the birds roost, often carry potentially deadly fungi and bacteria. Construction workers working on historic buildings have become ill and even died because they attempted to clean up pigeon feces without the correct precautions (Waldorf 2008).

Anyone involved with historic buildings needs to be aware that pigeons pose a serious problem. If pigeons are present, they should be removed and prevented from returning. Any effort to clean up pigeon dung and debris needs to be performed by professionals wearing approved protective suits and masks.

Keeping pigeons away from buildings can be quite a challenge. The most important course of action is to ensure the birds have no opportunity to access the interior of a building. They can enter through broken or missing windows, gaps in screens and grilles, and through any hole in the building envelope that is bigger around than the pigeons are. All historic buildings, whether in use or not, should be sealed against pigeons, because once they enter a building they pose a significant health risk. Even if a building contaminated with pigeon debris were to be demolished, the act of demolition would release their

Figure 8.13. Pigeons roosting on historic building in Jaipur, India. Pigeons live all over the world. Source: Photograph by Peter B. Dedek, 2012.

hazardous fecal material into the air. Rehabilitation can also release dangerous pathogens when pigeon leavings are disturbed without the necessary precautions.

Numerous methods of keeping pigeons away from historic buildings exist and have various degrees of success, including the use of spikes to keep them from landing on horizontal surfaces, poisoning them, using chemical repellants, installing nets to keep them out of areas of buildings where they like to nest, playing recordings of the calls of raptors that prey on pigeons, and even just shooting them. It should be noted that the use of "colored flags, balloons, ultrasonic sound, magnetic pulses, and various kinds of scarecrows" (such as plastic snakes or owls) have been shown to be utterly ineffective (Jones 2007, 11). When dealing with most invasive animals, the employment of someone experienced in removing and blocking the return of pigeons is necessary to keep them at bay.

INTRUSIONS BY PLANTS

While plants and vines can look quaint growing on or close to historic buildings, they are quite destructive to historic building fabric. If not controlled and managed, plants damage historic structures in a variety of ways. A significant part of maintaining any building, particularly a historic building, is keeping plants from damaging its foundations, walls, and roofs. The most common source of damage comes from roots, which can push up foundations, penetrate walls, and create gaps in roofs. Several types of plants are particularly destructive to historic architecture.

Vines

Vines, such as wisteria, English ivy, poison ivy, and Virginia creeper, often cause significant damage to buildings by creating damp areas between their leaves and stems and the historic walls and roofs that they cling to. This moisture tends to invite rot and insects. Vines also send out roots that penetrate building materials, such as brick, stone, and wood (Figure 8.14). The roots break away pieces of masonry and promote rot in wooden siding. In regions with active freeze-thaw cycles, moisture trapped by vine roots and stems freezes and expands, accelerating the cracking and breaking process. Sometimes the vines themselves will force their way into seams or cracks in a building's exterior and widen existing cracks and gaps as they grow. In addition, an enzyme found in the roots of all vines dissolves lime, a critical component in historic brick mortar, and leaves only the sand, which then erodes quickly away.

Despite their aesthetic qualities, vines should not be allowed to grow on the walls of historic buildings. They need to be removed or grown on arbor structures that are separate from the wall. Whenever vines are present near historic buildings, they have to be carefully managed, as they tend to grow fast, and will readily attach to building exteriors. Some will even grow into interiors through cracks and gaps in windows.

Care must be taken when removing vines from walls and other architectural elements, because the tendrils that they have inserted into walls and window frames will bring material with them if pulled out too forcefully. Before removal, the vine should be cut and allowed to dry out, and once the vines are taken off the wall, their roots should be removed from the ground and the area managed to prevent the vines from growing back.

Figure 8.14. Vines should be removed from all historic buildings. They crack masonry, invite water into walls and roofs, and have tendrils that tear at the outer surface of bricks, stone, and mortar. Source: Photograph by Peter B. Dedek, 2010.

Bushes

Volunteer bushes (wild plants) and shrubbery (purposely planted ornamental bushes), can easily grow too large or too close to buildings and end up damaging them. Volunteer plants are not only found in the ground next to buildings but can sometimes grow on top of buildings or into cracks and gaps in their walls. If shrubs grow directly against historic siding or masonry, they usually invite pests, such as carpenter ants and termites; trap unwanted moisture; and cause abrasion to the building when blown by wind. Also, if the root systems are allowed to penetrate foundations, they cause damage by inviting in moisture and destabilizing the foundation.

Shrubs should be pruned to keep them from growing against walls and removed if they grow too large and their roots start to compromise foundations.

Trees

Like shrubs, trees can damage historic buildings and landscape features. Because of their size, they have the potential to do more damage than shrubs. The most common type of damage trees create is when their roots penetrate the materials of foundations and walls and additions, such as porches. If present, roots widen cracks, displace piers, and introduce moisture. If trees are allowed to grow too close to buildings, they can also block gutters and clutter roofs with leaves and fallen branches. If left unpruned, their branches can also rub against roofing and damage it, especially if the roof is made of brittle materials, such as slate, asbestos tile, and ceramic tile.

As with shrubs, trees located close to historic buildings should be pruned and even removed if they are harming a building. In cases where it is historically, environmentally, or aesthetically desirable to have tree branches projecting over the roofs of historic buildings, gutters should be checked and cleaned on a routine basis and roofs periodically swept to clear leaves, twigs, branches, nuts, seeds, and any other plant detritus that might be there.

Lichens and Mosses

Lichens and mosses found growing on historic buildings are sometimes an indication that excessive water is being allowed to penetrate the building materials upon which they are growing. In some cases, lichens and mosses exacerbate damage done by moisture and cause the outer surface of masonry or stucco or paint to peel off. A number of products are available to kill and remove lichens and mosses; however, it's very important to find and correct any underlying water issues before removing the lichens and mosses or they will simply grow back, and the moisture may cause other types of damage.

EARTHQUAKES

In the United States, earthquakes pose the most significant threat in the western states and Alaska, but some areas in the east, midwest and south have experienced damaging earthquakes as well. Examples include Massachusetts, 1755, Missouri, 1811, and South Carolina, 1886 (Look, Wong, and Augustus 1997). Historic buildings tend not to withstand earthquakes as well as newer buildings that are designed to withstand earthquakes and may have to be upgraded for safety in earthquake-prone areas. Earthquakes tend to cause cracks, shear brittle unreinforced masonry, and topple elements such as brick chimneys and gable ends. The better maintained a building is generally, the less chance it will receive significant damage in the event of an earthquake. In some locations, such as California and western Washington state, however, many historic buildings require structural modifications in the form of seismic retrofits to be safe places to live or work.

Whenever a seismic retrofit is planned, care must be taken to preserve a building's historic integrity as much as possible in the process. A common retrofit technique is installing steel anchor bolts that tie exterior walls to each other and to the roof so that in the event of an earthquake, the building will shake as a unit rather than vibrating more vigorously in some areas than in others, which tends to tear the structure apart. Other retrofit techniques involve infilling unstable windows, reinforcing exterior ornamentation, constructing exterior or interior buttresses made of steel posts and beams, and reinforcing floors and roofs (Figure 8.15) (Look, Wong, and Augustus 1997).

These measures have the potential to detract from a building's historic qualities, but if designed in a way that harmonizes with the original appearance of the building, they can be made to blend in and not negatively impact the building's historic integrity. Preservationists should work closely with the structural engineers who design such retrofits to ensure that they maintain the significant features of the building to the greatest degree possible while still making the building as safe as possible in the event of an earthquake.

FIRE

Since increasing numbers of historic buildings have been preserved rather than demolished in the past few decades, fire is becoming a growing serious threat, because older buildings often have aging wiring and HVAC systems and contain more flammable materials. Sometimes the cause of fire is natural, such as lightning, but much more common causes of fire are faulty wiring or defective heating systems.

Most fire codes in the United States are modeled on the National Fire Protection Association (NFPA) Code for Safety to Life, often referred to as NFPA 101 or the Life Safety Code. The Life Safety Code is primarily concerned with providing fast and easy routes for people to get out of burning buildings and with the provision of fire protection equipment. Other building codes, such as the International Building code, also address fire-related issues.

Figure 8.15. This historic building in San Francisco has been reinforced on the inside with steel braces to prevent damage from earthquakes with little negative impact to the historic qualities of the building. Source: Photograph by Peter B. Dedek, 2008.

According to a paper issued by the Advisory Council on Historic Preservation, the priorities in retrofitting fire safety features in historic buildings are first, "to provide for the protection of life; second, to protect the property; and third, to ensure that the installation of fire safety devices has minimal impact on the historic features of the property" (Advisory Council 1989, 5).

Modern buildings are designed according to contemporary fire codes that allow the building's occupants to exit rapidly in the event of a fire and require the use of modern materials in new commercial construction that are fire rated and highly regulated. Because their designers didn't use modern versions of the Life Safety Code, adapting historic buildings while retaining their historical character can be a challenge. The code requires features such as fire-rated escape corridors and closed, rated fire stairs, which often do not exist in historic buildings. Many historic buildings have historically significant features, such as grand open staircases constructed of wood, which are combustible and can help fire travel from one floor to the next. The challenge is to preserve these major features while making the building safe for its occupants. In the past, fire officials often required that unsightly exterior fire-escape stairs that marred their

Figure 8.16. This historic building façade in Asheville, North Carolina, has been compromised by intrusive fire escapes. Source: Photograph by Peter B. Dedek, 2008.

appearance be added to the street façades of historic buildings (Figure 8.16). Today, rated fire exits are usually placed within a historic building's interior or sometimes enclosed fire-rated staircases added to the rear or to another secondary façade. Cutting a compliant fire stair through the interior of a historic building can have a dramatic impact on the interior, particularly of buildings with a relatively small footprint.

Fire safety codes vary according to building occupancy, meaning that the standards for building types and uses that pose significant dangers to their occupants—hospitals, chemical factories, hotels, and crowded theaters—are more stringent than those for other types of buildings, such as retail stores. Fire safety codes also address the flammability of interior finishes. Many types of fabrics, wall coverings, and floor coverings that are commonly used in residential applications are not allowed to be installed in commercial or institutional interiors. Because many historic interior finishes are not fire resistant enough to pass standard flammability tests and meet code, exceptions to fire standards must be made in some cases in order to retain or replace them in kind. However, if a serious safety issue exists because a historic interior finish may pose a fire hazard, then safety should always take precedence, and the interior designer should specify that material be removed or encapsulated and replaced or covered with an identical or at least similar reproduction made of a material that is properly fire rated.

Because historic buildings were not constructed according to contemporary fire codes, they can be less safe than their modern counterparts. Generally, building codes are not enforced for existing buildings until they are substantially rehabilitated inside or out. However, technically, according to the Life Safety Code, existing buildings are required to comply with the code in most jurisdictions even if they're not being renovated. At the point where significant changes are made, the building will certainly have to be brought up to code, although in some cases, rehabilitation of historic buildings does not require full compliance with building and fire codes used in new construction so long as the authority with jurisdiction deems that no unsafe conditions will be present in the building when the work is complete.

Sometimes negotiations are undertaken among the parties involved that balance code requirements with protecting the historic integrity of the building. Many of these compromises are based on the concept of equivalency, which appears in most building codes. The NFPA describes **code equivalency** as "an alternate means of providing an equal or greater degree of than that afforded by strict conformance to proscribed codes and standards" (Watts 2003, 24). In other words, if a significant historic feature would have to be destroyed or adversely altered in order to adhere to a specific code requirement, an alternative treatment may be used so long as it provides the same or greater level of safety and is agreed upon by the relevant code officials.

The team in a major rehabilitation or renovation project usually includes building managers, building occupants, architects and interior designers, historic preservation specialists, fire protection engineers, and review authorities (Advisory Council 1989). In some cases, the historic preservation specialist is also an architect or interior designer. Since fire safety retrofits in historic buildings can be tricky and complicated, a good deal of research and consultation and project coordination should occur among the professionals involved.

Relatively simple additions (many of which are required by law) can greatly improve the fire safety of a historic building. These include the proper installation of smoke and fire detectors, the provision of fire extinguishers and other fire suppression devices, and clear signage that leads people to fire exits.

To help prevent fires, a part of any building rehabilitation should be the examination and replacement of all old and dangerous wiring. Many historic buildings have antiquated wiring, such as the **tube-and-knob wiring** used in the early 20th century, which consisted of bare wires strung on ceramic insulators located in attics and within walls, floors, and ceilings. Outdated and faulty wiring accounts for a significant percentage of fires, and bringing the electrics up to current standards goes far in protecting historic buildings and their occupants. Although the United States lacks vital statistics on how many historical buildings burn each year, Historic Scotland estimates that Scotland loses one listed building a month due to fire (Watts 2003). Given that the United States is much larger than Scotland, and we have a greater percentage of wooden buildings, we probably lose a far greater number of historic buildings to fire each month. Electrical modernization is required in large projects, but it should be a part of any rehabilitation or renovation.

STORMS AND FLOODING

Hurricanes, tornados, and other violent storms routinely damage historic buildings and districts in the United States. In fact, historic buildings are often more likely to be damaged by hurricanes and floods than buildings in general, because many older cities and settlements were built along the coasts and beside rivers, as evidenced to the damage done to historic districts in New Orleans in 2005 by Hurricane Katrina and the damage done to historic Galveston, Texas, by Hurricane Ike in 2008. While storm and flood damage can't always be prevented, good maintenance practices and plans for preparation for storms can help.

Floods brought on by hurricane storm surges or high amounts of rain often do the most damage. When a building has been flooded, it is important to inspect it as soon as the floodwaters have receded and it is safe to go inside. For historic buildings, the inspection should be done

A SURVIVOR IS RESTORED

The S.D. Robinett Building, a vernacular brick commercial building, was one of only two historic buildings in Greensburg, Kansas, to survive a severe tornado that hit the town in May 2007. Constructed as a "fireproof" building in 1915, the structure has foundation walls three feet thick and load-bearing brick walls 13 inches thick, with floors and a roof made of heavily reinforced concrete. Its unusually solid construction allowed the building to survive the tornado. The building was listed on the National Register of Historic Places in 2010.

After the storm destroyed nearly 95 percent of the town, its residents decided to rebuild as a model green community, including new features such as a wind farm and a subdivision of "eco-houses." As part of this rebuilding project, the historic S. D. Robinett Building was to be saved and reused. It underwent a $124,653 rehabilitation completed in 2010. The sustainable rehabilitation included rebuilding the damaged brick parapet at the rear, installing energy efficient windows to replace ones damaged in the tornado, installing new insulation and an energy efficient HVAC system, and adding bamboo flooring to the interior. Significant damage had occurred to the interior due to water infiltration, which was addressed. The rehabilitated building currently houses an antique store on the first floor and a private apartment on the second and stands as a sustainable symbol of Greenburg's history and its emergence as a thriving, progressive community after the catastrophe.

Figure 8A. S.D. Robinett Building after the tornado. Source: City of Greensburg, KS.

Figure 8B. S.D. Robinett Building after rehabilitation. Source: City of Greensburg, KS.

Figure 8C. Rehabilitation of interior. Source: City of Greensburg, KS.

by someone qualified to determine what damage has been done to the historic fabric and what the ramifications are, such as a historical architect or a structural engineer. It is also important to clear out any mud or soggy items such as rugs and furniture and then to let the building dry out slowly. Rapid drying can cause cracks and warping, which will amplify the damage. In addition to replacing interior plaster and other repairs, if a building has been flooded, the electrical wiring in all affected areas will also have to be replaced. Many historic buildings damaged by flooding have been successfully rehabilitated.

MAJOR HUMAN THREATS TO HISTORIC BUILDINGS

People cause at least as much damage to buildings as natural factors. Vandalism, demolition, arson, and wars have destroyed millions and millions of historic buildings. While preventing much of this damage is impossible, in many situations, preservationists and designers can work to limit the destruction through good preservation and security practices.

NEGLECT AND VANDALISM

Buildings require routine maintenance to survive over the long term, especially in rainy and humid climates. As stated earlier, the best way to keep a building from deteriorating is to keep it occupied by people who have an interest in the building's maintenance. In addition to the dangers from natural sources described earlier, neglected and vacant buildings can become "crack houses" or other types of squats where otherwise homeless people camp or where people go to party and take drugs (Figure 8.17). If a building is neglected or abused by its occupants, it becomes blighted and a menace to the area where it is located, and this may be used as a

Figure 8.17. This historic roadside building located in West Texas has been abandoned and vandalized and is now falling victim to demolition by neglect. Source: Photograph by Peter B. Dedek, 2012.

justification to tear it down. Another reason often cited for the demolition of such properties is that they have become a legal liability for their owners who are afraid someone will be injured within the building and sue them. Squats also commonly succumb to arson or fires lit inadvertently by their occupants.

One method of keeping unoccupied historic buildings from decaying is called mothballing. When owners mothball an unoccupied building, they are planning on keeping it vacant by choice or by necessity for a period of time while still hoping to preserve it for possible use in the future (Figure 8.18). A building may be mothballed because no viable use can be found for the building at the time or perhaps during a period while money is being raised for its rehabilitation. The point of mothballing is to keep the building safe from threats, such as vandals, water intrusion, and destructive animals, while it is vacant. In order to mothball larger buildings the expertise of a historical architect and or a structural engineer will probably be required, and to protect a building effectively, mothballing must be done carefully and properly. Common mothballing techniques include securely boarding up windows with thick plywood panels that cover the window openings completely, installing new roofs when necessary, erecting strong fences around the site to keep people out, shutting off water and electricity, and installing durable and dependable security lighting.

Figure 8.18. With a new roof and boarded-up windows, this historic building in Alpine, Texas, has been mothballed for future use. Source: Photograph by Peter B. Dedek, 2012.

IMPROPER REPAIRS

Many well-meaning people make inappropriate repairs, which end up doing more harm than good. For example, when water is seeping in through a wall in a building's basement, one fairly common "repair" is to seal the inside surface of the wall with a waterproof sealant. This actually makes the problem worse, because water still seeps in from the earth outside and instead of dripping out or evaporating on the surface, the water gets trapped in the wall behind the barrier where it further weakens the concrete or stone or brick that the cellar wall is made of. Eventually, water pressure will force the sealant barrier off, probably taking some of the wall surface along with it, causing greater damage.

The key to any successful repair to historic buildings is to address the root causes of a problem at its source. In the case of the cellar wall, a proper repair would mean digging a trench on the outside of the wall and installing a French drain and or a robust water barrier to the outside of the wall to prevent water from entering the building in the first place. Another example of an ineffective repair is using caulk to seal an expanding crack in a masonry wall. In the short term, the caulk may seal the crack, but if the building continues to settle and the wall keeps shifting, the crack will simply get larger than the caulk bead, and the bead will fall off. The cause of the crack, which often requires much more sophisticated and expensive remedy than the crack itself, must be addressed to solve the problem.

Improper repairs to historic brick walls cause serious damage. As described in Chapter 10, the *Secretary of the Interior's Standards* advise that historic materials should be repaired as the first choice and be replaced in kind if for some reason they can't be repaired. For a repair or replacement material to last, it doesn't only have to match the original in appearance, but it has to be compatible in other ways as well. For example, if mortar in historic brick is decayed and falling out, the replacement mortar not only has to match the original in color, it is even more important that it match the original in consistency and hardness (Figure 8.19).

Figure 8.19. Improper repairs to historic brick using Portland mortar are not only unattractive, but can cause damage to the brick. Source: Photograph by Peter B. Dedek, 2008.

Historic mortar (in buildings built before the 1930s) was made up of lime, sand and sometimes ground-up brick, animal hair, and in the early 20th century, masons sometimes added some cement to the mix. Historically, mortar was a relatively soft, sandy material and, as described in Chapter 7, historic bricks were softer than today's as well. A major ingredient in modern mortar is Portland cement, which is a hard stonelike material first manufactured in the United States in 1872. If contemporary mortar is used to repair a historic wall, the new mortar will be harder than both the old mortar and the brick. The historic mortar and brick expand and contract as the temperature and humidity changes, but Portland does not. Over time, the bricks will start to break apart because the Portland mortar won't give when the bricks expand, often causing serious damage to the bricks (Figure 8.20). When repointing historic brick and adding replacement mortar, a sample of the historic mortar should be sent off to one of several laboratories in the United States that analyze the contents of historic mortar, and the new mortar should be formulated to match the existing. This way, not only will the mortar look authentic, it will expand and contract in harmony with the bricks and protect the wall.

Other improper repairs can cause damage or just end up looking bad. A process similar to the mistake of using Portland mortar to repoint old brick walls is the practice of using hard modern stucco to cover old brick walls described in Chapter 7. At first the hard stucco seems attractive, because it is denser and more weather resistant and should last longer than traditional stucco, which, like traditional mortar, was made with a combination of lime and sand, but the Portland stucco has the same problem as Portland mortar in that it doesn't expand and contract with the porous brick wall behind and will eventually crack and break off.

In some instances, synthetic materials such as fiberglass can be used effectively to repair historic buildings. Once such case is when lost or severely damaged decorative cornices are replaced by copies made of fiberglass. Once painted, the fiberglass looks identical (from the

Figure 8.20. This brick is spalling because of improper repointing with Portland mortar. Source: Photograph by Peter B. Dedek, 2012.

street below at least) to the original wood or metal, and if attached properly to the façade it can last for a long time.

Other damaging repairs include using inappropriate filler epoxies on rotten wood that eventually fall out and replacing historic plaster with wall board when it could have been repaired with plaster that matches the historic material. Repairs need to preserve the historic integrity of both exterior and interior features while also preventing the return of factors, such as water intrusion and pests, that caused the damage in the first place.

HARSH CLEANING AND STRIPPING

Dirty buildings look ugly, and people, particularly in the United States, often like to give even very old buildings a nice clean and tidy look. Harsh cleaning, such as sandblasting and using high-pressure water, can seem like the perfect solution to beautify a dirty historic building. Unfortunately, harsh cleaning often does serious damage to historic building materials, such as brick, stone, and wood. As described in Chapter 10, the *Secretary of the Interior's Standards* advise against harsh cleaning, because it can tear into and pit the exterior surface of the building.

Take old brick for example. As stated earlier, brick made before the 1930s is softer than today's brick, and the farther you go back in history, the softer the brick was. Using a sandblaster or high pressure washer strips the brick's hard exterior away, exposing the softer interior layers, which are then more prone to erosion after the cleaning is finished. Harsh cleaning also pits the surface of the brick which will actually cause it to collect more dirt more quickly than before. Harsh cleaning also washes away some of the historic mortar, which, as we know, was softer than today's Portland cement mortar.

Harsh cleaning damages wood by gouging out the softer, lighter parts of the wood grain. A common goal of harsh stripping on wood and brick is in the removal of old paint. The use of spinning metal brushes on drill heads and mechanical scrapers damage old wood. Hand scraping, perhaps using mild chemicals to dissolve the paint, is the preferred (and admittedly more expensive) method of removing paint from wood, and in many cases it's simply impossible to satisfactorily remove paint from old brick without damaging the brick itself, requiring that the paint be left on.

Another damaging practice is to use industrial power sanders on historic pine and hardwood floors. Unless used with caution by experts, these sanders often scratch and gouge the floor surface and remove the historic patina, which reduces the historic feeling of the room. Using small, hand-held sanders or simply retaining the historic finish is recommended.

VINYL AND ALUMINUM SIDING

People install vinyl siding on historic houses and other buildings because it seems like an easy way to avoid having to repair and periodically paint and repair the wooden siding beneath. Siding made of artificial materials gives the impression that a building is clean and in good repair and also has a neat, modern look. Although it may seem that aluminum and vinyl siding are indestructible, they actually fade in sunlight and also can warp in areas with hot temperatures

Figure 8.21. As evidenced by this old building in upstate New York, aluminum siding not only harmed the historic integrity of the building, but also proved to lack durability. Source: Photograph by Peter B. Dedek, 2008.

(Figure 8.21). Because it is applied in sheets, vinyl siding is more difficult to repair than wooden siding, because whole sheets have to be replaced and if the siding has faded, the color of replacement panels will not match that of the siding already on the wall. This may mean that the vinyl must be painted, which defeats much of the purpose of installing it in the first place.

The installation of vinyl siding can damage significant features of historic buildings and can also exacerbate and conceal problems within the walls it covers. Usually, vinyl is installed on buildings that have peeling paint, rotting boards, and other maintenance issues. Applying the siding simply covers these issues up without addressing them, allowing problems such as water intrusion, rot, and termite infestation to continue beneath the surface unchecked. In fact, the application of vinyl siding often makes matters worse by trapping moisture inside walls. If problems such as condensation of water within walls, rising damp, or infestation by termites or carpenter ants continue unabated beneath the false serenity provided by vinyl siding, major and expensive structural repairs will eventually be required to prevent parts of a building from collapsing. Even if the structure remains intact, water migrating into walls behind the siding from broken gutters, roof leaks, or rising damp is likely to damage interior finishes, making paint peel and wallpaper bubble up, and eventually water will ruin the plaster beneath. Water present inside a wall will also reduce the insulation value of most types of thermal insulation (Myers and Hume 1984).

Another problem with vinyl siding on historic buildings is that siding installers sometimes destroy significant historic features, such as moldings and cornices, and even remove entire windows during the installation process. This reduces the historic integrity of a building and the damage caused can sometimes be very difficult or impossible to reverse. In addition, vinyl siding also has a different look and feel than historic siding, which further reduces the historic

Figure 8.22. The installation of aluminum siding harmed the historic integrity of this historic church by covering up or destroying most of its architectural details. Source: Photograph by Peter B. Dedek, 2012.

integrity of a building (Figure 8.22). Vinyl siding, particularly if it is poorly installed, makes a building appear as if it is wearing a poorly fitting plastic coat.

ACID RAIN

Acid rain, which results from air pollution generated by industry and vehicles, can damage decorative architectural features and sculptures, especially those rendered in soft stone, such as limestone or marble; however, hard stone such as granite can also be damaged over long periods of time (Figure 8.23). This damage can be greatly accelerated by the presence of certain species of birds such as pigeons and English sparrows, because their acidic dung mixes with the rain and accelerates the erosion of stone or metal and hastens the rot of wood. Also, if exposed to acid rain, traditional lime-based mortars used in brick and stone walls dissolve more quickly over time, doing potentially serious damage to the wall.

Chemical treatments, such as silanes, silicates, silicon resins, and acrylic emulsions that increase the strength and cohesion of the material can help protect

Figure 8.23. This sculpture has been damaged by acid rain. Source: Photograph by Peter B. Dedek, 2009.

stone architectural elements and sculptures from the effects of acid rain. The chemicals usually work by reducing the size of the pores of the stone. Care should be taken not to plug the pores completely, however, because that would not let water evaporate out of the stone, which is required to prevent moisture building up in the material (Croci 1998).

When stone is treated with chemicals, the stone element is usually removed from the building and dipped in a bath of chemicals in a process called **consolidation**. In other cases, the chemicals are carefully applied with brushes like paint. If chemicals intended to protect stone from acid rain and erosion are applied incorrectly, they can actually make the erosion and wear more severe, and therefore chemicals used in consolidation should be applied only by experienced conservators.

VIBRATIONS FROM TRAFFIC AND MACHINERY

In some areas of the country the vibrations created by heavy trucks and trains can shake historic buildings and cause damage, especially to those with masonry walls and traditional plaster with wooden lath. Vibrations are particularly damaging in areas with thick, loamy soils and a lot of heavy traffic. Another common source of damaging vibration that can occur anywhere comes from nearby construction or demolition. Activities such as driving piles and blasting have the potential to harm historic buildings in the area. The plaster in historic ceilings is particularly vulnerable to vibrations. Even minor shaking can loosen and crack ceiling plaster, especially if it has decorative elements such as molded plaster medallions.

The best way to control vibrations is at the municipal level by working for lower speed limits, weight limits, and lower traffic counts on roads near vulnerable historic buildings. Danger from pile driving and blasting needs to be addressed by working with regulators and general contractors to find alternative construction methods.

If the vibrations themselves can't be limited, then it may be possible to install vibration absorbing layers under the foundations of affected buildings, however this is very involved and expensive. Or it may even be possible to pad nearby roads. The installation of absorbent rubber pads beneath an adjacent heavily trafficked road protected the Villa Farnesina in Rome from road vibrations (Feiden 2003). Perhaps an easier solution would be to route heavy traffic away from historic areas.

CONCLUSION

An ability to identify common threats to historic buildings is critical to successful design solutions. Because of their age and a greater variety of building construction types and materials, historic buildings often require more attention and care than their newer counterparts. Designers who work with historic buildings and their interiors deal with a lot of specific issues that require specialized knowledge and skills not required when designing new buildings. This adds complexity and greater challenges but also adds a fascinating aspect to the work of a designer or architect.

STUDY QUESTIONS

1. Water is the most common threat to historic buildings. Name five ways in which water can enter historic building fabric, and name a few ways this intrusion can be detected.

2. In what ways can pigeons endanger historic buildings and their occupants?

3. What are the three basic types of termites are found in the United States, and what are the primary ways of protecting historic wood from infestation from each?

4. What are some of the implications for a historic building that has a horizontal crack in a masonry wall that is growing wider by the day?

5. What is "differential settling," and what are some potential causes for it?

6. Why shouldn't masonry walls be completely sealed and made fully waterproof on all surfaces?

7. What are some types of damage caused by sandblasting to historic stone, brick, and wood?

8. Name some reasons why preservationists frown on the use of vinyl siding.

9. Discuss the reasons why leaving a building vacant endangers it.

10. Why are historic buildings statistically more likely to be damaged in hurricanes and floods than newer buildings?

VISUAL QUIZ

CASE STUDIES

A series of six photographs of endangered buildings is presented that show damage from sources discussed in the chapter.

1) For each photograph, list the types of damage present and probable causes for the damage.	2) What possible measures might be taken to minimize further damage and correct the situation for each condition identified in question 1?

Answers and explanations found in Instructor's Guide.

Figure 8.24. A series of six photographs of endangered buildings showing damage from sources discussed in the chapter. Source: Photograph by Peter B. Dedek, 2012.

Figure 8.25.

Figure 8.26.

Figure 8.27.

Figure 8.28.

Figure 8.29.

SOURCES

Advisory Council on Historic Preservation and the General Services Administration. 1989. "Fire Safety Retrofitting in Historic Buildings" 27. Washington, DC: US Government Printing Office.

Croci, Giorgio. 1998. *The Conservation and Structural Restoration of Architectural Heritage.* Advances in Architecture Series. Southampton, UK: Conceptual Mechanics Publications.

Feiden, Bernard. 2003. *Conservation of Historic Buildings.* Third edition. Amsterdam: Architectural Press.

Greensburg Greentown. 2010. "In Depth Case Studies: S.D. Robinett Building." Accessed November 29, 2013. http://greensburg.buildinggreen.com/overview.cfm?projectid=2064.

Hooper, Mary. 2010. "Greensburg Residents from Kiowa County United to Help Small Businesses." Accessed November 29, 2013. http://www.thelegendmagazine.com/Spring10/kiowa10.html.

Jones, Frank T. 2007. "Understanding and Controlling Feral Pigeons." *Avian Advice,* Winter edition. Center of Excellence for Poultry Science, University of Arkansas Cooperative Extension. Accessed June 27, 2012. http://www.avianadvice.uark.edu/AA%20PDFs/avianadvice_wi07.pdf.

Look, David W., Terry Wong, and Sylvia Rose Augustus. 1997. "The Seismic Retrofit of Historic Buildings Keeping Preservation in the Forefront." Preservation Brief 41. Washington, DC: National Park Service.

Myers, John H. 1984. "Aluminum and Vinyl Siding on Historic Buildings: The Appropriateness of Substitute Materials for Resurfacing Historic Wood Frame Buildings," rev. by Gary L. Hume. Preservation Brief 8. Washington, DC: National Park Service.

Ohio General Health District. "Vector Borne Disease Control-Mice." Accessed September 7, 2012. http://www.clermonthealthdistrict.org/VectorBorneMice.aspx.

Technical Preservation Services, NPS. 2010. "Tax Credits Help with Tornado Recovery: Featured Case Study: S.D. Robinett Building." Accessed on November 29, 2013. http://www.nps.gov/tps/tax-incentives/case-studies.htm#robinett.

Waldorf, Phil. 2008. *Health Hazards from Pigeons, Starlings, and English Sparrows.* Second edition. Boonton, NJ: Diversi-Comm.

Watts, John M., Jr. 2003. "Fire-Risk Indexing: A Systemic Approach to Building-Code 'Equivalency' for Historic Buildings." *APT Bulletin* 34(4): 23–28. Association for Preservation Technology International.

Winston, Mark L. 1999. *Nature Wars: People vs. Pests.* Boston: Harvard University Press.

DATING A HISTORIC BUILDING

OBJECTIVES

- Outline some common methods of visually investigating the exteriors and interiors of historic buildings.

- Describe the materials visible in historic buildings that assist in determining their approximate age.

- Identify methods of determining the age of a building using evidence from specific materials, construction techniques, traces of removed features, and mechanical systems.

A major factor in deciding whether a building should be considered historic is its age. According to the National Register guidelines, a building over 50 years old is potentially eligible for listing, although age is only one factor among many, such as the building's style, history, and level of historic integrity. Knowing the age of a building helps one understand what kinds of materials and craftsmanship may be found there and assists in the determination of what level of special care should be used during rehabilitation or renovation.

There are many methods of making an educated guess as to the age of a building. Archival evidence is very important if it can be found. Before doing a visual inspection of a site, archival historical research should be done first to find out if there is any available documentary evidence, such as old building contracts, deed transfers, period photographs, relevant letters, and the like, to establish and document the history and the age of a building. Chapter 4 describes this process. The use of architectural style field guides can also help an investigator identify a building's form and style and hence be able to estimate its approximate age, since specific styles belong to approximate periods in history. In addition, especially where little historical information can be found on a property, it is useful to perform a physical survey of the building and its surroundings in order to gather clues about its history and to help estimate its age and character (this process is described in Chapter 11).

Many aspects of historic buildings and their contexts offer evidence about their history. However, since old buildings often undergo repairs, alterations, and additions over time, new materials may cover a building that is older than it looks. A good strategy is to examine a building's most fundamental structural elements, such as its frame, load-bearing walls, and foundations, and estimate a building's age based on these, because the basic structure of a building is relatively difficult to replace or alter significantly. For example, if an old building has a heavy timber frame it was probably built before 1860, even if it has more superficial elements such as windows and interior finishes that date from later periods. It is also important not to try to guess the age of a building based on just one or two individual features. A credible case for the age of a building can be made when many of the building components discussed in this chapter are investigated and information about them combined to create a relatively complete picture of how and when a building was constructed. This chapter provides a brief explanation of how to ascertain the age of a historic building based on its context, appearance, materials, and methods of construction.

NEIGHBORHOOD AND REGION

By examining and researching the history of the neighborhood and geographic region in which a building is located, one can discover the first clues as to when it may have been built. The first indicator to consider is the region where the building is. Because New England was first settled by Europeans in the early 1600s, a historic house located in eastern Massachusetts could possibly be over 300 years old, while a house built by people of European or African ancestry in Wyoming cannot date from before the mid-1800s, because such people did not build substantial buildings there before that time. This sounds straightforward, but individuals involved with historic buildings have believed a building to be older than is possible given the area where it is located. A member of a local preservation group once argued that a cut-stone bank building located in Midland, Texas, was built in 1810. Since people who lived in that area were nomadic before the railroad arrived in 1880s, such an early date of construction could be eliminated due to the building's location (Leffler 2012).

Specific types of development occurred at different times in different places, and having knowledge of the overall evolution of certain building types within a region can help to determine the general time frame in which a particular building was most likely to have been constructed. This knowledge can be obtained by researching the history of the region, state, and community where the building in question is located using available resources, such as books, the Internet, and other materials available at repositories, such as libraries, archives, and state and local historical societies.

HISTORIC FUNCTION

Another clue to the approximate age of a building is its original function and any other functions it may have served throughout its history, if known. If, for example, a house was used as a hospital during the Civil War, then obviously it was built before 1865. If a historic building started out as a garage, car dealership, or had any other original function related to automobiles, then it must date to sometime after the beginning of the 20th century; many auto-related buildings, such as old gas stations and car dealerships, can be identified easily by observing features such as stained concrete floors, garage doors, and picture windows, although it is always possible these features were added to an older building (Figure 9.1). In addition, a historic building may be associated with a certain stage of a community's development, such as an economic boom period brought on by the coming of the railroad or as part of a commercial area that

WILSON'S TEXACO TRUCK STOP
U. S. HIGHWAY 11 NORTH, HATTIESBURG, MISSISSIPPI

Figure 9.1. This historic gas station in Hattiesburg, Mississippi represents a distinct period in the development of the automobile landscape, which helps place the building and its associated surroundings in the mid-20th century. Source: Peter B. Dedek Collection

sprung up after a highway was constructed. Understanding a building's historical context and functional associations within its community and among its neighbors can help place it in time.

STYLE

Historical architectural styles spanned distinct eras. For example, the Greek Revival style began about 1820 with the construction of architect William Strickland's Second Bank of Philadelphia (1820) (Figure 9.2) and ended in the 1870s, earlier in northern states. Therefore, gaining a working knowledge of American historic architectural styles can help in efforts to date a building. A number of excellent books are available that provide detailed information on American architectural styles (See Appendix A).

An investigator must be careful, however, because some later styles, such as colonial revival style, which dates from about 1920 to the 1950s, can mimic earlier styles, such as the Georgian style, which dates from about 1720 to the 1780s. In regions where Georgian houses were built

Figure 9.2 William Strickland's Second Bank of Philadelphia (1820). Source: Library of Congress Prints and Photographs Division Washington, D.C. 20540 USA http://hdl.loc.gov/loc.pnp/pp.print. Historic American Buildings Survey/Historic American Engineering Record/Historic American Landscapes Survey. Reproduction Number: HABS PA,51-PHILA,223—42.

and still exist, such as in New England, it is possible to confuse the copy, colonial revival, with an original Georgian. Where such confusion is possible, other evidence, such as the age of the neighborhood (if a house is surrounded by similar houses built in the 1920s, then it probably also dates from the 1920s), and looking closely at physical elements of the building, such as its windows, frame, and foundation, can help solve the riddle. Of course, if a house that looks like a Georgian is located in California, it cannot possibly be an original Georgian, and other possibilities need to be investigated. There were also a good number of buildings constructed in North America in the late 1800s and early 1900s in the Beaux-Arts and classic revival styles that can both be easily confused with earlier styles, such as the Federal and Adamesque styles, which date to the late 1700s and early 1800s.

Another point of caution is that a building may have been remodeled and might exhibit elements that date to a period later than its original period of construction. In order to find a reliable estimate, in addition to surveying façades and major rooms, unfinished interior spaces, such as attics and basements, need to be examined.

WINDOWS

One of the easiest and most telling methods of determining the age of a building is examining its windows. In general, when looking at buildings from the 1700s and 1800s, the windows in these older buildings tend to have small panes with wavy, thick, and bubbly glass. This assumes, of course, that the existing windows are not later replacements. The windows of many old buildings have been changed over time. However, if multipane, wood-sash windows with panes of wavy glass with bubbles exist on a building that otherwise appears to be old, then it is likely that the building dates back at least to the mid-1800s.

Buildings constructed before the late 1800s had multipane windows. The earliest buildings built before the early 1700s found in regions such as New England and New York State and in Mid-Atlantic states such as Virginia, Maryland, and Delaware, usually had multipane **casement windows**, which are hinged on the sides and open outward from the middle. By the 1700s, many buildings constructed in the east had single-hung sash windows, in which the bottom sash opens by sliding up. Single-hung windows came in various configurations, such as nine panes over six, or twelve-over-nine, nine-over-nine, or twelve-over-twelve (Figure 9.3). In the early 19th century, the six-over-six configuration became common throughout

Figure 9.3. Multipane windows, such as this twelve-over-twelve pane single-hung window, are often found on buildings built prior to 1850. Source: Peter B. Dedek, 2011.

Figure 9.4. Six-over-six windows like this one were common from around 1800 to about 1880. Source: Peter B. Dedek, 2008.

most of the areas of North America occupied by the settlers from Europe and their decedents (Figure 9.4). The panes themselves began to grow in size as glass-making technology advanced. Before around 1860, only the bottom sash could be moved up and down, but after that time, double-hung windows came into use where the upper sash slid up and down as well for better ventilation and easier cleaning.

The availability of more advanced glassmaking technology and the ability of people to afford larger panes of glass varied by area and was determined by the affluence of a building's owners or builders. In rural and poorer areas, glass panes tended to remain smaller for longer, and were upgraded less frequently.

In the Gulf South from Louisiana westward into the Southwest, most early buildings, which had French and Spanish influence in Louisiana and Spanish influence in Texas through California, continued to have casement windows even after 1700. In these regions, casement windows were commonly used into the mid-1900s.

Having larger and clearer window panes on one's house or commercial building became a status symbol in the late 1800s, and around 1865 a new type of window came into use. The two-over-two double-hung sash window was only popular from about 1865 to about 1880, but it was installed widely during its short period of dominance (Figure 9.5). If a building has this type of window, it probably dates back to this period, except in rural areas where it might date to 1890 or even 1900. Like most single- or double-hung windows made since about 1820, the bottom sash of these windows was made easier to open and to keep open by the presence of cast-iron counterweights suspended on ropes and located inside the sides of the window (behind the jambs) that moved down as the window's bottom sash was pushed up. When in good working order, the weights kept the sash from needing to be propped up when open.

Around 1880, the wooden one-over-one double-hung window was introduced. These operated in the same manner as six-over-six and two-over-two windows and became very popular. As the decades passed, glass became clearer and free of defects such as waves and bubbles. All of these historic windows had wooden sash with a single thickness of glass (**single glazed**) and were fitted with detachable storm windows in areas with cold winters. Single-glazed wooden one-over-one double-hung windows were commonly used until around the 1980s, especially in residential construction, but are rare today in new construction where **double-glazed** (with two panes of glass filled with an inert gas) metal or vinyl sash windows are often used.

Figure 9.5. The presence of a historic version of two-over-two windows such as these indicates that a building dates from around 1865 to about 1890, unless the window replaced an earlier multipane window. Source: Peter B. Dedek, 2011.

During the 1900s, new types of windows emerged—such as those with metal sashes—that were sometimes casement windows or of the double-hung variety, or were fixed in the wall with or without an operable section (Figure 9.6). Single-glazed metal windows were popular in both commercial buildings from the 1920s to the 1960s.

In addition to the number and sizes of panes, the type of glass used in windows can be a good indicator of how old the windows are. The technology of glassmaking evolved in a number of distinct steps over the past three centuries.

Crown Glass Windows

Between 1700 and the early 1800s, **crown** or **table glass** was produced for use in windows. To make these windows, a glassblower would hand-blow a lump of molten glass in a way similar to how they created bottles at the time. The worker would then spin the glass out into a thin disc using centrifugal force and, after it cooled, would cut the resulting plate, which could be as large as four feet in diameter, into rectangular panes. At the center, the disk

Figure 9.6. Multipane metal windows were popular in the early to mid-20th century, particularly on commercial or industrial buildings. Source: Peter B. Dedek, 2008.

had a "bull's-eye" that was essentially useless and was often remelted in the furnace. The resulting panes of glass were thick, bubbly, and wavy, and usually somewhat thicker on one side than the other.

Cylinder Glass Windows

Cylinder glass was produced from the early 1800s to around 1920. Glassworkers created cylinder glass by blowing a long tube of glass and then cutting it along the entire length of the cylinder, reheating it, and letting it fall flat on a table. Because cylinder glass could be made into larger and more uniform panes, it gradually replaced crown glass in windows. As this technology improved, the production of thinner and larger sheets of glass became possible, and glass windows became less expensive and more common. Although still wavy by today's standards, cylinder glass was clearer, thinner, and less bubbly than crown glass (Black 1998).

Plate Glass Windows

Plate glass dates from around 1860 and is still manufactured today. To make plate glass, molten glass is poured onto large tables then rolled flat into sheets. Then, after the sheets cool, industrial machinery grinds and polishes them on both sides. This process produces a large and much more uniform sheet of glass than the crown or cylinder processes. The introduction of plate glass allowed for large, relatively inexpensive windows and enabled the widespread use of one-over-one and single-pane shop windows. Plate glass is less wavy than cylinder glass and has no bubbles.

Float Glass Windows

Float glass has been produced since the mid 1900s and, like plate glass, continues to be manufactured today. In the float process, molten glass is poured across the surface of a vat of molten tin where it flattens into nearly flawless sheets. Float glass, which is perfectly transparent, is the type often used for large picture windows and for the glass curtain walls of modern buildings.

FOUNDATIONS

Historic buildings often have brick or stone foundations. The material chosen usually depended on the availability of a given kind of masonry in the local area. The presence of brick or stone as a structural material suggests a building built before the mid-20th century. Also, generally, the older the building, the softer the brick used and the softer the mortar present; grainy mortar was also used in early stone foundations. In addition, many old wooden structures were set on brick or stone piers.

If a building or a section of a building has a concrete foundation, it probably dates from around 1900 to the present, although some earlier buildings with concrete foundations and walls do exist. Also, it is possible that a building that appears to be older than 1900 that has a concrete foundation might have been moved from its original location and placed on a new foundation or the building may have been jacked up in place and its foundation replaced.

As described in Chapter 7, from around 1905 to 1930, some foundations and entire buildings were constructed out of molded hollow concrete blocks that were designed to look like cut stone blocks or even to mimic brick. Concrete cast-stone blocks were used for a limited time, and their presence can be a strong indication that the building dates to the early 20th century (Simpson 1989). If a building has an original foundation of standard undecorated concrete masonry units (CMU), commonly known as cinder blocks, the building dates from the 1930s or later and most likely from after the Second World War.

Sometimes, in addition to the basement construction materials, items often found in basements and crawlspaces, such as old furnaces, coal storage bins, vintage pipes, and old electric wiring, can offer clues as to the age of the building. Random objects, like old furniture, or boards, doors, and windows previously removed from the building, found stored in a basement or attic can also provide valuable information about the building and its history.

MASONRY WALLS

Many early buildings had load-bearing masonry walls made of brick or stone or a combination of the two. After the mid-20th century, most walls that appear to be brick or stone are actually veneers, one layer thick. Since 1900, some masonry walls have been made of concrete.

Brick

As noted, older bricks are soft. They also have a somewhat rough texture and are less uniform in shape than more recent bricks. Early bricks were pushed into a wooden mold and later fired in a wood-burning kiln. Around the mid-19th century, a process where bricks were molded in machines and fired in kilns using coal and other modern fuels was adopted. If brick is rough and irregular and soft, it is evidence that a building may date from before the mid-1800s. Older bricks were often fired at inconsistent temperatures, which made them sometimes have varying shades, and some bricks may have deteriorated faster than others found on the same building.

Also, if the mortar is a soft sandy material, this indicates an older wall. The presence of hard Portland cement suggests a wall that dates from the late 1800s or later, although some earlier bricks have been **repointed** (the process of replacing mortar between bricks) with Portland at a later time. Bricks are also laid in different patterns called "bonds" (see Chapter 7). Certain bonds, such as Flemish and English bonds, indicate early dates of construction, and some decorative brick patterns and brick finishes are characteristic of certain styles and periods.

Another indicator of age is whether a brick wall is load-bearing. Brick walls built until around 1930 tend to be of the thick load-bearing type, which are several bricks thick, while more recent brick walls often have a brick veneer, which is only one brick thick.

Stone

Stone walls can be identified in much the same way as brick in that thick load-bearing walls with soft lime-based mortar usually indicate a building constructed before the 20th century

Figure 9.7. Stone construction such as this room that functioned as a jail at Fort Stockton in Fort Stockton, Texas, dates to the 19th century. In most Victorian buildings, this stone would have been plastered over on the interior. Source: Peter B. Dedek, 2010.

(Figure 9.7). As with brick, more recent buildings with a stone exterior usually have a stone veneer, with some other material holding the building up. Precise evaluation of the age of stone construction can be complicated, however, because the kinds of stone available vary by region, and a wide variety of building methods were used. In the United States, a building constructed of stone that was not locally quarried indicates the building was probably erected after the arrival of railroads to its location, unless, perhaps the building was constructed in a port city or near a shipping canal.

FRAME TYPE

Wooden buildings and the wooden elements of masonry buildings were constructed using timber-frame construction prior to the mid 1800s. Timber-frame buildings have a structural system made up of heavy timbers consisting of thick posts and beams and braces that are attached together by mortise and tenon construction (see Chapter 7). Through the 1800s, wooden framing evolved in several distinct phases.

Hand-Hewn Timber-Frame Buildings

Hand-hewn timber-frame buildings are held up by heavy beams hewn from logs and shaped using a broad axe with hand-chiseled mortise and tenon joints. The entire frame was made up of thick timbers, often with mud, stone, or brick sandwiched between them. The technique was based on European, especially English, building methods from the Middle Ages (Figure 9.8). Early timber-frame buildings often had simple foundations usually made of piled fieldstone, and had large, long posts and beams, because wood was common in eastern North America

Figure 9.8. Hand-hewn-timber framing in America was based on English building techniques such as those used here in Lavenham, England, in the 1500s. The timber structure was often visible from both within and without. Source: Peter B. Dedek, 2011.

where most Europeans were settling in these times. In urban areas and in more significant buildings, the foundations were more substantial. This kind of construction is mostly concentrated in buildings built before about 1800 located in states along the Atlantic coast, although hand-hewn buildings were constructed until much later in remote areas that did not have access to sawmills. If hand-cut beams are present in a building in a town or city it indicates an early date of construction, but this also depends on which part of the country the building is found; the more urban and farther east, the older it probably is.

Timber-Braced-Frame Buildings

Timber-braced-frame construction with sawed timbers replaced hand-hewn timber frame in urban areas first. Timber-braced-frame construction still used heavy timbers and mortise-and-tenon joints, but with an added system of sawn **studs** (comparatively thin vertical members such as two-by-fours and two-by-eights used within the walls for additional support). Timber-braced-frame buildings usually had more sophisticated, solid foundations made of mortared masonry. In addition, timber-braced frames had numerous diagonal braces that were notched into the main timbers. Timber-braced framing was used well into the 1850s, especially in rural areas and is found in a lot of historic barns dating into the late 1800s.

Balloon Frame Buildings

As described in Chapter 7, in balloon-frame buildings, heavy timbers were replaced by long, lighter sawn studs (such as two-by-fours and two-by-eights) that supported the building. These boards were arranged vertically, often spanning two or more floors, and were also used as beams. Heavy elements, such as corners and posts, were made up of several thin boards nailed together. Balloon frame construction did away with mortise-and-tenon joints in favor of nails, which had become much less expensive due to new industrial production methods. Balloon-frame buildings were much cheaper and easier to build and were constructed across America from the 1860s until around 1930. Balloon frame can be identified by the presence of sawn but unplaned boards with rough-cut studs that span up more than a single floor.

Stud- or Platform-Frame Buildings

Stud-frame or platform-frame construction, in which each story is framed out and constructed individually, replaced balloon frame in the 1930s and is the system still used today. Stud framing helps improve structural rigidity and makes a building more resistant to fire (Center for Historic Preservation 2002). Newer stud-frame buildings built after about 1950 use smooth, planed boards.

SAW CUTS

The types of marks left by saws over the decades can help an investigator identify how long ago a board was cut. Woodcutting technology evolved in identifiable ways. As with looking at the frames themselves, the best place to find saw marks is in cellars and attics. Many early buildings also had hand-hewn beams instead of, or along with, saw-cut boards.

Pit Saws

The earliest European settlers used **pit saws** to rip boards, which cut with an up-and-down vertical motion and were powered by hand. Settlers continued to use them for decades. To "rip" a board is to cut it lengthwise, along the grain. These saws were used in some places until around 1800. Wood cut by pit saws left slanted (but not curved), irregular grooves that are not particularly distinct.

Water-Powered Saws

Water-powered sawmills became widespread in the early 1800s. They used up-and-down "sash saws" (something like a giant jigsaw) that cut wood much more efficiently. These saws left uniform, completely vertical, distinct grooves on boards. They were replaced by circular saws in many places by the mid-1800s, but continued in use in some rural areas until around 1900.

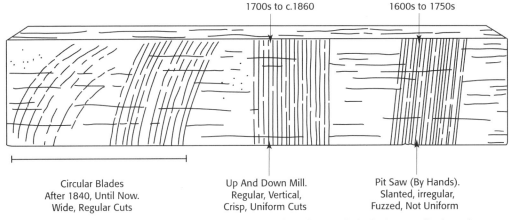

1700s to c.1860

1600s to 1750s

Circular Blades
After 1840, Until Now.
Wide, Regular Cuts

Up And Down Mill.
Regular, Vertical,
Crisp, Uniform Cuts

Pit Saw (By Hands).
Slanted, irregular,
Fuzzed, Not Uniform

Figure 9.9. Saw marks indicate the time period when a piece of wood was milled, which is usually about the time a building was constructed; however, sometimes wood was reused in later buildings.

Circular Saws

Invented in the early 1800s, circular saws cut wood faster than sash saws. Often powered by water power or steam and later by electricity, these saws came into use in most areas by the 1850s. Circular saws leave diagonal circular arcs on unplaned boards. They continue to be used to this day, however, now their saw marks are usually removed in the wood planning process. (Center for Historic Preservation 2002) (Figure 9.9).

FLOORBOARDS

The floorboards found in older buildings tend to be wider than those used in later buildings. When old-growth lumber was common, wide-plank floors were practical. Many early floors were made of pine, while in the late 1800s floors were increasingly made of narrow strips of hardwood such as elm, ash, and chestnut, especially for more formal rooms, where parquet was sometimes used. **Parquet floors,** which originated in baroque France in the 1600s, are made up of hardwood designed in geometric patterns. The boards became narrower and often had tongue-and-groove seams, because flooring could be manufactured with steam power.

Old floorboards in high-traffic areas often show wear, indicating their advanced age. Also, one may look for saw marks (as described) on the bottom sides of floorboards to help ascertain how old they are. Patterns of tack holes on wooden floors can indicate that certain types of flooring, such as linoleum or carpet, were once installed over the planks.

INTERIOR WALLS

The materials and construction techniques used in interior walls can offer hints as to the age and evolution of a building. If intact, the design of historic baseboards, trim, and cornices can indicate the style and the status of a building. Thick and ornate trim indicates age and status.

Figure 9.10. Elaborate staircases, thick trim, and high ceilings, can suggest a Victorian-era room, like this one in the Caldwell County Courthouse in Lockhart, Texas. Source: Peter B. Dedek, 2010.

Interior walls with plaster built in the 1700s and early 1800s were usually plastered after the finished trim had been installed, meaning that if the trim is removed, there is no plaster present behind it. After the early 1800s, trim was normally applied after the walls were plastered. Trim in houses built by middle- and high-income people and in many commercial buildings was particularly substantial and ornate during the Victorian era, which lasted from the 1830s to around 1900 (Figure 9.10). Thin, beveled baseboards and minimal trim, combined with drywall, suggests a house built or remodeled after the Second World War, particularly between about 1950 and 1980. Many buildings built before the mid-1900s, especially the homes of lower-income people and buildings in rural areas, had interior walls that consisted of planks of wood (similar to simple plank flooring) that was often covered directly by cloth or wallpaper. The type and style of wallpaper present (some of which might be concealed by layers of paint and other wall coverings) can also be examined and analyzed to indicate the age of a building.

It is important to note, however, that interiors were often altered and remodeled, meaning that interior features may date from a later period than the building. One way to investigate if this is the case is to look for evidence of "ghosting" or shadows left by removed trim and other features on walls, floors, or ceilings. Sometimes evidence of earlier features, such as the original trim, can be found behind the existing trim, sometimes having been used as blocking or shims (McDonald 1994).

The type of wall material can indicate the approximate date of construction. The use of wet-wall plaster and various types of lath (see Chapter 7) indicates that a building probably dates from before the 1930s, whereas wallboard was often used from the 1930s on, although certainly not always. An easy way of telling if a wall is plaster or drywall is to hit it with a fist. Plaster makes a low thump when struck, while drywall has a louder, hollow knocking sound.

NAIL TYPES

The technology used to make nails has evolved in many discernable steps over the past few centuries. Nails can be found somewhere in virtually all buildings and can be a good indicator of a building's age. Attics and basements are the best places to find exposed nails that can be pulled out and identified. There are several major types of historic nails.

Hand-Wrought Nails

Hand-wrought nails date from the time of the first settlement by Europeans to about 1800. These nails were made by hand by blacksmiths who hammered each one out on an anvil. Although they were generally replaced by cut nails at the turn of the 18th century, these nails did not break easily when bent and were therefore used until about 1850 for special applications that required a great deal of tensile strength. Hand-wrought nails can be identified by their rounded heads and small dents from having been hammered into shape by hand during manufacture. Their shaft also tapers in on all four sides and they have either a sharp point or a flat, spade-type point. They vary greatly in style and in form.

Machine-Cut Nails with Hand-Made Heads

Machine-cut nails with hand-made heads were first introduced around 1790. They came into use because hand-wrought nails were difficult to produce and expensive. Machine-cut nails with hand-made heads were produced until about 1820. They can be identified by their shafts, which are rectangular in section and had sides that taper in toward the point on the wide side but do not taper in on the narrow side. Their heads are rounded and so are their points, and the shafts do not exhibit hammer marks, but their heads do. These nails are quite brittle and break fairly easily when bent. Both hand-wrought and cut nails have rectangular shanks, but the corners of a hand-wrought nail are tapered toward the pointed end on all four sides, whereas on a cut nail, the corners are tapered on just two opposite sides (Mercer 1923).

Machine-Cut Nails with Machine-Hammered Heads

Machine-cut nails with machine-hammered heads came into use around 1810. They look like machine-cut nails with hand-made heads except that the heads are more uniform and are flatter because they were applied with water-powered machines. The tips are rounded. These nails were produced until about 1840. These look identical to machine-cut nails with hand-made heads except the heads are flat and have only one hammer mark on them.

Machine-Headed Cut Nails

Machine-headed cut nails came into use in around 1825. These nails were made by machine in one piece with a single operation and have flat heads with no hammer marks. The heads were comparatively thin from about 1825 to 1835 and were usually asymmetrical and not always perfect. After 1835 or so, the heads became thicker and squarer and uniform (Mercer 1923). They look like machine-cut nails with machine-made heads, except that they are more uniform, have square tips, and can be bent without as much risk of breaking. They were in use until about 1900.

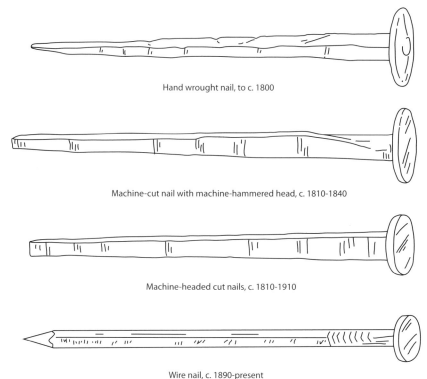

Hand wrought nail, to c. 1800

Machine-cut nail with machine-hammered head, c. 1810-1840

Machine-headed cut nails, c. 1810-1910

Wire nail, c. 1890-present

Figure 9.11. Nail types.

Wire Nails

Wire nails started replacing machine-headed cut nails around 1890 and are still in use. They have round shafts, flat heads, pointed ends, and are far cheaper to make than square nails (Figure 9.11). (Center for Historic Preservation 2002).

SCREW TYPES

Screws were first made in significant numbers around 1800. Screws made before the 1850s had no point and were called **blunt point screws**. In the middle 1800s, these were replaced by screws with sharp points, making pilot holes less necessary with the new design. Although screws sometimes are replaced over time, the presence of a blunt point screw in a building, especially if it has a timber frame, indicates that it may have been built before the mid-1800s (Center for Historic Preservation 2002).

Until the 1930s, all screws had a single slit for use by a flat-head screwdriver. In the 1930s, Henry Phillips designed the **Phillips-head screw**, which has a crossed slit in the head that allows the screwdriver to not slip off as easily. First used in industry, the Phillips-head screw started making its way to buildings by around the 1950s.

EXAMPLES OF BUILDING INVESTIGATIONS
FROM PICTURES

Analysis: The house in this picture appears to be in the Queen Anne style, with a bay window, turned posts, and gingerbread brackets, ornate trim, clapboard siding, and wooden-shingle siding in its gable. The Queen Anne style was popular between around 1870 and 1910, placing the probable time of construction between those dates. The window shown has a one-over-one, double-hung wooden sash, which appears original. If so, this type of window was introduced around 1880, narrowing the probable date of construction to 1880–1910. To better determine the construction date, the type of foundation and framing, along with interior materials and finishes could be examined.

Analysis: This room has a functional fireplace with a simple vernacular style. Since fireplaces of this type weren't constructed much after 1900, the building in which this room is located was probably built before that date. In addition, the floorboards look about nine or so inches wide. Wide floorboards were used normally until around the time of the Civil War, after which narrower hardwood floors were more common. Since the room is fairly stylish (in a country sort of way) one can assume it would have narrower floorboards if built after about 1870. The windows appear to have small panes and look original, also indicating a construction date before the 1870s. Further factors to look for would be saw cuts on the backs of the floorboards and nail types.

This picture, taken in a basement, shows hand-hewn-timber construction, indicating a construction date from the 1700s through the early 1800s, although if the structure was built in a rural area it could date up to about 1850. Note the wide flooring. To narrow the estimated date of construction, one could look at saw cuts on the backs of the floorboards and at nail types.

Analysis: Often when buildings are deteriorated or missing finishes it is often easier to determine their date of construction. Here we see load-bearing brick walls, thick rough-cut joists, and an old-style vernacular classical fireplace. These factors indicate a construction date before 1900, with the fireplace style

suggesting an earlier date of sometime in the mid- to late-1800s. Looking at the saw cuts on the joists, roof framing, nail types, and the overall style of the house would help narrow the date further.

Analysis: This picture shows rough-cut framing with tube-and-knob wiring, both of which indicate a date of construction before the late 1930s. Wooden lath is also present, which was also not used much past 1930 or so. In the upper left-hand corner, a thin wooden siding called waterfall siding is visible, which was popular in the 1920s and early 1930s. While it is clear from the picture the building was constructed before 1930, further investigation of factors such as its foundation, saw cuts, flooring types, and nail types would be needed to determine how much earlier it was built.

Analysis: This house shows balloon construction. indicating a construction date of between 1860 and 1930. The windows are boarded and appear to be replacements, offering no help. A look at the brick piers and the age of the neighborhood may shed more light, however the interior is missing, as are most of its exterior stylistic features.

CONCLUSION

By carefully investigating a building and finding multiple clues based on its location, style, building materials, and building techniques, one can make an educated guess as to when it was first constructed and when it may have been remodeled or added to.

In some cases, a simple visual inspection of a building will yield plenty of information; however, sometimes more elaborate and intrusive techniques such as x-raying walls to identify nail types or using small mirrors or cameras to look in tight spaces need to be employed. Sometimes more destructive techniques, such as removing materials, like trim, siding, or plaster, are used to evaluate materials and conditions underneath, but this should not be done unless all nonintrusive measures have been exhausted, and should be done only by experienced professionals.

Examining historic buildings in ways described in this chapter is useful in determining its age and character. However, without documentation using historical archival evidence, such as building contracts or historic photographs, any date assigned remains speculative. A broad range of investigative techniques need to be employed to accurately assess the history and historical significance of a property.

STUDY QUESTIONS

1. If a house located in New England looks like a colonial Georgian house, does this mean it was built in the 1700s? What are some ways to verify this?

2. What is the approximate earliest period a building that originally functioned a gas station can date to? Why?

3. Which building is older, one with nine-over-six windows or one with two-over-two windows? Is your answer true in all cases? Why or why not?

4. If a building has old, bubbly multipane windows and a concrete foundation, what might this mean?

5. Describe the structure of a braced-timber-frame building.

6. What are the three major types of saw marks and approximately what periods do each date from?

7. A room that functioned as a parlor, which has high ceilings, thick ornate trim, and solid plaster walls, probably dates from which historical era?

8. Describe a machine-cut nail with hand-made head. How does it differ from a machine-headed cut nail?

9. If a floor was screwed down with flat-tipped slot-head screws, about when does the floor probably date from?

10. If a contractor asks you to tear off a fireplace mantel in an old house to determine what kind of bricks were used in the chimney and shed light on how old the building is, what steps should you take before going through with this extreme measure?

EXERCISE: IDENTIFY APPROXIMATE DATE OF BUILDING SHOWN IN IMAGES

You may want to consult a guide to styles of American architecture as well as this chapter while completing the exercise. Choose one of the following ranges of date for each Image:

A. Before 1800 _____   C. 1850–1900 _____   E. 1950–2000 _____

B. 1800–1850 _____   D. 1900–1950 _____   F. After 2000 _____

Answers and explanations found in Instructor's Guide.

SOURCES

Black, Gordon. 1998. "Glass in the Past." *Old House Journal*, August.

Center for Historic Preservation. 2002. "Construction Dating Information." Accessed August 13, 2012. http://campusarch.msu.edu/?p=1305

Leffler, John. "Midland, TX." *Handbook of Texas Online*. Accessed October 05, 2012. http://www.tshaonline.org/handbook/online/articles/hdm03,

McDonald, Travis C. 1994. "Understanding Old Buildings: The Process of Architectural Investigation." Preservation Briefs 35, Technical Preservation Services: National Park Service.

Mercer, Henry C., SC.D. 1923. "Dating Old Houses." Doylestown, Pennsylvania. Accessed October 5, 2012. http://www.philipmarshall.net/Teaching/rwuhp482/mercer_1923.htm

Simpson, Pamela H. 1989. "Cheap, Quick, and Easy: The Early History of Rockfaced Concrete Block Building." *Perspectives in Vernacular Architecture*, Vol. 3: 108–118

10

APPROPRIATE DESIGN: APPLYING THE *SECRETARY OF THE INTERIOR'S STANDARDS*

OBJECTIVES

- Explain the application of the *Secretary of the Interior's Standards for the Treatment of Historic Properties,* which are the national guidelines for designers working with historic buildings.

- Describe how each of the 10 standards is applied in the process of rehabilitating and designing new spaces within and when adding to historic buildings.

The Secretary of the Interior's Standards are a set of rules and preservation guidelines and are the basis for appropriate preservation design in the United States. Originally written by a committee of preservationists in 1976 and revised in 1992 by the National Park Service (NPS), which is under the Department of the Interior, the standards act as a fundamental set of rules for architects, interior designers, building owners, builders, and anyone else actively involved in the preservation, rehabilitation, restoration, or reconstruction of historic buildings. The standards encourage a set of ten practices designed to minimize harm to historic buildings and structures during the planning, design, review, and execution of projects. The NPS maintains four versions of the standards: distinct versions for preservation, rehabilitation, and restoration, and a set that guides historic reconstructions. Each version of the standards differs somewhat, with those for restoration being more strict than those for rehabilitation. The version addressing rehabilitation is the one most commonly used by architects and designers and is the one presented and explained in this chapter.

The *Standards for Rehabilitation* are widely used. For example, they are applied in evaluating whether a project qualifies as a Certified Rehabilitation in for the Federal Investment Tax Credit (explained in Chapter 2). The *Standards for Rehabilitation* are also employed by federal agencies for rehabilitation work on federally owned historic properties and by state and local officials, such as historic district and planning commissions, when reviewing rehabilitation projects on historic landmarks and buildings located within local historic districts.

Even though they are concise and clearly written, applying the standards is not as straightforward as one might imagine. Within the preservation and design fields, they are subject to differing interpretations, something like the way constitutional amendments are given various interpretations in the courts. The requirements of individual standards may mean different things to different people and sometimes become the focus of debate among professionals. It is not unusual, in fact, for experienced preservationists to argue how the standards should be applied in specific instances. One person may assert that a certain standard dictates a particular course of action while another may disagree. For example, an architect could site Standard 9, which states, "New additions, exterior alterations, or related new construction will not destroy historic materials, features, and spatial relationships that characterize the property," as requiring that some unsightly additions to a 1910 courthouse added in the 1970s by a local architect be removed, while to another preservationist, Standard 9 might be interpreted to support the additions' retention because, although the style of the additions does not match the historic building, their materials and scale are compatible. The preservationist arguing for the retention of the additions might also contend that, since the additions date from the early 1970s and are approaching 50 years old, they should be retained under Standard 4, which states, "Changes to a property that have acquired historic significance in their own right will be retained and preserved." Interpretations vary, but as with laws, over the past few decades precedents and case studies have established a fairly consistent general understanding of how the standards should be applied across the preservation field in various situations.

THE SECRETARY OF THE INTERIOR'S STANDARDS FOR REHABILITATION

As stated earlier, the standards are particularly important to designers because they address design decisions and conservation practices encountered in the course of building rehabilitations. Each of the ten standards concerns a specific aspect of historic design or preservation, such as designing additions to historic buildings (Standard 10) and cleaning historic building materials (Standard 7). The application and meanings of the standards sometimes overlap from one standard to the next, but each addresses distinctive issues and applications. A list of the ten standards and explanations of how they are interpreted follows.

STANDARD 1

A property will be used as it was historically or be given a new use that requires minimal change to its distinctive materials, features, spaces, and spatial relationships.

According to Standard 1, ideally, historic buildings should be used for their historic purpose. For example, if a building's historic purpose was a movie theater, the building should remain in use as a movie theater, if possible. The reason for this is if the building continues in its originally intended use, then it is likely fewer damaging changes will have to be made to it than if it were converted to a new use (Figure 10.1) (Figure 10.2).

Figure 10.1. The New York Central Train Station, Poughkeepsie, New York, has continuously retained its historic function since its construction in 1918. Although passenger traffic declined in the 20th century, keeping the building in service as a commuter rail station has allowed the building to retain its historic integrity. Source: Peter B. Dedek, 2011.

Figure 10.2. The historic 1929 Arizona Biltmore Hotel in Phoenix, designed by Albert Chase McArthur, with some very influential consultation with Frank Lloyd Wright, continues in its most appropriate use, as a hotel, and the Grand Ballroom, shown here, as a grand ballroom. Source: Peter B. Dedek, 2010.

Figure 10.3. The Battery Park Hotel, built in 1924 in Asheville, North Carolina, was converted to housing for the elderly during the 1980s and retained much of its historic integrity and context in keeping with Standard 1. Source: Peter B. Dedek, 2008.

If the traditional use cannot be continued for practical or economic reasons, Standard 1 requires that the new use be as close in character to the traditional function as possible. For example, it would be more in keeping with Standard 1 to rehabilitate an old hotel into housing for senior citizens (Figure 10.3). Why? The changes required to convert an old hotel into a shopping mall, for example, would change the basic character of the building, particularly its interior, because malls require large open interior spaces, which would require the removal of most, if not all, of the hotel's guestrooms. In another example, it would be difficult to convert an old movie theater into an office building. The slanted floor found in most movie theaters would have to be leveled, at least in places, for use as office or lobby space, and, in most cases, the large theater space would have to be subdivided to create offices, conference rooms, and the like—a process that would require significant, unsympathetic alterations to the building. Designers and occupants of offices also usually desire natural light, which would require that windows be added to the previously windowless walls, diminishing the integrity of the exterior and probably harming the interior walls, which in theaters are usually decorative. Skylights might be added instead, but they would probably adversely affect the ceiling, which, like the walls, often have significant decorative features. Also, new mechanical systems, such as HVAC ducts would require changes that might harm significant interior architectural features.

This is not to say that significantly altering a building's historic use is always impossible without damaging the building's historic integrity. However, the more incompatible and radically different the new use is, the more designers are challenged to be able to follow the standards and preserve the adaptively used building's integrity.

Another example of a new use for a building that probably won't conform to Standard 1 is converting a historic church into lofts to house students at a university (Figure 10.4). Converting this historic church into such an incompatible use transformed the spatial quality of the interior into something unrecognizable as a church and destroyed the outer context of the building by altering the "spaces and spatial relationships" around the building. Also, as can be seen in the photo, "distinctive materials and features" have been unsympathetically altered on the exterior of the historic building itself.

Figure 10.4. In 2006, developers converted the First Baptist Church, built in San Marcos, Texas, in 1927, into the Sanctuary Lofts, a student housing complex. Although the project probably saved the church from demolition, the new use was so incompatible with the original building that the site lost its integrity and context. Source: Peter B. Dedek, 2008.

STANDARD 2

The historic character of a property will be retained and preserved. The removal of distinctive materials or alteration of features, spaces, and spatial relationships that characterize a property will be avoided.

Probably one of the reasons Standard 2 was written has been the rampant installation of aluminum and vinyl siding to historic houses across North America starting in the 1950s (Figure 10.5a). The original siding is important to retain (Figure 10.5b). The removal and replacement of historic windows is also a common design decision that has been widely

Figure 10.5a. This little building near West Point, New York, has lost its historic integrity due to the addition of aluminum siding and replacement of historic windows and doors. Source: Peter B. Dedek, 2008.

Figure 10.5b. With the exception of its metal roof, this historic house has retained its original exterior materials, including wooden siding and historical details in keeping with the standards. Source: Peter B. Dedek, 2011.

Figure 10.6a. The replacement of historic windows and the original doors has reduced the historic integrity of this firehouse building in Seguin, Texas. Source: Peter B. Dedek, 2012.

Figure 10.6b. The historic windows and the original doors are significant aspects of the historic integrity of this house in upstate New York. Source: Peter B. Dedek, 2011.

interpreted as breaking Standard 2 (Figure 10.6a). Windows remain a particular point of contention because old single-glazed windows tend not to be as energy efficient as their new vinyl or metal double- and triple-glazed counterparts, however historic windows are a major defining characteristic of most historic properties (Figure 10.6b), and it is very difficult to replace windows with modern ones without significantly altering the building's appearance. Even the new glass itself looks different than historic glass, especially if it is of the "low-e" variety often favored by architects and builders, especially in hot climates.

Replacing historic windows is often not even all that practical, because historic windows, particularly those from the 19th century or earlier, were made of high quality old-growth narrow-grain wood, which, if properly maintained, can last for centuries, while many new wooden or vinyl windows are prone to failure due to cheap construction and materials. Historic windows are not always less energy efficient than new ones, either, since, if kept in good repair, old windows are usually tight, and new elements designed to reduce heat loss, such as interior storm windows, can be added.

Another common issue is the removal or significant alteration of porches. Porches, which are often very important features on historic buildings, tend to fall victim to poor maintenance, water intrusion, and differential settling (see Chapter 8). Porches all too often get removed rather than repaired, or at least parts of them end up being taken off, such as the columns, which have been replaced with incompatible materials such as cheap wrought iron. Altering the porch, especially if it adorns the front of the building, can make a historic building difficult to recognize and appreciate and also can adversely alter its function and relationship to the street (Figure 10.7a). Retaining significant features creates a very different impression (Figure 10.7b).

Finish materials, such as wood, brick, and stone; distinctive features such as doorways, porches, and rooflines; and spatial relationships, such as building heights, courtyards, and proximity to the street are critical to the character of a historic building. When designing or evaluating a rehabilitation under Standard 2, the designer should carefully examine the exterior and interior of the building to be rehabilitated to identify the materials, features, and spatial

Figure 10.7a. This double shotgun house in New Orleans has lost its integrity and identity due to remodeling. Windows above the doors have been blocked, historic windows changed, and aluminum siding and a concrete porch added. Source: Peter B. Dedek, 2013.

Figure 10.7b. This double shotgun house in New Orleans on the same street and likely by the same designer as Figure 10.7a has retained more of its original features and materials, including wooden siding and original windows. Source: Peter B. Dedek, 2013.

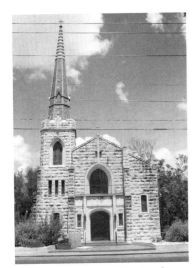

Figure 10.8a. Exterior of National Register–eligible church built circa. 1900. Source: Peter B. Dedek, 2012.

Figure 10.8b. Interior of the nave (former worship space) of the same church, remodeled insensitively for adaptive use as a school. Source: Peter B. Dedek, 2012.

relationships that give the building its historic character and then plan for the preservation of those elements. Sometimes, while the exterior of a building has been left largely intact, the interior has been altered beyond recognition and loses its historic connection and harmony with the character of the exterior (Figures 10.8a, 10.8b).

STANDARD 3

Each property will be recognized as a physical record of its time, place, and use. Changes that create a false sense of historical development, such as adding conjectural features or elements from other historic properties, will not be undertaken.

The French architect Eugène Emmanuel Viollet-le-Duc (1814–1879), regarded by some as the first preservation architect, believed that buildings should be restored not to what they actually were but to what they "should have been." When restoring medieval churches, including Norte Dame in Paris, he often added new statues, and "perfected" the building to rational 19th-century standards. Viollet-le-Duc saw restoration as a "means to reestablish [a building] to a finished state, which may in fact never have actually existed at any given time," (Viollet-le-Duc 1854, 195). Not all of Viollet-le-Duc's contemporaries agreed. John Ruskin, who was English and another early preservationist, believed that historic architecture should be mostly left alone in its authentic state with minimal intervention to preserve it. Ruskin wrote "It [restoration] means the most total destruction [that] a building can suffer" (Ruskin 1849). The standards take a more moderate and more sophisticated position between the extreme opposing views of Viollet-le-Duc and John Ruskin.

Standard 3 abandons Viollet-le-Duc's intrusive approach, because such speculative rehabilitation diminishes the historical integrity and authenticity of a building and reduces its ability to teach us about the past as it actually was. The significant aspects of historic buildings and interiors give them their unique character and altering them to suit a contemporary design ideal or myth about what a building should have been creates a fiction that is not true preservation.

The most common problem that occurs in relation to Standard 3 is the impulse of building owners and some architects and interior designers to make a building look special and even monumental, perhaps more special and monumental than it ever did during its period of historical significance. For example, a group associated with a university located in Appalachia planned to restore a historic four-room cabin to depict and portray a "living" late-19th-century farm in the Blue Ridge Mountains. Their idea was to create a visitor's center where Appalachian music could be performed within a "living history" historic farm context where the visitor would be treated to an authentic 19th-century Appalachian farm experience. When asked what the floors inside would be, members of the committee said, "polished hardwood;" and when asked where the animals would be housed, they said, "What animals?" They planned to create a slick and cleaned up version of rural Appalachian farm life in a house that was to look like a 21st-century visitor's center presented as a historic farmstead. Such a project would run counter to Standard 3, because polished floors, a nice sod lawn, and no animals would give a "false sense of historical development" on a site that was supposed to represent and interpret an unpretentious Appalachian farmhouse in the middle of a working farm.

Another common design activity that does not conform to Standard 3 is the erection of fancy "historic" streetlights, which been done in many American towns and cities within the last 30 or so years. In most cases, such ornate fixtures never existed historically in the places where they are added to create a "historic" feel. In order for the installation of historic reproductions of street lighting to conform to Standard 3, research would have to be done using historic photographs and other records to determine exactly what kind of lights and other street fixtures actually existed during the historic period being emulated in the specific locations where the lights are proposed to be added. Then, if desired, lights resembling the documented originals should be remanufactured to specific specifications and erected in approximately the same locations where they existed historically. One of the key methods of adhering to the standards is to back up design decisions with solid historical research.

STANDARD 4

Changes to a property that have acquired historic significance in their own right will be retained and preserved.

Standard 4 concerns features of historic buildings that were added after the building was constructed or after its period of historical significance (see Chapter 4). These include such elements as attached siding, new porches, drywall partitions, retrofitted storefronts, replacement windows, suspended ceilings, landscape features, and additions. Buildings evolve over time, and very few historic buildings have survived unchanged since being erected. Some additions are innocuous and some have become historic in their own right, while others are distracting and reduce the historic integrity of the building. Deciding which is which can involve a lot of thought and research.

Standard 4 is one of the more difficult to interpret and is sometimes open to debate. The most direct way of interpreting this standard is to use the definitions of historic properties as outlined in the Criteria and the Criteria Considerations for eligibility for listing on the National Register of Historic Places (described in Chapter 4). To interpret Standard 4, questions should be asked, such as: Is a given addition over 50 years old? Are any significant persons or events associated with the additions or other changes made to a building? Are the materials, scale, and orientation of the added elements compatible with those of the historic building?

For example, suppose an 8-foot drywall drop ceiling were added to the parlor of an 1870 Victorian house in 1962 when the house was converted to offices. The ceiling has commercial florescent lights embedded in it and conceals the upper part of a decorative chimneypiece over the fireplace. An inspection reveals that the original ceiling is 12 feet high and has decorative plasterwork, which has been damaged. Is the drop ceiling over 50 years old? Yes. Does it impede the historic character and feel of the room? Unfortunately, the answer is also yes. In this case, Standard 3 would require that the drop ceiling be removed and the historic plaster restored to its original appearance unless there were some compelling historical justification for retaining the ceiling, such as the ceiling was present when a famous person, such as Martin Luther King Jr., used the house, making the house's primary period of significance the 1960s. This scenario would be very unusual, though, as usually the older aspects that define the character of a building should be restored where possible.

Addressing issues of historical significance helps clarify whether an added aspect of a building should be retained or removed in the process of a rehabilitation. In some cases, both the original building and its addition or other alterations will be historically significant and should be preserved together. In other instances, the addition or alterations, as with the drop ceiling

Figure 10.9. This recent addition to a historic building in Asheville, North Carolina (the balcony on the upper right), is not in keeping with the historic and stylistic qualities of the building, but if left for longer than 50 years, it might become historic in its own right. Source: Peter B. Dedek, 2008.

described, may be so detrimental to the historic feeling and character of a property that they need to be removed, even if they have some potential to be historically significant in the future (Figure 10.9).

In the end, most of these decisions are based on the philosophies and ethics of historic preservation. It is a good practice to include the input of as many stakeholders and professionals as possible, though not everyone involved will always agree. Generally, from a preservation point of view, the most conservative option is usually the best. If the addition or element is less than 50 years old and has no significant associations with people or events, it is often best to remove it, especially if it does not complement the historic qualities of the building.

STANDARD 5

Distinctive materials, features, finishes, and construction techniques or examples of craftsmanship that characterize a property will be preserved.

Sensitivity and respect are vital to the appropriate treatment of historic buildings. Since we are discussing the *Standards for Rehabilitation* and not the *Standards for Restoration* here, some non-character-defining historic features and materials of the building may be removed, and the rehabilitation will still stay true to Standard 5. However, the features that define the building's historic character need to be retained. These include but are not limited to historic windows, porches, columns, rooflines, dormers, siding, railings, trim, and front doors (Figure 10.10). The more ornate or unique or characteristic of a particular style the feature is—be that Queen Anne, Art Deco, or Bauhaus—the more it needs to be preserved. When an architect or builder designed a given building, significant features were important to the function and the appearance of the final building. The loss of such elements will distort the original intent of the building's designer. The goal is to keep a building easily recognizable for future generations. Features such as carved stone, ornate brickwork, milled wooden moldings, decorative columns, and molded plaster help allow us to identify a building as historic and interesting and worthy of preservation.

As more and more 20th-century buildings become historic, traditional features are not the only type that need to be considered by preservation designers today. Modern elements, such as plate-glass windows, road signs, and concrete walls, will also have to be identified and preserved. In modern-style historic buildings, the structure (such as a steel frame) is often exposed, requiring that it will need to be repaired where necessary and preserved. In

Figure 10.10. The removal and replacement of the doors of this historic church near West Point, New York, breaks Standard 5 and reduces the historic integrity of the building. Source: Peter B. Dedek, 2008.

some cases modern codes come into conflict with historic integrity. When this occurs, the least destructive strategy should be used that satisfies the code requirement.

When programming and construction for a rehabilitation is undertaken it is important that significant historic materials, features, finishes, and construction techniques first be identified and documented, then be protected from damage during construction, and then be repaired as necessary and preserved in their historical locations and functions, be they structural, decorative, or both.

STANDARD 6

Deteriorated historic features will be repaired rather than replaced. Where the severity of deterioration requires replacement of a distinctive feature, the new feature will match the old in design, color, texture, and, where possible, materials. Replacement of missing features will be substantiated by documentary and physical evidence.

MATERIALS PARK, THE ASM INTERNATIONAL HEADQUARTERS, MID-CENTURY MODERN LANDMARK RESTORED

Materials park. Source: © Jeff Goldberg / Esto

Interior before rehabilitation. Photo courtesy of The Chesler Group, Inc.

Interior after rehabilitation. Source: © Jeff Goldberg / Esto

Materials Park has been home to the headquarters of the American Society for Metals (ASM) International since its construction in 1959. The building is an amazing example of mid-century modern design. Located on a 45-acre site in Russell Township, Ohio, 20 miles east of Cleveland, the semicircular 50,000-square-foot building has an 11-story-high geodesic dome, the largest such open-work dome in the world. The building has stylistic features, such as stainless steel sunscreens, extensive expanses of glass, and a concrete base, that integrate the building into the hillside (ASM 2011). Two prominent modernist architects collaborated in the design of the building, John Terence Kelly and R. Buckminster Fuller. Mr. Kelly envisioned a structure that would bring nature and technology together. Mr. Fuller engineered the giant geodesic dome to express a mastery of modern materials and technology. The building was listed on the National Register under Criterion C for architecture in 2009 (NPS 2011).

The rehabilitation, which began in 2010, cost approximately $6.2 million. The building's mechanical systems were refurbished. A new green roof was installed above the garden level of the building, which lies below grade. The historic light fixtures, designed by Kelly, needed no work and were retained. The rehabilitation restored many of the building's original features, including its brass screens, historic door handles and hinges, a conference table with stainless ASM medallion inlays, and 32 vintage Steelcase chairs. During the rehabilitation, 7 brushed-aluminum mural panels commissioned in 1953 from artist Nikos Bel-Jon (1911–1966) titled the "History of Iron" were discovered and rehung throughout the building (Calkins 2013). This historic rehabilitation is a demonstration of the significance and value of preserving architectural monuments from the recent past.

The message here is to be conservative. If a feature can be repaired, repair it. If a feature needs to be replaced, replace it, but only with an element that looks as close to the original as possible and is preferably made of the same material. However, Standard 6 implies but does not openly state is that if a new feature is replacing a structural element that is not made of the same building material, it is usually fine to use so long as the element is hidden from view.

For example, when repairing many of the wide eaves on the prairie-style houses of Frank Lloyd Wright which tended to sag over time, many historical architects have opted to replace the historic wooden rafters within the eaves with metal trusses. Even though the new material is different than the original, this does not pose a problem, because the changes are hidden from view and will help to make the building's roof structure more resistant to failure in the future. A problem would emerge if the metal bracing were applied to the exterior, such as on this example of "preservation" on Beale Street in Memphis, Tennessee (Figure 10.11). If the metal structure were a temporary solution designed to stabilize the façade, it would be acceptable, but this does not work as a permanent solution. Also, the rest of the building behind the façade was demolished, breaking a number of the standards, including Standard 5.

Figure 10.11. Although this looks like a construction site, the façade of this building on Beale Street in Memphis, Tennessee, has been "preserved" in this manner for at least a decade. The original windows are lost as are the roof, side walls, and interior. *The Secretary of the Interior's Standards* were written to discourage insensitive treatments such as this. Source: Peter B. Dedek, 2007.

Special epoxies are sometimes used to consolidate rotting historic wood and other deteriorating materials. With recent improvements in the quality of these epoxies, they often make an effective, and hidden, method of repairing and not replacing historic features, such as brackets and decorative trim.

When a historic element is missing and needs to be replaced, it is very important that its replacement matches the original in design and materials as it actually existed on that particular building as closely as possible. To accomplish this, the best empirical evidence, such as historic photographs, must be used wherever possible. If no such evidence can be found, it is often best to use the least obtrusive solution. For example, a local historical society in the Hill Country of Texas restored a small farmhouse. The house, built in the 1860s, had one-over-one double-hung windows that were clearly not original to the house and were probably added sometime in the early 20th century. The historical architect decided to replace the existing 20th-century sash with new, speculative multipane four-over-four sash because similar windows could be found on houses of the same vintage in the immediate vicinity. When the historical society applied to have the restored house given state historic landmark status, the state Historical Commission refused, because it asserted that the addition of the speculative windows was not in keeping with Standard 6. The historical association and their architect responded by reinstalling the old one-over-one 20th-century sash, because it represented the only windows known to have existed on the house historically and soon thereafter the landmark application was approved. It is important to avoid speculation and go with the known historic condition of a particular building, even if what is present is not ideal. If a historic photograph showed the Hill Country farmhouse with four-over-four windows, then it would have been perfectly acceptable to have windows matching those in the picture manufactured and to install them.

STANDARD 7

Chemical or physical treatments, if appropriate, will be undertaken using the gentlest means possible. Treatments that cause damage to historic materials will not be used.

A key rule in preservation is don't ever sandblast or use high-pressure water (over 400 PSI) on a historic building. Fortunately, through decades of effort and education, most architects, engineers, and contractors that work with historic buildings already know not to sandblast, but other destructive cleaning methods—using power sprays on materials such as marble and old brick, both of which are soft, porous materials—are unfortunately still sometimes used. The only historic building material that can be sandblasted safely is iron, and iron elements, such as porch railings and brackets, should be removed from the building before sandblasting to avoid damage to adjacent materials, and reinstalled once cleaned up and repainted.

Harsh mechanical tools, such as grinders, rotary sanders, heat torches, and grit blasters, should also not be used on historic buildings to clean surfaces or remove paint. Preservation Brief 1, available on-line from the National Park Service states:

> Since the abrasives do not differentiate between the dirt and the masonry, they can also remove the outer surface of the masonry at the same time, and result in permanently damaging the masonry. Brick, architectural terra-cotta, soft stone, detailed carvings, and polished surfaces, are especially susceptible to physical and aesthetic damage by abrasive methods. Brick and architectural terra cotta are fired products which have a smooth, glazed surface which can be removed by abrasive blasting or grinding. (NPS Technical Preservation Services 2000).

Although it is more time consuming and expensive due to the cost of labor, historic buildings should be hand-cleaned using only mild cleansers and low-pressure washers, and paint should be removed with hand scrapers with the help of relatively mild chemicals intended for use on historic building materials.

Using abrasive cleaning methods on wooden buildings can be at least as destructive as using them on masonry buildings because wood is a soft organic material that has particularly soft material between the grain, which can be easily eroded or scraped away by harsh tools and pressure washing, causing irreparable damage.

Figure 10.12. Harsh cleaning can destroy delicate historic building fabric such as this brick wall. Sandblasting pits the surface of old brick, damaging it and making it collect dirt faster than it did before the cleaning. Source: Peter B. Dedek, 2009.

Harsh cleaning can literally destroy the exterior surface of a historic building (Figure 10.12). The effects of harsh cleaning on historic materials, such as brick, stone, and wood are also discussed in Chapters 7 and 8.

STANDARD 8

Archeological resources will be protected and preserved in place. If such resources must be disturbed, mitigation measures will be undertaken.

If there's any possibility that archeological artifacts and potential to yield archeological information exists on a site, before digging or otherwise disturbing the ground consult with a contract archeologist or one employed by the state highway department (if it is involved) or the state historic preservation office (SHPO). If the potential archeological site is located on federal land or land within an Indian reservation, then the Native American Graves Protection and Repatriation Act (NAGPRA) (see Chapter 1) may apply, in which case the federal agency owning the land should be contacted. If the site may contain Native American graves or any historical burials—even on private land—state and local laws may apply, and those responsible for their possible disturbance should contact their SHPO, which may require research and "mitigation" before work commences.

If a site must be disturbed, the mitigation measures usually undertaken generally involve "salvage archaeology," where the area is excavated by qualified archaeologists prior to construction to gather as much information about the site and the people who occupied it as possible before it is either destroyed or covered up.

STANDARD 9

New additions, exterior alterations, or related new construction will not destroy historic materials, features, and spatial relationships that characterize the property. The new work shall be differentiated from the old and will be compatible with the historic materials, features, size, scale and proportion, and massing to protect the integrity of the property and its environment.

Designing additions to historic buildings can be tricky and controversial. Determining whether an addition meets this standard can be a matter of interpretation. However, some additions are clearly inappropriate due to their incompatibility with their historic counterparts in scale, materials, and style (Figure 10.13a). Other additions are more in keeping with Standard 9 (Figure 10.13b).

One of the most difficult concepts contained in Standard 9 is, "The new work shall be differentiated from the old." Many design professionals and others believe that an addition to a historic building should match the original design. Why, they may ask, should the addition stand out from the historic building? Won 't that be distracting and interfere with the historical feeling of the site? The answer is that the goal of the authors of the *Secretary of the Interior's Standards* was that an addition to a historic building should not confuse viewers by creating a false

Figure 10.13a. The use of plate glass and modern brick on this addition to this Victorian era house in Columbia, South Carolina, breaks Standard 9, because the modern materials do not match the historic. P Source: Peter B. Dedek, 2007.

Figure 10.13b. This recent addition to a historic stone church in New Braunfels, Texas, matches the original building in materials and respects the scale of the historic building while still being easily identified as a later addition. Source: Peter B. Dedek, 2012.

historic impression. If the addition matches the historic building too well, then it will appear as if the addition itself is historic. For example, if a nonprofit adding to a small Appalachian farmhouse while rehabilitating it for use as offices were to design the addition to match the original building too well, then an observer might believe that the entire building is historic and would not be able to understand or appreciate its history as a humble farmhouse, but believe instead that the people who resided there when it was a farm were much more affluent than they actually were; or the building might look as if it were historically a boarding house or even a hotel, rather than what it actually was. If an addition were designed to complement the house in scale and materials, but had, say, more modern looking windows and a concrete foundation, then someone viewing the building would be likely to understand that the addition is relatively new and that it is attached to what must have been a small residence.

The term "contextual" is often applied to new architectural additions that fit in with the built environment surrounding them. In order to be contextual, and to conform to Standard 9, the addition should adhere to the following principles:

- The scale of the addition should not overpower the existing building. A 10,000-square-foot addition to a 2,000-square-foot building should not be constructed, not aboveground at least. A 40-story monster should not be placed atop a humble historic commercial building unless extreme measures (such making the addition appear to be a separate building) are taken (Figure 10.14).

- The scale of elements within the addition, such as windows and porches, should also not overpower those of the existing building. Even if the addition itself doesn't overpower

Figure 10.14. This humble building on Market Street in San Francisco (at center, embedded in the newer building) has completely lost its context. Retaining the old façade even serves to impair the architectural integrity of the modern skyscraper around it. Source: Peter B. Dedek, 2008.

the existing structure, contemporary elements, such as plate-glass windows can dwarf the scale of elements on the original building, such as historic double-hung windows.

- The materials used, while not necessarily identical, should be compatible with those of the historic building. While the new materials do not have to be, and probably should not be, identical to the historic, similar materials in scale, texture, and application should be used. For example, adding to a 1920s bungalow with a structure covered with metal panels and plate-glass windows will not jibe with the original house or the intent of Standard 9. Using cedar shingles or even synthetic siding that resembles cedar clapboards would be more appropriate. Attaching steel and glass and other modern materials and forms directly to the facades of historic masonry buildings is not appropriate (Figure 10.15).

- Usually an addition should be separated from the historic building by a hyphen or walkway rather than being directly attached to a large section of the historic fabric. The use of a hyphen helps to divide new from old and communicate that "this is an addition to a building that existed independently for decades or even centuries." The hyphen also ensures that less historic fabric will be removed from the existing building during construction, preserving more of the historic exterior.

Figure 10.15. This recent addition to a Beaux-Arts building in San Francisco is inappropriate in style, scale, color, and materials. Source: Peter B. Dedek, 2008.

- The architectural details of the addition should tend to be less intricate than those on the original building, especially if the building is of a historical revival style. This keeps the focus on the original building rather than the addition and helps avoid the historical confusion discussed earlier by visually differentiating old, ornate, and from newer, simpler, and more modern.

- The features of the historic building shouldn't be a parody or mockery of its historical companion. One of the impulses of the postmodern movement was contextualism. Another postmodern urge was to create visual parodies and "coded" commentaries on classical or otherwise traditional architecture. If done subtly, these messages are harmless, but if done to excess such detailing can severely diminish the historical feeling and character of the site (Figure 10.16a). The addition should usually be constructed to the side or rear rather than in front or in any location that blocks the primary façade of the historic building. Again the principle should be that the new construction is the addition and not the other way around, and the new construction should not dominate (Figure 10.16b).

- If the site has a significant garden or view or other related historic feature the addition should avoid impacting it. Often the context of a historic building can be as important as the building itself in conveying the feeling and character of a historic site. For example, if Mount Vernon were surrounded by a suburban Washington D.C. office park, much of the visitor experience would be lost.

Figure 10.16a. This circa 2002 addition to Sage Hall at Cornell University in Ithaca, New York, parodies the historic building and reduces its historic integrity. Source: Peter B. Dedek, 2005.

Figure 10.16b. Only yards away on the Cornell University campus, this addition is a perfect example of a modern addition that conforms to the standards. Located at the rear of the historic music building away from its front that faces the quadrangle, this addition is scaled to the historic building, respects its massing and its materials, but also is clearly newer, as shown by its more modern windows and simpler detailing. Source: Peter B. Dedek, 2005.

A basic concept for architects to keep in mind when dealing with additions to historic sites is that according to the Secretary's Standards, designers should create an addition that is visually and spatially secondary to the original structure. This means that, in some cases, the natural and understandable impulse that many architects and designers have to make a statement and to express their individual design style must be suppressed. The addition has to be, above all else, a good neighbor. There is a certain elegance that results when a new design shows deference to the work of a historic designer.

STANDARD 10

New additions and adjacent or related new construction will be undertaken in such a manner that, if removed in the future, the essential form and integrity of the historic property and its environment would be unimpaired.

Reversibility is a key tenet of all preservation activity. The principle of reversibility allows later generations to remove later additions and restore an earlier appearance as easily as possible should they choose to. The most important thing to keep in mind is that if someone were to remove a given addition, could the site be restored to its previous condition (Figure 10.17).

With modern machines, materials, and construction techniques, it has become increasingly easier to wipe out entire contexts with very little effort—someone with a modern bulldozer can destroy centuries of history in hours. With this in mind, it is important that architects, designers, and contractors are sensitive to the natural and built environments they work with. At times, even when historic elements must be replaced, the originals are preserved and even displayed, such as with these beams in the medieval Mezquita (mosque) in Cordova, Spain (Figure 10.18). This allows the historic features of a building to be retained as educational tools.

Figure 10.17. The interior of this Beaux-Arts building was gutted and the roof removed to transform this classical edifice into a courtyard for the skyscraper behind it. This is an example of exactly what *not* to do to conform to Standard 10. Source: Peter B. Dedek, 2008.

Figure 10.18. These deteriorated beams from the Mezquita in Cordova, Spain, an eighth-century mosque, were preserved and displayed after they were replaced. This way they continue to contribute to the historic feeling of the site. Source: Peter B. Dedek, 2008.

In addition to removing historic materials and retaining them, another method of adhering to Standard 10 is to encapsulate the historic elements. When this is done, the historic features and materials are just covered over without disturbing or damaging them in a manner that if any new construction is removed in the future, the old elements will remain. A simple example of this would be covering an old mosaic floor in a high traffic area with a replica of the mosaic applied directly over the historic one, but not adhered to it, so that the new floor could be removed at any time without harming the historic flooring beneath.

CONCLUSION

The *Secretary of the Interior's Standards* are regarded as the universal rules regarding the proper treatment of historic buildings at the federal, state, and local levels in the United States. The standards are used by most historic tax credit and grant programs and form the basis of the 2,500 or so local preservation ordinances that exist throughout the United States today. The standards serve to preserve the historic integrity of America's historic resources. When designers understand and apply the standards, they advance the cause of historic preservation.

STUDY QUESTIONS

1. Who wrote the *Secretary of the Interior's Standards* and why?

2. What four types of building treatments are covered by the *Secretary of the Interior's Standards*? Which one is the most exacting? Which is the least intrusive?

3. Do all preservationists agree on how the *Secretary of the Interior's Standards for Rehabilitation* should be applied? Why or why not?

4. Which new use would be most appropriate under Standard 1 for a historic gymnasium, a roller skating rink or a music school? Why? Name a few more uses that might be compatible with a historic gymnasium.

5. If a client in a Historic Investment Tax Credit project asked you as the designer to remove all of the historic plaster from a Victorian commercial building's interior to expose the brick walls beneath, and the

plaster is in good shape, would you comply? Why or why not?

6. If you were asked to design a porch for an early-20th-century building that is listed on the National Register to replace a porch that was once there, what steps would you take in order to be in keeping with *Secretary of the Interior's Standards for Rehabilitation?*

7. If a building is failing structurally, do the standards allow its foundation to be replaced with a new one? What sorts of design decisions would you be required to make in such a case?

8. If an early-20th-century commercial building has an ugly 1950s storefront, it should be replaced with one that looks more like it was from 1900. Is this true? In what circumstances might you be able to do such a thing, according to the standards?

9. If a contractor wants to sandblast elements of a historic building, which materials can she sandblast safely?

10. An architect you are working with has designed an addition that matches the historic building perfectly. He is so proud. How do you advise him?

EXERCISE: HISTORIC REHABILITATION CRITIQUE

Locate a potentially historic (one at least 50 years old) building that has been restored or rehabilitated or remodeled within the last 15 (or so) years and, using this chapter, critique the rehabilitation according to the *Secretary of the Interior's Standards for Rehabilitation of Historic Buildings.* Use the standards and go through each standard to see if elements of the rehabilitation (or remodeling) complied or not.

First, briefly describe the building by answering the following questions:

How old is it? (If you can't find out, make an educated guess)

What style is it?

What was its use historically?

What is it being used for now?

What is it constructed of? i.e., brick, stone, wood, a combination?

Does the interior appear to be original? If not, when do you think it might have been altered?

When reviewing compliance with each standard describe the treatment of the following features if they are visible on or within the building:

1. Exterior walls

2. Interior walls

3. Windows

4. Foundation

5. Porches

6. Doors

7. Floors

8. Staircases

9. Interior finishes

10. Landscaping/context

11. Historic floor plan

12. Roof (materials/additions)

13. Additions

Organize your answer according to the *Secretary of the Interior's Standards* and USE THEIR NUMBERS in order when critiquing different aspects of the building. When discussing a particular treatment refer to the specific standard and explain how the feature conforms or violates that standard.

Also consider these questions:

Is the rehabilitated building aesthetically pleasing?

If you were the designer, how would you have done it differently?

Answers and explanations found in the Instructor's Guide.

SOURCES

American Society of Materials (ASM), 2011. "Materials Mastery:The Renaissance of Materials Park." Accessed November 29, 2013. http://www.asminternational.org/portal/site/www/renovation/

Calkins, Bel-Jon. 2013. "Nikos Bel-Jon." Accessed on November 29, 2013. http://bel-jonstudios.com/

Morton, Brown W. and Gary L. Hume. 1976, rev. 1990. *Secretary of the Interior's Standards for Rehabilitation and Guidelines for Rehabilitating Historic Buildings.* Washington, D.C.: U.S. Department of the Interior, National Park Service Preservation Assistance Division.

National Park Service (NPS). "Introduction to Standards and Guidelines." Accessed June 8, 2012. http://www.nps.gov/hps/tps/standguide/overview/choose_treat.htm

———"Featured Case Study: ASM International Headquarters: Mid-Century Modern Landmark Preserved." Technical Preservation Services. accessed November 29, 2013. http://www.nps.gov/tps/tax-incentives/case-studies.htm#asm-international.

Ruskin, John. 1849. *The Seven Lamps of Architecture.* Dover Publications: 1989.

Viollet-le-Duc, Eugène-Emmanuel. (1854) 1990. *The Foundations of Architecture.* Translated by Kenneth D. Whitehead, 95. New York: George Braziller

11

DOCUMENTING, PROGRAMMING, AND MANAGING HISTORIC DESIGN PROJECTS

OBJECTIVES

- Outline the various roles of professionals in historic preservation projects.

- Describe various types of preservation-related activities.

- Describe how to perform a physical survey of a building.

- Communicate methods of documenting historic buildings prior to the commencement of rehabilitation work.

- Describe the phases of the design process as they apply to historic building design projects.

- Outline the special aspects of programming and project management of a historic design undertaking.

THE ROLES OF PROFESSIONALS
IN PRESERVATION PROJECTS

In order to understand the process of programming and managing preservation projects, it is important to be aware of the range of professionals involved and the roles they commonly play. All but the smallest preservation projects involve more than one person. Most projects, especially those that include design and construction, require a team of professionals with various backgrounds who specialize in different aspects of the undertaking. The optimal composition of the team depends on the nature of the project.

THE TYPES OF PROFESSIONALS INVOLVED
IN HISTORIC PRESERVATION

A variety of people with varying education, training, and experience are commonly included in preservation projects. Each member of a team brings specific skills and knowledge that will help achieve the goals of the project. The professionals who most commonly participate in preservation projects include architects, historical architects, interior designers, archeologists, structural engineers, preservation specialists, historians, architectural historians, contractors, curators, and architectural conservators, among others.

Architects

According to the American Institute of Architects (AIA), "An architect is a licensed professional with specialized skills who designs buildings and cityscapes and helps make real the unique vision of their clients and communities." Architects design buildings and often supervise their construction. They must have a professional degree in architecture and possess a state license to practice. After receiving their degree, they must work under a licensed architect for a period of time and pass a state licensing exam in all 50 states.

Architects who are not experienced with historic architecture can successfully participate in preservation projects that involve new construction or major rehabilitations to a building if they work closely with other professionals more familiar with preservation practices and standards. Architects contribute knowledge in the principles of design, architectural materials and structures, and building codes.

Historical Architects

Historical architects are registered architects who have specialized training and experience with historic buildings. Historical architects have the same professional requirements as any architect except, according to the National Park Service professional qualification standards, they also should have "graduate study in architectural preservation, American architectural history, preservation planning, or closely related field" or "at least one year of full-time professional experience on historic preservation projects." Historical architects should have extensive knowledge about the

National Register Criteria and the *Secretary of the Interior's Standards,* as well as the characteristics of historic architectural styles, historic building materials, and construction techniques.

Historical architects often take leadership roles in rehabilitations and restorations, managing restoration and historic design projects. They also consult with other architects, interior designers and other professionals who are working with historic architecture.

Interior Designers

Interior designers perform many of the same roles as architects. The main difference is that interior designers are not qualified to design or alter the structural aspects of a building, and normally work exclusively within a building's shell. Interior designers are specifically trained to work with interior space planning, furniture selection and arrangement, and specification of interior finishes and colors.

Interior designers normally hold a bachelor's or master's degree in interior design or architecture with coursework in interior design. Some interior designers possess two- or three-year associate's degrees in interior design or entered the field by gaining experience on the job. Some states regulate and register interior designers and some do not. The national credential for interior design is successful completion of the NCIDQ exam, which is taken after a required combination of college-level education and work experience in interior design.

As with architects, interior designers contribute an understanding of the principles of design and can invent and execute design solutions. Working on a preservation design project, interior designers often perform interior space planning, furniture selection and placement, and specifying interior materials and finishes. Interior designers can also combine their design education with coursework and experience in historic preservation and architectural history to expand their roles in preservation undertakings.

Archeologists

Archaeologists conduct excavations or "digs" to uncover, study, and conserve artifacts from historic or prehistoric sites, such as ancient ruins and encampments. They study man-made objects, such as tools and ceramics, in order to learn about past cultures. The minimum qualification for entry-level positions is normally a bachelor's degree in archeology or anthropology, but most archeologists have graduate degrees.

Archeologists usually become involved in a project when buried artifacts are found that need to be studied and better understood. Archeologists are often called in when in the course of a construction project at a historic site historic or prehistoric artifacts are inadvertently dug up, or when they are believed to exist in an area about to be excavated. Archeological investigations can also be planned into a project and become an integral aspect of it.

Structural Engineers

Structural engineers design and evaluate the structural components of buildings and other man-made constructions. As practitioners within a branch of civil engineering, structural engineers are qualified by education and experience to ensure that even the largest structures are built or modified in ways that make them sound and safe.

Structural engineers generally require a minimum of a bachelor's degree in engineering and a state license to practice structural engineering. There are different types of engineers, and it is important not to confuse structural engineers with other types, such as electrical engineers.

Structural engineers are required to be involved when any significant structural work is required. Although architects have training in structures, engineers are the true experts and should be consulted in large projects and those that involve historic properties with structural issues such as settling, cracks, and subsidence.

Preservation Specialists

Preservation specialists are people qualified by education and experience to perform a wide range of preservation activities.

Preservation specialists normally have a master's degree in historic preservation, public history, or a related field and have working experience in preservation. They are usually not designers or architects, but do have significant knowledge of preservation issues, concepts, and practices.

Preservation specialists perform activities such as writing National Register nominations, surveying historic properties, and consulting with architects, interior designers, and engineers in preservation projects. They also manage grant programs and write grants, manage preservation organizations or divisions within those organizations, conduct research, advocate preservation, and supervise volunteers and interns. Sometimes they are also qualified architectural historians or even archeologists.

Historians

Historians are professionals with academic training in history. Many historians specialize in a particular aspect of history, such as a specific period like the Renaissance, or a particular location, such as the history America's Midwest. The field is divided between academic historians, who focus on the study and writing of history, and public historians, who focus more on writing history for presentation to the public at places like museums and historic sites. Many public historians work in preservation.

According to the National Park Service professional qualification standards, historians should have a "graduate degree in history or closely related field; or a bachelor's degree in history or closely related field plus one of the following; at least two years of full-time experience in research, writing, teaching, interpretation, or other demonstrable professional activity with an academic institution, historical organization or agency, museum, or other professional institution; or substantial contribution through research and publication to the body of scholarly knowledge in the field of history."

Historians research the history of historic sites and their occupants, study their lives, lifestyles, life ways, and material culture. The work of historians often makes up the basis upon which design and conservation decisions are made in historic design projects. The work of historians is especially relevant in restorations.

Architectural Historians

Architectural historians are historians who have specific formal training in architectural history. According to the National Park Service professional qualification standards, architectural historians should possess a "graduate degree in architectural history, art history, historic preservation, or closely related field, with coursework in American architectural history; or a bachelor's degree in architectural history, art history, historic preservation or closely related field plus at least two years of full-time experience in research, writing, or teaching in American architectural history or restoration architecture with an academic institution, historical organization or agency, museum, or other professional institution; or substantial contribution through research and publication to the body of scholarly knowledge in the field of American architectural history" (NPS).

Architectural historians perform historic surveys; identify the style, age, and other characteristics of historic buildings; research historic buildings; write National Register nominations; consult with other preservationists; and write about and document historic architecture.

Contractors

Contractors coordinate and execute construction projects. General contractors usually supervise an entire project, while subcontractors specialize in certain areas of a project, such as excavation or kitchen installation.

Contractors require experience and a reputation in managing construction projects and a license.

Contractors implement the plans of architects and interior designers and contribute their expertise in construction methods and management and in building codes. Some contractors specialize in projects involving historic buildings.

Curators

Curators assemble and manage collections and exhibits. A graduate degree in a related field such as art history or history and work experience in a museum setting are required to be a curator.

Curators are normally involved in restorations where the finished project will be exhibited, and they work closely with architects, interior designers, historians, and conservators to create an authentic and rewarding experience for visitors to historic sites while protecting the artifacts and historic environments being displayed, stored, or archived.

Architectural Conservators and Craftspeople

Conservators and craftspeople do the hands-on preservation work when specialized skill is required. They tend to focus their abilities on certain types of resources or materials, such as wall paintings or historic plaster.

While many college and university degrees exist in conservation, many conservators and craftspeople get the experience needed to restore and preserve specific architectural elements and historic artifacts while working for others experienced in the field.

Like curators, conservators are most often involved in restorations, however they may also work in rehabilitations when specific significant historic elements, such as a historic painted ceiling or fresco or a stained-glass window need to be carefully restored and preserved.

TYPES OF PRESERVATION ACTIVITIES

Preservation projects come in many forms and often have different goals. Some are more focused on historical research, some on historic surveys and identifying historic resources, while others are more concerned with active restoration or rehabilitation. In any case, a preservation project involves some kind of activity designed to promote the conservation of a historic resource or group of resources. There are a number of common types of preservation activities, each of which stresses different skills or combinations of skills.

Documentation

Historic resources often need to be recorded for various reasons, such as for being listed on the National Register or recorded as part of a mitigation package in Section 106 cases. It is very important to carefully document the condition of historic buildings and interiors before any work on them begins. Recording can involve various media, such as written descriptions, photography, drawings, maps, and architectural plans. Documentation is most often performed by preservation specialists, architectural historians, and curators.

Reviews

Preservationists review properties to determine whether they should be considered historic using the National Register Criteria (see Chapter 4) and also evaluate construction projects to determine if they are historically sensitive and appropriate using the *Secretary of the Interior's Standards* (see Chapter 10). Historic reviews to determine National Register eligibility are most often performed by architectural historians and preservation specialists. Reviews of preservation design projects are usually done by historical architects, preservation specialists, or interior designers with significant preservation training and experience.

Historic Surveys

Historic surveys are usually conducted in order to create new historic districts or heritage areas or as part of Section 106 projects (see Chapter 2). They involve locating, identifying, documenting, and evaluating historic resources such as buildings, structures, and landscapes located within a given geographical area. An example of a historical survey would be an examination of a neighborhood in an area about to be potentially impacted by a highway project to determine whether historic properties exist in the area. Architectural historians and preservation specialists are the professionals who usually perform historic surveys.

The National Register process (see Chapter 4) involves identifying and researching a property, district, or landscape to determine its history, its significance, and its condition and degree of historic integrity The process of writing a National Register nomination requires knowledge of history, architectural history, and the ability to evaluate the historical significance, integrity, and evolution of buildings and to document them with written descriptions and photography. Architectural historians, preservation specialists, and sometimes historians and historical architects or teams made up of various professionals usually write National Register nominations.

Historic Structure Reports

Historic structure reports are book-like documents that record and preserve the history of a specific building and its site. They are usually written by historical architects but can be authored by others, such as preservation specialists, engineers, or interior designers with training and experience with historic buildings. Historic structure reports also evaluate a building's condition and make recommendations for how it should be maintained or rehabilitated and preserved in the future. Historic structure reports include detailed and specific information about a building's features and condition. As tools used in preservation planning, historic structure reports are created as guides for designers, owners, and building managers to help them understand and care for a building or group of buildings. The reports include information about management options for the use of the property. In order to write a historic structure report, the steps of researching and inspecting historic buildings described later in this chapter are undertaken and are added to the report. They are usually prepared by historical architects, preservation specialists, or interior designers who are experienced with historic architecture (Reed 1982).

Historic structure reports usually follow a general format, which is similar from one report to the next.

Rehabilitations

Rehabilitations, which are described in detail in Chapter 6, involve repairing and altering historic buildings or structures for a contemporary use, which may be the same or different from its historic purpose. When used in a preservation context, rehabilitation means that a property is renewed in a sensitive manner that respects its significant character-defining features but does not necessarily meticulously restore all aspects of the structure to their historic condition. Historical rehabilitations are usually supervised by historical architects, carried out by contractors, and often involve professionals from all areas of the preservation field, such as engineers and preservation specialists. Rehabilitations involving only nonstructural changes to interior spaces may be supervised by an interior designer with preservation experience in consultation with other preservation professionals.

Restorations

The term restoration, also described in greater detail in Chapter 6, involves actively bringing a property back to its condition during a specific period of time in history. Care is taken to

THIS IS AN EXAMPLE OF A TYPICAL TABLE OF CONTENTS FOR A HISTORIC STRUCTURE REPORT

INTRODUCTION

Purpose of the report
Preservation objectives
Basic information about the property including its location, type, and style

BRIEF HISTORY OF THE PROPERTY

Historical significance and historic events
Local, regional, or national people associated
Ownership history

CONSTRUCTION HISTORY

Original construction, and subsequent alterations

Chronology of building events

Historical documentation cited (letters, diaries, vouchers, newspaper articles, etc.)

Site work (including ordering of materials, construction, unusual craft work, etc.)

Reference to craftsmen/builders/architects associated with the property

Early views, photographs, etc., showing appearance at different periods

Physical investigation (e.g., analysis of paint layers relative to construction events) (See Chapter 13)

ARCHITECTURAL EVALUATION

Assessment of all exterior and interior features and finishes.

Identification of those architectural features.

Materials and finishes that are character defining and therefore significant and should be preserved in the course of project work.

The order of priority of these features (premiere, important, contributing, noncontributing).

A room-by-room evaluation, including identification of materials, construction techniques, features (e.g., lighting, paneling, wainscoting, radiators, glazing, cabinetwork, fireplaces) and finishes.

The order of priority of architectural significance of spaces (premiere, important, contributing, noncontributing).

Description and evaluation of building mechanical systems (heating, lighting, plumbing, electrical, etc.).

EXISTING CONDITIONS

Analysis of existing conditions, damage, structural problems, materials deterioration, etc.

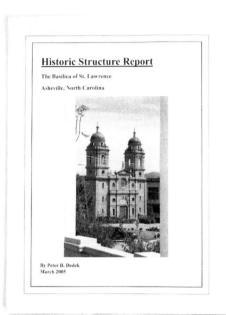

The order of priority of repair/ stabilization work

Assessment of the need for materials conservation

MAINTENANCE REQUIREMENTS

Outline of the need for a plan and program for general and periodic maintenance, recognizing that deferred maintenance is not an option for historic resources.

ARCHEOLOGY

Depending on the nature of the property, its site and setting, and on potential funding sources, it may be desirable or necessary to include this section to address any archeological concerns associated with any proposed stabilization plans or project work.

PROPOSED WORK

Design recommendations for any proposed work based on existing conditions and preservation objectives, which might include a list of work priorities, phasing, and estimated costs. Categories of work: architectural, structural, mechanical, electrical, archeological, conservation, and others.

DRAWINGS AND PHOTOGRAPHS

Copies of original drawings and specifications, along with similar documentation of subsequent alterations are of great importance. Drawings of the existing facility are also important. Historic and current photographs are of critical importance.

An extensive set of current photographs in 35mm format, including all building elevations, major interior spaces, and details.

Bibliography (as needed)

References (as needed)

Appendices (as needed)

(California Office of Historic Preservation 2012)

base all design decisions on historical evidence, and modern intrusions are kept to an absolute minimum, with technology such as modern HVAC and lighting systems kept absent or as hidden as possible. Restoration can involve a whole building or just certain aspects of a building, its interior, or specific interior elements, such as wallpaper, woodwork, or a painted ceiling. Restorations often involve historical architects, interior designers, structural engineers, preservation specialists, historians, architectural historians, contractors, curators, and architectural conservators.

PREPARATION FOR A PRESERVATION DESIGN PROJECT

Architectural rehabilitations and restorations are referred to as preservation design, because they normally involve both conservation of existing historic fabric and adding new architectural and interior elements. Once a rehabilitation project has been initiated, no work should begin until all buildings and other historic resources that may be impacted by the project have been researched and their significant features identified, understood, and documented. Appropriate members of the team, such as historians or preservation specialists should perform historical research on the building as described in Chapter 4, carefully inspect the building, and then document its significant features.

PHYSICAL SURVEY OF BUILDINGS

Historical research, the examination of a building and its site, and preliminary documentation of the building (photography, sketches, and measuring) often take place simultaneously. Specialized skill and knowledge is required to identify and evaluate many aspects of a historic building while performing a physical investigation. For example, while a preservation specialist, historical architect, or anyone trained in preservation can locate and identify cracks in masonry, a structural engineer is usually needed to diagnose the causes of the cracking and recommend measures to correct them. For minor projects, such as the cosmetic redo of an interior involving minor wall repairs, paint, and new flooring, the process of investigation is simple and can be performed by a contractor, conservator, or craftsperson. However, if even in the course of a small project, evidence of significant damage, such as cracking, rot or damage from animals such as termites is uncovered, other professionals will need to be called in. On the other hand, if a building requiring major rehabilitation is obviously in trouble, such having leaning walls or a collapsing foundation, the services of a structural engineer will be required from the beginning.

A building investigation for all but the smallest projects should be carefully planned. For safety reasons, it is advisable to have at least two people present while inspecting a historic building, especially if it is not occupied or is in less than pristine condition. Having a team also makes measuring easier, and team members can discuss and hopefully resolve situations where physical evidence found in a building is not clear, such as deciding if a particular wall treatment or decorative motif is original to the building or not. The team would ideally include someone trained in historic architecture, such as an architectural historian or preservation specialist, and at least one person trained in design, such as an architect or interior designer, or people possessing both kinds of training, like historical architects. For larger buildings or buildings exhibiting more problems and issues, a structural engineer and a mechanical engineer (to examine the type and condition historic and modern mechanical systems, such as furnaces and ductwork) should also be included (Friedman 2000).

Historic buildings about to be renovated and or rehabilitated need to be carefully examined for two major reasons:

- First, to determine type, style, structure, materials, and workmanship, and to find clues into its history and major and minor alterations made to it over time. The building's historic character and distinctive architectural features should be identified and documented to assess the historical significance of the building and to identify its defining characteristics (see Chapters 2 and 7).

- Second, it is necessary to access its condition inside and out from the foundation to the roof. This requires a thorough examination of the building's physical state to determine what significant features are intact, which may be threatened and which may require preservation, repair, or replacement.

Steps Involved in a Historic Building Survey

A building must be examined for its architectural qualities, including features of its design, setting, materials, workmanship, and overall feeling. The researchers should look at various aspects of the building's setting: Is it urban, suburban, or rural? Is it isolated in a district of related buildings? Is the building relatively intact or has it been greatly altered over its life? Combining any archival evidence found, such as historic photographs or descriptions, with physical evidence discovered within the building itself, carefully discern what elements appear to be original and which may have been added at later times and investigate to find out when any major changes were made.

While examining a building to determine its architectural character, evolution, and historical significance consider the following elements:

- Its overall **massing** (the volumes the building occupies), its overall shape, and the arrangement of windows and doors;

- The style and character of its roof, any projections, such as turrets or towers;

- The design of its trim, both inside and out;

- The materials used, both structural and decorative, inside and out;

- The structure type and material(s) of its foundation, walls, and roof.

Also, look for evidence of inventive or unusual use of decoration and materials, such as:

- Interesting brick or stone patterns and other unique design features in exterior walls;

- Distinctive motifs, trim, medallions, and the like in interior walls or ceilings;

- Examples of distinctive joinery, such as mortise and tenon construction;

- Outstanding exterior materials and finishes, such as slate or tile roofs or terra-cotta;

- Creative handicraft and interior finishes, such as carved staircases or wall paintings or historic wallpaper (Fram 2003).

The surveyors should use a checklist to examine and assess the condition of the structural and architectural features of the building, looking for evidence of issues such as stains, damp areas, rot, cracking, unlevel floors, and walls that are not plumb.

Since water intrusion is a common threat to historic buildings (see Chapter 8) a building should be inspected in wet weather as well as in dry, if possible. When rain is falling or shortly thereafter, water intrusion inside or pooling around the building becomes obvious, making any serious threats easier to identify.

The items on the surveyor's checklist should include a wide range of areas to be examined, which are listed here. For each item, any problems or issues observed should be noted on drawings and diagrams with enough detail and precision that the problem area can be easily found at a later time.

Building Site

- Water issues. Drainage around the building and any areas where water sprays or pours on the building because of, for example, a broken gutter or pipe, or where water collects in puddles (for more information about damage caused by wet conditions see Chapter 8).

- Vegetation. Look for vegetation, such as bushes and trees, adjacent to walls and foundations or reaching over roofs, that might damage the building or invite wood-damaging insects.

- Outside structures. Assess the condition of any garden or retaining walls or fences and outbuildings.

- Utilities and services. Look for utility connections, such as electric and gas lines. Are they present? Are they connected or broken? Do they need to be evacuated by people experienced with the specific utilities for safety?

Foundations

- Materials. What materials are present in foundation walls and or piers, such as brick, stone, or concrete or reinforced concrete? The material can help determine the age and design of the building and possible additions (see Chapter 9).

- Cracks and erosion. Are there cracks or bulges in the foundation? Any signs of crumbling, peeling, or splitting away of material? Is any wood in contact with the ground or otherwise touching soil?

- Structural integrity and settling. Are the foundation and the floors above them level? Are foundation walls or piers plumb?

Walls

- Materials. What material(s) are the walls made of? Is the material visible on the outside of the structural material, such as load-bearing brick or stone, or is it a decorative veneer? Sometimes this cannot be determined without going into and examining basements or attics.

- Structure. Is the structure load-bearing masonry, timber frame, balloon frame, stud frame, or another material and structure? Inspectors often must go into secondary and utility spaces, such as attics and basements, to determine the building's structure.

- Cracks or rot. Are any cracks present in walls? Are any areas of wood showing rot? Are all of the walls straight up and down or are some of them leaning?

- Mortar. If the walls are brick or stone, is the mortar (if present) crumbling? Has it been repaired with possibly damaging Portland cement (see Chapter 8)?

- Efflorescence. Are there any patches of powdered minerals present on wall surfaces inside or out? (See Chapter 8 for an explanation of efflorescence).

- Insect damage. Are there any areas that may have been hollowed out by termites or carpenter ants (see Chapter 8)?

- Decorative elements. Are any wood, stone, or brick decorative components and motifs, such as brackets or window moldings, chipped, rotting, cracked, or missing?

Roofs

- Roof type. What kind of roof or roofs cover the building—gable, hipped, flat? Are there dormers or chimneys? If so, note locations, type, materials, and condition.

- Roofing type. What roofing material is visible—asphalt, metal, slate, ceramic tile, wood shingle? Does the roof have a historic appearance, possibly having distinctive patterns or textures? Is there any evidence of any other roofing materials underneath?

- Roofing condition. Does the roofing material appear to be sound? Often, using a pair of binoculars or a ladder helps in this determination. Is there evidence of damaged flashing around chimneys, dormers or vents, or junctions? Are shingles chipped, cracked, or buckled?

- Roof structure. Are the rooflines along the ridge straight, or do they sway toward the center or undulate? Sagging rooflines often indicate substantial structural issues in the roof and possibly in the walls and foundations as well.

- Gutters and eaves. Are any gutters, eaves, fascia boards, rafter ends, or downspouts broken, rusting, rotten, or otherwise damaged? Are any gutters or downspouts blocked with leaves, sticks, bird droppings, or other debris? Is paint peeling on any of these elements?

- Chimney condition. Are any chimneys leaning or broken in places? Is the mortar intact? Are all flashings or caps present, secure, and waterproof?

Porches and additions

- Porches. Are porches sagging or settling? Are the materials such as decking and posts sound? Are porch steps settling or decaying? Does the porch appear to be original to the building (see Chapter 9 for estimating the age)?

- Additions. Are additions sagging or settling? Does their design interfere with the building's historical integrity? (See Chapter 8).

Windows and Doors

- Windows. Do the windows appear to be original (see Chapter 9 for estimating the age of windows)?

- Window condition. Is all of the glass intact? Are the window frames square and sound? Is the sash peeling anywhere or showing rot in the case of wooden sash or rust in the case of metal windows? Do the windows open and shut or are they not in working order? Do they appear to leak air? Are any of the glass panes cracked? Are there cracks in the lintels or walls above or near any windows (Figure 11.1)? Is there any evidence of condensation or stains on the sash or the sill?

Figure 11.1. Settling such as this should be noted in the survey. Such settling will require the involvement of a structural engineer. Source:Peter B. Dedek, 2010.

Basements (interior)

- Condition. Is the basement or crawlspace dry? Is the atmosphere musty? Is there any water present or efflorescence on walls or standing puddles on floors?

- Structural integrity. Do the walls or piers appear plumb from the inside? Are there any cracks or crumbling walls or piers? If a floor is present, is it level? Have any structural members, such as posts and beams, been cut into or removed during the installation of pipes and other utilities?

Interiors

- Security. Make sure that the interior is not accessible to people, such as vagrants, who may do it harm. If the building is vacant, look for evidence of intrusion, such as graffiti, trash, and discarded objects, such as food wrappers and drug paraphernalia.

- Floors and stairs. Are the interior floors level and even? (This can be tested by rolling a marble over them and also by visual inspection or using a level). Are there cracks in masonry floors or spongy areas in wooden flooring? Do wooden floors or stairs squeak when walked over? Is the finish material, such as linoleum or hardwood, in good condition? Does the flooring appear to be historic?

- Walls. What material is present in the walls—plaster, wallboard, wood, exposed brick, stone? Are there cracks in the plaster or other material? Is there peeling paint or stains on wall surfaces? Are any significant historic wall coverings present, such as distinctive wallpapers or hand painted patterning? What is the condition of the wall covering? Is there any evidence of removed features, such as the outline of missing staircases, lines in a floor or wall that indicate a wall has been removed, or holes left by historic fixtures, such as heating stoves, built-ins, or gaslights?

- Ceilings. What material is present in the ceilings—plaster, wallboard, wood, or another material, such as pressed metal? Are the ceilings cracked? Are they level? Are stains or peeling paint present? Are any ceiling areas crumbling or collapsed? Have any decorative elements, such as cornices or plaster medallions, cracked, or has material broken off (Figure 11.2)?

- Trim and doors. Does the trim appear to date from the building's period of significance? Is it intact? Is there peeling paint or missing parts? Are any doors missing? Do the existing doors match the trim or appear to be replacements? Do the doors open and shut correctly without binding or scraping the floor? Does the hardware, such as doorknobs, latch plates, and hinges, appear to date from the building's period of historic significance, or might they be replacements?

- Fireplaces. Are any fireplaces present? If so, do they have distinctive aspects, such as decorative tile, or marble mantels? Do they appear to date from the building's period of

Figure 11.2. Although this interior of this endangered historic church is in deteriorated condition, many historic materials and finishes, such as the wooden ceiling, the historic plaster and the window trim, remain. Flooring has been torn up, cracks are evident in the plaster, and significant interior elements, such as furniture and pews, are missing. Source: Peter B. Dedek, 2011.

historic significance, or have they been modified in some way, such as having the mantel replaced or the flue blocked up? Are there any cracks in any visible areas? Are the fireplaces operable? (Fireplaces in historic buildings should be inspected and cleaned periodically by an expert if they are used.)

- Fixtures. Do electrical fixtures such as built-in lighting appear to be historic? Are any historic sinks, bathtubs, or heaters present?

Attics

- Structure. What kind of frame is visible in the attic—timber, stud, balloon, something else? Do rafters, roof decking, posts, trusses, or other supports appear to sag or be broken or show rot? Are there any water stains on supports, roof decking, or flooring?

- Ventilation. Does the area appear to be properly ventilated? Do attic areas feel exceptionally hot or humid? Are there visible vents in the gables or along the roof line or in the roof itself? Do any pipes present in the attic appear to have water condensing on them and dripping?

- Insulation. Is any insulation visible? What condition is it in? Is the insulation present a pebblelike, pour-in product, light brown or gold in color? If so, it may be vermiculite insulation, which was used into the 1980s and is often contaminated with asbestos. Vermiculite poses a significant health hazard and must be removed by professionals. Is a vapor barrier present? On which side of the insulation is it located?

- Roofing. Is light visible through any part of the roof to the sky? Are stains present on the inside of the roof?

- Infestation. Is there any evidence of insect damage or infestation by other animals (see Chapter 8)? Look, particularly for sawdust, feathers, and animal droppings.

DOCUMENTATION METHODS

During and after an inspection, the appearance and condition of a historic building should be documented in a careful and systematic manner before any work begins. This way, if in the course of demolition and subsequent construction work, any historic features are damaged or destroyed, repairing or replacing them can be done using proper documentation, such as photographs, drawings, and notes, so they can be restored or replaced as authentically as possible. Sometimes contractors and construction workers damage historic features either through oversight or a lack of experience with working with historic buildings, making proper documentation key. Two major forms of documentation are measured drawings and photographs.

Measured Drawings

When documenting a historic building or historic interior in preparation for a rehabilitation or restoration project, the first step is to draw a plan of the building's site showing the footprint of the building, an outline of the property, a north arrow, and the location and relative size of any significant features on the property, such as outbuildings (Friedman 2000). The next step is to measure the building and draw accurate floor plans of it. Even if the original architectural drawings or a subsequent set of plans can be located for the structure, existing plans can often have inaccuracies and should be checked by taking new measurements based on the architecture itself in order to verify accuracy and revise the plans where needed. Existing plans can include architectural drawings, shop drawings, plans drawn for alterations to the building, and drawings made as the result of earlier investigations (Friedman 2000).

To create new as-built plans, it is best to start out by creating a sketch plan on grid paper. Using a tape measure 20 feet or longer, carefully measure the distances between and within all major architectural elements in the rooms, such as doorways, window openings, and pilasters, measuring from one to the next all the way around the room. Once this is complete, take independent measurements of the overall width and length of the room in order to check to see that the sum of all of the measurements taken on all sides of the room match the total width and length of the space. As measurements are taken for the entire work area, and the thicknesses of walls, ceiling heights, and the heights of other significant features are recorded, draw the plan out to scale on graph paper, carefully recording all dimensions down to the half-inch.

These preliminary plans will be used as the basis for drafting formal plans and other drawings, such as sections and elevations. The plans should include labels and notes describing the characteristics and condition of all relevant aspects and features of the building and its site. The notes should be keyed to the drawings. Aspects such as wall materials, thickness of walls, heights of ceilings, locations and composition of posts and beams, floor materials, surface finishes, and the estimated vintage of any features dating from after the original construction should be noted. In addition to overall plans, the investigator(s) may also desire to create detailed drawings of particularly interesting or particularly problematic building features.

Photographs

Photography is another important tool in documenting historic buildings. Before construction work begins, all significant features that might be possibly impacted by the work need to be carefully photographed in order to record their appearance, condition, and location. Photography in historic buildings that need work can often be difficult due to low light levels; obstructions in rooms, such as debris; or obstacles on the exterior, such as vines and other vegetation. For this reason, it is wise to take a number of pictures of a feature or space using different shutter speeds or aperture settings to help ensure that at least one usable photograph will result. After work begins, there may not be a second chance to take the picture (Friedman 2000).

Photographs should be taken in a methodical way to document the building and its features thoroughly. A clear documentary photograph should be taken of all visible façades of a building. Also, photographs should be taken of all defining features and all areas where a specific conservation issue, such as a roof leak or a cracked wall, has been discovered during an inspection. Photographs should also be made of all significant interior spaces and areas.

A high-resolution camera, such as a single lens reflex with a digital resolution of at least 10 or so megapixels should be used. Quality film cameras are also still fine to use. A tripod will be useful when photographing interior spaces with low light. All photographs must be carefully labeled and cataloged so it is clear exactly what they depict and where and when they were taken. Often the documentation of historic buildings prior to rehabilitation or restoration work is performed according to Historic American Buildings Survey (HABS) (see Chapter 2) standards. HABS documentation includes large-format photographs and measured drawings of the building before work begins. Video may be used in conjunction with photographs to better document the site.

PROJECT MANAGEMENT IN HISTORIC DESIGN

In general, all but the very smallest architectural projects go through a series of distinct steps, which do not always occur in exactly this order:

- Programming Phase (planning)

- Schematic Design Phase (initial design explorations)

- Design Development Phase (design refinement)

- Construction Documents Phase (solidifying the design)

- Bidding and Negotiation Phase (hiring contractors and suppliers)

- Contract Administration Phase (construction management)

The programming and management of design and construction projects involving historic buildings require more steps than are needed in most new construction projects. They also command greater caution and mindfulness, because the features and materials found in historic buildings are irreplaceable. Also, the many types of old construction methods and materials used in historic buildings require specialized knowledge to understand, preserve, and adapt to new uses successfully. During a restoration or rehabilitation, the welfare of the historic building fabric is always a priority, and care must be taken so that the building's historic integrity is reduced as little as possible in the process of design and construction. It is also important for all members of the design team to visit the construction site on a regular basis throughout the design and construction phases to ensure destructive practices, such as harsh cleaning and improper repairs, do not occur on the site (Figure 11.3).

The following procedures should be followed when programming and managing a historic restoration, rehabilitation, or adaptive-use project:

Figure 11.3. The tool being used in to remove the existing mortar in preparation for repointing this brick is an angle grinder, which is very likely to cut into and damage the historic bricks. Hand tools are preferred. Correcting practices such as this is a significant aspect of construction management in historic preservation projects. Source: Peter B. Dedek, 2010.

PROGRAMMING PHASE

Thorough planning should be completed before any features of a historic building are altered or demolished. Once the historical significance of every aspect of the building has been assessed and its importance to the historical integrity of the site and the project understood, the various historic features should be ranked in terms of their importance to the overall historical integrity of the building and preserved accordingly throughout the project. Regardless of other programming and design considerations, the character-defining historic features of the building should always be of the utmost importance. For example, a prominent doorway should not be removed to comply with fire codes unless every possible method of mitigating the code violation—without impeding the safety of the building or destroying the feature—has been considered. Or, for example, if a client suggests removing all of the historic plaster in the interior of Victoria-era commercial building because she likes the textural quality of the brick, the best preservation practice would be to recommend the retention of the plaster and suggest an alternate, removable finish, such as an interesting wall covering that has deep color and strong texture but preserves the historic plaster in place (Figure 11.4). Structural brick was almost never left exposed in habitable spaces during the Victorian era and to do so creates a false historical impression.

Assess Condition and Stabilize

Once the building has been inspected, measured, and photographed, the next step is to identify any of its aspects that are in immediate danger and take steps to mitigate such threats immediately. For example, if a door is broken and vandals are entering the building through it, immediately have the door repaired or the opening boarded over to prevent further danger to the building. If a roof leak has been discovered, have the leak fixed before other work is done, as water can cause serious damage to a building very quickly and may cause delays and expensive repairs during the project. Such repairs can be temporary, with more permanent measures taken in the course of the construction phase of the project. If initial repairs are not designed to be permanent, the designer should ensure that any emergency repairs are done in a reversible manner and do not cause any damage to the building or its distinctive historic features or materials.

Figure 11.4. In the Victorian era, nearly all habitable interior surfaces had a plaster surface. While removing the plaster may be aesthetically appealing to many today, to do so reduces the historical integrity of the building. Source:Peter B. Dedek, 2011.

Feasibility Study

Once a building has been examined and documented and the programming phase is under way, a feasibility study should be done to investigate and determine what historic preservation programs, such as Investment Tax Credits or historic preservation regulations, the project falls under. The technical and economic feasibility of the project should also be evaluated (AIA 2013)

Contemporary Needs and Historic Spaces

The **programming phase** of the design process involves delineating what functions a historic building must fulfill in its new role and determining the kinds of spaces will be needed to meet these functional requirements. In addition to specific spaces, a program also describes such design elements as circulation, furnishings, lighting, acoustics, and desired aesthetics.

Most construction projects that include historic architecture involve adapting old buildings to contemporary uses, which are often not the original intended use. Changing the use often requires significant design alterations to a building, especially to interior spaces. As discussed in Chapter 10, the *Secretary of the Interior's Standards* recommend that any new uses be compatible with the historic design of the existing building wherever possible. However, a high degree of compatibility is not always possible, and designers often have to create innovative design solutions in order to accommodate pragmatic program requirements needed to make a building economically viable. All of this must be accomplished while still retaining a building's historic integrity.

Some design solutions that may seem the most efficient require alterations that are incompatible with good historic design. These should be reevaluated in terms of historic integrity and alternative possibilities considered. Architects and interior designers who design projects within or in the proximity of historic buildings should control any desire to express their own aesthetic if that aesthetic clashes with the character of the historic architecture. Good historic preservation requires having respect for the significant work of architects, designers, and artisans of previous generations. When dealing with our nation's built heritage, contemporary designers should work carefully to balance contemporary design aesthetics and functional considerations with historical considerations. When this balance is accomplished, the building often looks and functions better than in cases where a historic structure is butchered in the name of current fashion or efficiency. "Less" can often indeed be "more."

The basic functional aspects of a building, such as existing circulation and entry patterns, should be retained where possible. For example, if a historic double parlor is to be reused as a modern living room, it is appropriate to leave the historic walls in place rather than tearing them out in order to open the space up in the manner that most living rooms would be designed today. Often the peculiarities of older buildings, such as seemingly useless entry halls, formal staircases, arched doorways, and ornate fireplaces, add interest and create a sense of wonder and excitement in people who experience them.

When programming projects that alter historic buildings, the spaces within should be ranked according to their historical significance, their defining characteristics, and how prominent and accessible they are within the project. Wherever possible, the most significant spaces, such as lobbies, banquet rooms, and parlors, should be given to new uses for which they must be altered the least, and plainer, less visible spaces, such as utility rooms, attics, and lofts, should accommodate uses that require more alteration. This keeps incompatible modern adaptations as hidden as possible. For example, if a historic church is to be converted to an office building, the main sanctuary should be retained as a lobby or perhaps as an open office area with removable partitions, while the closed office areas would be best housed in areas formerly designed as church offices, Sunday school areas, or used for other activities that did not require a large aesthetically pleasing space. Also, if any new additions are planned, it is usually optimal that utilitarian functions and service zones, such as elevators and handicapped accessible bathrooms, which often require a lot of space and significant building alterations, be located within the addition rather than within the historic building itself.

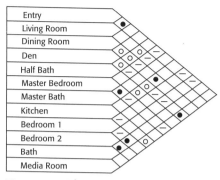

Legend
- ● Direct/Primary Adjacency
- ○ Convenient/Secondary Adjacency
- − Distant/Remote Adjacency

Entry
Living Room
Dining Room
Den
Half Bath
Master Bedroom
Master Bath
Kitchen
Bedroom 1
Bedroom 2
Bath
Media Room

Figure 11.5a. Adjacency matrix.

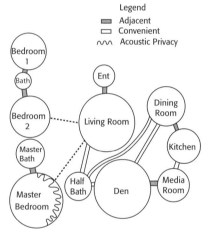

Legend
- Adjacent
- Convenient
- Acoustic Privacy

Figure 11.5b. Bubble diagram.

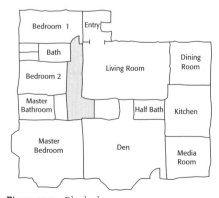

Figure 11.5c. Block plan.

CONCEPTUAL DESIGN PHASE

Based on information gathered and decisions made during the programming process, all architects and interior designers involved should collaborate to create a set of conceptual or preliminary design alternatives. These should include planning the overall changes to be made to the floor plans, exteriors, and spaces to adapt the building to its proposed functions. The **conceptual design phase** involves creating and evaluating design alternatives using visual tools such as adjacency matrices (Figure 11.5a), which show how various functions and spaces should relate to one another; bubble diagrams (Figure 11.5b), which are graphic representations of the possible arrangement of spaces based on adjacency matrices; and block plans (Figure 11.5c), which are loose drafts of possible final architectural plans based on bubble diagrams. Sketches, such as sections, elevations, and perspectives, may be used to further explore the various design alternatives (Historic Preservation Subcommittee 2013).

The proposed design solutions resulting from the conceptual design phase should be examined and discussed by all stakeholders, including the design team, contractor, consultants, possible future users, and the client(s). The client is the person, people, or organization paying for the project. The examination of alternatives eventually produces a preferred conceptual design.

DESIGN DEVELOPMENT PHASE

Once a conceptual design has been chosen, a preliminary cost estimate can be developed. As this is being done, the design team continues refining the design. At this point, architectural drawings, such as hardline plans, sections, and elevations, can begin to be created and modified.

The impact of the proposed design on the historic building and its future function is often reassessed at this stage in the process, in consultation with all stakeholders. If needed, the design is altered in order to minimize the project's impact on the historic integrity of the property and to maximize its functional and aesthetic effectiveness. Depending on the nature of the historic building and the type of project, this may involve consultation with outside parties, such as a local architectural review board, a municipal government, the state historic preservation office, the Advisory Council on Historic Preservation, or the National Park Service.

The team members utilize their specific skills as they work together. Among other tasks, the interior designer makes certain that furniture, fixtures, and equipment (FF& E) are compatible with the design and character of the historic building and scaled appropriately to its important historic features, such as doorways, ceiling heights, and floor spaces within rooms. In some cases, an interior designer might specify furnishings that purposefully contrast with the style of a building. This can be appropriate and allow for a healthy measure of design creativity, so long as the building itself does not need to be damaged to accommodate the selected furniture and any significant changes required are reversible.

CONSTRUCTION DOCUMENTS PHASE

Once the preferred design has been developed, the architects, interior designers, and their associates create detailed construction documents, which take the form of a final set of plans including architectural plans, mechanical plans, sections, elevations, detail drawings, and the like. During this phase, the construction documents are examined and coordinated with any known preservation issues to ensure continued respect for the integrity of the building. A full budget for the project is also completed at this time, and the bidding or negotiation phase for construction work begins in which qualified and competent contractors are selected (Burley 2000). Architects and interior designers specify many of the materials and finishes to be installed during construction in this phase.

CONTRACT ADMINISTRATION PHASE

Often exterior work and work on the interior can be performed simultaneously, but both activities must be closely coordinated. Following is a list of preferred practices and the proper order of work to be considered during the construction phase on the exterior and the interior:

Order of Construction Management on Exterior

- As described previously, inspect the entire building before work begins and document all significant architectural features.

- Educate all contractors and workers about the historic significance of the property.

- Repair any remaining immediate threats to the building or to construction workers, such as significant foundation settling, broken windows, or roof leaks, that have been identified in the survey and pump out any standing water from any areas where it has been found (Figure 11.6).

- Secure and cordon off all unsafe areas and cordon off or remove loose building components.

- To ensure fire safety, remove all flammable solvents and debris, make fire extinguishers and other fire suppression systems available, and clear all fire exits and ensure they are operable.

- Employing appropriately certified professionals, remove or **encapsulate** (meaning to cover up and seal away) any hazardous materials, such as asbestos or lead.

- Complete any needed permanent repairs to the roof and permanently mitigate any major structural deficiencies.

- Construct any exterior additions called for in the program.

- Clean the exterior, if necessary, using the most gentle means.

- Repair exterior masonry and ornamental woodwork and metal elements.

- Repair any damaged windows.

- Stain and then paint exterior finishes that require paint.

- Inspect all completed work.

- Create a building maintenance manual that documents building systems, and creates a regular inspection and maintenance schedule.

Figure 11.6. Certain conditions such as broken windows should be temporarily repaired before construction begins. Windows in this condition invite water and damaging animals, such as bats and pigeons, inside. Source:- Peter B. Dedek, 2010.

- Mask and protect all aspects of the building, especially significant features such as ornate woodwork and stairways against being damaged in construction.

- Remove all elements slated for removal or demolition, retaining any potentially historic elements for storage in case future work calls for their return.

- Employing appropriately certified professionals, remove or encapsulate any hazardous materials, such as asbestos, lead, or pigeon dung.

- Install heating, ventilation, and air conditioning (HVAC) equipment, upgrade electrics, plumbing, gas lines, etc., as needed.

- Install any required moisture or vapor barriers inside basements, attics, or the inside surfaces of exterior walls.

- Clean up all construction debris.

- Seal and caulk and install new interior finishes or refinish old surfaces where called for.

- Prime and paint where required.

- Reinstall repaired or reconditioned salvaged historic fixtures.

- Install new FF&E.

- Repair and refinish all fixtures and finishes that were masked and left in place.

- Clean interior and inspect work (Fram 2003).

CONCLUSION

Historic restorations and rehabilitations are sophisticated and complicated, requiring a great deal of expertise from researching history, to ensuring a structure is engineered correctly. The process of historic design parallels that of other architectural projects, but involves additional steps and precautions. Surveying and documenting historic sites is a key component of the historic design process, because these activities form the basis of all of the decisions that will be made during the entire design process from the schematic design phase through design development and construction management.

Understanding a building itself and its significant features requires a systematic process of investigation, discovery, and evaluation of design alternatives. It is the process of balancing contemporary needs with preserving the historical integrity and value of historic architecture that makes historic design challenging but also rewarding and interesting. When well-trained and informed designers proceed with care and sensitivity toward historic resources while keeping in mind the needs of their clients, successful projects are bound to result.

STUDY QUESTIONS

1. How do the roles of architects and interior designers differ in historic design projects? How are they the same?

2. List the types of building professionals likely to be involved in a large historic building restoration. Describe their likely roles.

3. Why are historic structure reports written? What are their three major purposes?

4. What is the first major step in the process of rehabilitating a historic building once the project has been initiated?

5. What are the two major reasons intensive surveys are done of the exteriors and interiors of historic buildings before any rehabilitation work begins?

6. Why are attics an ideal place to look for those evaluating the structure and the condition of a historic building?

7. Describe how best to go about measuring the interior of a historic building. What steps does one take? What tools does one need?

8. What are the reasons why historic design projects require a greater level of caution and mindfulness than many projects involving only new construction?

9. Describe what happens in the Design Development phase of the design process.

10. In what sorts of spaces within a historic building or its additions should utilitarian aspects, such as elevators and accessible bathrooms be located if possible?

EXERCISE: MATCH PHASES OF THE DESIGN PROCESS WITH ASSOCIATED ACTIVITIES

Match the following phases of the design process with each activity listed in the right-hand column that should be performed during that phase:

A) Programming phase

B) Conceptual Design phase

C) Design Development phase

D) Construction Documents phase

E) Contract Administration phase

1 _____ Create preliminary cost estimate

2 _____ Develop full project budget

3 _____ Feasibility study

4 _____ Begin bidding phase

5 _____ Bubble diagramming

6 _____ Create construction documents

7 _____ Access condition and stabilize

8 _____ Complete all permanent repairs to building

9 _____ Identify significant historic features

10 _____ Draw first hard-line plans

11 _____ Access client needs

12 _____ Complete building maintenance manual

13 _____ Create block plan

14 _____ Install heating, ventilation, and air conditioning

Answers and explanations found in Instructor's Guide.

SOURCES

Burley, Robert, and Dan L. Peterson. 2000. "Historic Preservation," *The Architect's Handbook of Professional Practice.* 13th Ed., New York: John Wiley & Sons, Inc.

California Historic Preservation Office. "Historic Structure Report Format." Accessed November 29, 2013. http://ohp.parks.ca.gov/pages/1069/files/historic%20structure%20report%20format.pdf

Fram, Mark. 2003. *Well Preserved: The Ontario Heritage Foundation's Manual on Principles and Practice for Architectural Conservation.* Third Ed., Erin, Ontario, Canada: Boston Mills Press.

Friedman, Mark. 2000. *The Investigation of Buildings: A Guide for Architects, Engineers, and Owners,* New York, NY, John Wiley & Sons, Inc.

Reed, Paula Stoner. 1982. "Documentation of Historic Structures," *Bulletin of the Association for Preservation Technology.* 14 (4): 19–22. Historic Structure Reports.

Historic Preservation Subcommittee. "Whole Building Design Guide: Apply the Preservation Process Successfully." National Institute of Building Sciences. Updated October, 22, 2013. www.wbdg.org/design/apply_process.php

UNIVERSAL DESIGN, THE AMERICANS WITH DISABILITIES ACT, AND HISTORIC BUILDINGS

OBJECTIVES

- Explain the issues involved when historic buildings are retrofitted in order to provide access for mobility impaired people.

- Address and balance preservation and accessibility.

- Explain regulations and standards and the legal rights of the handicapped.

- Outline the ADA Alternative Standards for Historic Buildings and their applications.

Efforts to adhere to universal design principles and to comply with the Americans with Disabilities Act (ADA) can cause significant obstacles for good preservation design in historic buildings. Because no accessibility laws or standards existed when historic buildings were constructed, their designers gave little or no consideration to the sensory or mobility impaired. Many old buildings possess a great number of architectural barriers. They are often accessed by staircases (Figure 12.1), possess no elevators, have changes in floor levels, have noncompliant bathrooms and kitchens, and have narrow hallways and pinched doorways.

Despite the architectural barriers often found in historic buildings, they can be upgraded to allow for greater accessibility. However, such alterations can easily damage a building's historic integrity by removing significant features that make them historic and special. For example, if a historic county courthouse has a wide, ornate staircase leading up to its main entrance, replacing that staircase with a giant, zigzagging ramp would remove a major character-defining characteristic of the building's design and severely harm the building's historic integrity. For this reason, the ADA and other accessibility laws include some exceptions for historic buildings. But even when designers take advantage of these exceptions, retrofitting historic buildings to conform to modern accessibility standards while not destroying their historic qualities can be very challenging.

Figure 12.1. This historic art museum is normally accessed by these grand stairs, which are an architectural barrier for the mobility impaired. To replace all or some of the steps with an ADA-compliant ramp, which can only rise by one inch for every foot of length, would severely alter the historic qualities of the façade. Source: Peter B. Dedek, 2009.

It is important to note, however, the importance of making historic buildings that are open to the public accessible to the mobility impaired. Accessibility has become a priority in the last few decades because it is a matter of human rights and equal access for opportunities, goods, and services. Because of architectural accessibility laws, many people who would be literally prevented from using many commercial and instructional buildings can now take full advantage of the opportunities to shop, seek entertainment, and do business in many of the same ways as anyone else. If architectural barriers are removed from within and around historic buildings in a sensitive way, including historic museums and tourist sites, it will increase their value to society.

UNIVERSAL DESIGN

Universal design is a philosophy that supports the idea that consumer products, architecture, and interiors should be designed to be easily usable by a wide range of people with varying physical and sensory abilities, to the greatest extent possible. Universal design also encourages that this be done with a minimum of obvious clumsy adaptations or indiscreet specialized features (Figure 12.2). Not a law or a code, but a set of goals for design professionals, the intent of universal design is to simplify everyone's lives by reducing architectural barriers for the widest

Figure 12.2. This ramp is not in keeping with the historic nature of the building in materials, location, or color and is not in keeping with the Secretary's Standards. Source: Peter B. Dedek, 2010.

Figure 12.3. This ADA-compliant ramp for the handicapped on the historic Texas capitol building in Austin preserves a set of historic granite stairs while being dignified and reasonably discreet. Source: Peter B. Dedek, 2008.

range of people as possible at a reasonable cost. In general, universal design features should be virtually invisible, or if that is not possible, the features should be not be obvious and should seem to fit in naturally with a building's exterior or interior design. Universal design integrates all users and avoids the "handicapped only" stigma. For example, according to universal design concepts, everyone—both the able-bodied and the mobility-impaired—should be able to use the same entrance to any building that is open to the public. Universal design can be compatible with preservation, in that both seek to make accommodations for the handicapped as discreet as possible (Figure 12.3).

THE AMERICANS WITH DISABILITIES ACT

The first comprehensive national legislation dealing with accessibility to non-federally owned facilities came in 1990 with the passage of the **Americans with Disabilities Act of 1990** (ADA), which was designed to protect the civil rights of Americans with disabilities. Discrimination in employment, access to places of public accommodation, services, programs, public transportation, and telecommunications were prohibited by this law.

The design, rehabilitation, and use of historic architecture is impacted by the Americans with Disabilities Act, because the act seeks to reduce the physical barriers that impede access to all public places, including private businesses open to the public, and requires that, even in existing buildings, many such barriers must be removed wherever they exist. The ADA was designed to create a uniform nationwide standard that ensures a level of accessibility across the nation, regardless of local conditions and attitudes.

Shortly after the passage of the ADA, the Architectural and Transportation Barriers Compliance Board issued a set of specific accessibility guidelines for architecture in 1991 based on the provisions of the law. The U.S. Department of Justice adopted these guidelines with some modifications, and these became the enforceable ADA Standards for Accessible Design. Probably in an effort to prevent a spike in government bureaucracy and to lower the cost of the law, the ADA created no federal agency to enforce its accessibility requirements. The law is enforced by plaintiffs who object to specific violations in individual court cases and is not policed by the federal executive branch or by local officers. Most states, however, have their own architectural accessibility laws, many of which are directly enforced by agencies at the state level. The state-specific guidelines and regulations of these codes are similar to those in the ADA, but some requirements are stricter than the ADA, and many state codes are triggered when any new construction or significant renovation work takes place.

The ADA applies to most buildings that are open to the public, including businesses and institutions such as retail stores, offices, museums, hospitals, and hotels. However, certain small businesses, such as bed and breakfasts where the proprietor lives within the building, and very small hotels with five or fewer rooms, private clubs, and religious facilities are exempted (Tully 1998). All purely residential buildings, including apartment houses, are also not subject to the ADA.

ACCESSIBILITY AND HISTORIC BUILDINGS

The ADA requires that state and local governments remove barriers to handicapped accessibility in state and local facilities by relocating their services and programs to accessible buildings or by retrofitting existing buildings to make them accessible. The ADA also requires that private owners of "public accommodations" make any "readily achievable" changes, regardless of whether they intend to remodel or alter the buildings in which their businesses are located. In this context, "readily achievable" changes are those that can be made without excessive cost, such as installing small ramps, providing signage, rearranging furniture and displays, equipping bathrooms with grab bars, and adding lever hardware on doors. When major restoration or rehabilitation work is undertaken, a higher level of accessibility requirements is triggered.

In some historic buildings, especially those that have only one story open to the public, the alterations needed to conform to the ADA and other accessibility laws may be as minor as providing signage for the handicapped, perhaps adding a short, removable plywood ramp to traverse a step or two, and the installation of an accessible restroom with grab bars, sufficient space to maneuver, and lever hardware in some secondary portion of the building. In other instances,

Figure 12.4. In cases such as the one shown here, a poorly designed and integrated ramp can dominate a historic building and negatively impact its historic context. Source: Peter B. Dedek, 2010.

however, the alterations required to historic buildings may be extensive and potentially harmful to the building's historic integrity (Figure 12.4).

In general, the concepts of barrier-free design focus on access to the functional aspects of buildings, allowing the mobility-impaired to benefit from the basic facilities that are used by the general public, such as restrooms, retail store sales areas, museum displays, food service areas, and so on. What this means is that not every space within a given building needs to be made fully accessible. Focusing on the most public and necessary spaces rather than on opening an entire building to handicapped individuals can save money and also help preserve the significant features of historic buildings, because with good planning, many of a building's public functions can be clustered in more easily accessed areas or even in new additions, leaving historically sensitive or difficult to reach spaces untouched.

THE ADA FOR HISTORIC BUILDINGS

In order to balance the need for accessibility with the requirements for good historic preservation, Congress included alternative standards for historic buildings. In the ADA, Congress directed that any changes to historic buildings done in order to make them more accessible that are funded all or in part by federal money or require a federal license be subject to Section

106 review (see Chapter 2), and if the state historic preservation office finds that the proposed changes would cause an "adverse effect," then the project's designers would be allowed to use the ADA exceptions for historic buildings.

Under the ADA, in cases where alterations to qualified historic buildings and facilities (those listed or eligible for listing on the National Register or deemed historic by state or local law) do not involve federal funding or permits and are not subject to Section 106 of the National Historic Preservation Act, the alternative standards may be used "if the entity undertaking the alterations believes that compliance with the requirements for accessible routes (exterior and interior), ramps, entrances, or toilets would threaten or destroy the historic significance of the building or facility." In this case, the entity should consult with the State Historic Preservation Officer. If the State Historic Preservation Officer agrees that compliance with the accessibility requirements for accessible routes (exterior and interior), ramps, entrances or toilets would threaten or destroy the historical significance of the building or facility, the alternative requirements (the historic preservation minimum requirements) may be used (Americans with Disabilities Act of 1990).

The ADA also encourages "consultation with interested persons" in projects involving historic architecture. The law states, "Interested persons should be invited to participate in the consultation process, including State or local accessibility officials, individuals with disabilities, and organizations representing individuals with disabilities" (Americans with Disabilities Act of 1990). For projects on historic buildings under the jurisdiction of a Certified Local Government (CLG), the responsibility of determining whether the ADA exceptions for historic buildings should be used may be carried out by local CLG government officials.

THE ADA ALTERNATIVE STANDARDS FOR HISTORIC BUILDINGS

In passing the ADA, Congress prescribed these provisions as exceptions to the standard ADA standards for historic buildings:

Entrances

The exceptions require that "at least one accessible route [complying with standard ADA requirements] from a site access point to an accessible entrance shall be provided." Normally under the ADA, the main or primary entrance, or at least an entrance that is commonly used by the public, is required to be made accessible by a ramp or another means to the mobility impaired and must have at least 32 inches of clear width and have lever hardware. This universal design principle ensures that most buildings don't have a "special" handicapped entrance in the back of the building or through some side alley or beside the loading dock or in another subordinate location that is likely to make handicapped individuals feel like second class citizens. However, the main entrances of historic buildings commonly have stairs or steep slopes leading up to them, and these stairs are often historically significant, character-defining elements. Therefore, the ADA exceptions allow a single alternative accessible entrance to be placed in a secondary location if it is necessary to maintain the historic character of a building. Any handicapped entrance must have signage leading to it and cannot be locked during business hours. The entrance also is required to have an intercom system or another type of "notification system" with "remote monitoring" if needed for security reasons.

Ramps

Normally under the ADA, accessible ramps are required to have no greater slope than a one-inch rise for every foot of length. Under the exceptions for historic buildings, "a ramp with a slope no greater than 1:6 for a run not to exceed 2 ft (610 mm) may be used as part of an accessible route to an entrance." This allows a shorter ramp than usual for relatively low climbs. These shorter ramps are easier to install on historic sites, which can be more constricted and crowded than the sites around new buildings.

Bathrooms

"If toilets are provided, then at least one toilet facility complying with [standard ADA regulations] shall be provided along an accessible route . . . Such toilet facility may be unisex in design." This exception allows for the installation of a single, lockable, unisex bathroom if altering the main restrooms to make them accessible would damage the historic qualities of a building. Among other requirements, an accessible bathroom must have a turnaround for wheelchairs (5 feet or greater), have sinks of the proper height to accommodate a wheelchair (34 inches maximum), and have toilets with proper clearances to accommodate a wheelchair and grab bars. Without this exception, the requirement to install standard accessible bathrooms would harm the historic integrity of many historic buildings, especially small ones.

Access to Upper Floors

Under the exceptions, the ADA requires that "accessible routes from an accessible entrance [be provided] to all publicly used spaces on at least the level of the accessible entrance . . . Access shall be provided to all levels of a building or facility in compliance with [standard ADA regulations] whenever practical." This is important, because the second and subsequent floors of historic buildings are often difficult to access without damaging the building. Usually a costly elevator has to be added, which can harmfully alter significant interior spaces, particularly in relatively small buildings. In historic museums, for example, if the upper floors can't be made accessible without damaging the historic integrity of the building, then videos or remote cameras may be used to allow handicapped individuals to gain some experience of the areas that they can't access in person.

Displays and Interpretive Materials in Museums

In museums and businesses located in historic buildings, the ADA requires that "displays and written information, documents, etc., should be located where they can be seen by a seated person. Exhibits and signage displayed horizontally (e.g., open books), should be no higher than 44 inches (1120 mm) above the floor surface" (Americans with Disabilities Act of 1990). This is designed to allow people in wheelchairs to access the same level of information as anyone else.

POPLAR FOREST RETROFIT

Poplar Forest was the second home of Thomas Jefferson. Jefferson built the octagonal house in 1806 on property he had inherited in 1773. One of only two houses Jefferson designed, he used the residence as a retreat from his much busier estate at Monticello. A nonprofit organization, the Corporation for Jefferson's Poplar Forest, currently operates the National Landmark property as a historic house museum.

Figure 12A Poplar Forest. Photograph courtesy of The Corporation for Jefferson's Poplar Forest.

In order to make Poplar Forest accessible to the mobility impaired, handicapped visitors needed a mechanical lift to allow access to the entrance, because a ramp near the house would have significantly harmed its historic integrity. Originally, architects working at Poplar Forest recommended a lift with a shaft buried 15 feet in the ground, which the management saw as too expensive. With the goal of finding a less expensive lift that was also nonobstructive and would do little to harm the historic integrity of the site, Poplar Forest's manager asked a company that sells industrial lifts if it could customize one with folding rails and a cover, but it said it could not.

The Corporation for Jefferson's Poplar Forest decided to buy a standard hydraulic scissors lift. Once the lift was received, the corporation had a local steel fabrication company install custom folding railings and a folding cover

on the lift, creating an elevator that was only 10 inches above the ground when not in use.

Figure 12B Lift in use. Photograph courtesy of The Corporation for Jefferson's Poplar Forest.

With this lift in place, when a person in a wheelchair arrives, a staff member opens the cover, puts up the railings, and uses a remote control to raise it to the wing deck level where they can then open the gate. The ramp, which does little to impair the historical context of the house, has worked perfectly and cost less than $10,000. Installing the lift on the grounds away from the house prevented the need to install ramps or other intrusive accessibility implements that would have harmed the integrity of the historic house's exterior or its interior.

Figure 12C Lift not in use. Photograph courtesy of The Corporation for Jefferson's Poplar Forest.

PROCEDURES IN DEALING WITH ACCESSIBILITY IN HISTORIC BUILDINGS

When determining what issues will be involved in making an apparently historic building that is open to the public accessible and compliant with the ADA and possible state or local accessibility regulations, the first step is to determine whether the building is already compliant with the standard ADA accessibility requirements or if it can be easily brought up to those standards without harming the building's historic qualities. If either is true, then there is no reason to be concerned with the ADA historical exceptions in that particular building. If making a particular building fully compliant clearly does not hurt its historical qualities, then it should simply be made compliant.

In some cases, simple retrofits, such as adding removable lever attachments to doorknobs or installing automatic door openers, adding a sidewalk and perhaps a short and innocuous ramp to the doorway, or rearranging the fixtures in a bathroom, is all that is needed. To determine whether any proposed alterations would damage a building's historic characteristics, the *Secretary of the Interior's Standards* (see Chapter 10) should be used. If there is any question as to whether making a building compliant might harm its historic character, then a thorough study of the potential historical status of the building and the possible effects of making it accessible should be undertaken by a historical architect or another qualified professional, such as an interior designer, who is familiar with historic buildings and designing for handicapped accessibility.

If there is some question as to whether making a building accessible and compliant with the ADA will harm it, then an important step is to determine if the building in question is indeed historic. If a building is listed on the National Register, is on an official state register, or has been designated as a local historic landmark or as a contributing structure in a local or National Register historic district, then the building is considered historic under the criteria in the ADA. If the building has not been so designated, then the state historic preservation office (SHPO) should be contacted. If provided with documentation of the history of the building and with photographs and other evidence of its appearance and condition, the SHPO can make a determination of whether or not the building is eligible for the National Register. If the SHPO determines that the building is eligible, then it will be considered historic for the purposes of the ADA. Once its historical status has been established, an architectural historian should perform an evaluation of the building to determine which of its elements are character-defining and need to be retained and preserved to ensure that the building keeps its historic integrity while it is made more accessible.

The next step is for a historical architect or another qualified preservation professional in conjunction with a designer familiar with ADA standards to determine what alterations will be needed to make the building accessible. Also, any applicable state or local accessibility requirements should be investigated and taken into consideration if necessary. Each potential alteration should be evaluated to determine what potential effects it may have on any character-defining qualities of the building. While some changes that represent minor impacts to historic integrity can be made to all but the most preserved and highly historic buildings (such as Mount Vernon or Independence Hall) those changes should not be such that they significantly impair the historic integrity of the building, its interior, or its grounds. For example, ramps or lifts should not impact the main façades or be placed in highly visible locations as the ramp pictured does in this historic mansion in upstate New York (Figure 12.5). Also, ramps and lifts should not replace historic staircases. In addition, original doors and doorframes should be retained, and major lobbies and original hallways should be retained relatively unaltered wherever possible.

Factors that should influence a decision regarding use of the exceptions include how large the structure is and how well it would be able to absorb alterations necessary under the conventional standards; whether the historic building will have primarily a public or private use; how the cost of full compliance compares to the cost of accessibility using the alternative standards; and how much increased accessibility full compliance will provide. If after these questions are considered, the players involved determine that one or more of the exceptions for historic buildings need to be used to preserve the integrity of the building, then the SHPO should be consulted. If the SHPO agrees the exceptions should be used, then the exceptions should be employed in a manner that best preserves the building while still allowing for the maximum

Figure 12.5. This wheelchair lift located near the main entry of the historic Mills mansion in upstate New York adversely affects the historic integrity of the building. The ramp detracts from the historic feeling of the house's grand portico and front door. Because of the lift's ugliness and awkward position, it also stigmatizes anyone who is forced to use it to gain access to the house. Source: Peter B. Dedek, 2008.

possible level of handicapped accessibility. All work done should be designed and overseen by a historical architect or an interior designer trained in preservation.

Federal resources, such as tax credits for small businesses, tax deductions for any kind of business, and community development block grants for local governments are available to help offset some of the costs of making buildings accessible under the ADA. If combined with sensitive historic design, these programs can be used to finance more effective and less damaging accessibility alterations to historic buildings (Tully 1998). In some states and localities, grants may also be available for accessibility projects in historic buildings.

In some instances, when a historic building cannot be made compliant without damaging its integrity, a new addition may be required to house many of the functions in spaces that need to be accessible.

Any addition to a historic building should be designed in accordance with the *Secretary of the Interior's Standards*. This allows features, such as handicapped restrooms and elevators, to be located in the addition, keeping the historic building largely intact. If the addition is located adjacent to a secondary part of the building and is constructed in a reversible manner so that it could be removed in the future without significantly damaging the historic building, it may be an ideal tool to achieve the goals of both accessibility and preservation. Care should be taken, however, to maintain the historic main entrance and to preserve the traditional relationship that the building has with the street and its other surroundings and with those viewing and approaching it.

In otherwise historic buildings that have already been altered with nonhistoric features, such as remodeled rooms or additions, the most altered and previously redone areas are normally the best places to concentrate intrusive accessibility measures, such as elevators, ramps, and accessible restrooms (Jester and Park 1993). It is important that designers, contractors, their clients, and any other participants go through the consultation process described here before starting any work on a building or site. The parties involved should keep a written record of the process so that if needed, they can demonstrate having made a good faith effort to comply with the intent of the ADA in case there is ever a complaint.

CONCLUSION

It is important to balance the needs of historic preservation with the needs of people with disabilities. Handicapped people have as much right to access public facilities as anyone, and every reasonable effort should be made to accomplish the goals of accessibility and universal design. Using the concepts of universal design, creative solutions can be found that address both accessibility and preservation by emphasizing that alterations and accommodations made for accessibility look as invisible and natural as possible. Sometimes, relatively subtle changes in landscaping or the layout of spaces can make buildings as accessible as they need to be. In cases where major changes are required to make a historic building accessible, the use of the exceptions for historic buildings in the ADA can help reduce the adverse effect of those changes. In any case, design creativity and flexibility are required to avoid unnecessary damage to historic resources.

STUDY QUESTIONS

1. Is the Americans with Disabilities Act (ADA) a building code? If not, what is it and why did Congress pass it?

2. In what ways does the concept of universal design differ and perhaps go beyond the ADA?

3. Name three types of businesses that are exempted from the ADA.

4. Name five minor accommodations that have little chance of damaging the integrity of a historic building that could be added to comply with the ADA.

5. Under what circumstances does Section 106 of the National Historic Preservation Act of 1966 come into play when ADA upgrades are being planned for historic buildings and sites?

6. List and briefly explain the five exceptions to the standard ADA standards for historic buildings.

7. What are the requirements for a property to be considered historic under the ADA?

8. What role does the SHPO play when ADA compliance may harm a historic building?

9. Under what circumstances might it be advisable to design a sympathetic new addition to a building to comply with accessibility standards?

10. As a designer, what factors must be considered to achieve successful design solutions while making significant changes to historic buildings to address accessibility issues? How might a designer address access to a building that is reached by the public via historically significant front stairs? How might accessible bathrooms be installed without harming the historically significant floor plan of a small house?

EXERCISE: IDENTIFY POTENTIAL BARRIERS
TO ACCESSIBILITY

List potential accessibility issues visible in the four photographs below. Assume the building is going to be made open to the public.

Photo A

1) _____

2) _____

Photo B

1) _____

Photo C

1) _____

2) _____

3) _____

Photo D

1) _____

2) _____

Answers and explanations found in Instructor's Guide.

SOURCES

Americans with Disabilities Act of 1990 (Pub. L. 101-336)

Jester, Thomas C., and Sharon C. Park. 1993. "Making Historic Properties Accessible," Preservation Brief 32. National Park Service.

Tully, Tania A., Jane Brinkerhoff, ed. 1998. "Adapting for Access: ADA Compliance in Historic Structures." Salt Lake City: Utah State Historic Preservation Office.

HISTORIC PRESERVATION, THE ENVIRONMENT, AND GREEN BUILDING

OBJECTIVES

- Describe how historic preservation and protection of the natural environment are related and complementary.

- Explain the historical connection between the preservation and the environmental movements in terms of their origins and goals.

- Explain how historic preservation promotes environmental protection by saving cultural landscapes, reducing urban sprawl, conserving energy, and reducing waste.

- Introduce the concepts of embodied energy and life cycle costs.

Preservation is environmentally friendly. When a historic building is preserved rather than torn down and a new one built in its place, whether voluntarily or because of preservation regulations, reusing and maintaining the existing structure saves a tremendous amount of energy, building materials, trees and shrubs, and landfill space. In fact, when one compares historic preservation to contemporary green design standards for new construction, historic preservation is the greenest design of all. In addition, although the two fields are often viewed as being separate, the environmental movement and the preservation movement have related histories.

PRESERVATION AND ENVIRONMENTAL ETHICS

The preservation movement in the United States began with 19th-century activists working to memorialize historic people and events by saving individual properties associated with them; however, by the 20th century, preservationists had begun trying to preserve whole districts and by century's end, entire landscapes. Initially, the motivation for historic preservation had little to do with saving the environment. When preservation groups such as the Mount Vernon Ladies Association and the Ladies Hermitage Association sought to save the homes of dead presidents from decay and demolition, they could effectively state that the site should be saved and preserved as a museum, shrine, and memorial to the memory of a "great man," and this was the only argument they needed. To preserve larger historic areas, such as the ruins of Native American sites in the Southwest and historic districts that encompass whole neighborhoods and large portions of active downtown areas, the history argument has rarely sufficed to stop looters in the first case and developers in the second. More sophisticated arguments and often government protection became necessary.

As with environmental conservation, historic preservation benefits greatly from a mentality and social ethic that values the welfare of a community as a whole over the private interests of unrestrained personal profit. Without that basic understanding among members of society, preservation of anything more than a few isolated historic sites exists in a hostile environment and will probably not be very successful. From the 1950s through the 1970s, significant historic landmarks and entire historic neighborhoods fell to the wrecking ball because a majority of the population had not yet decided that it was in the public good to preserve historic properties if it meant that someone might have to forgo making a profit. However, things have changed: it would be difficult to imagine Americans accepting the massive destruction to America's historic cities and towns caused by the construction of interstate highways and urban renewal programs today.

Although over the past few decades historic preservationists have made great progress in saving historic sites due to their historical and cultural value, adding the significant role that historic preservation can play in the conservation of natural resources can further bolster the preservation cause. With oil in ever shorter supply and with the increasing recognition that global warming due to human activities threatens the well-being of future generations, the pressing need to protect the environment through the conservation of energy and other natural resources is becoming widely recognized. Given this, historic preservation is no longer merely an issue of history or aesthetics. Preserving the built environment can play a significant role in protecting the health and welfare of the population of the entire world through helping to address issues such as energy conservation, efficient land use, minimizing solid waste, and reducing the release of greenhouse gasses. It is becoming evident that a unified approach to sustainability needs to be developed across a wide range of disciplines as diverse as ecology, interior design, architecture, urban planning, and this list should certainly include historic preservation.

THE EVOLUTION OF THE PRESERVATION AND ENVIRONMENTAL MOVEMENTS

The history of the American preservation movement has been linked more closely to the environmental movement that many may assume. With the closing of the frontier after 1890, a movement to conserve the natural resources of the American West began as many educated people started to realize that the nation was unlikely to expand into much more new territory, and that rather than being there for the taking, America's natural areas and resources were going to become increasingly finite as the population grew.

The movement to set aside natural areas that slowly evolved in the 19th century and began to take hold in the 20th, was largely in response to the impending loss of unique natural resources. The conservation movement sprung up because of a widespread threat to wilderness areas due to logging, settlement, and mineral extraction.

Similarly, the preservation movement arose because of the destruction or impending destruction or neglect of historic sites such as Civil War battlefields, Mount Vernon, and Southwestern Indian ruins. The Progressives, who supported conservation in the first decade of the 20th century, began the long and still controversial journey away from the 19th-century concept of individual autonomy in land ownership and virtually unlimited exploitation toward government regulation to ensure that owners use their land and the structures upon it in a responsible manner that preserves some resources for future generations. For the Progressives, the term "conservation" was used to describe the preservation of both natural and cultural resources. For the first time in American history, Progressives emphasized the management of society, nature, and historic sites by professionals.

The conservation promoted by the Progressives was not the full-blown environmentalism of people such as Henry David Thoreau and John Muir that eventually took hold in the 1960s. On the contrary, it stood for wise and efficient allocation of natural resources for practical reasons, such as sustainable economic growth and tourism. The Progressives' cultural conservation was utilitarian: in 1905, Congress placed the new U.S. Forest Service under the U.S. Department of Agriculture. When Progressives moved to protect Indian ruins by passing the 1906 Antiquities Act, it was primarily so that qualified archeologists would get a chance to excavate them before pot hunters destroyed the archeological information contained there. In addition, conservation advocates argued that tourism in national monuments and parks might generate more revenue over the long run than could be made by exploiting limited mineral resources.

Despite its limitations, Progressive political thought marked a shift away from unmitigated competitive individualism to a more holistic, socially-oriented ideology. By the Progressive era, the mood in Washington had changed dramatically from earlier decades. The Progressives who passed the 1906 Antiquities Act represent the first effective political manifestation of the conservation ethic.

Around the time of passage of the 1906 Antiquities Act, natural conservation laws were passed often supported by the same people. For example, Congressman John F. Lacey of

Iowa, who would sponsor an Antiquities Act in 1900 and again in 1905, sponsored legislation designed to prevent the shipment of bird plumage from birds illegally killed across state lines. The Lacey Act of 1900 was the first federal attempt to save endangered species of animals. (Sellars 2008). Sites of both "historical" and "scientific" interest were worthy of withdrawal from development, and reservation for "future generations" under the 1906 Antiquity Act, which both Theodore Roosevelt and Lacey supported.

Nowhere is the connection between natural and historic preservation as clear as in the case of the United States National Park Service, which has been involved in both types of conservation since its inception in 1916. Congress established the National Park Service (NPS) as a bureau under the Department of the Interior "to conserve the scenery and the natural and historic objects and wild life" within the areas it was designated to manage. The initial mission of the NPS was to protect and administer the national park system. However, it was gradually given responsibility for the management of most federally-owned properties, including national parks, national monuments and historic sites such as Revolutionary and Civil War Battlefields, historic corridors such as the C & O Canal in Maryland, and even the White House. Although it administered historic sites right from the beginning, the NPS did not employ professional historians until 1931: it has employed hundreds since. As discussed in earlier chapters, the Park Service also plays a key role in historic preservation across the country. From the founding of Yellowstone National Park in 1872 and the Forest Protection Act of 1891, through passage of the 1906 Antiquities Act and the Historic Sites Act of 1935 and the 1966 Historic Preservation Act, the federal role in historic and natural conservation has served to unite these two goals, often within the same geographical areas and the same agencies.

Today, the environmental and historic preservation movements face political challenges at least as significant as the ones they faced in 1906. There are still forces in society, such as the property rights and so-called "wise use" movements, that do not share the philosophy that well-conceived government regulations of land use can actually benefit all of society, including individual landowners. Many people still cling to the 19th-century notion that liberty simply means people doing with their property whatever they see as being the most economically profitable no matter how destructive it is to their neighbors' health and well-being. This radical anti-regulation ideology threatens both the built and the natural environments equally. The shared philosophy between natural and cultural preservation should be recognized and promoted to create a new united front against the forces of irresponsible resource development and short-term planning. The preservation movement should be viewed as an integral part of the environmental movement, promoting the conservation and stewardship of cultural landscapes, cultures, communities, historic buildings, and their associated landscapes.

PRESERVING LANDSCAPES AND THE BUILT ENVIRONMENT TOGETHER

In order for the preservation and the environmental movements to function together, entire communities and regions need to be considered in preservation projects, not merely specific sites. The sight of an old brick or stone building with its fancy detailing and 19th-century human scale surrounded by gigantic glass-faced skyscrapers or cinder-block warehouses is testament that preserving specific structures without regard to their contexts can be folly (Figure 13.1). A historic building without a sympathetic, respectful context can be a pathetic sight, something like the experience of seeing a caged tiger entirely devoid of context and purpose. A historic structure, no matter what its history, is merely an oddity if it is left alone in a sea of glass, steel, and concrete, and seeing a historic marker that commemorates the site of a building long demolished can even be worse (Figure 13.2).

This is not only true within cities and towns: Historic buildings located in rural places lose their significance and meaning when their context is destroyed or severely altered. A historic farmhouse is only a sad reminder of a lost and dead past without at least some of its original open landscape left around it. Preservation should not be practiced to memorialize the past but for present and future appreciation and enjoyment.

Figure 13.1. The materials and scale of the tower behind this small 19th-century building in San Antonio, Texas, destroy the building's historic context. Source: Peter B. Dedek, 2008.

Figure 13.2. The historic cabin that this historical marker in San Marcos, Texas, commemorates is long gone, making the marker more of an epitaph than a celebration. Source: Peter B. Dedek, 2008.

CULTURAL LANDSCAPES

Geographic areas that contain both natural features and evidence of human occupation and activities are referred to as cultural landscapes. **Cultural landscapes** are places where people have altered the natural environment in visible ways. They embody the connection between historic preservation and environmental conservation (Figure 13.3). A cultural landscape is an identifiable area that includes intact cultural and natural resources that enhance contemporary people's understanding of a historic event, long term human activity, or the life of a historic person or group of people. The NPS defines four types of cultural landscapes:

Historic Sites

Historic sites are landscapes significant for their association with a historic event, activity, or person. Examples include battlefields and associated structures, such as Gettysburg; houses of famous people with associated grounds, such as Mt. Vernon; and places where a significant cultural event took place, such as the farm in Bethel, New York, where the Woodstock Festival was held in 1969.

Historic Designed Landscapes

Historic designed landscapes are areas of land in the country or in a city that were created by human designers. Examples include city parks, such as New York's Central Park; college campuses, such as the historic Harvard Yard; large estates, such as the grounds of the Biltmore Estate in Asheville, North Carolina; and entire planned cities, such as the center of Washington, D.C.

Historic Vernacular Landscapes

Historic vernacular landscapes evolved organically due to human activity over a long period of time. In such landscapes, the function and interaction between people and the local

Figure 13.3. Cultural landscapes combine both natural and man-made features and show how human activity is integrated with nature. The road portrayed is a remnant segment of the Old Spanish Trail, an early 20th-century highway that went from Florida to Southern California. The railroad also has also impacted this landscape near Columbus, Texas. Source: Peter B. Dedek, 2012.

environment play an important role. Examples include historic farm complexes, such as a cluster of slave cabins and associated structures; a district of related farms associated with a natural or man-made feature, like along a river or a historic road, such as the old plantations along the Mississippi River in southern Louisiana; or a mine or quarry, such as the historic coal mines of southwestern Pennsylvania.

Ethnographic Landscapes

Ethnographic landscapes are areas that contain natural and cultural objects that a people, such as an Indian tribe, define as being part of their heritage. Examples include villages, such as the village green in a small New England town; sacred sites, such as the Big Horn Medicine Wheel in Wyoming; and even mountains, such as Tucumcari Mountain in New Mexico or Enchanted Rock in Texas, both of which have religious significance to Native Americans.

An example of a cultural landscape that is also a historic designated landscape, the Blue Ridge Parkway, is a 469-mile-long scenic parkway in Virginia and North Carolina planned and initially constructed as part of Roosevelt's New Deal in the 1930s. As with all cultural landscapes, with the Blue Ridge Parkway, the line between the preservation of historic resources, such as the road and the Works Progress Administration structures associated with it, and natural resources, such as the mountains and forests visible from the parkway become two very closely integrated pursuits.

Cultural landscapes are important because they provide a critical link between the preservation and environmental movements and often unify their objectives. In considering cultural landscapes, programs can be developed to protect cultural and natural features while carefully considering and preserving their contexts. This allows the buildings, sites, and scenes from our past to continue to exist and evolve and to convey meaning and enjoyment indefinitely. An example of the union of historic preservation and natural conservation in a cultural landscape can be seen in the forested hills and valleys visible from Monticello, Thomas Jefferson's home near Charlottesville, Virginia. The natural landscape and vegetation have been protected to preserve the atmosphere and feeling of this rural historic site as it existed during Jefferson's life (Figure 13.4).

Figure 13.4. The Refractory at Monticello. Experiencing the natural landscape as Jefferson saw it is critical to the visitor experience, unifying natural conservation and historic preservation. Source: Peter B. Dedek, 2007.

THE PROBLEM OF URBAN SPRAWL

New development in the United States since the Second World War has emphasized suburban expansion into open land based on the nearly universal use of the automobile. Called **urban sprawl,** America's towns and cities have expanded rapidly over vast amounts of land through the development of subdivisions, shopping centers, and roads. The advance of sprawl, often pioneered by new car sales lots, manufactured home sellers, and warehouses, has eaten up massive amounts of former farmland, natural areas, and historic cultural landscapes in the past few decades. The primary culprit is our dependence on the automobile, and only recently has the problem been seriously addressed by the planning and design disciplines, although all one has to do is take a domestic flight and look out the window at the suburbs of cities such as Atlanta, Dallas, Las Vegas, and Phoenix to see that urban sprawl continues to expand at an alarming rate (Figure 13.5).

Since the 1950s, rural and suburban areas of the United States have undergone a steady and dramatic transformation due to the coming of the interstate system. Even today, fields, forests, and historic structures continue to be replaced by wide access roads, barren parking lots and bland, sprawling cinder block buildings. We are rapidly becoming a nation of massive one-story warehouse-like supermarkets, super-sized department stores, sprawling trucking distribution

Figure 13.5. Urban sprawl is nearly as bland and dehumanizing from the air as it is from the ground. Source: Peter B. Dedek, 2008

centers, truck stops, chain restaurants, spread-out corporate office buildings, corrugated steel-clad factories, self-storage complexes, and strip shopping centers. These buildings are inevitably surrounded by extensive parking lots. This destruction of the natural and historic landscape seems to go unnoticed by the majority of people who appear to accept it as necessary.

Car-related development dominates and destroys large amounts of land because the use of cars takes up so much more land than pedestrians or bicycles. A standing pedestrian occupies only about two square feet, a parked bicycle about four. Cars, on the other hand, require 70 to 100 square feet of barren, lifeless ground just to be parked, and the number of redundant parking spaces makes matters worse. In the state of Pennsylvania, for instance, there are about six parking spaces for each of the nearly 7 million registered cars in the state (Hylton 1995, 26). If one takes the number of registered cars in the country—250,272,812 in 2010—and multiplies that number by 6, the result is the approximate number of parking spaces in the United States—about 1.5 billion. That's more than four spaces for every man, woman, and child in the country (Bureau of Transportation Statistics 2012). In some areas of the nation, the situation is even worse than the average; for example, the city of Houston provides nearly 30 parking spaces per resident, Detroit 13. In contrast, Paris provides only one space per three residents (Beaumont 1994, 3). Parking lots are the ultimate monoculture, a single use for land that makes it inorganic and dead, killing virtually all potential to support life and add oxygen to the atmosphere or promote human well-being.

Urban sprawl is not necessary for economic development and in some cases can actually impede it, especially now that fuel costs have increased. Sprawl centers do not always represent prosperity or jobs and are often not even well-maintained. About 12 percent of the space sheltered by retail warehouse structures was vacant in 1990 (Beaumont 1994, 3), and between 1990 and 2005, the amount of retail space in the United States doubled (Institute for Local Self-Reliance 2012).

As urban sprawl continues nearly unabated, farmland, animal habitats, and historic structures continue to be destroyed in the United States at a rate comparable to the destruction of tropical rain forests. Preserving and reviving historic areas helps to direct development activities away from the edges of towns and cities back toward the center, promoting energy savings through reducing dependence on cars. Most established cities have public transportation and where cars are used, travel distances are usually shorter than in the suburbs. In addition, many historic buildings are surrounded by large old trees that are often cut down if the building is demolished and replaced with a new building. Preservation discourages the clearing of land, which destroys carbon-consuming trees, and saves the energy that might be used to demolish old buildings and construct new ones.

Because the majority of historic buildings are located in or near the traditional centers of cities and towns, preservation focuses development in concentrated areas and therefore discourages urban sprawl. When centrally located neighborhoods and business districts become more desirable, the focus of development shifts from the periphery, saving rural areas including historic cultural landscapes and other historic sites from destruction. When historic farms are preserved along with their rural context, this saves open space. The environmental impact of preservation is not only limited to the saved historic buildings themselves, but to the places spared when development is focused in traditional urban areas. Reducing development at the edges of towns preserves open land, reduces fuel consumption by cars and trucks, reduces the need for additional and costly infrastructure such as highways and bridges, and promotes greater cultural interaction and racial integration. According to Mike Jackson, FAIA, of the Illinois SHPO, "In terms of density and land planning, the city of the 2060s may be more like the city of 1860 than the city of 1960" (Jackson 2008).

HISTORIC PRESERVATION AND GREEN BUILDING

While the pursuit of historic preservation can help preserve aspects of the environment through the recognition and designation of cultural landscapes, and the reduction of urban sprawl, preservation can also play a significant role in the growing green building movement.

Green architecture was developed to address the vast environmental impact that the construction and operation of buildings has. Buildings and construction have a huge impact on the consumption of natural resources. According to the U.S. Green Building Council, in the United States alone, buildings account for:

- 72 percent of electricity consumption

- 39 percent of energy use

- 38 percent of all carbon dioxide (CO_2) emissions

- 40 percent of raw materials use

- 30 percent of waste output (over 136 million tons annually)

- 14 percent of potable water consumption (U.S. Green Building Council 2012)

Because buildings have such a significant impact on the environment, green building has received increasing attention in the design professions in the past two decades. However, until recently, green design and historic preservation have been treated as if they were two separate pursuits. One of the reasons for this is the way the two disciplines evolved, with preservation having a traditional focus on history and aesthetics and green building emphasizing recycled building materials and energy efficiency. The field of architecture has mostly evaluated sustainable design with a focus on new construction. The main standard used in the United States since 2000 is the United States Green Building Council's (USGBC's) LEED (Leadership in Energy and Environmental Design) evaluation tools.

LEED is a certification program that evaluates the construction and operation of green buildings by giving them an evaluative rating in points. According to the USGBC's official website:

LEED certification provides independent, third-party verification that a building, home or community was designed and built using strategies aimed at achieving high performance in key areas of human and environmental health: sustainable site development, water savings, energy efficiency, materials selection and indoor environmental quality.

Currently, a building can be given a designation as a green "LEED certified" project or building in a number of categories, such as new construction and major renovations, existing buildings, and commercial interiors, out of a possible 100 points from "certified," 40 or more points; "silver," 50 or more points; "gold," 60 or more points; and "platinum," 80 or more points (United States Green Building Council 2012). The points are awarded for the use of sustainable design in a number of areas, such as the specification of sustainable building materials and finishes, energy efficiency, and access to public transportation.

Although the system created an effective, standardized method of evaluating the environmental impact of architecture projects, LEED emphasizes new construction and does not currently attribute very much value to the reuse of buildings. Under version LEED 2009, the guidelines in use at this writing, reusing the core of an existing building in a construction project is assigned only 1 to 3 points out of 100 (up from 2 points under the previous guidelines), not much more value in points as "merely using environmentally-friendly carpet" (Moe 2008). And although many historic projects have been awarded one or two points for reusing existing walls, few have even been awarded all three of the points (Roberts 2007). Architect Barbara Campagna of the National Trust for Historic Preservation cites three reasons why LEED green building standards insufficiently address preservation. The rating system "overlooks the impact of projects on cultural value, does not effectively consider the performance, longer service lives, and embodied energy of historic materials and assemblies, and is overly focused on current or future technologies, neglecting how past experience helps to determine sustainable performance" (Campagna 2008). However, the National Trust for Historic Preservation worked with the U.S. Green Building Council to create the LEED 2009 guidelines, which did increase the density credit awarded to projects in urban settings, from just 1 to a potential of 1 to 5 points. LEED 2009 also increased the public transportation credit, which is awarded to projects constructed near mass transit, from 1 to a potential of 6 points (Farwell 2009).

In addition, the U.S. Green Building Council has added an entire Neighborhood Development rating system to LEED for communities, which indirectly promotes preservation by encouraging construction in dense, walkable neighborhoods in or near existing towns and cities. Even this system, however, only provides 1 point for historic adaptive use and 1 for existing building reuse. This adds some weight in the LEED system for preservation projects and planning, but preservation as a significant environmental value is still not apparent in the LEED rating system. Despite this disadvantage, a number of buildings renovated and certified under the federal Investment Tax Incentives have also won LEED certification. Examples include the Christman Construction Headquarters in Grand Rapids, MI; the Big D Construction Headquarters in Salt Lake City, Utah; and the Ecotrust Building in Portland, Oregon (Young 2011).

HISTORIC BUILDINGS ARE GREEN

One factor that LEED has yet to take into account is that existing buildings, particularly those built before the Second World War, have many inherent green attributes that are not always matched by newer buildings. Older buildings were constructed often using traditional natural and local materials, many of which would be difficult or impossible to replicate today. Also,

MCCORMICK GOODHART MANSION

HISTORIC MANSION PROVIDES A GREEN HOME THAT PROVIDES SOCIAL SERVICES

Figure 13A Parlor before rehabilitation. Source: Ward Bucher, AIA

Figure 13B Parlor after rehabilitation. Source: Kenneth M. Wyner

Built in 1924 and designed by leading Washington D.C. architect George Oakley Totten, the Georgian Revival-style McCormick-Goodhart Mansion in Langley Park, Maryland, stood vacant for many years and had become badly damaged by water intrusion, a fire, and vandalism over time. The 3-story, 19,000-square-foot mansion was originally the seat of the 565-acre Langley Park estate and has a mostly Tudor-style interior. After the death of the original owners, the mansion was used as a seminary, later as a Montessori school, and then as a child care center before becoming vacant. Periodic remodeling had caused the original walls in many significant rooms to be covered with Masonite paneling and ceilings with acoustical-tile. Fire damage in the lobby had been concealed behind drywall, and many of the historic mantels and doors had been removed. When it rained, waterfalls in the

Figure 13C Restored mansion. Source: Kenneth M. Wyner

corners of many major rooms damaged plaster and decayed the wooden structure.

The mansion was listed on the National Register in 2008 under Criterion C as an example of a great country house of 1920s Maryland (NPS 2008). Soon thereafter, CASA de Maryland (CASA) a nonprofit dedicated to providing resources and opportunities for low-income immigrants and their families acquired the house for reuse as an administrative and social services center. CASA used federal historic tax credits when rehabilitating the building. The work restored the exterior and saved much of the historic interior, especially the highly decorative significant spaces of the first floor, such as the lobby, dining room, main stair, library, and ballroom. The project preserved the house's decorative interior details, among the most significant of which are ornate neoclassical interior moldings, hardwood floors, and molded plaster ceilings.

Figure 13D Grand stairway, an interior defining characteristic

The rehabilitated building provides administrative offices, conference spaces, and specialized training rooms. Service and storage areas were remodeled, and since a large meeting room could not be located in the historic house without harming significant spaces, an underground multipurpose addition was constructed in the rear. The project both rehabilitated and retained the significant historic features of the house and also earned LEED Gold certification. The green aspects of the rehabilitation include a green roof on the flat roofs of the modern additions, drought tolerant landscaping, the use of sustainable building products, and a geothermal HVAC system (Star Democrat 2011).

their siting and design attributes sometimes took advantage of prevailing winds, which help ventilate and cool them without the need of air conditioning, and they were sometimes built to take advantage of passive solar gain, which helps heat them without the use of fossil fuels. Many historic buildings also have usable porches, significant roof overhangs, awnings, and many are located adjacent to mature trees, all of which provide shade and can reduce the energy required for cooling, especially in warmer parts of the country. Some historic buildings, such as many old factories, have operable windows and sometimes skylights that can save on energy on lighting. According to architects John Krieble and Laurie Kerr of the Office of Sustainable Design at New York City's Department of Design and Construction, artificial lighting can account for 30 to 50 percent of a building's energy usage, so having sources of natural light such as large historic windows can significantly reduce the energy it consumes (Krieble and Kerr 2004).

The durable materials, such as old growth wood, brick, plaster, and solid stone commonly used in historic buildings, often last longer and age more gracefully than their modern equivalents. Historic building materials, such as brick and stone, also have thermal mass and often act as "heat sinks," which absorb heat during the day and release it at night, helping to moderate interior temperatures in northern climates. While LEED does encourage the reuse and recycling of architectural elements salvaged from old buildings, even in LEED-certified projects this usually makes up a small percentage of materials used in new construction (Young 2011).

In addition, the design and arrangement of historic buildings is often more compact than that of their contemporary counterparts, with many sharing party walls making them easier to heat and cool. A 2008 study by the U.S. Energy Information Agency indicated that buildings built prior to 1920 are, on average, more energy efficient than buildings built between 1920 and 2000 (Young 2011). However, the same study found that buildings constructed between 1960 and 1990 use significantly more energy than both their older and their newer counterparts, meaning that as these buildings become historic, they will often require significant energy efficiency upgrades if they are to be preserved and operated in an environmentally-friendly manner. A 1999 study by the General Services Administration of the U.S. government found that utility costs for historic buildings operated by the federal government were 27 percent less than those for more recently-built buildings (Moe 2008).

ENERGY EFFICIENCY AND EMBODIED ENERGY

Even though new buildings that are built to LEED standards will be more energy efficient on an operational basis than most historic buildings, this is not the only consideration when it comes to the overall consumption of energy in architecture. New construction consumes a lot of energy. Trees have to be cut, processed, and transported; the materials needed for concrete have to be quarried, processed, and transported; stone has to be quarried, cut and moved to the site for installation; bricks must be fired, and so on.

Embodied energy is the energy that has already been consumed in the past when existing buildings were constructed. The energy is embodied in the historic building, and if the building is destroyed, that energy is lost. The energy saved by not demolishing a historic building and the energy saved by not constructing a new one in its place often tips the scale in terms of energy conservation in favor of preservation. Even if a new building has a gold or platinum LEED rating and is very energy efficient, how green is it if it replaced an existing historic building that had a vast reserve of embodied energy?

Embodied energy calculations need to become a vital part of the equation. According to Richard Moe, former president of the National Trust for Historic Preservation, the Advisory Council for Historic Preservation estimates that 80 billion BTUs of energy are retained in a typical 50,000-square-foot commercial building, which is the equivalent of 640,000 gallons of gasoline. This constitutes the embodied energy that would be wasted if the building were to be demolished. In addition, the act of demolition itself and constructing a new building in its place uses additional energy. Construction activity also uses up natural resources and releases pollutants and greenhouse gases. Moe reports that "constructing a 50,000-square-foot commercial building releases about the same amount of carbon into the atmosphere as driving a car 2.8 million miles" (2008).

It is important to realize that the answer to saving the environment is often to do less and not more. Constructing a massive "green" building still uses a tremendous amount of resources, especially if historic buildings are destroyed in the process. Moe points out

> You might think that all the energy used in demolishing an older building and replacing it is offset by the increased energy efficiency of the new building—but . . . . recent research indicates that even if 40 percent of the materials are recycled, it takes approximately 65 years for a green, energy-efficient new office building to recover the energy lost in demolishing an existing building [and] . . . . Most new buildings aren't designed to last anywhere near 65 years (2008).

In addition to using a lot of energy, demolitions also create a tremendous amount of waste that needs to be disposed of.

WASTE CAUSED BY DEMOLITION

According to the Environmental Protection Agency, approximately 136 million tons of building-related construction and demolition debris was generated in the U.S. each year in the 1990s and by 2003, the amount of waste was estimated to have been 325 million tons, an increase of almost 250 percent. In addition, the EPA reports that building demolitions accounted for 48 percent of this amount or 65 million tons a year. Construction and demolition debris makes up roughly 24 percent of the municipal solid waste stream (Frey 2007). It is no wonder, since demolishing a single 50,000-square-foot building creates nearly 4,000 tons of waste, enough to fill 26 rail-road boxcars (Moe 2008). According to various estimates, building-related waste accounts for between 10 and 30 percent of the total waste stream being transported to the nation's landfills (Montana State University Extension 2008). This percentage is much higher in some places; for example, over 60 percent of the solid waste generated in New York City comes from construction and demolition waste, which is greater than national average due to New York's large stock of old buildings. To make matters worse, the city often ships this waste to Pennsylvania and Virginia, consuming a vast amount of energy in transportation to fill up landfills in those states (Krieble and Kerr 2004).

Disposing of this waste squanders energy as heavy debris is trucked to landfills that occupy land that could be used for better purposes or left in a natural state. The waste created by razing a typical commercial building that is about 25 feet wide and 120 feet deep takes up as much landfill space as not recycling around 1.3 million aluminum cans (Young 2011). By simply allowing historic buildings to remain in place and rehabilitating them, we do the environment a great service.

HISTORIC WINDOWS AND LIFE-CYCLE ANALYSIS

A major area where preservation and green design come into conflict is the question of whether to retain or replace historic windows. In virtually all cases where historic windows are present, the *Secretary of the Interior's Standards* and other historical guidelines and regulations recommend or require their retention (see Chapter 10). The reason for this is that historic windows are an integral part of the historic look and character of most buildings (Figure 13.6). The problem is that historic single-glazed windows tend not to

Figure 13.6. Historic windows are an integral defining characteristic of most historic buildings. This 1934 drug-store building in Hollywood, California, possesses the original horizontal windows on its second level, which help identify and define it as an art modern-style building. Reused as a medical building, it has lost its original storefront windows at the street level, reducing its over-all historic integrity. Source: Peter B. Dedek, 2008.

be as energy efficient as new double- or triple-glazed windows. While this is true, historic windows, especially those made of old-growth wood or metal, tend to have a longer lifespan than newer ones. Whether made of metal or old growth wood, the materials used in historic windows tend to be very durable (Figure 13.7).

The concept of life-cycle analysis, which is important to design professionals and preservationists alike, is very important in green design. **Life-cycle cost** analysis refers to the total cost of purchasing and maintaining an architectural element over its entire life. Therefore, using life-cycle cost analysis, new windows that will probably need to be replaced every 20 years may end up costing the building owner more in money, energy, and waste than retaining historic windows, which, with routine maintenance, can last hundreds of years. It is important when evaluating both preservation and green building decisions that the life-cycle cost—the total cost of installing, maintaining, and possibly reinstalling over time—is taken into account. Every time anything is manufactured or built, energy is expended and waste is generated, so even if historic windows lose more energy than new ones, replacing them may be harder on the environment in the long run. Also, the manufacture of typical vinyl and PVC replacement windows creates a lot of toxic waste (Sedovic 2005).

Figure 13.7. With proper care, historic windows such as this one can last for centuries. Source: Peter B. Dedek, 2011.

A common argument for replacing historic windows is that new windows often have "low-e" glass, which reflects long wavelengths in sunlight, causing heat gain in the interiors of buildings in summer months. Window shades can often do much the same job, and in some instances where low-e windows are necessary, the glass can be changed while retaining the historic sash and window frames in place, which reduces the loss of historic integrity (Sedovic 2005). However, from a preservation perspective, it is preferable to retain historic glass, especially in buildings dating from before the 1940s and to use reversible solutions such as the aforementioned window shades or canopies.

To keep heat in, in most cases, historic windows can be retained and new interior storm windows can be added to increase energy efficiency while retaining the historic appearance of the exterior. Even adding removable exterior storm windows that alter the appearance of the building is a better solution than replacing historic windows. But the question in many cases is, do historic windows need to be replaced at all? A common argument for replacement windows is that they seal the building envelope from outside air. However, on average as much as 50 percent of heat loss is due to cracks and leaks in and around windows, not heat passing through the glass itself, meaning that much energy can be conserved by keeping historic windows in good repair and using simple solutions such as weather stripping (Fisette 1998). Adding insulation to attics and sealing gaps in all areas of a historic building is a less expensive, more environmentally friendly, and usually more effective way to reduce energy consumption than replacing historic windows.

CONCLUSION

Although the preservation movement and the environmental movement may appear to have differing goals, the two pursuits are actually very compatible. Because preservation reduces urban sprawl, conserves embodied energy, and reduces landfill waste, retaining historic buildings, neighborhoods, and cultural landscapes is good for the environment. Historic preservation needs to be raised to the forefront in the green building and environmental movements. Unless urban sprawl with its accompanying demolitions and loss of farmland and natural areas can be brought under control, the effort to reduce greenhouse gasses and thus slow global warming will be stymied. Preservation is a critical tool in the rethinking of our environmental policies and the creation of a greener future.

STUDY QUESTIONS

1. How did the goals and methods of conservation during the Progressive Era differ from the goals and methods of the environmental movement today?

2. What is a cultural landscape? What are the four types of cultural landscapes indentified by the National Park Service?

3. What are the LEED green building ratings and what is their goal?

4. How significant is historic preservation in the LEED system?

5. In what ways has United States Green Building Council increased the significance of historic presentation in its 2009 LEED ratings?

6. What is embodied energy and how does preservation help conserve it?

7. What evidence suggests that preserving historic buildings saves energy and space in landfills?

8. What is life-cycle cost analysis and how does it work?

9. Is replacing old windows with new ones always the best solution in terms of saving energy? Why or why not?

10. In what ways are green design and historic preservation comparable?

EXERCISE: CONCISE DEFINITIONS

Define the following terms found in the chapter in 12 words or less:

1) Cultural landscapes _____

2) Historic designed landscapes _____

3) Historic vernacular landscapes _____

4) Ethnographic landscapes _____

5) Urban sprawl _____

6) Green _____

7) LEED _____

8) Embodied energy _____

9) Life-cycle cost _____

Answers and explanations found in Instructor's Guide.

SOURCES

Beaumont, Constance. 1994. *How Superstore Sprawl Can Harm Our Communities and What Citizens Can Do about It.* Washington D.C.: National Trust for Historic Preservation.

Bureau of Transportation Statistics. "Table 1-11: Number of U.S. Aircraft, Vehicles, Vessels, and Other Conveyances." Accessed June 15, 2012. http://www.rita.dot.gov/bts/sites/rita.dot.gov.bts/files/publications/national_transportation_statistics/html/table_01_11.html

Campagna, Barbara. 2008. "New Version of LEED to Incorporate Better Metrics for Historic & Existing Buildings." Accessed July 23, 2010. http://blog.preservationnation.org/2008/03/24/new-version-of-leed-to-incorporate-better-metrics-for-existing-historic-buildings/#.UpZabyfxDjE

Farwell, Jennifer. 2009. "The Latest on LEED: How the Points System Is Changing," *Preservation,* March/April. Accessed June 15, 2012. http://www.preservationnation.org/magazine/2009/march-april/latest-on-leed.html

Fisette, Paul. 1998. "Understanding Energy Efficient Windows." *Fine Homebuilding,* 68–73.

Frey, Patrice. 2007. "Making the Case, Hiastoric Preservation as Sustainable Development," National Trust for Historic Preservation. Oct. 15. http://www.heritagecanada.org/sites/www.heritagecanada.org/files/Making%20the%20Case%20-%20Frey-%20Discussion%20Paper%202007.pdf

Hylton, Thomas. 1995. *Save Our Land, Save Our Towns: A Plan for Pennsylvania.* Harrisburg: RB Books.

Institute for Local Self-Reliance. 2007. "FACTSHEET: Big-Box Blight: The Spread of Dark Stores," BIGBOXTOOLKIT.com. Accessed June 15, 2012. http://www.ilsr.org/wp-content/uploads/2008/12/bbtk-factsheet-blight.pdf

Jackson, Mike. "Reduce + Reuse = Preservation: A Presentation Concerning Green Preservation." Illinois Historic Preservation Agency. Accessed July 22, 2010. http://www.state.il.us/hpa/PS/green_preservation.htm

Krieble, John and Laurie Kerr. 2004. "Back to the Future: Greening Historic Buildings." GreenHome NYC, April 21. Accessed July 23, 2010. http://greenhomenyc.org/forum/backtothefuture%3agreeninghistoricbuildings-april21%2c2004/

Moe, Richard. "Sustainable Stewardship: Historic Preservation's Essential Role in Fighting Climate Change." Lecture, delivered at the First Church of Christ, Scientist, Berkeley, CA, March 27, 2008.

Montana State University Extension, "Building—Related C&D Waste Characteristics." Accessed July 22, 2010. http://peakstoprairies.org/p2bande/construction/c&dwaste/whatsC&D.cfm

NPS National Register form, 2008, "Langly Park." National Park Service. Accessed November 29, 2013. http://www.nps.gov/nr/feature/weekly_features/LangleyPark.pdf

Roberts, Tristan. 2007. "Historic Preservation and Green Building: A Lasting Relationship," *Environmental Building News January.* Accessed October 9, 2010.

http://www.buildinggreen.com/auth/article.cfm/2007/1/2/Historic-Preservation-and-Green-Building-A-Lasting-Relationship/

Sedovic, Walter, and Jill H. Gotthelf. 2005. "What Replacement Windows Can't Replace: The Real Cost of Removing Historic Windows," *APT Bulletin*, 4: 25–30.

Sellars, Richard West. 2008. "A Very Large Array: Early Federal Historic Preservation—The Antiquities Act, Mesa Verde, and the National Park Service Act." *The George Wight Forum,* 1: 65–120.

Star Democrat, 2011. "Local Residents Honored for Restoration Work." Accessed November 29, 2013. http://www.stardem.com/real_estate/article_4bee672e-c2f6-56e5-81bf-9fde61a36d3d.html

United States Green Building Council. "What Is LEED?" Accessed June 15, 2012. http://www.usgbc.org/articles/about-leed

Young, Robert A. 2011. "Historic Preservation and Adaptive Use: A Significant Opportunity for Sustainability" Architecture Research Centers Consortium, ARCC 2011, Spring Conference, Detroit , MI. Conference Paper, Refereed, Presented, 04/2011.

IN WITH THE OLD, OUT WITH THE NEW: EMERGING TRENDS IN HISTORIC PRESERVATION IN THE 21st CENTURY

As the 21st century matures, the practice of preservation design is changing. Among the forces driving this change is green design and sustainability, climate change, New Urbanism, a growing appreciation for 20th-century modernist architecture, an ever-increasing diversity of historic resources, property right issues, and cuts in governmental funding and involvement.

GREEN DESIGN, SUSTAINABILITY, AND CLIMATE CHANGE

As discussed in Chapter 13, environmental conservation and protection is already a significant aspect of historic preservation, and this trend is likely to continue to grow. Not only will more old buildings be reused, but the methods and materials employed to restore them will be greener. Future work on historic buildings will include more recycled elements, better energy efficiency, and a more holistic and synergistic design process.

A number of significant efforts to better integrate historic preservation with environmental conservation have been undertaken in recent years. In 2009, the National Trust for Historic Preservation created its Preservation Green Lab in Seattle to study, develop, and promote practices such as creating better energy codes for historic buildings, weatherproofing rather than replacing historic windows, and doing "deep energy retrofits" to historic buildings. A major goal of the Green Lab is to help minimize the amount of carbon being emitted due to construction activity and other sources related to the built environment. The project seeks to encourage reductions in direct emissions by conserving old buildings and upgrading their energy efficiency without significantly reducing their historic integrity. Another goal of the Green Lab is to encourage the planning and development of more sustainable rural and urban communities that incorporate historic resources.

The National Park Service (NPS) has also recently initiated a program to promote sustainability in historic structures. These measures include working to identify a sample of approximately 20 typical NPS historic structures and holding a design charette "that will provide recommendations for sustainable treatments for those typical examples," developing general guidance on best practices in making sustainable changes to historic buildings, and working to "identify, protect, and preserve the historic assets most at risk to climate change" (NPS 2012). Efforts such as these are likely to be repeated and expanded at the national, state, and local levels as energy costs continue to rise, the climate continues to change, and the role of preservation in sustainability becomes increasingly apparent.

NEW URBANISM

A trend that first emerged in the 1980s, **new urbanism** is an effort by city planners and some developers to recreate the urban density and diversity or the pre automobile era in new and existing neighborhoods in order to fight urban sprawl (see Chapter 13) and improve the livability and sustainability of cities and other communities. The American Planning Association describes new urbanism as: " . . . a time-tested planning practice that incorporates interrelated patterns of land use, transportation, and urban form to create communities that foster the most desirable characteristics of human habitation: neighborliness, environmental sustainability, economic efficiency and prosperity, historic preservation, participation in civic processes, and human health." (APA 2012). This approach has impacted and will continue to impact preservation in a number of ways. Although the idea has been in circulation for a while, only a limited number of new urbanist projects, such as Stapleton, developed on the site of the old airport in Denver, Colorado (2001), and Mountain House located near Tracy, California (2001), have been implemented. While most new urbanist projects have been designed and built independently on large sites outside historic city centers, some new urbanist planning takes place in existing urbanized areas, such as in San Antonio, Texas, and Miami, Florida, where many historic buildings and districts are located. Although there have been some conflicts in recent years between new urbanist planners and preservationists, in the long run, the further implementation of new urbanism is likely to encourage preservation because most historic neighborhoods built before the Second World War already possess many new urbanist characteristics.

However, new urbanism can also draw some resources away from historic urban centers, because so many new urbanist communities are developed from scratch in suburban and rural areas. It will be important for preservationists to emphasize the value of practicing a sympathetic form of new urbanism in historic areas and not focusing as much on the creation of completely new development. In addition, if many of the mid-20th-century developments built in the 1950s and 1960s currently becoming historic were reconstructed under new urbanist guidelines, this would likely negatively impact the historic integrity of those places. Strangely, preservationists may soon find themselves defending the kinds of auto-related modern structures and landscapes they have spent decades fighting. As this occurs, it is likely many will gain new appreciation for such places.

GROWING HISTORIC SIGNIFICANCE OF 20th-CENTURY MODERNIST ARCHITECTURE

A major factor impacting the practice of preservation and the work of designers is the changing nature of what is considered a historic resource. As discussed in Chapter 2, the age at which a site has the potential to be considered historic is 50 years. Hundreds of buildings, subdivisions, and commercial districts built in the 1960s are becoming eligible to be considered historic every day. This not only means that the style and configuration of these buildings is different from the kinds of properties preservationists are used to defending and working with, but also that the materials preservationists and designers will be working with will also be different. While rehabilitating a modern historic building, a designer will end up studying how to preserve plate-glass, reinforced-concrete, and vinyl floor covering, rather than the more traditional wooden-sash, old brick, and plank flooring. This will require the creation of new preservation technologies and also will involve preservation designers having to become accustomed to a different, more modern aesthetic. It is even possible that preservationists and environmentalists may clash at times over the preservation of certain postwar 20th-century places, because glass box buildings and strip malls, which usually have large single-glazed plate-glass windows and little insulation, often waste energy and occupy land that might be impacted by new urbanist developments or alternative energy sites. There have already been cases where property owners within historic districts have opposed the construction of green intrusions, such as electric generating windmills and solar panels within or near the district.

THE EVER-INCREASING DIVERSITY OF HISTORIC RESOURCES

Along with modern design becoming historic, the general diversity of historic resources in need of identification, documentation, protection, and rehabilitation will continue to expand. The sheer amount of development that took place after the Second World War will mean that preservationists will be swamped with an enormous volume of potentially historic resources ranging from old gas stations to chain restaurants, water towers, shopping centers, entire subdivisions of tract houses, and even interstate highway overpasses, the types of historic resources never envisioned by those who created historic preservation in America in the 1920s through the 1960s. This will require innovation, flexibility, and a sincere concern for history and conservation on the part of all preservationists, including architects and designers.

PROPERTY RIGHTS

So far, historic preservation has largely avoided becoming the specific target of any political agenda; however, as discussed in Chapter 5, the issue of private property rights has always been a significant obstacle to the survival and enforcement of laws designed to protect historic buildings. The conflict between preservation protections and property rights advocates continues. For example, in 2012 a preservation battle involving the property rights argument was underway in Phoenix, Arizona, about an owner's plans to demolish the David and Gladys Wright House designed by Frank Lloyd Wright in 1951 (Haldiman 2012). The owner wanted to redevelop the property despite the house's national significance and was willing to go to court to do so. While private property rights need to be safeguarded, the right of all Americans to enjoy the beauty and the environmental benefits of retaining significant historic buildings, such as the David and Gladys Wright House, also needs to be protected. The property rights argument and the issue of where the balance lies between the rights of landowners and the need for preservation will continue to be a significant debate that will likely result in future controversies and court cases.

CUTS IN GOVERNMENTAL FUNDING AND INVOLVEMENT

Another political factor that has already affected preservation in recent years is a decreasing role of government in the field due mainly to budget cuts and a shift in priorities at the federal level and in some states. For example, as mentioned in Chapter 1, the 1990s federal program Preserve America, and the 2000s initiative Save America's Treasures, both of which provided preservation grants nationwide, have lost their funding. In addition, a number of states, such as Texas, have cut much of the funding for their State Historic Preservation Offices, forcing them to cut back on staff and programs. The federal tax incentive program passed in 1978 and revised in 1986, which has spawned billions of dollars in private investment to rehabilitate historic buildings, has even come under fire in recent years. If this trend continues, private organizations, such as the National Trust for Historic Preservation, will have to take up the slack, but it is uncertain if they are willing or even able to do so. It seems that political advocacy will be a key component in ensuring that preservation activities continue. Historic preservation will have many challenges, especially with government funding and private property conflicts, but also many opportunities, such as a broader range of resources to protect and better coordination with the environmental movement.

PRESERVATION DESIGN OF THE FUTURE

Ultimately, the future of preservation depends on people personally caring about America's historic resources. For preservation to succeed, professionals and their clients involved in all areas of design and building will have to want to respect and preserve historic architecture and landscapes. In the end, the most important preservation activity is educating people about the merits of preserving. As more people care, preservation laws will be tested less frequently and conflicts will become more scarce. Preservation practices that were once exceptional, such as following the *Secretary of the Interior's Standards* and incorporating green design practices when rehabilitating buildings, will become commonplace, making the future bright.

SOURCES

American Planning Association (APA). "New Urbanism Division." Accessed on November 23, 2012. http://www.planning.org/divisions/newurbanism/

Haldiman, Phillip. "Frank Lloyd Wright Home Debate Pits Preservation vs. Property Rights." *The Republic.* Accessed on November 23, 2012. http://www.azcentral.com/community/phoenix/articles/20121007frank-lloyd-wright-home-debate.html#ixzz2D554UTm7

National Park Service (NPS). "Sustainable Operations and Climate Change." Accessed on November 23, 2012. http://www.nps.gov/sustainability/sustainable/structures.html

GLOSSARY

501(c)3 charitable nonprofit organizations: charitable groups not organized or operated for the benefit of private interests where no net earnings may inure to the benefit of any private shareholder or individual.

Advisory Council on Historic Preservation: a federal agency with 23 official members, 21 of which are appointed by the president. The council is dedicated to promoting the preservation of all types of historic properties across the nation.

adobe: sun-dried clay used as a load bearing building material.

ambrotypes: photographs printed on a sheet of glass and easily identified because of the glass, and the fact they have a black paper backing. Patented in 1854, ambrotypes were produced until the 1880s.

American common bond: a method of laying up brick which has occasional all header courses separated by five or so all stretcher courses.

Americans with Disabilities Act of 1990 (ADA): a law designed to protect the civil rights of Americans with disabilities. Discrimination in employment, access to places of public accommodation, services, programs, public transportation, and telecommunications were prohibited by this law.

anticipatory demolition: when owners of potentially historic buildings demolish them proactively because they believe the building will soon be designated as historic and believe the designation will limit their rights as property owners.

architectural terra-cotta: a relatively soft blend of fired clays commonly used in the late 19th and early 20th centuries to construct and decorate buildings.

archival research: the act of investigating written sources, such as those found in archives and libraries.

Area of Potential Effect (APE): the geographical area in which a Section 106 project has the potential to impact any historic property that may be present.

area of significance: the overall theme into which a property falls. Examples of commonly used areas of significance include agriculture, architecture, commerce, education, the heritage of a particular ethnic group, exploration and settlement, industry, military history, religion, and transportation.

asbestos: an inorganic fiber now known to be very hazardous used as a fireproof building material from the beginning of the 20th century until the 1970s.

ashlar masonry construction: walls and other elements made of stone cut into blocks.

association: a property's documented or observable links to the past.

balloon framing: structural construction using long rough-cut boards used as studs and beams held together by nails.

bedding/face bedding: layers within certain kinds of stone that resembles wood grain and runs in a particular direction.

binder: a glue-like substance in paint that holds the compound together and helps it stick to and grip the surface to which it is applied.

blunt point screws: screws made before the 1850s that had no point.

boring bees: a variety of large bee that looks something like a bumblebee and makes its nest by boring holes into wood.

brick: a common masonry material in historic buildings, essentially rectangular blocks of fired clay mixed with sand to increase dimensional stability.

building: A building is a relatively permanent construction built to shelter any type of human activity, such as living, selling goods, or producing goods. Buildings include houses, barns, churches, factories, office blocks, and other types of shelters that are designed to be fixed to one location (although buildings are sometimes moved) and are usually made of heavy materials such as wood, brick, metal, stone, or concrete.

bundle of rights: the many-faceted set of rights that a landowner may possess.

canales: hollowed logs that project through the parapet walls of Spanish colonial buildings that direct rain water off the roof and out away from the walls of the building.

carpenter ants: wood-dwelling ants that prefer moist timber. They do not eat the wood itself but destroy the material by making tunnels in order to nest in it.

casement windows: windows hinged on the sides that open outward from the middle.

cast iron: refined iron ore that is melted and poured into molds to create diverse shapes.

cast stone: also called "artificial stone," unreinforced concrete formed into blocks designed to mimic ashlar stone.

Certified Historic Structure: a building or structure that has been individually listed on the National Register or has been determined to be a "contributing" building located within a National Register district.

certificate of appropriateness: a document issued by a municipal authority that allows rehabilitation work to begin on a regulated historic property, which is either within a local historic district or is a designated historic landmark.

Certified Local Government Program: a federal program that encourages local governments to participate in the national historic preservation program, create local historic districts, and to utilize national preservation standards, such as the *Secretary of the Interior's Standards,* in their decisions regarding historic properties.

character-defining features: significant elements of a building, such as historic porches, windows, rooflines, decoration, and in the case of districts, historic blocks and street configurations that help people identify them as being historic.

client: the person, people, or organization paying for a project.

code equivalency: an alternate means of providing an equal or greater degree of protection than that afforded by strict conformance to proscribed codes and standards.

compressive strength: the ability of a given material to resist force or weight that presses directly down on it, as when stone blocks are piled up: the stone at the bottom will have to resist greater compressive stress than the blocks above.

conceptual design phase: a creative stage in the design process that involves creating and evaluating design alternatives using information gathered in the programming phase and visual tools such as adjacency matrices, bubble diagrams, and block plans.

conservation district: designated districts within towns and cities with distinct geographical boundaries that have less stringent regulations than historic districts. They usually limit demolitions and the scale of new development.

consolidation: when stone is treated with chemicals, and the stone element is usually removed from the building and dipped in a bath of chemicals.

construction documents phase: the step in the design process in which detailed construction documents are created.

contract administration phase: the step in the design process in which interior designers and architects help supervise and monitor construction activity and make changes to the design or design specifications when needed.

contributing: a term applied to a property, usually a building, located within a historic district that is deemed to be historic.

crown or **table glass:** glass produced in the 1700s and early 1800s for use in windows from hand-blown lumps of molten glass spun out into a thin disc using centrifugal force and later cut into rectangular panes.

cultural landscape: a place where people have altered the natural environment in visible ways in an identifiable area that includes intact cultural and natural resources that enhance contemporary people's understanding of a historic event, long-term human activity, or the life of a historic person or group of people.

cylinder glass: glass produced from the early 1800s to around 1920 created by blowing a long tube of glass and then cutting it along the entire length of the cylinder, reheating it, and letting it fall flat on a table.

daguerreotypes: the first type of commercially made photograph from 1839 to the 1890s, were etched on a copper sheet plated with silver.

defendant: the party (person, corporation, or governmental entity) whose actions (or lack of action) have caused someone else to sue them.

demolition by neglect: when building owners purposely or inadvertently allow buildings to deteriorate to the point that it is no longer feasible to rehabilitate them.

Design: the overall form and features that make an interior, historic building or historic district distinctive.

design development phase: a part of the design process in which the design chosen during the conceptual design phase is refined.

differential settling: when sections or parts of the building to settle to a greater degree and at different rates than others causing a destructive condition where the structure splits apart.

double-glazed: windows with two panes of glass filled with an inert gas.

efflorescence: a powder or stain, usually whitish in color, that collects on the surface of masonry as the result of water intrusion.

embodied energy: the energy that has already been consumed in the past when an existing building was constructed and is lost if it is torn down.

encapsulate: to cover up and seal away hazardous materials, such as asbestos or lead.

English bond: a method of laying up brick which has alternating courses each consisting of all stretchers and all headers.

English Cross or **Dutch bond:** a method of laying up brick which has alternating courses of headers and stretchers.

ethnographic landscape: an area containing natural and cultural objects that a people, such as an Indian tribe, define as being part of their heritage.

façadism: when only the historic street façade is retained with just a thin strip behind it, while the rest of the building is demolished and replaced with a totally new structure.

Federal Historic Preservation Tax Incentives: a federal program that provides financial incentives for preservation and the implementation of accepted preservation practices in commercial development projects, which has saved thousands of significant American historic buildings.

Federal Preservation Institute: a federal program that provides government officials and other interested parties with training in subjects related to historic preservation.

feeling: a property's ability to communicate its period of historical significance and to remain unique to the time in which it was created or the time when it hosted famous events or people.

finish coat: a finish coat of fine plaster usually only about 1/8-inch thick, providing a smooth interior surface.

Flemish bond: a method of laying up brick which has stretchers and headers alternating with one another within each course.

Float glass: large sheets of nearly perfect glass that have been produced since the mid-1900s and, like plate glass, continue to be manufactured today

footer drain: a perforated drainage pipe that runs underground below the level of a basement or footer wall that drains water away to a location downhill from the building or to a sump pump.

Formosan termites: termites that originated in China and can be found in the South, mostly in coastal areas, and in Hawaii.

French drain: a ditch filled with gravel containing perforated pipes that carry water away from the foundations and walls of buildings.

green architecture: sustainable architecture designed to minimize harmful environmental impacts due to the construction and operation of buildings through planning, energy efficiency, the use of sustainable materials, and conserving development space.

hand-wrought nails: nails made by hand by blacksmiths who hammered each one out on an anvil, date from the time of the first settlement of America by Europeans to about 1800.

historic designed landscapes: areas of land in the country or in a city that were created by a human designer.

historic structure reports: book-like documents that record and preserve the history of a specific building and its site.

historic surveys: locating, identifying, documenting, and evaluating historic resources, such as buildings, structures, and landscapes, located within a given geographical area.

historic vernacular landscape: a place that evolved organically due to human activity over a long period of time, where the function and interaction between people and the local environment play an important role.

galvanic corrosion: occurs when cast or wrought iron was welded or otherwise connected with non-ferrous metals, such as lead and copper and exposed to moisture causing an electrochemical reaction that deteriorates the iron.

gentrification: when artists and other "urban homesteaders" who are attracted by the unique aesthetic qualities and location of a low-income neighborhood, move in and drive up property values, often forcing many of the traditional residents to leave.

hardwood: varieties of wood that come from deciduous trees (those that drop their leaves in the winter).

headers: bricks laid down perpendicular to the direction of the wall so only their short ends show.

highest and best use: the idea that land is supposed to be used for the purpose that provides the greatest economic return.

historic district: a defined geographical area made up of a significant concentration, linkage, or continuity of sites, buildings, structures, or objects that are united historically or stylistically by events, design, function, or physical development.

historic integrity: the degree to which a property has retained its original historic features. To have integrity, a building has to look similar to the way it did when it was constructed or at least resemble the way it looked during its period of historical significance.

historic property: any building, structure, site, object, or district that has historical, architectural, archeological, or cultural significance.

historic site: the physical location where a historically significant event took place, where a prehistoric or historic occupation or activity happened, or where buildings, structures or objects (whether intact, in ruins, or no longer evident) stand or stood.

historical context: a property's connection to wider historic events, noteworthy people, its surroundings, or architectural trends.

hydraulic cement: a kind of cement that can dry while damp and can even set up when submerged under water in some applications, first invented by the ancient Romans around 200 BC.

Igneous stone: a kind of rock created deep in the earth directly by volcanic activity. It tends to be hard and durable such as granite and basalt.

Infill: new buildings constructed within historic neighborhoods.

in situ: a preservation term that means "in place," or without having been moved.

jurisdiction: the area (geographical or governmental) where a legal body (such as a court) or a political entity (such as a city council) possesses the authority to deal with legal matters. **laches:** a legal term referring to the timeliness of a case. In some cases, plaintiffs are barred from maintaining a lawsuit if they have unreasonably delayed bringing action, and this delay may cause prejudice to defendants if the suit were allowed to go forward.

lath: a material that plasterers attach to the interior surface of a wall to provide a rough surface for the wet plaster to attach onto.

LEED: a certification program created by the United States Green Building Council that evaluates the construction and operation of green buildings by giving them an evaluative rating in points.

life cycle cost: the total cost of purchasing and maintaining an architectural element over its entire life.

lime: a fine, white powder that is manufactured by grinding up limestone or oyster shells and firing the resulting grit at high temperature in a kiln.

limestone: a relatively soft, easily worked sedimentary stone that comes in a number of colors including white, grey, and red, but is usually white or tan.

liquid vehicle: material that allows paint to be spread thinly over a surface.

local historic district: multiple historic properties located within a specific and contiguous geographical area designated and regulated by local municipal law.

Local historic landmark: Individual property designated by local authorities as historic and regulated by local municipal law.

machine-headed cut nails: nails made by machine in one piece with a single operation, with flat heads and no hammer marks, came into use around 1825.

Main Street Program: a program of the National Trust for Historic Preservation that promotes economic revitalization through the rehabilitation and sympathetic reuse of historic downtowns.

marble: a metamorphic stone created when limestone is subjected to heat and pressure underground.

masonry: made of heavy materials, including stone, adobe, brick, and concrete, derived from the earth, usually with good compressive strength.

massing: the volumes a building occupies, its basic volumetric design.

Memorandum of Agreement (MOA): a document drafted and signed by all involved parties at the end of the Section 106 process. The MOA officially documents a final agreement.

metal lath: a method of holding up plaster that consists of a metal grid or screen that is attached to the wall. It creates a strong bond because it holds a greater density of plaster keys than wood lath.

metamorphic stone: rock created when already existing igneous stone is subjected to extreme heat and pressure deep underground and "metamorphosed" into a new stone such as marble or slate.

missing tooth syndrome: the condition where buildings are removed and the lot left empty, breaking the historic spatial arrangement of the streets, the blocks, and the rows of buildings.

mitigation: measures taken to reduce or compensate for adverse effects during the Section 106 process.

mootness: when a lawsuit is deemed frivolous or otherwise unnecessary.

mortises: squared-off chiseled holes used to join timbers in timber framing.

National Heritage Area: a place designated by the United States Congress where natural, cultural, historic, and recreational resources combine to form a cohesive, nationally-distinctive landscape arising from patterns of human activity shaped by geography.

National Historic Landmarks: properties also listed on the National Register but enjoying added status. They must have historic significance at the national level.

National Park Service (NPS): a federal agency under the jurisdiction of the Secretary of the Interior that manages U.S. National Parks and national monuments and has a critical role in historic preservation in the United States.

National Register Bulletin: a series of informational booklets published by the National Park Service to guide individuals writing National Register nominations and completing the National Register nomination form.

National Register nomination: a file created through research and documentation with the purpose of listing a historic property on the National Register of Historic Places.

National Register of Historic Places: the nation's official list of historic properties deemed worthy of preservation.

National Register Criteria Considerations: types of properties generally considered not eligible for the register, but which may be eligible under extraordinary circumstances. They include religious buildings, buildings that have been moved, birthplaces or graves of historical figures, cemeteries, reconstructed buildings, monuments, buildings and structures that achieved their significance less than 50 years before the time the National Register nomination is made.

National Register Criteria for Evaluation: the four distinct classifications (historic events, noteworthy people, distinctive architecture, and archeology) under which a property may be deemed eligible for the National Register.

National Transportation Act: an act of Congress, passed in 1966, that was the first transportation law to address historic preservation.

National Trust for Historic Preservation: a national preservation organization established as a public-private venture in 1949. The purpose of the National Trust is to provide leadership, education, and advocacy to save America's diverse historic places and revitalize communities.

non-contributing: a term applied to a property, usually a building, located within a historic district that is deemed not to be historic. **object:** a potentially movable artifact, often artistic in nature and usually relatively small in scale compared to buildings, constructed in a simple manner.

parquet floor: Wooden flooring that originated in baroque France in the 1600s made up of hardwood designed in geometric patterns.

period of significance: the time span during which the historic events or association with historic people or construction episodes that makes a particular property or district historically significant took place.

permeable membrane: Streets or public squares with commercial and public buildings that allow the public to enter from the street. This makes a city or town more pleasant for pedestrians. **Phillips-head screw:** a screw with a crossed slit in the head that allows the screwdriver better purchase on the screw.

pigment: material that provides the color in paint.

pit saws: early saws used to rip boards, cut with an up-and-down vertical motion and powered by hand.

plaster: a material used to cover interior walls and ceilings in order to provide a paintable, durable interior surface.

platform framing: when the structure of each successive story of a building is constructed separately using short studs and posts.

plaintiff: the party that starts the lawsuit. A plaintiff must claim injury or otherwise negative effect from the actions or lack thereof of the defendant.

plate glass: dating from around 1860 and still manufactured today, molten glass is poured onto large tables then rolled flat into sheets.

plumb: when a wall or other vertical object is perpendicular to the ground or straight up and down.

police power: the right of government to compel citizens to act or to force them not to act in certain ways.

powderpost beetles: beetles that make small holes in usually unfinished wood, such as wall studs and other framing elements.

preservation: the process of maintaining a building so that it continues to exist and function in good condition for decades and perhaps even centuries without ever falling into disrepair or being substantially altered in any way.

preservation easement: legal agreements where a property owner donates or sells an aspect or a number of aspects of property rights to another entity, usually a local government or private preservation organization.

primary sources: documents dating from the historical era being studied. Examples include historic photographs, old letters, period newspaper articles, and original documents such as building contracts and architectural plans.

programming phase: an early step in the design process during which future functions and other requirements are determined and the kinds of spaces and other architectural features required to meet these needs are defined. Programming involves of information gathering and interpretation of data.

rebar: iron rods imbedded in concrete that reinforce the concrete and give it greater tensile strength.

reconstruction: the total rebuilding of a historic building or complex of related structures that once existed on a given site.

regulatory taking: a term property rights advocates apply to any situation where a government regulation, such as the rules enforced in a historic district, limits the owner's use of that property in a manner that costs him or her money.

remedy: the action or payment plaintiff is seeking when filing a lawsuit.

repointing: the process of replacing mortar between bricks.

restoration: the activity of taking a building and its grounds back to the way they appeared during a particular period in its history.

revolving fund: a monetary tool where money is loaned to the buyers of historic buildings, paid back, and then loaned again to others to promote their preservation projects. Sometimes a revolving fund is used to purchase a historic building in order to add preservation easements to its deed and resell it.

ripeness: before a court case is ripe, a plaintiff must try using all administrative remedies (other possible legal means) before resorting to a lawsuit.

rising damp: a situation where water wicks up into wall material from below in a process similar to when water soaks up into a cotton swab or a washcloth that has been partially dipped in water.

rock lath: a method of holding up plaster used extensively after 1930 that comes in the form of sheets made up of compressed gypsum board faced with paper. Rock lath sheets are nailed to the studs and have a rough surface to hold onto or "key" the plaster.

rubble masonry construction: construction made of rounded or natural stones usually mortared together.

running bond: a method of laying up brick which has continual courses of stretchers that are just one brick thick and alternate with the bricks centered over the ends of the bricks in the preceding courses.

sandstone: a relatively hard sedimentary rock that comes in various colors including tan, pink, and brown.

sense of place: unique places and sites in the social and topographical sense, that help give a community its identity. For example, a historic village square has a sense of place, while a big box retail store does not.

scratch coat: the primary or rough coat that forms the bulk of a plaster wall.

Section 106 of the National Historic Preservation Act: a law requiring all federal agencies or other entities that engage in projects or "undertakings" using federal funds or needing a federal license to allow the Advisory Council to have "the opportunity to comment" on the project before it is built.

Secretary of the Interior's Standards: a set of rules and preservation guidelines that are the basis for appropriate preservation design in the United States.

Section 4(f) of the National Transportation Act: a part of a law originally passed in 1966 and retained in the federal transportation statutes passed since then created to protect historic sites from demolition caused by transportation-related federal undertakings.

secondary sources: documents and other media containing information already gathered and interpreted by other researchers or authors usually not dating from the time period being studied.

sedimentary rock: stone created when silt or sand or fossils or a combination thereof settles in layers that gradually compress and harden into new kinds of stone, such as sandstone or limestone.

setting: the location of a historic property referring to its immediate physical surroundings, its context.

significance: a term that means the factors that make a property historic, such as association with a historic event or a famous person or possessing distinctive architecture can be applied to a particular property.

single glazed: glass set in sash with a single thickness.

softwoods: varieties of wood that come from conifers, commonly known as pine trees.

spalling: when water freezes inside a brick or other material and expands causing the face of the material to crack and break off in a process.

stack bond: a method of laying up brick which courses of all stretchers that do not overlap from course to course but with bricks placed directly above one another.

standing: the right to sue in court. In order to file a lawsuit a plaintiff must prove standing.

State Historic Preservation Offices: created by the National Historic Preservation act of 1966, state agencies that manage the historic resources and preservation programs within their states.

stereograph: devices that feature two identical photographs mounted over a cardboard backing to create the illusion of a three-dimensional scene when seen through a viewer designed for the purpose. They date from around 1851 to the 1930s.

stretchers: bricks laid with their long sides parallel to the wall.

stucco: a plaster-like material that is applied to the exteriors of buildings to both beautify and protect them.

studs: comparatively thin vertical members such as two-by-fours and two-by-sixes used within walls to support them.

stud-frame construction: also called **platform framing,** a method of wood construction where each successive story of a building is built separately using studs and posts, rather than the tall vertical studs that extend up two or more floors used in balloon framing.

structure: constructions distinguished from buildings because they are permanent constructions designed for purposes other than creating routine shelter for human activities; examples include bridges, monuments, and most towers.

style: distinct decorative systems that are applied to both the exteriors and interiors of buildings.

takings: when a governmental entity confiscates someone's property without compensation to the owner. Takings are prohibited by the Fifth Amendment of the United States Constitution.

tensile strength: how well a given material will hold up when being sheared by force.

tenons: squared off chiseled projections used to join timbers in timber framing.

timber-frame buildings: have a structural system made up of heavy timbers consisting of thick posts and beams and braces that are attached together by mortise-and-tenon construction.

Tintype: a type of early photograph with a sheet-metal backing used until about 1900.

tout ensemble: a French term meaning "taken together" used by a Louisiana court to describe how the integrity of historic districts can be diminished by non historic intrusions, such as business signs.

travertine: a hard, often colorful kind of rock with holes in it that forms when minerals collect in springs and waterfalls over millions of years.

Tribal historic preservation officers: the heads of tribal preservation agencies that manage the historic resources and preservation programs within the territories of specific Native American tribes.

tromp l'oeil: a French term for a method of rendering that attempts to make a two-dimensional painting or print look three-dimensional, thus "tricking" (*trompe*) the eye (*l'oeil*).

tube-and-knob wiring: a kind of wiring used in the early 20th century that consisted of bare wires strung on ceramic insulators located in attics and within walls, floors, and ceilings.

universal design: a philosophy that supports the idea that consumer products, architecture, and interiors should be designed to be easily usable by a wide range of people with varying physical and sensory abilities.

urban sprawl: new development in the United States since the Second World War that has emphasized suburban expansion into open land based on the nearly universal use of the automobile.

vapor barrier: a water- and air-resistant film placed between the interior plaster or wallboard and the interior structure of the wall to prevent condensation within the wall.

vigas: log beams set into the upper section of the adobe walls with their ends sometimes projecting outside that support the upper floors or roof.

vitrification a process in which clay is heated to high temperatures, normally from about 1000 to 1500 degrees Celsius where the material becomes less porous, smaller in volume, and achieves greater strength and resistance to water .

wet wood termites: the most common in North America, including subterranean native termites, require moisture to survive.

wire nails: nails with round shafts, flat heads, and pointed ends, started replacing machine-headed cut nails around 1890 and are still in use, far cheaper to make than square nails

wood lath: a method of holding up plaster consisting of narrow strips of rough wood that are nailed to the studs or joists and subsequently covered with layers of plaster.

wrought iron: iron formed into rods and pounded by a blacksmith into bars that can be twisted or hammered into various shapes.

zoning: an urban planning tool introduced by municipalities to separate residential, commercial, and industrial areas in order to increase the quality of life and the property values within protected areas

INDEX

Bauhaus style, 269
Beachfront Management Act
    (1988), 126
Beacon Hill, 15
Beale Street, Memphis, Tennessee,
    271*f*
Beat Generation, 111
Beaux-Arts style, 95, 241
    interior, 278*f*
    Pennsylvania Station, 16, 16*f*
    post office in New Orleans, 150*f*
    San Francisco, 276*f*
    terra-cotta, 178
bedding, 174
bees, boring, 216
beetles, powderpost, 216
Bel–Jon, Nikos, 270
Big Horn Medicine Wheel,
    Wyoming, 333
binder, 193
birthplaces, 102, 104
Blind Girls' Home, 44
Blue Ridge Mountains, 266
Blue Ridge Parkway, 333
blunt point screws, 252
bonds, 245
books and articles, 110–11
boring bees, infestation by, 216
Boston, historic, 17, 17*f*
brass, 184
Breuer, Marcel, 20, 21*f*
brick, 167–70, 274*f. See also*
    masonry
    load-bearing walls and
        foundations, 168–69
    masonry walls, 245
    preservation issues, 169–70
    walls and interior plaster, 45–46
bronze, 184
building, 2
building materials
    adobe, 165–67
    architectural terra-cotta, 176–79
    asbestos, 197–98
    ceramic tile, 192–93
    compressive strength, 164
    concrete, 174–76
    fired brick, 167–70
    glass, 184–86
    historic integrity, 264–65

maintaining historic integrity,
    274–77
masonry, 165–79
metals, 182–84
nonmasonry, 179–86
paint, 193–95
plaster, 189–91
pressed metal ceilings, 192
stone, 170–74
stucco, 186
tensile strength, 164–65
wallpaper, 195–97
wood, 179–82
wood in interiors, 187–89
building site, preservation project,
    294
bundle of rights, 125
Bush, George W., 24
bushes
    intrusions, 219
    preservation project, 294
business literature, 114
Buttnick v. City of Seattle (1986),
    135
Byzantine revival style, 129

C & O Canal, 330
Cabildo, 14
Café du Monde, 78
California. *See also* San Francisco,
    California
    Hollywood, 341*f*
    Pasadena City Hall, 69*f*
Cambria Steel Mills, 47
canales, 94, 167
Capital Building, Washington, D.C.,
    65
carpenter ants, infestation by, 215
Carson Pirie, Scott, & Company
    Building, 95*f*
CASA de Maryland (CASA), 338
Casa Grande, National Park Service,
    7–8
casement windows, 241
cast iron, 182–83
cast stone, 175–76
ceilings
    preservation project, 297
    pressed metal, 192

cemeteries, 102, 104, 183*f*
census records, 115–16
Central Train Station, New York,
    261*f*
ceramic tile, 192–93
certificate of appropriateness, 67
Certified Historic Structure, 42
Certified Local Government
    Program (CLG), 47, 50, 58
chain of title, 116
character-defining elements, 150
character-defining features, 99
Charleston, South Carolina, The
    Battery, 13–14, 24, 60
Charleton white, paint, 193
chemical treatments
    acid rain, 231–32
    standards, 272–73
Chickamauga Battlefield, 8
Chicora Wood Plantation, 93*f*
Church of Latter Day Saints, 116
Church of the Immaculate
    Conception, 72
circular saws, 249
*Citizens to Preserve Overton Park
    v. Volpe* (1971), 38, 132–33
City Beautiful Movement, 95–96
city directories, 114–15
city lithographs, 115
City of New Orleans v. Pergament
    (1941), 133
Civil War, 6, 8, 47, 87, 90, 239, 253,
    329, 330
cleaning, harsh, 229
climate change, 347–48
Clinton, Bill, 23
code equivalency, 223
Colburn School, 147*f*
College of William and Mary, 10
Colonial Williamsburg, 10–11, 154
Colorado Cliff Dwellers
    Association, 7
commercial histories, 112
Commission on Chicago
    Landmarks, 71–72
common bond, 168, 169*f*
compressive strength, materials, 164
conceptual design phase, project
    management, 304

concrete, 174–76. *See also* masonry
    cast stone, 175–76
    load-bearing walls and
        foundations, 175
    preservation issues, 176
concrete masonry units (CMU), 245
conservation, 156
conservation areas, 3
conservation districts, 68–69
conservators, preservation projects,
    287–88
consolidation, 232
construction documents phase,
    project management, 305
construction history, historic
    structure report, 290
construction management
    exterior, 305–6
    interior, 307
constructive use, 37
contextual, 275
contract administration phase,
    project management, 305–7
contractors, preservation projects,
    287
contributing, 59
copper and copper alloys, 184
Cornell University, Sage Hall, 277f
Corporation for Jefferson's Poplar
    Forest, 319
cracking
    natural threat, 206–7, 208f
    preservation project, 294, 295
crack monitor, 207, 208f
craftspeople, preservation projects,
    287–88
crazing, terra-cotta, 178
Crockett, Davy, 91
crown glass windows, 243–44
Crystal Palace, London, 182
cultural landscapes, 332–33
Cultural Resources Stewardships
    and Partnerships Program, 12
Cunningham, Ann Pamela, 6–7, 8
curators, preservation projects, 287
cylinder glass windows, 244
Cynthia Woods Mitchell Fund for
    Historic Interiors, 72

daguerreotypes, 114
dating historic buildings, 238–52
    floorboards, 249
    foundations, 244–45
    frame type, 246–48
    historic function, 239–40
    interior walls, 249–50
    investigations from pictures,
        253–54
    masonry walls, 245–46
    nail types, 250–52
    saw cuts, 248–49
    screw types, 252
    style, 240–41
    windows, 241–44
David and Gladys Wright House,
    350
*The Death and Life of American
    Cities,* Jacobs, 18
decorative plaster, 190
defendant, 122
Delta Queen steamboat, 86, 86f
demolition, 97–98
    active, 142–43
    oppositions to, 77–78
    passive, 140–42
    waste caused by, 341
demolition by neglect, 61, 61f, 125,
    140–42, 225f
    abandoned house, 142f
    cases involving, 134–35
    Unity Hall, 141f
Department of the Interior, 260, 330
Derby House, Massachusetts, 84f
design, 99–100
design development phase, project
    management, 304–5
design projects. *See* preservation
    projects; project management
    in historic design
Detroit, Michigan, 142
differential settling, 205
dissertations, 111–12
*District of Columbia Preservation
    League v. Department of
    Consumer and Regulatory
    Affairs* (1994), 135
diversity, 349

documentation
    measured drawings, 299–300
    photographs, 300
    preservation activity, 288
Dolan v. City of Tigard (1994), 126
doors, preservation project, 296, 297
double-glazed windows, 242
double shotgun house, New
    Orleans, 265f
drawings
    documentation, 299–300
    historic structure report, 291
Drayton, John, 157
Drayton Hall, 157
    Georgian paneling, 187f
    handcrafted plaster medallion,
        191f
dry wood termites, infestation by,
    215
Dutch bond, 168, 169f

earthquakes, 220–21
Edison, Thomas, 11
Edison Institute, 11
efflorescence, 209f
    preservation project, 295
    water damage and, 208–13
Eiffel Tower, 65
El Rancho Hotel, New Mexico, 158f
embodied energy, 340
Empire State Building, 65
*Employment Division of Oregon v.
    Smith* (1990), 129
encapsulate, 306
encapsulated, 194
Enchanted Rock, Texas, 333
energy efficiency, 340
English bond, 168, 169f
English Cross, 168, 169f
enhancement grants, National
    Transportation Act, 36–37
entrances, ADA (Americans with
    Disabilities Act) alternative
    standards, 317–18
environment
    energy efficiency and embodies
        energy, 340
    historic windows and life-cycle
        analysis, 341–43